Clinton's Foreign Policy

This volume is a detailed account of President Clinton's foreign policy during 1992–2000, covering the main substantive issues of his administration, including Iraq, Bosnia and Kosovo.

The book emphasises Clinton's adaptation of the elder Bush's 'New World Order' outlook and his relationship to the younger Bush's 'Americanistic' foreign policy. In doing so, it discusses in detail such key policy areas as foreign economic policy; humanitarian interventionism; policy towards Russia and China, and towards European and other allies; defence priorities; international terrorism; and peace-making. Overall, the author judges that Clinton managed to develop an American foreign policy approach that was appropriate for the domestic and international conditions of the post-Cold War era.

This book will be of great interest to students of Clinton's administration, US foreign policy, international security and IR in general.

John Dumbrell is Professor of Government at Durham University. He specialises in the study of US foreign policy.

Contemporary security studies
Edited by James Gow and Rachel Kerr
King's College, London

This series focuses on new research across the spectrum of international peace and security, in an era where each year throws up multiple examples of conflicts that present new security challenges in the world around them.

NATO's Secret Armies
Operation Gladio and terrorism in Western Europe
Daniele Ganser

The US, NATO and Military Burden-Sharing
Peter Kent Forster and Stephen J. Cimbala

Russian Governance in the Twenty-First Century
Geo-strategy, geopolitics and new governance
Irina Isakova

The Foreign Office and Finland 1938–1940
Diplomatic sideshow
Craig Gerrard

Rethinking the Nature of War
Edited by Isabelle Duyvesteyn and Jan Angstrom

Perception and Reality in the Modern Yugoslav Conflict
Myth, falsehood and deceit 1991–1995
Brendan O'Shea

The Political Economy of Peacebuilding in Post-Dayton Bosnia
Tim Donais

The Distracted Eagle
The rift between America and old Europe
Peter H. Merkl

The Iraq War
European perspectives on politics, strategy, and operations
Edited by Jan Hallenberg and Håkan Karlsson

Strategic Contest
Weapons proliferation and war in the greater Middle East
Richard L. Russell

Propaganda, the Press and Conflict
The Gulf War and Kosovo
David R. Willcox

Missile Defence
International, regional and national implications
Edited by Bertel Heurlin and Sten Rynning

Globalising Justice for Mass Atrocities
A revolution in accountability
Chandra Lekha Sriram

Ethnic Conflict and Terrorism
The origins and dynamics of civil wars
Joseph L. Soeters

Globalisation and the Future of Terrorism
Patterns and predictions
Brynjar Lia

Nuclear Weapons and Strategy
The evolution of American nuclear policy
Stephen J. Cimbala

Nasser and the Missile Age in the Middle East
Owen L. Sirrs

War as Risk Management
Strategy and conflict in an age of globalised risks
Yee-Kuang Heng

Military Nanotechnology
Potential applications and preventive arms control
Jurgen Altmann

NATO and Weapons of Mass Destruction
Regional alliance, global threats
Eric R. Terzuolo

Europeanisation of National Security Identity
The EU and the changing security identities of the Nordic states
Pernille Rieker

International Conflict Prevention and Peace-building
Sustaining the peace in post conflict societies
Edited by T. David Mason and James D. Meernik

Controlling the Weapons of War
Politics, persuasion, and the prohibition of inhumanity
Brian Rappert

Changing Transatlantic Security Relations
Do the US, the EU and Russia form a new strategic triangle?
Edited by Jan Hallenberg and Håkan Karlsson

Theoretical Roots of US Foreign Policy
Machiavelli and American unilateralism
Thomas M. Kane

Corporate Soldiers and International Security
The rise of private military companies
Christopher Kinsey

Transforming European Militaries
Coalition operations and the technology gap
Gordon Adams and Guy Ben-Ari

Globalization and Conflict
National security in a 'new' strategic era
Edited by Robert G. Patman

Military Forces in 21st Century Peace Operations
No job for a soldier?
James V. Arbuckle

The Political Road to War with Iraq
Bush, 9/11 and the drive to overthrow Saddam
Nick Ritchie and Paul Rogers

Bosnian Security after Dayton
New perspectives
Edited by Michael A. Innes

Kennedy, Johnson and NATO
Britain, America and the dynamics of alliance, 1962–68
Andrew Priest

Small Arms and Security
New emerging international norms
Denise Garcia

The United States and Europe
Beyond the neo-conservative divide?
Edited by John Baylis and Jon Roper

Russia, NATO and Cooperative Security
Bridging the gap
Lionel Ponsard

International Law and International Relations
Bridging theory and practice
Edited by Tom Bierstecker, Peter Spiro, Chandra Lekha Sriram and Veronica Raffo

Deterring International Terrorism and Rogue States
US national security policy after 9/11
James H. Lebovic

Vietnam in Iraq
Tactics, lessons, legacies and ghosts
Edited by John Dumbrell and David Ryan

Understanding Victory and Defeat in Contemporary War
Edited by Jan Angstrom and Isabelle Duyvesteyn

Propaganda and Information Warfare in the Twenty-first Century
Altered images and deception operations
Scot Macdonald

Governance in Post-Conflict Societies
Rebuilding fragile states
Edited by Derick W. Brinkerhoff

European Security in the Twenty-First Century
The challenge of multipolarity
Adrian Hyde-Price

Ethics, Technology and the American Way of War
Cruise missiles and US security policy
Reuben E. Brigety II

International Law and the Use of Armed Force
The UN charter and the major powers
Joel H. Westra

Disease and Security
Natural plagues and biological weapons in East Asia
Christian Enermark

Explaining War and Peace
Case studies and necessary condition counterfactuals
Jack Levy and Gary Goertz

War, Image and Legitimacy
Viewing contemporary conflict
James Gow and Milena Michalski

Information Strategy and Warfare
A guide to theory and practice
John Arquilla and Douglas A. Borer

Countering the Proliferation of Weapons of Mass Destruction
NATO and EU options in the Mediterranean and the Middle East
Thanos P. Dokos

Security and the War on Terror
Edited by Alex J. Bellamy, Roland Bleiker, Sara E. Davies and Richard Devetak

The European Union and Strategy
An emerging actor
Edited by Jan Hallenberg and Kjell Engelbrekt

Causes and Consequences of International Conflict
Data, methods and theory
Edited by Glenn Palmer

Russian Energy Policy and Military Power
Putin's quest for greatness
Pavel Baev

The Baltic Question During the Cold War
Edited by John Hiden, Vahur Made, and David J. Smith

America, the EU and Strategic Culture
Renegotiating the transatlantic bargain
Asle Toje

Afghanistan, Arms and Conflict
Post-9/11 security and insurgency
Michael Bhatia and Mark Sedra

Punishment, Justice and International Relations
Ethics and order after the Cold War
Anthony F. Lang, Jr

Intra-State Conflict, Governments and Security
Dilemmas of deterrence and assurance
Edited by Stephen M. Saideman and Marie-Joëlle J. Zahar

Democracy and Security
Preferences, norms and policy-making
Edited by Matthew Evangelista, Harald Müller and Niklas Schörnig

The Homeland Security Dilemma
Fear, failure and the future of American security
Frank P. Harvey

Military Transformation and Strategy
Revolutions in military affairs and small states
Edited by Bernard Loo

Peace Operations and International Criminal Justice
Building peace after mass atrocities
Majbritt Lyck

NATO, Security and Risk Management
From Kosovo to Khandahar
M.J. Williams

Cyber-Conflict and Global Politics
Edited by Athina Karatzogianni

Globalisation and Defence in the Asia-Pacific
Arms across Asia
Edited by Geoffrey Till, Emrys Chew and Joshua Ho

Security Strategies and American World Order
Lost power
Birthe Hansen, Peter Toft and Anders Wivel

War, Torture and Terrorism
Rethinking the rules of international security
Edited by Anthony F. Lang, Jr and Amanda Russell Beattie

America and Iraq
Policy making, intervention and regional politics
Edited by David Ryan and Patrick Kiely

European Security in a Global Context
Internal and external dynamics
Edited by Thierry Tardy

Women and Political Violence
Female combatants in ethno-national conflict
Miranda H. Alison

Justice, Intervention, and Force in International Relations
Reassessing just war theory in the 21st century
Kimberly A. Hudson

Clinton's Foreign Policy
Between the Bushes, 1992–2000
John Dumbrell

Clinton's Foreign Policy
Between the Bushes, 1992–2000

John Dumbrell

LONDON AND NEW YORK

First published 2009
by Routledge
2 Park Square, Milton Park, Abingdon, Oxon OX14 4RN

Simultaneously published in the USA and Canada
by Routledge
270 Madison Ave, New York, NY 10016

Routledge is an imprint of the Taylor & Francis Group, an informa business

© 2009 John Dumbrell

Typeset in Times by Wearset Ltd, Boldon, Tyne and Wear

All rights reserved. No part of this book may be reprinted or reproduced or utilised in any form or by any electronic, mechanical, or other means, now known or hereafter invented, including photocopying and recording, or in any information storage or retrieval system, without permission in writing from the publishers.

British Library Cataloguing in Publication Data
A catalogue record for this book is available from the British Library

Library of Congress Cataloging in Publication Data
A catalog record for this book has been requested

ISBN10: 0-415-35984-8 (hbk)
ISBN10: 0-203-00789-2 (ebk)

ISBN13: 978-0-415-35984-9 (hbk)
ISBN13: 978-0-203-00789-1 (ebk)

Contents

	Acknowledgements	x
	List of abbreviations	xi
1	Perspectives on Clinton and his foreign policy	1
2	Foreign policy between the Bushes	21
3	The globalisation president	41
4	Making war, avoiding war: 1993–96	62
5	Ancient enmities: the Balkans and Northern Ireland	81
6	Beyond the Cold War: dealing with old enemies	99
7	Alliance politics and borderless threats	123
8	The Middle East	146
9	Bill Clinton's foreign policy	165
	Notes	172
	Select bibliography	203
	Index	210

Acknowledgements

Colleagues at the universities of Keele, Leicester and Durham have all made important contributions to this project. I have delivered papers of relevance to this book at the University of Oxford (Rothermere Centre for American Studies), at the American Politics Group annual conference, at the Transatlantic Studies Association annual conference, and at the 2005 Hofstra University Eleventh Presidential Conference, 'William Jefferson Clinton: The "New Democrat" From Hope'. The Hofstra conference included important contributions from leading administration figures, including Madeleine Albright, William Perry and President Clinton himself. I have drawn on my notes from the conference where appropriate. Gratitude is also due to my editors at Routledge for their patience and professionalism.

Some of the key ideas for the book were developed for my 2005 Eccles Centre lecture at the British Association for American Studies annual conference, held at Cambridge University. I thank Professor Phil Davies, Director of the Eccles Centre for American Studies at the British Library, for inviting me to present the lecture.

John Dumbrell

Abbreviations

ABM	Anti-Ballistic Missile
ACDA	Arms Control and Disarmament Agency
AFL–CIO	American Federation of Labor–Congress of Industrial Organizations
AID	Agency for International Development
AIPAC	American Israeli Public Affairs Committee
APEC	Asia-Pacific Economic Cooperation
Bush41	President George H. W. Bush
Bush43	President George W. Bush
CANF	Cuban American National Foundation
CARICOM	community of (anti-communist) Caribbean countries
CEA	Council of Economic Advisers
CENTCOM	US Military Central Command
CIA	Central Intelligence Agency
CINC	commanders in chief
CIS	Commonwealth of Independent States
CNN	Cable News Network
CNTBT	Comprehensive Nuclear Test Ban Treaty
CPL	available on Clinton Presidential Library website
CQA	*Congressional Quarterly Almanac*
CQWR	*Congressional Quarterly Weekly Report*
CWC	Chemical Weapons Convention
EC	European Community
EU	European Union
FA	*Foreign Affairs*
FBI	Federal Bureau of Investigation
FoB	Friend of Bill
GATT	General Agreement on Tariffs and Trade
GDP	Gross Domestic Product
GOP	Grand Old Party (Republican Party)
G-7	Group of seven leading industrial nations
G-8	G-7 plus Russia
IAEA	International Atomic Energy Agency

ICC	International Criminal Court
IMF	International Monetary Fund
INA	Iraqi National Accord
INC	Iraqi National Congress
IRA	Irish Republican Army
JCS	Joint Chiefs of Staff
JFK	President John Fitzgerald Kennedy
KLA	Kosovo Liberation Army
LBJ	President Lyndon Baines Johnson
MFN	Most Favoured Nation (trading status)
NAFTA	North American Free Trade Agreement
NATO	North Atlantic Treaty Organisation
NEC	National Economic Council
NGO	non-governmental organisation
NJ	*National Journal*
NMD	National Missile Defense
NORAID	Northern Irish Aid Committee
NPT	Nuclear Non-proliferation Treaty
NSA	National Security Adviser
NSC	National Security Council
NYRB	*New York Review of Books*
NYT	*New York Times*
OAS	Organization of American States
OSCE	Organisation for Security and Cooperation in Europe
PDD	Presidential Decision Directive
PfP	Partnership for Peace
PIRA	Provisional Irish Republican Army
PLO	Palestinian Liberation Organisation
PNTR	permanent normal trading relations
RMA	revolution in military affairs
SDI	Strategic Defense Initiative
SNOG	Senate NATO Observers Group
START	Strategic Arms Reduction Treaty
TAFTA	transatlantic free trade area
UN	United Nations
UNOSOM	United Nations Operation, Somalia
UNPROFOR	United Nations Protection Force (Bosnia)
USIA	US Information Agency
USSR	Union of Soviet Socialist Republics
WMD	weapons of mass destruction
WP	*Washington Post*
WTO	World Trade Organisation

1 Perspectives on Clinton and his foreign policy

The presidency of Bill Clinton belongs to that most remote of historical periods: the day before yesterday – the day before the 9/11 terror attacks, the day before the invasion of Iraq, the day before the presidency of George W. Bush. Clinton's presidency constitutes the era from which political analysts, journalists and political scientists have retired, and to which professional, document-oriented historians have yet to direct their attention. In some respects, the final decade of the twentieth century, preoccupied by the 'culture wars' and with the sexual activities of the American nation's Chief Executive, seems like a lost world. In other ways, Bill Clinton and the memory of his presidency remain the very warp and weft of contemporary US politics. So, from differing viewpoints, Bill Clinton was the president who failed to protect Americans from international terrorism; the president who sacrificed American jobs and economic self-sufficiency to the ravages of unrestrained global economics; the president who valued alliances, and whose ambassadorial skills enhanced America's international standing; the president who squandered a brilliant foreign policy inheritance, bequeathing to his successor a hollow military and a directionless diplomacy. Adapting the titles of various articles written from a variety of points across the political spectrum during the 1990s, the 42nd president of the United States was a leader who presided over 'foreign policy as social work' and the 'end of idealism'. He was a 'new moralist on the road to hell', a president distinguished by 'fatal distraction', the 'bully of the free world'.[1]

The purpose of this book is to provide an account of Clinton's foreign policy, viewed from sufficient distance to establish a sense of perspective. My standpoint is that of the contemporary historian, writing well before most relevant documentation has become available, but still willing to offer interim judgements. This first chapter discusses Clinton's changing reputation and offers some reflections on how to assess presidential leadership of foreign policy. It will introduce the leading personalities associated with Clinton's foreign policy and also consider a major preoccupation of the entire study: the peculiar nature of foreign policy and foreign policy-making in the post-Cold War era – the period 'between the Bushes'. Chapter 2 provides a brief survey of policy context and development, as well as of Clinton's decisional style and organisation and the role of Congress. The discussion will then move on to the search for an integrating philosophy in a globalising

2 Clinton and his foreign policy

economic environment and to economic foreign policy (Chapter 3); to early defence policy, military action in Somalia and Haiti, and debates about humanitarian intervention (Chapter 4); to the Balkans and Northern Ireland (Chapter 5); to Clinton's stance towards old enemies from the Cold War (Chapter 6); to alliance politics, borderless threats (including terrorism) and second term defence issues (Chapter 7); and then to policy in the Middle East (Chapter 8). The final chapter will attempt to answer a series of overarching questions: Does the Clinton foreign policy deserve its reputation for sloppiness and lack of direction? Did the Clinton administration supply the United States and the world with a foreign policy which was appropriate to the post-Cold War era? Did Clinton actually have clear foreign policy objectives, and, if he did, to what extent did he achieve them? Did he squander the legacy from George Bush senior? What was his legacy to George Bush junior?

Clinton's changing reputation

Some indication of Clinton's standing towards the end of his presidency may be gleaned from a Chicago Council on Foreign Relations public opinion survey, published in 1999.[2] In many respects, this survey adds to our sense of the 1990s as a period from the remote past. The public's lead answer, by 21 per cent, to a request to name the biggest foreign policy problem facing the US was 'I don't know.' Clinton was named as the top post-1945 foreign policy president, ahead of, in order, Kennedy, Reagan, George H. W. Bush, Truman, Eisenhower, Nixon, Carter, Johnson and Ford. The temper of the times was also caught in a piece written by Jacob Weinberg, also in 1999, in the *New York Times Magazine*. According to Weinberg, Clinton was most likely to be remembered as 'the first in line of domestic presidents who followed the Cold War'.[3]

Despite his impeachment and despite the intense political partisanship of the period, Clinton's public standing at the end of his years in office was high, and his popularity extended to foreign affairs – possibly precisely because the 42nd president was seen as having achieved a proper balance between the foreign and domestic policy arenas. Bitter partisan divisions made it tricky to isolate a consensus elite judgement. However, a series of articles, published in the *New York Times* (*NYT*) in December 2000, tried to provide such a judgement. Todd Putnam noted the overwhelming shame of impeachment, but also saw Clinton as the saviour of enlightened presidential activism:

> in the face of a citizenry sceptical of governmental action at home and wary of commitment abroad, Mr Clinton managed to shape a new kind of limited executive activism that kept the presidency in the thick of things, whether in modest domestic initiatives or efforts to promote peace and trade around the world.[4]

For Richard Stevenson, Clinton was the economics-first president who had the good sense to 'let the good times roll', attaching himself to the 'widespread sense that times, for most people, have never been better'.⁵ David Sanger argued that Clinton's success was rooted in his clear-headed focus on the interpenetration of global free trade, American internationalism and the historic march of democracy. Clinton's message never varied, whether he was 'in an Irish village, a Vietnamese industrial park or at Beijing University': 'Prosperity would create choices, choices would lead to a demand for information, and that information, provided at the speed of the Internet, would bring political change.'⁶ These *NYT* articles certainly reflected that newspaper's generally favourable view of Clinton. Yet they also encapsulated most of what was to become the common currency of assessments of this president: spectacular personal gifts balanced by spectacular demons; flair balanced by indiscipline; the pragmatic vision to ride the global economic rollercoaster balanced by a deeper lack of direction and an inclination to trust to luck; successful internationalism balanced by an odd mixture of spineless caution and occasional adventurism. David Broder's assessment in the *Washington Post* (WP) made the familiar link between performance and character. Clinton's foreign policy, for Broder, had many good features; it also had 'too many jagged edges'. The fundamental failing was Bill Clinton's underpinning and unswerving belief in his own indestructible status as 'fortune's favored child'.⁷

Negative assessments of Clinton's foreign policy legacy and practice tended to concentrate on the perceived sacrifice of policy coherence to the needs of domestic agendas, as well as the reactive character of the Clinton policy in general. For Henry Kissinger, for example, Clinton's foreign policy was 'a series of seemingly unrelated decisions in response to specific crises'.⁸ Clinton, according to Christopher Hitchens, simply *had* 'no big plans, no grand thoughts, no noble dreams'.⁹ In the words of W. G. Hyland: 'In the absence of an overall perspective, most issues were bound to degenerate into tactical manipulations, some successful some not.'¹⁰ In an essay published in 2000, Emily Goldman and Larry Berman speculated that perhaps 'muddling through may be the best one can hope for'. Their general verdict was a tough one: 'Absent a strategic guidepost, Clinton's foreign policy has been broad but shallow; many international initiatives underway but few resources and little time devoted to any one because of a lack of priorities.'¹¹ Some internationalists on the right deplored Clinton's indecisiveness even as they admitted that at least he had kept America out of the hands of isolationists. Owen Harries, editor of *The National Interest*, put it as follows: 'Clinton's foreign policy is not an unmitigated disaster. It is not even a mitigated disaster. It is merely quite bad in certain ways that have limited consequences.'¹² In their 2000 book on assessing presidents, Marc Landy and Sidney Milkis left the reader in no doubt as to which president they had in mind when they condemned 'leaders who prostrate themselves before the nation', following rather than leading opinion.¹³

More positive judgements and apologies emanated from the inevitable rush of memoirs coming from former Clinton employees.¹⁴ Also countering some of the negative judgements, Stephen Walt in 2000 echoed E. M. Forster's verdict on democracy by offering 'two cheers' for Clinton's foreign policy. In Walt's view, domestic and international context was all. He emphasised the strategic, post-Cold War uncertainty of the 1990s and pointed to what he called the 'paradox of unipolarity'. In the early 1990s, the US was in a position of 'unprecedented preponderance'. The US economy was around 40 per cent larger than that of its nearest rival. American defence spending was greater than that of its next six competitors combined. For Walt, the paradox was that the US enjoyed 'enormous influence but has little idea what to do with its power or even how much effort it should expend'. The public in 1992 elected a president who, compared to his predecessor, 'promised to spend less time on the phone with foreign leaders and more time on domestic issues'. Americans also, to some extent in 1992 but more obviously in 1994, 'elected a congress whose disdain for foreign affairs is almost gleeful'. Some Republican Members of Congress actually boasted about their insularity. Against this background – strategic uncertainty, a disengaged public and a narrowly nationalist Congress – Clinton (according to the line of analysis offered by Walt) kept America credibly internationalist. The North Atlantic Treaty Organization expanded and found new purpose. Progress was made in curbing the proliferation of weapons of mass destruction (WMD), notably in the former Soviet Union, though not in India and Pakistan, both of whom tested nuclear weapons in 1998. Responsible internationalist, multilateralist and free trader that he was, Clinton's foreign policy deserved at least a muted acclamation.[15] In their end-of-the-second-term report, the editors of the journal, *Foreign Policy*, accused President Clinton of short-termism and inattention, rather than with lacking 'vision'. However, policy focus was too often allowed to slip. The *Foreign Policy* editors quoted former National Security Adviser (NSA) Tony Lake: 'in the Clinton White House, politics was too often seen as an end in itself.'[16]

In December 2000, with time running out for his Middle East peace initiatives, Bill Clinton, in remarks recorded by Sidney Blumenthal, mused: 'Sometimes, time is your friend. Sometimes, time is your enemy.' In Northern Ireland – with long-term factors working in the direction of peace – time, according to Clinton, was a friend; in the Middle East, as the 2000 election deadline approached, it had become the enemy.[17] Extending Clinton's frame of reference, it seems that time has largely been a friend to the reputation of America's 42nd president. As John Harris pointed out in *The Survivor*, by 2005, Clinton's reputation had already gone through at least two cycles of decline and revival.[18] Clinton's departure from the White House was overshadowed by controversy over the issuing of pardons (notably that of Marc Rich, American tax fugitive and friend of Israeli leader Ehud Barak). By the time he opened his Harlem office in mid-2001, however, the press was reporting a wave of Clinton-era nostalgia. 9/11 stimulated accusations that the 42nd president had left America exposed to terrorist threat. Opposition to the invasion of Iraq in 2003 led, however, to more positive reassessments of Clinton.

In Europe in particular, but also to an important degree in the US, negative assessments of the Bush43 response to 9/11 worked to the benefit of Clinton and his reputation. Questions about the putative continuity or discontinuity of policy between the elder Bush, Clinton and the younger Bush will be addressed throughout the course of this book. Suffice it for the moment to point out that, by the time of the 2003 invasion of Iraq, Clinton had, for many Europeans, become the 'anti-Bush', the American leader who 'talked European' and sought transatlantic cooperation. Clinton's great virtue, according to Michael Cox, lay in knowing 'how to sell American power to others'.[19] Conveniently forgotten in some of the European re-evaluations of the Clinton record was Bill's early transatlantic reputation as a country-bumpkin president who wished to shift American priorities from Europe to the Pacific. For many American opponents of the George W. Bush 'revolution' in foreign policy, Clinton represented the kind of cooperative 'liberal world order' and internationalist pragmatism which had been jettisoned by the new century's neo-conservatives and offensive nationalists. For Ivo Daalder and James M. Lindsay, for example, Clinton stood for 'a continuation of the traditional Wilsonian approach of building a world order based on the rule of law'.[20]

Despite the kindling of the Clinton flame among opponents of the younger Bush, the critical consensus in the early years of the new century was a familiar one. The Clinton foreign policy was not indefensible, but it had huge lapses, such as woeful inaction regarding Bosnia in the first term, and was characterised by inattention and imprecise purpose. Clinton continued to experience pincer attacks from both left and right. One strand of criticism was dominated by the impeachment and by the perceived failure of moral leadership, in both foreign and domestic arenas.[21] For many conservatives, Clinton continued to be the 'counter-culturalist in chief'. From the liberal side, however, the thesis argued by George Stephanopoulos in his 1999 White House memoir, *All Too Human*, continued to hold sway. Clinton was the leader who had betrayed his generation's liberalism by compromising with the Republicans, by over-compensating in terms of his dealings with the US military, and generally by embracing a strategy of short-term opportunism.[22]

If one burst of Clinton assessment accompanied the president's exit from office, another burst was stimulated by the publication in 2004 of *My Life*, the presidential autobiography. As seems almost inevitable with Clinton, links were frequently drawn between policy performance and the presidential character. A much quoted review in the *NYT* saw *My Life* as a reflection of the Clinton presidency itself: 'lack of discipline leading to squandered opportunities; high expectations, undermined by self-indulgence and scattered concentration.'[23] Rambling and poorly organised, the book was like the man: undisciplined, sentimental, superficial. The publication and critical reception of *My Life* coincided with the death of Ronald Reagan, causing several commentators to draw rather unlikely parallels between the two leaders. Joe Klein, author of *Primary Colors*, for example, described the irreducible optimism of the two small-town sons of troubled families.[24] William Berman was struck by the former Democratic president's shallow optimism: Clinton appeared to like 'virtually everybody whose name he mentions in the memoirs save Saddam Hussein and Kenneth Starr'.[25] With *My Life* degenerating in its second half into a diary-list of meetings and events, the impression of a random and reactive approach to foreign policy was reinforced. Reviewing the book, Garry Wills wrote that Clinton's foreign policy had been 'wise'. However, his 'vision had so little hold upon the public that (George W.) Bush was able to discard it instantly when he came in'.[26] British journalist Tim Hames recalled Theodore Roosevelt's dismissal of President McKinley as a man with 'the backbone of a chocolate éclair'. According to Hames, 'Mr Clinton's foreign policy had the spine of a raspberry pavlova'.[27] For John Harris, Clinton's opportunism was both his strength and his weakness. Clinton 'understood the transformational character of his times', but he sustained too many 'self-inflicted wounds' and exhibited too much in the way of directionless, defensive drift to be admitted to the 'elite gallery' of great presidents.[28]

Following the 1999–2000 assessments, and the 2004–05 judgements of the Clinton record which were provoked by the publication of the autobiography, yet another wave of implicit evaluation of White House leadership in the 1990s attached itself to Hillary Clinton's 2008 presidential election campaign. Bill's role in the primary campaign against Barack Obama injected energy and controversy, as well as a touch of humour. Pictures of Bill snoozing at a Martin Luther King memorial service provoked the immortal headline, 'Bill Has a Dream'. Was Bill in effect running for a third term? Placards at some Hillary Clinton rallies protested Bush–Clinton dynasty-building: 'The White House Is Not a Time-Share.' Hillary found herself confronted by accusations that she stood for 'old politics' – essentially the politics of outmoded 'culture wars'. Bill and Hillary were 'the Clintstones'. The perceived hostility of many low-income Democrats – for example, in the Pennsylvania primary of April 2008 – to the North Atlantic Free Trade Agreement caused Hillary to distance herself from Bill's record as a prophet of globalisation and champion of global free trade. Around this time the second volume of Nigel Hamilton's biography of Bill Clinton appeared, with its emphasis on Bill's capacity for learning in the White House.[29] David Phillips offered an extraordinarily upbeat account of Bill's charismatic and super-sensitive leadership.[30] Biographies of Hillary Clinton abounded, while in 2007 Sally Bedell Smith offered an analysis of what was in her view virtually a joint presidency. This was 'Clinton Incorporated'.[31] Zbigniew Brzezinski, NSA to President Carter and foreign policy adviser to the 2008 Obama campaign, offered a familiar interpretation of Bill Clinton's international efforts: 'the impotence of good intentions' meeting 'the price of self-indulgence'. For Brzezinski, Bill Clinton had, in his commitment to democratised globalisation, a genuine vision. Yet his strategy was compromised by intellectual vagueness and laziness: 'Complacent determinism, personal shortcomings, and rising domestic political obstacles overcame his good intentions.'[32]

Assessing Clinton and his foreign policy

The quest for benchmarks by which to judge presidential performance has generated a considerable body of specialist literature.[33] This literature involves judging presidential performance in-the-round – domestic as well as foreign policy; so let us start this section with some general discussion of those qualities which are widely regarded as constitutive of good presidential performance, relating the discussion to Clinton.

The presidential ranking debate centres on problems of subjectivism in the would-be presidential ranker, and on the difficulties of finding objective tests to determine presidential success or failure. The point is frequently made that the game of rating presidents is bedevilled by an unstated bias towards liberal activism. 'Great' presidents, it is often argued, are not the consolidators, but leaders who secure rafts of innovative legislation, expanding the scope of the federal government's authority and generally 'getting the country moving'.[34] 'Great' leaders are 'transformative' leaders, leaders who are largely concerned to assert, even to expand, the full powers of the executive office. On the face of it, Bill Clinton, the activist leader with a liberal reputation, would seem well placed to gain advantage from this supposed bias in the ratings game. Yet, despite some overhang from the radical politics of the 1960s, and despite the liberal orientation of the White House staff early on in his presidency, Clinton was nothing if not a pragmatist and a militant man of the centre. As Joseph Nye – the Harvard professor who also worked in the Pentagon under Clinton – noted, Bill was a president with an 'inspirational style' but with 'incremental objectives'.[35] A liberal activist who specialised in the politics of 'triangulation' and compromise is perhaps unlikely to attain 'great' status. As Arthur Schlesinger wrote in 1996: 'Middle-roading may be fine for campaigning, but it is a sure road to mediocrity in governing.'[36]

What virtually all writers on presidential performance agree upon is that chief executives must have a clear purpose and must be decisive. To quote Schlesinger once more: 'To succeed, presidents must have a port to seek and must convince Congress and the electorate of the rightness of their cause.' Looking towards the second Clinton term, Schlesinger advised that, in order to 'make a mark on history', Bill 'must liberate himself from polls and focus groups'.[37] On matters of decisiveness, there clearly are questions about Clinton's decisional habits and style. Leon Panetta, White House Chief of Staff between 1994 and 1997, commented after he left government service that 'Clinton's nature is to constantly assess and assess again, depending on who's talking to him and depending on the thoughts they presented.'[38] Describing the chaotic White House decision-making of the pre-Panetta years, Elizabeth Drew concluded: 'It wasn't policy-making. It was group therapy.'[39] Of course, all vices can, with a shift of perspective, be magically transformed into virtues. In her memoirs, *Living History*, Hillary Clinton did just that when she wrote: 'One of Bill's greatest strengths is his willingness to invite disparate opinions and then sort them out to reach his own conclusion.'[40] In this line of argument, fuzziness of purpose and failure of directed thinking are transmogrified into creative pragmatism. However, the conventional wisdom rather credits Bill Clinton with, to adapt Michael Heale's memorable phrase, 'sinuous' rather than 'creative' pragmatism.[41] On these issues of decisiveness and clarity of vision – leading rather than following – let us simply admit at this stage that Bill Clinton has a case to answer.

A 1999 Pew Research Center public opinion survey found the following characteristics heading the list of 'essential qualities Americans want in a president': 'sound judgement in a crisis' (rated by 78 per cent of respondents); 'high ethical standards' (63 per cent); 'compassion for the average citizen' (63 per cent);

8   *Clinton and his foreign policy*

'saying what one believes, even if unpopular' (57 per cent); 'having consistent positions on issues' (50 per cent); and 'forcefulness and decisiveness' (46 per cent).[42] During the year in which this survey was taken, Clinton enjoyed a Gallup public approval rating of 61 per cent. (This compared to 47 per cent in 1995. Bush41's scores oscillated between a high of 70 per cent in 1991 and 41 per cent in 1992; his son scored 78 per cent in 2002, crashing to the low 30s in his second term.) What is striking here is not only that Clinton was popular during the impeachment proceedings at the end of his presidency, but also that he was popular at precisely the time the Pew respondents were so clearly valuing 'high ethical standards'. It is also worth noting that three of the qualities identified in the 1999 poll – 'say what one believes, even if unpopular', 'having consistent positions on issues' and 'forcefulness and decisiveness' – touch directly on the received view of Clinton as 'sinuous pragmatist' and opportunist. The conclusion may be that we should not confuse elite and mass judgements; more persuasively, it may be that economic security – the later 1990s 'Clinton boom' – trumped all other considerations in public perceptions of Clinton's performance.

In regard to the top quality on the 1999 list – 'sound judge in a crisis' – it may be that Clinton was fortunate, compared to his Cold War predecessors and to Bush43 on 11 September 2001, in not having too many crises to handle. Clinton was the first American leader since the 1920s to assume office in a situation where the US was neither experiencing severe economic depression nor waging global war (whether 'hot' or 'cold'). The foreign policy crises that Clinton faced were real, while also, no doubt, to some extent manipulated to maximise presidential control over them. But they were less than existential. If this meant that he was denied some of the 'rally round' effect that benefited other leaders, it also seems to have allowed him slowly to accumulate an impressive reservoir of public approval. It seems also that Clinton scored well in the remaining category from the top six qualities identified in the 1999 Pew survey: 'compassion for the average citizen.' Talking to 'ordinary' Americans, in all their variety, about domestic and foreign issues is a vital part of the president's job. A good president must, in Erwin Hargrove's phrase, find 'culturally appropriate' means of presenting his political and programmatic case.[43] On this issue of empathy with 'ordinary' Americans, it is at least worth recording that Clinton, unlike the two Bushes, was no child of privilege. Whatever its weaknesses, his autobiography, *My Life*, no less than Ronald Reagan's *An American Dream*, plausibly presents its author as the liver and exemplification of the American Dream.[44] Of course, as the example of Franklin Roosevelt will attest, an American leader does not have to demonstrate humble origins in order to achieve empathy and democratic credibility. It is also true that, in terms of the passions surrounding his presidency, Clinton followed Reagan in dividing as much as uniting his fellow countrymen. Yet, surely one of Clinton's strengths was his 'common touch' and ability, despite the brutal partisan divisions of the 1990s, credibly to embrace American diversity and openness. It was in this rhetorical, 'culturally appropriate' vein that, in his 1993 Inaugural Address, the newly elected Clinton rededicated the US to 'the very idea of America ... an idea ennobled by the faith that our nation can summon from its original diversity, the deepest measure of unity'.[45]

Foreign policy assessments raise profound problems of structure, agency and of levels-of-analysis in international relations. At the macro-level, US foreign policy unquestionably is more the product of shifting American geopolitical and economic interests, not to mention of the global structure of power, than of the vision of any particular president. By the same token, one would have to be a very arch-determinist indeed to accord no meaningful scope to domestic pressures and to individuated presidential decisions. Leading neo-realist thinkers in fact tend to allow considerable weight to such factors in explaining both success and failure in US foreign policy.[46] As Stephen Skowronek argues, the US presidency is a 'blunt instrument', well suited to the disruption of established structures.[47]

How should we judge the president's part in shaping foreign policy decisions? Much turns on questions of context. What was the nature of the legacy inherited from the former chief executive? Did the president rise to the opportunities presented by the international and domestic political context in which he operated – in Clinton's case, of course, the opportunities inherent in the post-Cold War international order? A good foreign policy president needs to display 'contextual intelligence': 'a capability to discern trends in the face of complexity and adaptability while trying to shape events.'[48] Good presidents need to keep a degree of control over complex decisional structures: to lead the actors in the foreign policy process – including the bureaucracy, and indeed the US military – towards the achievement of goals set in the White House. Presidents should at least aspire to rationality in foreign policy decision-making: notably the careful weighing of options (always including the option of benign neglect). They should exercise good judgement, defined by Richard Haass thus: 'the ability to assess a situation accurately and, where applicable, prescribe a course of feasible policy that does the most to advance recognized interests and bring about desirable outcomes at the lowest possible direct and indirect costs'.[49] Presidents should be aware of the constant threats to rationality: the inevitable impact of complex bureaucratic politics; the inherent ambiguity of American 'national interests' – a particularly acute problem in the uncharted waters of the post-Cold War era; time constraints; and so on.[50] They should aspire to run a procedural tight ship, taking opportunities to learn and adapt. Presidents will also be judged according to their ability to build domestic and international consensus, including the management of alliance structures; according to their ability to achieve democratic legitimacy, including the observance of domestic and international law and the achievement of productive relationships with the US Congress.

Much of the literature on the assessment of presidential foreign policy takes a strong psychological turn. Alexander and Juliette George pose the following test for judging the quality of foreign policy leadership: 'To what extent is the leader's response to a particular set of circumstances reasonable, given its situational context and, conversely, to what extent is it the response dictated by the idiosyncratic requirements of that leader's personality rather than by the requirements of the situation?'[51] Good leaders are ones who are aware of their own personality, cognitive style and 'character' and who are able to develop a decisional process which minimises their attendant distortions.[52] Foreign policy decisions to a very high degree involve 'value complexity' – the trading-off of values: presidential and congressional agendas have somehow to be reconciled; free trade values can conflict with the commitment to promote democracy.[53] Again, successful presidents will bring rationality and open process to bear on these problems. To do so, they must be *aware* of them. They must avoid narrow procedural 'groupthink' and promote 'multiple advocacy' in their advisory structures.[54] Human beings cannot avoid thinking in analogical terms: relating current crises to past events and experiences. The good president is the one who rationally adopts *appropriate* and 'testable' analogies, never becoming their prisoner.[55] All this may sound like a counsel of perfection, and to some degree it is. Yet presidential foreign policy needs to be judged against just such formulations. Such judgements will be made implicitly as we survey different elements of Clinton's foreign policy. They will be made explicitly in the final chapter. We turn now to the leading personalities, focusing particularly on key foreign policy experiences and beliefs.

Personalities

The presidency of Lyndon Johnson was labelled by Hugh Sidey 'a very personal presidency'.[56] Though much more frequently compared to JFK than to LBJ, Bill Clinton also presided over an exceptionally personalised administration. Presidential assistant Bill Curry later described how the procedural rhythms of the White House replicated the Clinton personality traits which had been forged in the Arkansas of the 1950s and 1960s: 'We were all living in Hot Springs, every one of us.'[57] Like the people who worked for LBJ, Clinton's staff lived in dread of random outbursts of temper – with Bill issuing 'cusswords for five minutes' – followed (at least in Clinton's case) by a swift lifting of the darkness, though never quite by an apology.[58]

Charm in buckets, the need for approval, recklessness (especially in sexual matters), quickness of intellect, a tendency towards self-indulgence: these aspects of the presidential character require little further emphasis. The testimony of former associates from Arkansas came to have a certain predictable and self-fulfilling quality. However, these testimonies do tend to run along similar lines. Here was a leader who, despite the outbursts of temper, craved consensus. As Benjamin Barber recalled, Clinton was a president who 'didn't like hard choices'. When forced to decide between competing views, he continued to believe 'deeply that he could always do "some of both"'.[59] Here also was a leader whose charm and inclusive empathy could apparently shift into slipperiness and duplicity. According to Arkansas news reporter Brenda Blagg: 'He doesn't like to make anybody mad and, of course, in the process of trying not to make anyone mad, he makes somebody mad all the time.'[60] Arkansas journalist Max Brantley recalled: 'He crawls into your soul for a minute or two, and then he looks over your shoulder for the next guy in the room he's going to do the same thing to.'[61] More brutally still, here is Bill Baker, former Arkansas labour leader: Clinton, according to Baker, would 'pat you on the back and pee down your leg'.[62] The upside here, from the viewpoint of good policy, was that charm could become a positive resource. As Sidney Blumenthal put it: 'He understood his effect on people while he was having it, a most unusual combination of instinct and self-awareness.'[63] The problem, of course, was the one identified by Brenda Blagg and expressed, in the polite tones of a Clinton supporter, by former Treasury Secretary Robert Rubin: 'Clinton listened so sympathetically that people who were unaccustomed to him often took it as duplicitous when he later came out against their positions'.[64]

James David Barber, doyen of academic analysts of presidential character, regarded Clinton as falling firmly into his category of 'active-positive' leaders: presidents who combine an activist expansionist view of the office with an ability to derive emotional satisfaction from its exercise.[65] Like other 'active-positives' such as FDR and JFK, Clinton had the proclivity to overreach. Clinton as president did experience difficulties deriving from a disorganisation which seemed to be associated with sheer wilful energy, leading to overwork. Robert Reich, Secretary of Labor between 1993 and 1997, recalled a cabinet meeting of February 1993: 'He can barely stay awake. ... His eyelids droop and his pupils move up under them, leaving nothing but a narrow sliver of white eyeball.'[66] 'Overreaching' was to become a common diagnosis of why the Clinton presidency ran into difficulties. In November 1996, *Time* magazine attributed his first term problems to his attempt to transform the 42 per cent of the vote he received in the 1992 presidential election into an 'imperial mandate to rearrange the planets'.[67]

Clinton's 'active-positivism' inevitably involved a degree of defensiveness and insecurity. He coped emotionally with the ultimate presidential humiliation of impeachment really very well, but his subsequent claims that everything was 'business as usual' in the White House were not entirely credible.[68] A certain southern defensiveness also came through in some of Clinton's rhetoric. He told the Southern Legislative Conference in August 1992: 'Let's show them that there is a New South and we're a lot smarter than they think we are.'[69] Despite this, what was very striking about Clinton was actually the absence of chips on his shoulder. He was also that comparatively rare animal in American electoral politics: a politico who combined an exhaustive knowledge of political minutiae, keen electoral skills *and* a genuine enthusiasm for policy. As Fred Greenstein wrote in 1995:

> It is as if the more cerebral side of John F. Kennedy's approach to leadership were writ large and amalgamated with Lyndon Johnson's proclivity to press the flesh, find ways to split the difference with his opponents and otherwise practise the art of the possible.[70]

Given his gubernatorial background, it is not surprising that Clinton's strong sense of confidence and personal efficacy was greater in domestic rather than in foreign policy. His foreign policy outlook, of course, was formed by the Vietnam War. Clinton seems to have taken some clear lessons from the war:

America should not become exposed in areas of the world far removed from its core interests, controversial foreign policy commitments require extensive public education, American power always has limits and fallibilities. Clinton's own account of his early days laid stress on his loyalty, pragmatism and moderation. When he first went to work for Arkansas Senator J. William Fulbright's Foreign Relations Committee in 1966, Clinton was prepared to give President Johnson 'the benefit of the doubt' on Vietnam.[71] Exposure to the anti-war positions being adopted by Fulbright and by Clinton's fellow staffers shifted Bill's position to the kind of moderate peacenikism which dominated his outlook into the mid-1970s. Clinton found a summer 1966 National Student Association convention at the University of Maryland 'full of people like me, who were uncomfortable with the more militant SDS' – Students for a Democratic Society – 'but still wanted to be counted in the ranks of those working to end the war'.[72] He was influenced by the within-the-system anti-war positions embraced by Allard Lowenstein, as well as by the conscientious objections to Vietnam service offered by fellow Oxford Rhodes scholar Frank Aller. It is a mark of the tempestuous nature of the times that both Lowenstein and Aller took their own lives.

For Clinton, 1968 was the turning point in the recent history of American politics: the year when, as he wrote in a revealing section of his autobiography, 'conservative populism replaced progressive populism as the dominant political force in our nation'.[73] Bill (born in 1946) and Hillary (born in 1947) were both of the generation of '68. For Bill, one lesson of the late 1960s and early 1970s appeared to be – despite Clinton's own role in the 1972 McGovern campaign – that principled 'progressive populism' needed to be treated with a strong dose of pragmatism. Clinton's own academic background in international affairs, at Georgetown University and at Oxford (despite the time spent by Rhodes scholars 'wondering what the devil we were doing there', living on time 'borrowed' from service in Vietnam) was very strong.[74] His stance towards the foreign policy issues of the later 1970s and 1980s was that of an informed New Southerner, far more interested in the modernisation of his region than in the shifting patterns of world politics. Even in 1991, his endorsement of President Bush's action in the Gulf was vague and disconnected.[75] In terms of his developing foreign policy orientation, it is difficult to improve on Sidney Blumenthal's account of Clinton's 'protean nature': 'He stood in concentric circles: the New South, post-Cold War America, and the generation of 1968 that was coming to power throughout the Western world. In each area, he was something new.'[76]

No First Lady, except perhaps Lady Macbeth herself, has been the object of as much critical investigation as Hillary Rodham, the other half of 'Clinton Incorporated'[77]. As part of 'Billary', supplying the *super-ego* to Bill's *id*, she exemplified for many conservatives the road trodden by so many in the 'Vietnam generation'. The Clintons, according to one conservative critic became 'paradigmatic 1960s Coat and Tie Radicals, spending their college days in protest, alienation and spelunking (*sic*), and applying to law school'.[78] As a former 'Goldwater girl', Hillary had a harder job than Bill in adjusting to the 1960s, yet their views on the war were converging even before they met at Yale in 1970. In her formal response to a 1969 address at Wellesley College by Edward Brooke, Hillary Rodham criticised the Massachusetts Senator for preferring 'empathy' to action over Vietnam. Brooke, at that time the only African American in the Senate, had moved to a mild anti-war position. As president of Wellesley Young Republicans, Hillary Rodham campaigned for Brooke in her freshman year. Now, in terms which one would not necessarily associate with her husband, she urged Brooke to 'practice politics as the art of making what appears to be impossible, possible'.[79] In 1970, following the Kent State killings, she urged Yale students to eschew 'disruption or "revolution"', while condemning the invasion of Cambodia as 'the unconscionable expansion of a war that should never have been waged'.[80]

In 1970, Hillary and Bill commenced a complementary balancing act that was to dominate the rest of their lives. A former student friend remembered the complementary dynamic thus: 'Hillary was very sharp and Chicago, and Bill was very *To Kill a Mockingbird*'. Many years later, Harold Ickes, Deputy White House Chief of Staff between 1993 and 1996 concluded: 'She is much harder-edged on issues, and he's much more accommodating.'[81] It is difficult to believe that Hillary's harder edge did not have some impact on key foreign policy decisions during the presidential years, notably in relation to the Balkans. She apparently told journalist Lucinda Franks, following the start of the Kosovo campaign in 1999: 'I urged him to bomb ... What do we have NATO for, if not to defend our way of life?'[82] The extent of her policy influence in the Clinton administration became a matter of intense debate during Hillary Clinton's 2008 election campaign. Greig Craig, former director of Policy Planning at State under Bill Clinton declared in 2008 that Hillary had never sat in on National Security Council (NSC) meetings and did not even enjoy security clearance. Countering Hillary's suggestion that she had been closely involved in 1999 negotiations to open borders for Kosovo refugees, Ivo Daalder, former Kosovo specialist on the NSC staff (and, like Craig, now advising Barack Obama), recalled that 'she had absolutely no role in the dirty work of negotiations'. On Northern Ireland, however, John Hume (former leader of the Social Democratic and Labour Party in the province) declared 'from firsthand experience' that she 'played a positive role' in the peace process.[83] The First Lady was linked into foreign policy decisions in ways which will become clearer once relevant archives are released. She consciously followed the trail set by Eleanor Roosevelt, writing in *Living History*: 'Wherever I ventured, Mrs Roosevelt seemed to have been there before me.'[84] Her most celebrated foreign policy venture was her public attack in 1995 on Chinese human rights policies at the Fourth United Nations World Conference on Women in Beijing. Her public foreign policy agenda concentrated on women's rights, foreign aid promotion and civil society development.[85]

When David Gergen, then counsellor to the president, asked Chief of Staff 'Mack' McLarty in 1993 to describe the White House organisational chart, he was told that 'three people' were in the 'top box': Bill Clinton, Hillary Clinton and Vice President Al Gore.[86] Tensions between the two junior 'top boxers' were evident from the start of the presidency.[87] Born in 1948, a year later than Hillary,

Al Gore developed a foreign policy outlook which was shaped by the debates surrounding the anti-war positions taken by his father, Senator Albert Gore Senior, Democrat of Tennessee. The junior Gore was unquestionably inspired by his father's anti-war stances on the Senate Foreign Relations Committee, but also appreciated the practical consequences of espousing policies – pro-civil rights as well as anti-war – which ran against the Tennessean grain in the late 1960s and early 1970s. Albert Gore Senior lost his Senate seat in 1970. The younger Gore served in Vietnam as a reporter for the military newspaper, *Stars and Stripes*, a job which exposed him to dangerous combat situations. As a Tennessean Congressman in the late 1970s and early 1980s, he became an expert on arms control. He opposed Reagan's Strategic Defense Initiative as a violation of anti-ballistic missile (ABM) agreements with the Soviets. Gore's successful Senate race of 1984 was accompanied by a degree of rethinking on Vietnam. Defending the granting of aid to the anti-communist *contra* rebels in Nicaragua in 1984, Gore declared: 'We've overlearned the lessons of Vietnam.' He later recalled:

> I didn't change my conclusions about the war being a terrible mistake, but it struck me that opponents to the war, including myself, really did not take into account the fact that there were an awful lot of South Vietnamese who desperately wanted to hang on to what they called freedom.[88]

In the Senate, Gore was a strong supporter of Israel and an opponent of the cautious Bush41 policies on the former Yugoslavia. He voted for military action in the Gulf in January 1991. After the Gulf War victory, he criticised the decision to allow Saddam Hussein to remain in power. The Iraqi dictator should not be allowed to remain 'an acceptable part of the landscape'.[89] In the Congress, Gore was not quite the eco-warrior he later became. He supported various Tennessee Valley projects of questionable environmental impact, and was far from being the most outspoken Senator on environmental issues in the 1980s.[90] However, his 1992 book, *Earth in the Balance*, was an agenda-setting personal manifesto on environmentalism, often couched in a mixture of apocalyptic and romantic language. Attacking the contemporary 'environmental holocaust', Gore urged an 'environmentalism of the spirit'.[91] His attraction to Clinton in 1992 was obvious. Gore was a New Democrat Washington insider with a record of service in Vietnam. He joined the Clinton ticket with a determination that environmentalism should be part of foreign policy. He also brought a strong commitment to reversing the Bush caution on Bosnia.

Describing the incoming Clinton team, Martin Walker wrote in 1992 that it represented 'both the maturing and the vengeance of the anti-Vietnam generation'.[92] The Friends of Bill – led by figures such as Strobe Talbott (born in 1946), Clinton's room-mate at Oxford, who became Ambassador at Large in the State Department in April 1993 – were indeed individuals whose international outlook had been shaped by the war. Clinton's first Secretary of State, however, was from the preceding Second World War/early Cold War generation. A lawyer from Los Angeles, Warren Christopher (born in 1925) had served as a deputy to Secretary of

State Cyrus Vance in the Carter years. He was known particularly for his work for President Carter in coordinating human rights policies at the interagency level and for his role in the Iran hostage diplomacy of 1979–80. He had also been closely involved in the diplomacy attending normalisation of relations with China. At 67, Christopher was a Democratic 'grey-head'; several commentators pointed out that he was exactly the same age as Clinton's deceased father (William Jefferson Blyth) would have been. Unveiling a portrait of Christopher in 1999, Clinton described his first Secretary of State as the first such figure in over 50 years to face 'the challenge of defining our foreign policy without a single, overriding threat to our security'. He added: 'Chris has the lowest ratio of ego to accomplishment of any public servant I've ever worked with.'[93] Stories circulated about his caution, mildness and fastidiousness. At a stop-over in Ireland, Christopher famously ordered a decaffeinated Irish coffee with no alcohol. His memoir, *Chances of a Lifetime*, was a model of controversy-avoidance.[94] For Madeleine Albright, Christopher was 'a lawyer's lawyer', always emphasising 'preparation, precision and perseverance'.[95] To many liberal Democrats Christopher seemed too much the bureaucrat, too little the original thinker who could devise foreign policy positions for the new era.[96] He described Washington as 'a cruel, unforgiving town that lacks a sense of balance', and constantly advertised his willingness to 'spread the limelight around' at the State Department.[97]

Christopher impressed Clinton by his work on the 1992–93 transition team. Compared to other candidates – such as former NSA Zbigniew Brzezinski and Senate Armed Services Committee chairman Sam Nunn – Christopher was a solid team player. He represented a credible link to the previous Democratic administration, but one whose relatively low profile lessened the possibility of divisions from the late 1970s being reignited. Christopher was actually younger than another possible candidate, Ed Muskie, who had served as Secretary of State in 1980. Christopher appealed to Clinton's cautious side. Though Nunn appeared at times to be a kind of Secretary of State in-waiting, Clinton clearly valued Christopher's reliability and dignified loyalty. According to Raymond Seitz, US Ambassador to London, Christopher stood out in the early Clinton crowd 'like an adult in a kindergarten'.[98]

The flamboyance of Clinton's second term Secretary of State, Madeleine Albright, contrasted sharply with the style of her predecessor. Albright had served on Jimmy Carter's NSC staff under Zbigniew Brzezinski, her former thesis adviser at Columbia University. She served as US Representative to the United Nations (UN) in the first Clinton term, becoming associated with the policy of 'assertive multilateralism'. Unusually for the American delegate to the UN, she was a Cabinet member and a full participant on the NSC. As UN representative she had a high public profile and developed a flair for public relations, commenting: 'CNN is the 16th member of the (UN) Security Council.'[99] Albright's 1997 appointment was aided by the support of the First Lady. Although widely regarded as extremely assertive and extrovert, her appointment was also probably assisted by the fact that, compared to her main rival, Richard Holbrooke – favoured by Vice President Gore as Christopher's successor – she was actually *less* inclined to grandstanding and freelancing. (Holbrooke, born in 1941, had worked in Carter's State Department; he was appointed by Clinton as Ambassador to Germany in 1993 and went on to serve as Assistant Secretary of State for European and Canadian Affairs, focusing on the Balkans, between 1994 and 1996, and as US Representative to the UN from 1999). Albright also had the advantage over Holbrooke of being more acceptable to Congressional Republicans. She was confirmed 99–0 by the Republican Senate in 1996 (Holbrooke was confirmed 81–6 in 1999 for the UN job, but only after long and acrimonious hearings). The other main rival to succeed Christopher was Senate Majority Leader George Mitchell. Albright mounted a concerted campaign for the post, consciously avoiding any suggestion that her appointment be 'made a litmus test of the President's commitment to women's rights'. Clinton had, by 1996, made numerous high-profile female appointments, and was likely to resent such an implication.[100]

Albright, born in 1937, was closer to the 'Vietnam generation' than Christopher had been, but famously described her own 'mindset' as 'Munich not Vietnam'.[101] She identified herself with the tough-minded stance of her mentor, Brzezinski, asserting the need not to forget either pre-Cold War ('Munich') or Cold War lessons in the post-Cold War era. Already in 1996, she was associated with the phrase, 'indispensable nation', to describe America's post-Cold War role. Clinton made a point of using those words when he introduced his new head of the State Department in 1996. The 'Munich not Vietnam' slogan also fitted in with Albright's extraordinary family history. As Strobe Talbott later put it:

> More than any of the rest of us, she was literally a child of the cold war: she had been eleven in 1948, when a Soviet-instigated coup d'etat forced her parents to gather up the family and flee their native Czechoslovakia.[102]

Brought up a Roman Catholic, Albright only discovered her Jewish origins after her appointment to Foggy Bottom. Like the Polish-American Brzezinski in the Carter administration, Albright's self-image was, in Thomas Lippmann's words, that of 'a tough-talking, straight-shooting "doer"'.[103]

Albright, as Representative to the UN, clashed frequently with Tony Lake, Clinton's first term NSA. If Albright was 'Munich not Vietnam', Lake (born in 1939) saw his role – which he described in self-deprecatory terms as 'national security adviser of the free world' – as reconciling the lessons of Munich with those of Vietnam. The US needed both to respond strongly to aggression *and* to recognise the limits to American power. Comparing his own early 1960s naivety over Vietnam to that of Graham Greene's 'Quiet American', Lake continued to uphold the need for moral purpose in foreign policy.[104] With his academic background at Harvard, Cambridge (England) and Princeton, Lake was an international affairs intellectual and a State Department Foreign Service Officer, who had worked in Vietnam between 1962 and 1965. He served on Henry Kissinger's staff under President Nixon, before resigning over the 1970 invasion of Cambodia. He became State Department Director of Policy Planning under

Carter, working for Cyrus Vance and inevitably partaking in Vance's intense rivalry with Brzezinski and his staff. Despite Lake's best efforts, it was not possible entirely to bury these old bureaucratic disputes, which flared up once more in the tension with Albright. Lake's outlook combined a degree of post-Vietnam caution with a real commitment to democracy-promoting humanitarian internationalism. With Gore, he supported a stronger line on Bosnia in the early stages of the Clinton presidency. Lake's style was low-key and, regarding the media in particular, often edgy and defensive. He later recorded his frustration at the media's damaging 'sequential hysteria', in relentlessly pursuing sensational and superficially 'new' news stories.[105] Lake's developing foreign policy outlook may be traced in his academic publications. In his edited volume, *The Vietnam Legacy* (1976), Lake warned of an overreaction to the Indochina disaster. The US must not take the view that it is 'inherently incapable of progressive action abroad': 'If Vietnam gives us more humility than self-hatred, caution rather than unconcern, then we shall have profited something from its horror.'[106] Surveying conflicts in the developing world in 1990, he urged external powers not simply to 'throw up their hands' at the intractability of ancient rivalries and enmities, but to pursue positive humanitarian engagement.[107] Uniquely for a NSA, Lake was also an academic expert on White House–State Department relations.[108]

Lake and Clinton had originally been brought together in 1991 by Sandy Berger, who served as Lake's deputy in the first term and succeeded him as NSA after the 1996 election. By the start of his second term, Clinton was concerned to be completely personally engaged in his own foreign policy. Against this background, Berger saw his role more as presidential enforcer, less as collegial, quasi-presidential equal in the Lake mould.[109] Sandy Berger (born in 1945) was a trade lawyer and former anti-Vietnam War activist. He worked on the 1968 campaigns of both Eugene McCarthy and Bobby Kennedy, as well as on the 1972 McGovern campaign, where he had first met Bill Clinton. He had also served as deputy to Lake on Carter's State Department Policy Planning staff, specialising in arms control. He had worked for Madeleine Albright, in her role as chief foreign policy adviser to the 1988 Michael Dukakis presidential campaign. When first appointed, his economics background – unusual in a NSA – was seen as complementing Albright's geostrategic outlook. Henry Kissinger's comment – 'you can't expect a trade lawyer to be a global strategist' – was quoted by journalists throughout the second term whenever the Clinton team was accused of lacking foreign policy direction. Clinton seems to have regarded Berger as a highly efficient Washington networker, and one without too much of a personal agenda. A long-standing Friend of Bill (FoB), Berger's virtues included an enormous capacity for long hours. His personal orientation was as a problem-solver who worried 'about today today and tomorrow tomorrow'.[110] Berger had actually been responsible for Clinton's 'first regular Washington institutional connection' – a position on the board of 'Democrats for the '80s', organised by Pamela Harriman (widow of Averell Harriman, Washington political hostess and eventual Clinton appointee as Ambassador to Paris). Berger presented himself as a pragmatic internationalist – less cerebral than Lake, but also more politically savvy and much more willing to take on the foreign policy media. In April 2005, Berger pleaded guilty to illegally removing classified material, relating to Clinton's anti-terrorist policies, from the National Archives in Washington DC.[111]

The history of Clinton's appointment of his Secretaries of Defense and Central Intelligence Agency (CIA) heads is complex and deeply affected by the partisan politics – and associated 'ethics panics' – of the 1990s. The first Clinton Secretary of Defense was 54-year-old Les Aspin, yet another former opponent of the Vietnam War and ex-chair of the House of Representatives Armed Services Committee. Aspin had taken the line of a conservative Democrat in the 1980s: voting both for MX missile funding and for aid to the Nicaraguan *contras*. His disorganised personal and working habits soon began to affect his bureaucratic effectiveness. Journalist Tim Weiner described him in 1996 as the 'absent-minded professor who had appalling relationships with the military'.[112] Aspin was succeeded in early 1994 by William Perry, following the unsuccessful nomination of Admiral Bobby Ray Inman. A former Deputy Director of the CIA, Inman was damaged by accusations concerning both his personal taxation affairs and his conduct at the CIA, where – according to journalist William Safire – he had in 1981 endangered Israeli security by denying Israel intelligence relating to Syria and Iraq. Perry (born in 1927) had worked for Secretary of Defense Harold Brown under Jimmy Carter, and was a respected expert on high-tech military procurement. Philip Zelikow, a member of Bush41's NSC staff, described Perry in 1996 as a 'strong defense secretary – the strongest in a generation'.[113] Perry in turn was replaced for the second term by William Cohen, former Republican Congressman and Senator from Maine. Cohen (born in 1940) was neither a Pentagon nor a Clinton insider. Clinton recalled Cohen as having played a key role in the military reorganisation legislation, the Goldwater–Nichols Act of 1986. He also 'wanted a Republican in the cabinet'.[114] Cohen conspicuously failed to defend the president during the impeachment process.

The appointment of James Woolsey to be head of the CIA in 1993 was rushed, and only finalised after Clinton was persuaded by a group of conservative Democrats that the initial foreign policy team already had too many liberals.[115] Woolsey's lack of CIA experience – he had worked for various foreign policy executive agencies and as a Senate staffer – seems to have appealed to Clinton's desire to reorient the Agency away from Cold War priorities, but Woolsey's generally neo-conservative policy outlook effectively ensured his marginalisation. David Gergen later wrote: 'When a small plane crashed on the White House lawn, people joked it was CIA director James Woolsey trying to get an appointment.'[116] Woolsey endorsed Republican presidential candidate Bob Dole in 1996 and in 2008 became a leading foreign policy adviser to the Republican presidential campaign of John McCain. Woolsey was succeeded in 1995 by John Deutch (born 1938), a former Pentagon official. The original choice to follow Woolsey was Air Force General Michael Carns, whose nomination failed, like several others in the Clinton administration, due to accusations about supposed legal irregularities regarding an immigrant household employee. Deutch in his turn eventually became embroiled in accusations of careless handling of classified information, and was pardoned by Clinton just before he left office in 2001. Deutch's departure in 1996 led to yet another unsuccessful nomination: this time of Tony Lake. Lake was ready to step down as NSA after one term and possibly not fully committed to the CIA job. He did not answer the partisan attacks – which almost inevitably included some minor ethics issues – from Senator Richard Shelby, Republican chair of the Intelligence Committee, with much in the way of combativeness, and withdrew his name from consideration. Clinton's final CIA head (1997–2001) was George Tenet, who had served as Deputy Director for two years and was considered a safe bet for a successful nomination. Even Tenet did not escape without minor financial irregularities being raised by the Intelligence Committee. Tenet (born in 1953) continued to lead the CIA into the Bush43 years, becoming controversially implicated in the controversies surrounding intelligence on the Iraqi development of WMD.[117]

What strikes us about the composition of Clinton's top foreign policy personnel? For one thing, despite Clinton's reputation for cronyism, few Friends of Bill were actually represented at the very top levels. Sandy Berger was a FoB, but Lake was not, nor were any of the Secretaries of State or Defense. Strobe Talbott probably could have become NSA in 1996/97, but seems to have declined the post precisely because of the ensuing complexity of working for his old and close friend. Talbott also (understandably, given the disarray at the CIA during the 1990s) showed little enthusiasm for the job of CIA head, following the withdrawal of Lake's nomination in 1997. We are struck by the degree of continuity with the Carter years, despite Clinton's famed lack of enthusiasm for 'Carter retreads'. The Carter administration, with its debilitating rift between Vance and Brzezinski, was not an attractive model to emulate. Yet where else was Clinton supposed to look for seasoned Democratic foreign policy personnel, if not to the ranks of the previous Democratic administration? Clinton was at first reluctant to bring Republicans into leading foreign policy positions, despite the flimsiness of his 1992 electoral mandate. Continuity with the Republican presidential years, of course, was achieved at a lower level in the career foreign policy bureaucracy. One of the most significant Bush41–Clinton holdovers was Dennis Ross, originally retained by Christopher to advise him on Middle Eastern issues. Though Ross had worked in the Reagan administration and had been close to Secretary of State James Baker under Bush41, he was a lifelong Democrat who, in true Clinton team style, had cut his political teeth in the antiwar campaigns of Bobby Kennedy in 1968 and McGovern in 1972.[118]

Following the Congressional elections of 1994 it became essential to pick candidates who were acceptable to the Republican Senate – a development which culminated in the nomination of William Cohen in December 1996. The fractious nature of nomination politics is evident from the foregoing narrative of the Clinton appointments. The challenge, certainly in the early years, was to recruit Democrats of experience and expertise without rekindling the old rivalries and hatreds. Ideologically, there were significant divisions, notably between democracy-promoting liberalism (Lake), extreme caution regarding intervention per se (Christopher), and unbridled assertion (Albright). Yet there was no 'great divide' on the scale of the Carter experience. The centre of gravity of Clinton's foreign policy team was, in Democratic Party terms, the New Democrat centre, represented by Bill and Hillary, as well as by Vice President Gore. Many of the key personnel had supported *contra* aid in the 1980s. Yet they also were internationalists with commitments to post-Cold War multilateralism, humanitarianism and democracy-promotion, even though these commitments would be severely put to the test. After all, even Christopher, in some ways the epitome of a European-style cautious 'conservative', was a veteran implementer of Jimmy Carter's global human rights policy. The Clinton team, even those with little direct experience of the Vietnam conflict, were all also concerned to respect the 'lessons of Vietnam'. Yet, as Lake had written as long ago as 1976, it was really unclear what exactly those lessons were.[119] Should the US really avoid all conflict that did not directly threaten core strategic interests? More crucially still, how did the onset of the post-Cold War redefine the scope of American interests?

2 Foreign policy between the Bushes

In March 1997, Sandy Berger attempted formally to spell out the foreign policy agenda for the second Clinton term. Speaking in Washington DC, he declared: 'I have come here today not only to praise the "Post-Cold War Era" but to bury it.' According to Berger, the period since the fall of the Berlin Wall had seen an unprecedented spurt of global integration: both economic and technological, and always underpinned by the expansion and ultimate universalisation of democratic values. So far, the world had been grappling with the new integrative dynamism, without fully appreciating the degree to which the new era was producing its own opportunities and problems – opportunities and problems with which the norms and institutions inherited from the Cold War years could no longer cope. The challenge now was 'to build up new institutions and understandings' – including the creation of an undivided, peaceful Europe, the achievement of a cooperative order in the Asia Pacific, accepting the 'inescapable reality that America can often be the decisive force for peace in the world, creating the multilateral means to combat 'transnational security threats', building 'an open trading system for the 21st century', and funding 'an American diplomacy fit for international partnership and 'sharing the burdens with likeminded nations'.[1]

From a twenty-first-century perspective, the 'post-Cold War era' seems less a transitional period, ending when global leaders woke up to these new challenges, but rather a distinct period of international history, beginning with the collapse of the Berlin Wall and ending with the 11 September 2001 terror attacks. From the point of view of US foreign policy, the period was distinguished by a continued American preoccupation with the affairs of Russia and, increasingly, with China. Berger himself envisioned China as the country whose development 'will have the biggest impact on our children'.[2] The post-Cold War era also saw the continuation of US 'Vietnam syndrome' inhibitions on the use of military power; various internal challenges to US presidential domination of foreign policymaking; the apparent replacement of geopolitics by geo-economics as the driving force behind US foreign policy; a conscious and complex public debate about the purpose of American alliance structures, and indeed of US internationalism generally; and, finally, the slow, but clear, emergence of the new, 'borderless threat' – from AIDS to refugees and international terrorism – agenda.

Post-Cold War foreign policy

Soviet negotiator Georgi Arbatov warned Washington in 1987 that Moscow, in bringing the Cold War to an end, would be doing 'a terrible thing to you – we are going to deprive you of an enemy'.[3] There is no question that the 'Soviet threat' had been both functionally constitutive of American identity, and a strong concentrator of America's foreign policy mind since the Truman presidency. Following the fall of the Berlin Wall, the notion that the US somehow had to 'construct' a new enemy to replace the Russian bear was a common theme in journalistic commentary and in undergraduate essays. More to the point, however, was George Kennan's observation that the onset of a world that 'appears to be devoid of anything that could be seen as a major great-power enemy' presented the US 'with a problem for which few of us are prepared'.[4]

Bill Clinton entered office in the middle of the national debate about the nature and purpose of American internationalism in the new era. The debate began in earnest under George H. W. Bush. Bush41's determination not overly to embarrass Soviet leader Mikhail Gorbachev by 'dancing on the Berlin Wall' combined with the recessionary economic climate of the early 1990s to stifle any climate of national rejoicing. However, as Robert Hunter wrote in 1992: 'There is no doubt that the United States won the Cold War, although Western leaders mute that point out of concern to avoid repeating with the Soviet Union the post-First World War experience in stigmatizing Germany.' In 1992, according to Hunter, 'the United States has a greater range of geostrategic choice than it has had since the beginning of the Cold War and in fact since before Pearl Harbor'.[5] While the Pentagon's 'No Rivals' plan, leaked in 1992, looked forward to a world of endless American primacy, other voices urged restraint.[6] Robert Tucker and David Hendrickson argued that post-Cold War America must resist 'the imperial temptation', with its familiar equation between US-guaranteed world-order with American security.[7] In a book published almost literally as the Berlin Wall collapsed, former Defense Secretary Robert McNamara advocated an immediate 50 per cent cut in the US military budget.[8] Various commentators wished to replace 'national security' with 'economic security', cashing in the post-Cold War 'peace dividend' in order to promote domestic regeneration.[9] American leaders were urged to prioritise Pacific over European policy; to resurrect the 'global community' agenda of the early Carter years; even to adapt to the threat posed by new nationalisms and a revived Islam.[10] In words that anticipated the concerns of Clinton's first term, Richard Gardner ventured the opinion in 1990 that there was 'now a broad bipartisan consensus that human rights should be part of the US foreign policy agenda'; how 'a nation treats its own citizens is no longer its own business alone'.[11] Above all, these were years where all seemed to be in flux. Old certainties and old political alignments were being re-made.

Bush41's legacy to Clinton was certainly, as Michael Mandelbaum described it in 1991, 'the greatest geopolitical windfall in the history of American foreign policy'.[12] To the new world which emerged from the rubble of the Berlin Wall, President George H. W. Bush (Bush41) responded with a cautious conservatism.

He sought a middle road between isolationism and 'globocop' imperialism, always stressing that 'our enemy today is uncertainty and instability'.[13] His central integrative concept for guiding US foreign policy in the post-Cold War context, the New World Order, was an attempt to reconcile the perceived need for US international leadership with burden-sharing and a rejuvenated UN. His approach – pragmatic, internationalist, the foreign policy of 'an American Tory'[14] – served America well, but did not remotely constitute a successor to anti-communist containment as an integrative conceptual apparatus for the future. In 1995, Richard Haass was still portraying the US as hovering between competing foreign policy options. He singled out the options of 'realism' (essentially world-order maximisation); 'economism' (where foreign policy is designed primarily to serve domestic economic ends; 'minimalism' (a new isolationist focus on domestic agendas, with both left and right wing variants); and 'Wilsonianism' (a foreign policy built around the perceived need to export 'freedom', variously conceived in a mixture of political and economic forms, to the rest of the world).[15]

Most commentators in the early 1990s felt that post-Cold War American leaders would have to confront a 'new isolationism' in American public opinion: possibly also an era of powerful neo-isolationist demagogues. President Bush anticipated Clinton in attacking notions of 'Fortress America': 'The notion that we can separate domestic and foreign policy rests upon a stubborn fantasy that we can live in an isolated island surrounded by a changing and developing world'.[16] One interesting feature of these foreign policy debates of the early to mid-1990s was the reluctance of virtually everyone to accept the label, 'isolationist'.[17] However, despite the almost universal avoidance of the 'I' word, the 'new populism' made its presence felt in the 1992 presidential nomination campaign in the persons of Jerry Brown (for the Democrats) and Pat Buchanan (for the Republicans). Both Brown and Buchanan criticised US policy on foreign aid, opposed the North American Free Trade Agreement (NAFTA) and argued that President Bush should not have fought the Gulf War. Brown declared that he would not 'give a penny' to foreign aid 'until every small farmer, businessman and family' in America was relieved of debt.[18]

There certainly was at least some evidence of a 'homeward bound' public opinion, although contemporary invocations of a 'new isolationism' in public opinion were more the product of rhetorical expediency than of concrete survey evidence. Ronald Steel in 1995 described a potentially dangerous 'chasm between a foreign policy establishment mesmerized by notions of American leadership and "global responsibilities" and an American public concerned by drug trafficking and addiction, jobs, illegal aliens' and the domestic economic agenda generally.[19] Public opinion surveys in the early 1990s did provide some basis for Steel's arguments. A 1994 survey undertaken at the University of Maryland found only 14 per cent of respondents prepared to agree with the proposition that 'the US should make sacrifices in an effort to help the world as a whole'.[20] Post-Vietnam public caution over troop deployment continued, despite Bush's success in the Gulf War.[21] Public opinion signals did not all point in the same direction. Support for the North Atlantic Treaty Organisation (NATO), for example, tended not to ebb with the end of the Cold War, especially if the case for international cooperation were linked to issues of burden-sharing. Though new technology tended to produce the 'CNN effect' of almost random public exposure to evidence of disaster and disruption abroad, the end of the Cold War inclined the American press to relegate international news away from the front pages.[22] From an internationalist perspective, the job of post-Cold War political leaders was clear: to lead the public and the political process away from introspection, alerting America to the requirements and opportunities associated with a world that was being re-shaped by new economic and technological forces.

The expectation of the early 1990s was that the form and process of foreign policy, as well as its substance, would alter in the new era. There was much talk of the possibility of a newly democratised process. In 1991, David Unger called on the American public to exploit the opportunities provided by the threat-free international environment and 'reclaim control of policy from the foreign policy establishment'.[23] With the likely future centrality of global economic and trade issues, it was widely anticipated that Congress would aspire to lead policy. State governments were even likely to enter the fray as advocates of local trade promotion policies. Presidents, moreover, would probably be less able to invoke near-permanent crisis as a way of shoring up executive authority. James Lindsay argued in 1994 that 'the demise of the Soviet Union ... lowered the perception of external threat and with it the political costs to members of Congress who choose to challenge the president.'[24] A bipartisan report on 'Public Engagement in US Foreign Policy After the Cold War' noted that America had inherited 'a conception of the "man in the Oval Office" hearing all the evidence, making lonely decisions, and then persuading the nation' of the wisdom of his foreign policy decisions. In post-1989 conditions, however, 'foreign policy making increasingly resembles the process by which domestic policies are made, and the president must be prepared to build mutually supportive coalitions at home and abroad that will give authority and legitimacy to his/her decisions'.[25]

The 1992 presidential campaign

Bill Clinton won the 1992 presidential election on a 43 per cent share of the popular vote, the lowest score for a winner of the presidential contest since the three-way contest of 1912, when Teddy Roosevelt ran on the Progressive ticket, giving Woodrow Wilson victory with 41.9 per cent of the popular vote. There was another three-way contest in 1992, with Independent Ross Perot playing the role of Teddy Roosevelt in splitting the vote in such a way as to ease a Democrat into the White House. In the 1992 election, Democrats retained their majorities in the House of Representatives (259–175) and in the Senate (57–43).

Despite his work for the 1972 McGovern campaign, Clinton, the Southern 'New Democrat' and former chairman of the Democratic Leadership Council, was an object of suspicion for many Northern liberals in 1992. George Stephanopoulos recalled how he associated the candidate from Arkansas with support for Nicaraguan *contras* in the 1980s and for the 1991 Gulf War.[26] Clinton's campaign in 1992 was centred on domestic renewal. Tony Lake recalled: 'Those of us doing foreign policy were always aware that we were a wholly owned subsidiary of the campaign.'[27] Clinton in 1992 certainly did not argue that foreign policy had ceased to matter with the fall of the Berlin Wall. A key theme was the interpenetration of the foreign and the domestic policy.[28] President Bush, according to the Clinton campaign, had not merely neglected the domestic agenda; he had also failed to understand the post-Cold War dynamics of domestic-foreign intermingling.

Clinton sought also to distance himself both from the foreign policy approach of the two previous Democratic candidates for the White House. According to Nancy Soderberg, the Clinton campaign saw itself as attempting to row back against the perception of nearly a quarter century of perceived Republican success in foreign policy: from Nixon's opening to China, through Reagan's negotiation from strength to President Bush's victory in the Gulf.[29] The only hiatus in this record of apparent Republican success was Jimmy Carter's single term. The Clinton campaign sought to establish a distance between itself and the previous Democratic administration, though some elements of the Cater record were acknowledged as a success. The Carter administration, after all, had actually pioneered, in its 'intermestic agenda', the notion of domestic-foreign policy interpenetration.[30] The former president's endorsement in April 1992 was a significant boost, especially since negative memories of the previous Democratic administration had been altered by positive public evaluation of Carter's conduct since leaving the White House. According to Clinton, the endorsement 'more than made up for the problems he had caused me during the Cuban refugee crisis in 1980'.[31] (Governor Clinton had clashed with President Carter over the resettlement of some 20,000 Cuban refugees at Fort Chaffee in Arkansas.) Clinton also avoided echoing themes sounded by the Michael Dukakis campaign of 1988. Dukakis's failed presidential bid raised memories of the uncharacteristically lame and 'teachy' speech made by Clinton at the 1988 Democratic convention.[32] Like Clinton (and indeed like Carter) Dukakis had presented himself as a 'New Democrat'. But where the Massachusetts Governor in 1988 attacked 'a defense establishment wasting money on duplicative and dubious new weapons', Clinton in 1992 resolved to defend 'the two qualities that make America's military the best in the world – the superiority of our military personnel and our technology'.[33] Clinton did question the need to keep around 150,000 troops in Europe and even, in December 1991, raised the prospect of doubling Bush's proposed Pentagon spending cuts over five years.[34] By the time he came to debate Bush in October 1992, however, he insisted: 'We're going to have to spend more money in the future on military technology and on greater mobility.'[35] Any cuts would be redirected 'back into jobs right here at home' and would not compromise Clinton's commitment to 'the world's strongest defence'.[36]

Clinton's assault on the Republican foreign policy produced some memorable phrases. The Grand Old Party (GOP) claim of having won the Cold War was ridiculed as the 'rooster taking credit for the dawn'.[37] Aside from the Republican record, Clinton's biggest problem with foreign policy related to his own inexperience. Pat Buchanan declared at the Republican convention in August 1992 that

Clinton's foreign policy background was 'pretty much confined to having had breakfast once at the International House of Pancakes'.[38] In a sense the whole orientation towards domestic renewal and to economics-first was an attempt to side-step the accusation of foreign policy inexperience. The implication was that the need for extensive foreign policy experience in the White House had ended with the Cold War. Clinton's relatively limited criticism of the Bush foreign policy early in the campaign reinforced this line of argument: US policy in key areas such as the Middle East and the former Soviet Union was more or less on track, and did not require radical and expert rethinking. Especially early on, the strongest assaults on the Bush foreign policy record tended to come from Al Gore rather than from Clinton himself. Gore attacked Bush's role in the Iran-*contra* scandal under Reagan, referring to a 'credibility canyon'. Special venom was reserved for Oliver North, the central figure in Iran-*contra*, who was now standing for a Senate seat in Virginia. For Gore, North was a 'liar', whose supporters came from the 'extra-chromosome right wing'.[39] Gore also led the attack on Bush's environmental record in speeches and interviews which denied any tension between environmental awareness and economic prosperity. Bush's policies were 'costing the United States millions of jobs by pretending that our strategy should be to protect the old, polluting, inefficient ways of the past'.[40]

Clinton did not entirely avoid specific undertakings. During the New York (NY) primary campaign in April, he promised to appoint a 'special representative to push for an end to the violence in Northern Ireland'.[41] He attacked Bush's record on China and in the Balkans, promising that, with Clinton in charge, America would 'never coddle tyrants, from Baghdad to Beijing'; it would champion 'the cause of freedom and democracy, from Eastern Europe to Southern Africa, and in our own hemisphere in Haiti and Cuba'. He undertook to reverse the current practice of refusing to accept refugees from Haiti.[42] In July 1992, Clinton urged Bush to seek UN authorization for selective bombing of Serbian targets in Bosnia.[43] Despite the odd specific promise, candidate Clinton managed to keep most foreign policy options fairly open. He did not even explicitly endorse the NAFTA until October 1992, by which time he had made various vague 'managed trade' remarks to labour audiences. In the October presidential debates, he presented himself as standing between Bush and Perot on NAFTA: 'Mr Perot says it is a bad deal. Mr Bush says it is a hunky-dory deal. I say, on balance, it does more good than harm.'[44]

Responding to Bush campaign attacks on his Vietnam record, Clinton managed to bring together several other lines of defence, notably regarding his foreign policy inexperience in general and his particular problems as a prospective commander-in-chief. He made an appeal to conscience: 'I was opposed to the war. I couldn't help that. I felt very strongly about it, and I didn't want to go to war at the time.' Many other presidents had not served in the military 'and had to order our young soldiers into battle, including President Wilson and President Roosevelt. ... Could I do it? Yes, I could'.[45] President Kennedy, of course, had served in the military with distinction, but Clinton, in his own self-narrative, was the JFK of the 'baby boomer' generation: the leader who could take the torch of national leadership and responsibility from the Second World War generation represented by President Bush. Perhaps only Clinton's generation – the 'Vietnam generation' – could really heal the wounds of the 1960s and 1970s: 'If I win, it will finally close the book on Vietnam.'[46] Tony Lake offered the following observations on the Vietnam legacy in July 1992: 'In the 1970s and the 1980s, we refought the Vietnam War within the (Democratic) party every four years. ... No more.'[47]

Although foreign policy struggled to rise up the agenda in Clinton's 1992 campaign, the Democratic candidate did make several important speeches devoted to international affairs. Where Clinton's stump speeches concentrated on economic renewal, with Bush cast as the president who was obsessed with the world beyond America's borders, foreign policy addresses were delivered to specialist audiences at venues such as Georgetown University in Washington DC and the World Affairs Council in Los Angeles. At Georgetown in December 1991, he outlined his intention – in the words of a commentary given by Leslie Gelb – to 'embrace much of the Reagan/Bush national security policy, pinch and poke it around, question its sincerity and then build it into his own strategy'. He called also for a doubling of already budgeted cuts in Pentagon spending over five years, as well as more emphasis on democracy-promotion.[48] In New York in April, he told the Foreign Policy Association that Bush had failed to 'offer a compelling rationale for America's continued engagement in the world'. The Bush team had 'invited a new birth of isolationism on the left and the right'.[49] By the time he addressed the Los Angeles World Affairs Council in August, the rhetorical assault on Bush was well-honed: 'From the Baltics to Beijing, from Sarajevo to South Africa, time after time this President has sided with the status quo against tyrants rather than those who would overthrow them ...'[50] At Milwaukee in October, Clinton declared that Bush had befriended 'potentates and dictators' and had been guilty of the 'appeasement' of Saddam Hussein in Iraq before 1990.[51] During the debate with Bush in St Louis, Clinton outlined his version of the 'democratic peace': 'We ought to be promoting democratic impulses around the world. Democracies are our partners. They don't go to war with each other.' Clinton attacked Bush for his timid reaction to the Tiananmen Square massacre in Beijing and also promised to consider lifting the arms embargo on the Bosnian Muslims. He noted, however, that the US 'can't get involved in the quagmire' of Bosnia.[52]

Clinton's foreign policy: the arc of development and the 1996 election

Clinton's foreign policy did – so this chapter section will argue – have some developmental consistency. All was not mere reactive and random confusion. In attempting to impose some degree of analytic order on the developing policy, however, it is important not to lose sight of the sheer relentlessness of the stream of problems with which the administration was forced to deal. To some extent, political leaders do choose their own agendas. Leaders should be judged by their ability to set clear priorities. Yet leaders should also be judged by the quality of their reaction to the bewildering unfurling of often seemingly random 'events'.

As presidents seek to provide coherent leadership, they are constantly confronted by a world where the domestic and the foreign policy agendas intermingle, and are themselves embedded in the ebbs and flows of domestic electoral politics. They are also confronted by a world in which the neat divisions between different types of foreign policy – security, economic, environmental, declaratory, regional, global and so on – also relentlessly intersect. As Clinton so often pointed out, this world of interaction and interpenetration actually constituted the post-Cold War policy environment.

Clinton's exasperation with the complex policy environment was most famously expressed in his early realisation that his prospects for reducing the federal budget deficit inherited from the Reagan–Bush era depended on global markets as well as decisions made by the (independent) Federal Reserve Bank, headed by Alan Greenspan: 'You mean to tell me that the success of the program and my reelection hinges on the Federal Reserve and a bunch of fucking bond traders?'[53] Clinton's exasperation betrayed, no doubt, a degree of naivety. It is also not irrelevant to note that, even if Clinton was beset by extreme global complexity, at least he was spared the intense crises – from Pearl Harbor to Cuban Missile Crisis to Tet Offensive to 9/11 – with which other presidents have had to cope.

At the level of detailed, quotidian problem-management, however, Clinton was assailed by intense complexity on a scale almost unimaginable to people working outside the Oval Office. We need only to examine short periods in the life of the Clinton administration to appreciate the sheer force of this complexity. Taking an example from the first term, on 26 February 1993, Clinton gave a long prepared address at the American University in Washington DC, in effect announcing the key theme of his first term. America must 'reach out' into the world, embracing the challenges of economic competitiveness and steeling itself to embrace the 'constant race towards innovation'. The speech deliberately echoed John Kennedy's 1962 address at the same university; it was a complex and rousing defence of American internationalism, rooted in Clinton's commitment to democracy-promotion and economic interconnectedness.[54] On that same day, in New York City, there occurred the first terrorist bombing of the World Trade Center, causing six deaths and over 1,000 injuries. Other presidential concerns on that day included the preparation of the medical health reform plan and the issue of gay rights in the US military. Two days later, agents from the Bureau of Alcohol, Tobacco and Firearms stormed the compound, near Waco in Texas, of the Branch Davidian religious cult, an action which provoked a backlash from the extreme, militarised American far right which was to last for the rest of Clinton presidency. Moving to the second term: within one week in early April 1998, Pakistan announced that it had successfully tested a nuclear weapon; the Good Friday Agreement was signed, following intense presidential lobbying, in Belfast; Clinton personally pressed the Senate to ratify the expansion proposals for NATO; and (in what Clinton was coming to call 'the parallel world of Whitewater'), important developments occurred in the various investigations and cases which were to culminate in the Senate impeachment trial of January 1999.

Yet, to reiterate, all was not reactive confusion. First term foreign policy concerns were dominated by two issues. One (global economics and free trade) was chosen by Clinton; the other (Bosnia) was assuredly not. Tony Lake recalled of the first term: 'I had often felt as if I had a "B" branded on my forehead, for Bosnia.' Clinton 'would almost visibly wince when the subject came up, as it did almost every day'.[55] Bosnian policy in the first term was indeed, as we shall see in a subsequent chapter, allowed to drift. The clear priority for action was free trade. NAFTA and the General Agreement on Tariffs and Trade (GATT) received Senate approval, while the administration negotiated numerous bilateral free trade agreements. Other first term priorities included multilateral 'enlargement' and democracy-promotion, from Mozambique to Russia; 'selective engagement' (involving, especially after the Haitian invasion and the setbacks in Somalia, the attempt to devise practical, usually domestic-oriented, criteria for assertive US international engagement); and military retrenchment, with Defense Secretary Aspin looking to cut defence spending levels, as a percentage of Gross Domestic Product (GDP), to roughly half the level for 1970. The dynamic of the first term ran generally in the direction of pragmatism (notably over China) and the recognition of limits: all leavened by a dose of neo-Carterist human rights, 'assertive humanitarianism' and the commitment to the vision of the democratic peace that Clinton had sketched out in the presidential election debate of October 1992.

The arc of development for Clinton's foreign policy was affected by at least three forces which were making their impact felt during the first term. One clear force for change was the conflict in the former Yugoslavia – a region which generally fell outside the administration's first term 'selective engagement' criteria. The patent inability of the European Union (EU) to take realistic steps to end the slaughter and disorder on its own doorstep; the growing US awareness that the region – uncomfortably close to the Russian sphere of influence, and also with implications for the Moslem Middle East – had significance for American security: these factors were important in provoking a shift towards diplomatic, and subsequently military, engagement in the Balkans in 1995. Also pushing Clinton towards altering his stance towards Bosnia was the threat of the new Republican Congress assuming policy leadership in this area. The Republican victory in the 1994 Congressional elections was the second major influence over the developing trajectory of the entire Clinton foreign policy. From January 1995, and throughout the rest of his presidency (since the GOP was to dominate both House and Senate into the new century), Clinton had to take due account of Republican Congressional preferences and pressures. Third, from about 1994/95 – ironically at the very time that Clinton's opponents were securing control of the legislative branch of government – the Clinton economic boom was beginning to be felt. Associated with the boom was a newly vigorous American internationalism. From 1994 onwards, although Republican strength in Congress hugely affected the way in which Clinton practised his new internationalism, the president no longer had to 'apologise' for the fact that America *had* a post-Cold War foreign policy. The computer revolution, the boom in consumer spending, and the inroads made into (and eventual elimination of) the Reagan budget deficit all contributed to a new confidence in US international power. Washington chatter was no longer about imperial decline, but about unipolarity.

The 1996 presidential election provided an opportunity for the administration and the nation to take stock of the progress Clinton had made towards achieving a viable foreign policy for the post-Soviet era. Writing in *Foreign Policy*, Richard Ullman gave the president a grade 'B', primarily as 'an acknowledgement of the extraordinarily difficult task of conducting foreign policy today'. Ullman regarded China and Bosnia as the major areas of policy failure. Yet it was hard to live with a Republican Congress and a disengaged public. Clinton had not yet managed to find a 'substitute for the snarly, menacing Russian bear as a concentrator of thought or as a justification for both action and sacrifice'.[56]

Clinton's 1996 victory over the 73-year-old Republican candidate, Senate Majority Leader Bob Dole was convincing. As Michael Heale put it: 'the exuberant Clinton excelled in what he did best, schmoozing the electorate'.[57] He outpolled the Kansan by over eight million votes; but, due to the 8 per cent of votes won by third candidate Ross Perot, this was another election in which Clinton fell short of 50 per cent support. The president proclaimed foreign policy successes in Haiti, Bosnia, North Korea, and in connection with NATO adaptation and the rescue of the Mexican *peso*. Progress, according to Clinton, had also been made in connection with nuclear proliferation and international terrorism. Special emphasis was placed on the construction of a new open trading system: 'I believe that decades from now people will look back on this period and see the most far-reaching changes in the world trading system in generations.' Clinton's campaign directed itself against the Republican unwillingness to accept America's role as the 'indispensable nation': 'I wish every American could see our country as much of the world sees us. Our friends rely upon our engagement. Our adversaries respect our strength.' Clinton related his emotional response to declarations by foreign athletes at the 1996 Atlanta Olympic Games who saluted 'the efforts the United States had made to foster peace in Bosnia, peace in Northern Ireland, peace in the Middle East'.[58] Endorsing Clinton for president, the *NYT* argued that the president had recovered from his early mistakes and confusions: 'Now he is regarded internationally as a leader with a sophisticated grasp of a superpower's obligation to help the world manage its conflicts and economic contests.' As evidence for this assertion, the *Times* offered Clinton's 'successful, high-risk' decision to 'throw political and financial support' behind Boris Yeltsin in Russia.[59] R. W. Apple commented that foreign policy was playing a 'meager' role in the campaign. Clinton was able to point to 53 per cent foreign policy approval ratings, the highest of his presidency, while Dole was finding it difficult to find foreign policy areas where Clinton was vulnerable.[60] Dole's personal internationalism was many miles distant from the preferences of a Jesse Helms (the Republican chairman of the Senate Foreign Relations Committee) or a Pat Buchanan (who had won the New Hampshire primary for the GOP). The Kansan denounced the Clinton team as 'would-be statesmen still suffering from a post-Vietnam syndrome'. He tried to develop coherent lines of criticism on policy areas ranging from Haiti to China;

however, as the *NYT* noted, the 1996 campaign was actually marked by 'convergence on foreign and defense matters'.[61]

As with most eight-year presidencies, the second Clinton administration witnessed an almost audible change of gear. The trajectory for the second term was set by those forces which had first made their presence felt around 1994/95: the realisation that chaos in the Balkans required an international leadership which only the US could provide; the need to accommodate to the realities of divided government at home; and the growth in confidence in American international power associated with the Clinton economic boom. The second term witnessed the playing out of these various pressures against a background of continued overarching strategic uncertainty. Two first term themes – 'assertive humanitarianism' and democratic free marketism – were reinforced, albeit within a conceptual framework which was more directly attuned to traditionally defined security agendas. The 1999 Kosovo bombing campaign reflected the 'lessons of Bosnia' and exemplified the administration's enhanced international confidence. Free market democratisation ran into trouble – most obviously at the 1999 World Trade Organisation (WTO) meeting in Seattle – in the shape of various leftist and rightist forms of globoscepticism.

Two other key second term developments embodied a deflection from, rather than a reinforcement of, first term priorities. Reflecting both Republican pressure and the new international confidence, the administration began to move in a unilateralist direction. On some issues, such as the Comprehensive Nuclear Test Ban Treaty (CNTBT; rejected by the Senate in October 1999), it was a matter of the US Congress applying its unilateralist stamp to policy. The administration also had little choice but to accept unilateralist measures such as the Helms–Burton legislation on Cuba. The new willingness (notably in the military actions taken against Sudan and Afghanistan, as well as in Kosovo) to act without UN sanction, however, was more the product of administration confidence than of any legislative pressure. Unilateral action by the sole remaining superpower was an expression of a global power environment where there was just one top dog, and where the administration in Washington was fully aware of its ability to go it alone. The second term also – and here GOP pressure was very important – saw a significant move towards remilitarisation. Aspin's defence projections were now forgotten. Presidential acceptance that more money was needed to fund America's global commitments was also an acceptance that, in this new era of confidence (and despite the strength of nationalist neo-isolationism in Congress), narrowly defined 'selective engagement' was a thing of the past.

The foregoing sketch of foreign policy development under Clinton does not establish that US internationalism in the 1990s was wise, skilfully executed or coherently conceptualised. It may, however, go some way to answering the charge that Clinton's foreign policy was all random reaction and no logical development.

Process

There is little dispute that the early Clinton foreign policy process was adversely affected by the lack of presidential attention to the traditional concerns of

American defence and foreign policy. Clinton seems to have taken very seriously the view that Bush had been undone by over-attention to foreign policy. Elizabeth Drew quoted a 'senior administration official' in 1994: 'We had hoped to keep foreign policy submerged.'[62] Dick Morris – the leading Clinton strategist in the first administration who ran into scandal after 1995 – recalled Clinton's 'episodic interest' in the subject of foreign policy.[63] The early national security operation suffered also from the general sense of staff disorganisation in the first two Clinton years. Philip Zelikow, who had worked on German reunification under Bush41, gave his opinion of the 1993–94 'national security apparatus': 'They didn't know what they didn't know.'[64] Elaine Sciolino reported in the *NYT* in November 1993 that 'even the ever-cautious Mr Christopher summoned up the courage to tell President Clinton point-blank that he has to become more engaged in foreign policy'. Vice President Al Gore was also widely reported as being concerned that his own considerable foreign policy involvement should not be allowed at function as a substitute for presidential engagement.[65]

Clinton's personal style was informal and face-to-face. Robert Rubin recalled his old boss liking to encounter policy positions 'not just in memo form, but actually to hear people on his team discuss and debate the options in front of him'.[66] The Clinton White House always threatened to revert to the state of a rolling seminar, with the president acting the part of a peripatetic philosopher accompanied by shifting and unstructured groups of aides and advisers. However, in organisational terms, Clinton, like Bush41, had a hierarchical system of handling foreign/national security policy within his NSC system. Issues were first raised and addressed in interdepartmental working groups, usually chaired by someone from the NSC staff rather than from the Pentagon or the State Department. Meetings were usually held in the White House. Issues and recommendations filtered up to deputies meetings, again held in the White House (usually twice weekly) and chaired by NSC staff personnel and attended by second level officers from (usually) the Pentagon, State and/or the intelligence community. Gore's national security adviser, Leon Fuerth, usually attended these meetings, along with the White House Chief of Staff. Above the deputies' meeting stood the principals' meeting: chaired by the president's NSC adviser and including relevant department heads and the Director of Central Intelligence. Principals' meetings sometimes included the president, but were more usually used to prepare advisory or informative material to be sent to Clinton. A Clinton NSC staffer interviewed by Bradley Patterson saw the main purpose of principals' meetings as providing a forum for frank discussion – 'people perhaps speak a bit more freely' without the presidential presence – and for the refining of issues which the meeting could then 'staff up' to Clinton.[67] Clinton tended to avoid the convening of formal NSC meetings. He also tended to communicate decisions informally, with formal presidential decision directives being reserved for high-profile, 'landmark' decisions or policy statements.

Clinton's formal process was initially designed to allow the president to concentrate on domestic issues; yet it was certainly not incompatible with close presidential foreign policy leadership. The formal process, after all, was very similar to that employed by Bush41, a president who is rarely accused of neglecting foreign policy. The move towards more intense presidential involvement began in the summer of 1994. *The Economist* noted in October that the president was 'performing with a foreign policy prowess that would have seemed unimaginable even a few weeks ago'. Clinton 'may actually be beginning to enjoy this aspect of his job'.[68] (The relevant article cited policy towards Haiti, North Korea, Iraq, Northern Ireland, Japan – the avoidance of a trade war – and China as examples of the new presidential sense of purpose.)

In very broad terms, Clinton's foreign policy advisory system was driven by the NSC staff in the White House. Tony Lake never pretended that a NSA could be merely a neutral broker, simply filtering competing views up to the president. Yet the system – again like Bush41's and unlike President Nixon's – was not designed to shut out the cabinet-level departments. Lake, as noted in the previous chapter, was a student of intra-administration bureaucratic conflict and was determined to avoid the damaging rifts of the Carter years. Yet, during 1993, there appeared to be tension between David Gergen (Clinton's White House counsellor, and a registered Republican) and Tony Lake. By July 1994, the WP was reporting 'bitter tension' between the White House and the State Department. The tension – arguably the flip-side of the increasing presidential foreign policy involvement – was illustrated in the transfer of Gergen to State, reportedly to provide the department with 'political reality checks'.[69] Christopher and Lake clashed over policy towards Haiti in 1994. As White House Chief of Staff Leon Panetta observed in 1995, when the NSA clashed with other members of the Clinton team, there were 'very few times that Tony ultimately is reversed or changed'. Tensions did become public, most damagingly in a loud shouting match between Lake and Tom Donilon, Christopher's Chief of Staff at the NY Waldorf-Astoria Hotel in September 1994.

Generally, however, rifts, personality clashes and debilitating 'bureaucratic politics' were held more or less in check. According to Bradley Patterson, 'Tony Lake, and especially Sandy Berger assiduously reached out to the secretaries of State and Defense, using constant and open communications to forge strong institutional and personal connections.' A State Department officer would accompany Berger on foreign trips, while an NSC staffer would join Madeleine Albright when she travelled overseas. Intra-administration cohesion was encouraged by the weekly 'pickle' (Perry/Christopher/Lake) meetings in 1994/95 and by the weekly 'ABC' (Albright/Berger/Cohen) lunches in the second term. The Berger–Albright relationship was grounded in agreed rules, which were designed to apply to all levels of State–NSC staff (and indeed NSC–State–Pentagon) relations: no public criticism of each other; 'walk ourselves back' – that is, retreat immediately from any public remark which is interpreted as criticism; 'presume innocence' – never assume dishonesty on the part of putative bureaucratic rivals; and 'no policy by press conference'. Berger and Albright talked frequently – sometimes as much as 20 or 30 times a day on their secure 'drop lines'.[70]

As noted in the previous chapter, Clinton's Secretaries of State could hardly have been more different in their political and management styles. Christopher's success resided in staying the course and riding out a period – roughly from the middle of 1994 to January 1995 – when he seemed to be on a kind of 'probation', pending replacement. Gergen's move to State was short-lived; he lasted only six months as 'counsellor' to Christopher. Yet it really did convey the impression that Clinton did not fully trust his Secretary of State. As Elaine Sciolino put it in June 1994: 'To hear Mr Gergen tell it, the President wants him to become a surrogate Secretary of State.'[71] Richard Holbrooke's high profile (both inside and outside the administration) in 1995 was widely interpreted as a rebuff for both Christopher *and* NSA Tony Lake.[72] Christopher, however, was always tougher than his manner suggested. His 1995 bureaucratic counter-attack included successful lobbying for a total trade embargo against Iran, tireless immersion in the details of the Middle East peace process, and high-level involvement (with Strobe Talbott) in the smoothing of rifts with Moscow over Chechnya and NATO enlargement.[73]

Clinton's two Secretaries of State were forced to go to battle with Congress for adequate funding for their department. Albright, nevertheless, made waves at Foggy Bottom, notably regarding the control she insisted on exerting over media contacts. She regarded her media liaison as US Representative to the UN as one of the more successful aspects of her tenure in that post, and took Jamie Rubin, her UN flack, with her to Foggy Bottom. Even Bill Richardson (US Ambassador to the UN, 1997–98) was required to clear media appearances. The Richardson–Albright relationship was, unsurprisingly, one of the more fraught foreign policy pairings within Clinton's team. Albright's own position in the cross-cutting battle for power at the top was not consistently secure. On Russia policy, Strobe Talbott always had a direct route to Clinton. Albright also tended to be marginalised in relation to the foreign economic policy agenda, rarely attending meetings of the National Economic Council (NEC), the body set up by Clinton to integrate global economics into foreign policy. She tended to respond to questions about her lack of influence in the areas of Russian and global economics by invoking the extraordinary nature of the times: 'My predecessors had a different world to deal with in which the parameters were fairly set.'[74] She was, therefore, forced to share authority in various arenas – notably the notoriously 'fuzzy' one of international economics. Reporting on Clinton's own increasing preoccupation with fending off second term scandals and investigations, Steven Erlanger wrote in September 1998 that it was 'not immediately clear who is in charge' of foreign policy. According to Erlanger, the consensus Washington view was that Albright was operating at a level of influence and effectiveness below that of Berger and Treasury Secretary Robert Rubin.[75] The press also relayed vivid stories about Albright's bureaucratic 'embattlement' during the early stages of action in Kosovo in 1999.[76]

An actor in the Clinton foreign policy process which experienced particular difficulties was the CIA. James Woolsey's particular problems of presidential access were noted in the previous chapter. The CIA was still widely seen as the agency which had failed – innocently or deliberately – to detect the weakening of Soviet power in the later stages of the Cold War. Woolsey, in fact, almost immediately after his appointment, ran into what journalist Tom Weiner called the 'buzz saw' of the Aldrich Ames scandal: the discovery of a spy at Langley who had long been selling secrets to Moscow.[77] The relationship between the White House and the CIA mirrored that between Clinton and the military; it drew on the 'culture clash' of the Vietnam War era, as well as on differing views on the role of intelligence in post-Soviet conditions. The problem extended to CIA–State Department relations. Loch Johnson, former staff member of the Congressional intelligence committees and leading academic expert on the CIA declared in 1996: 'I know people in State who think the CIA is a greater enemy than Russia ever was, and that feeling is reciprocated.'[78] Clinton's intelligence gathering operation was frequently the object of intense criticism: for example, in respect of the failure to anticipate the Indian nuclear weapon test in 1998.[79] Senator Daniel Patrick Moynihan (Democrat, NY), who had called for the abolition of the CIA following the end of the Cold War, described Langley in 1997 as 'an institutional collapse'.[80] Woolsey's successors enjoyed Cabinet status and far better presidential access. A procedural review led by John Deutch was designed to set the CIA back on course; yet reports and reviews continued to proliferate. Most reviews argued that American intelligence needs had not ended with the Cold War, but actually had become more complex. Reforms promoted by Deutch and by Congress concentrated on giving the Director of Central Intelligence more authority and on the streamlining and professionalisation of the CIA's workforce.

Bill Clinton's own decisional style was one of 'search and check' – 'search for information that will bring about good policy and check where relevant constituencies stand to see if consensus is possible.'[81] His instinct was always to *try* to solve problems, but not to commit to a course of action until consensus – certainly consensus in his own administration, but also as far as possible nationally and internationally – had been achieved. As we saw in the previous chapter, these decisional characteristics were rooted and formed in his early career. An Arkansas state senator recalled: 'That's Clinton. We reject one of his plans, and he comes right back at us saying, "OK, why don't we try to do it another way." '[82] 'Search and check' is a fine way of proceeding; at the least, it tends to minimise the dangers of foreign policy recklessness and hubris. 'Search and check' also tends to reinforce a rationally and slowly evolving world view, and to militate against erratic shifts of perspective.[83] Its downside, however, is a tendency towards indecision, procrastination and paralysing immersion in the process of consensus-building. To some degree, Clinton demonstrated an awareness of this deficiency; it is certainly arguable, for example, that he consciously used his more decisive Vice President as counter-weight to the negative aspects of 'search and check'.

The coherence of Clinton's foreign process was compromised not only by his own tendency to tolerate policy drift while awaiting the emergence of consensus; it also was adversely affected by his early disengagement and by his later preoccupation with Whitewater and the Lewinsky scandal. In some fairly celebrated instances – such as policy in Bosnia during much of 1994 – process and policy were in chaos. Procedural cohesion under Clinton was emphatically inferior to the record of the senior Bush. However, it compares reasonably favourably with

Carter, Reagan and Bush43. White House–State Department–Pentagon rivalries, divisions – even hatreds – existed under Clinton, but never approached the degree of conspicuous intensity which pertained to the latter three presidencies. Patrick Haney classifies foreign policy advisory systems as hierarchical, competitive or collegial – with all three having the potential both for success or failure.[84] Perhaps the best designation for the Clinton years would be: 'successful collegial sometimes descending into chaotic'.

Congress and foreign policy under Clinton

The idea that the post-Cold War policy environment would augment the Congressional role in foreign policy persisted into the later 1990s. In 1997, Robert Lieber saw a major and enduring characteristic of the new era as 'a reassertion of the Madisonian features of the American political system'.[85] There is no doubt that Clinton was forced, following Republican takeover of Congress in 1995, to pursue the remainder of his foreign policy in the teeth of three of the most assertive and oppositional Congresses (the 104th to 106th Congress, 1995–2001) in American history. Let us take a look at Congressional foreign policy under Clinton, concentrating on the ideas and impact of the post-1994 Republicans.

Clinton's relationship with Congress can be summarised by reciting his legislative 'box scores': the success rates in votes in Congress on which the White House took a position. Clinton's scores were 86.4 per cent success in 1993 (the highest success rate since Lyndon Johnson in 1965); 86.4 in 1994; 36.2 in 1995 (the lowest score since *Congressional Quarterly* began compiling the box scores); 55.1 in 1996; 56.62 in 1997; 51 in 1998; 37.8 in 1999; and 55 per cent in 2000.[86] These figures reveal general trends, but are also misleading. They do not reflect the intensity of White House support for particular measures, nor indeed the intrinsic importance of the various votes. Since foreign policy is legislated to a much smaller degree than domestic policy, it makes little sense to judge presidential foreign policy success in terms of the box scores. The post-1995 figures also reflect not only the fractious politics of divided government, but also Clinton's shifting tactics of compromise and confrontation.

Clinton's pre-1995 record in Congress included some important foreign policy successes: notably the 1994 NAFTA and GATT votes, as well as aid to Russia. As Senator Sam Nunn (Democrat of Georgia) put it in 1993, there was a widespread conviction, among Democrats as well as Republicans, that the Cold War era of foreign policy domination by the White House was over: 'There is the perception that there's more time for decision-making, more time for debate, and that inevitably means that Congress is going to be much more involved.'[87] The administration's budget request of $642 million, constituting the US contribution to UN peace-keeping funds, was cut to $402 million in 1993. Significant executive-legislative clashes took place over Somalia, Haiti and Bosnia. Yet military action in Haiti involved effective abdication of Congressional war powers – an occurrence which, as we shall see in following chapters, would be a feature of the entire Clinton era – with the president upholding an expansionist interpretation of his powers to commit troops.

The key test for the development of legislative–executive relations in a post-Cold War context emerged, of course, in the form of the post-1994 Republican Congress. In 1994, the GOP won eight Senate seats previously held by Democrats, picking up another when Richard Shelby of Alabama switched sides. This gave the Republicans a ten seat Senate majority. In the House, the Republicans achieved a lead of 230–204. (The 1996 Congressional elections produced Republican majorities of ten in the Senate and 24 in the House. The 107th Congress (1999–2000) had 55–45 Republican–Democrat split in the Senate, and a 223–211 split in the House). Clinton, according to Dick Morris, was 'devastated' by the 1994 results, blaming his own tactics and misjudgements: 'We never ran a truly national campaign: they had a national campaign. ... They had a two-word message: "less government". Our message took an hour to recite.'[88] The Republican programme, the Contract with America, was not primarily a foreign policy document, though the GOP takeover of Congress opened the way for intense legislative attacks on a range of administration policies: on defence priorities, normalisation of relations with Vietnam and Cuba, support for the UN and especially for UN peace-keeping, most-favoured trading status for China, foreign aid and State Department reorganisation, Bosnia, the role of the CIA, and so on. Many commentators drew attention to the attitudes of Republican freshmen. The 1992 and 1994 legislative elections saw the largest influx of new members since the elections of 1946 and 1948. By 1995, over half the House of Representatives membership had arrived since 1989. The new members were not necessarily all foreign policy amateurs, but they seemed rather unlikely passively to accept the internationalist consensus which had survived into the post-Cold War era. Freshman Republican Representative David Funderburk, who had actually served as Ambassador to Romania under President Reagan, spoke for the new intake: 'We're not saying we're protectionist or isolationist. We're just looking to put the interests of our district first. We represent the latest expression of populist feeling in this country.'[89]

At the time, the incoming House Speaker, Newton – 'Newt' – Gingrich was widely regarded as a 'bomb thrower', an oxymoronic 'conservative revolutionary'.[90] He effectively put himself forward as an American 'prime minister', leading the legislative charge by enacting the Contract. Yet in many respects, at least as far as foreign policy was concerned, Gingrich, who had supported NAFTA in 1993, was a force for internationalist moderation. He declared in 1995 his belief that if 'we don't lead the planet, there is no leader on the planet'.[91] According to Funderburk, both Gingrich and Senate leader Bob Dole had 'been inside the Beltway too long'.[92] In 1995, Gingrich persuaded John Kasich, chairman of the House Budget Committee, to reduce proposed foreign operations spending cuts by $2 billion.[93] Dole, prior to his 1996 presidential election campaign, resisted assaults, led primarily by his fellow Republicans, on foreign aid.[94] In fact, intra-Republican divisions – the famous conservative 'crack-up' – severely diffused the impact of the 1994 'revolution'. One important division was that between 'deficit hawks', keen to reduce all spending, and 'defence hawks', keen to increase military spending. Democratic Congressman Dave Obey neatly summarised the internal conflicts of House Republicans in his dissenting remarks on Pentagon appropriations in 1995: 'The majority party gnashes its teeth and sheds crocodile tears about the inadequacy of President Clinton's seven-year defense budget'; however, 'apparently, the Republicans can solve all of the national security inadequacies of the President's defense budget by increasing it by less than one percent'.[95] Gingrich described himself as a 'cheap hawk'. Unilateralist and nationalist Republicans in the House even raised the prospect of America leaving the UN. Congressman Joe Scarborough of Florida introduced legislation in October 1995, calling on the US to quit the organisation. Dana Rohrabacher of California declared: 'Everything done through the United Nations can be better accomplished on a bilateral basis.'[96] Veteran GOP internationalists, such as House Foreign Affairs Committee chairman Benjamin Gilman and Senator Richard Lugar of Indiana, resisted such de facto isolationism, insisting that their party remain committed to internationalism and free trade. Beyond Capitol Hill, neo-conservative intellectuals such as Robert Kagan and Joshua Muravchik presented their case for globalist American power promotion and criticised the narrow nationalism of the new Republican populists.[97]

Clinton's handling of the Republican onslaught was sensitive and effective, particularly in his winning of the public opinion battle against Gingrich. The president was helped by Gingrich's sexual indiscretions – the Speaker resigned his House seat at the end of 1998 – and by the Georgian's hyper-confrontational style in respect of Whitewater and the Lewinsky affair. The Republican majorities were not veto-proof, and the Senate tended to act as a cooler-off of House passions. Regarding foreign policy, Clinton had a number of other advantages. Despite their populist confrontationalism, many Republicans actually accepted that the legislature was not really equipped to deal with international crises. The post-1994 Republican majority in Congress was, after all, heir to a foreign policy tradition which for many years had exalted executive power and had criticised Congressional 'micromanagement'. Both Dole and Gingrich were committed to the *repeal* of the 1973 War Powers Resolution, describing it as an unconstitutional assault on presidential foreign policy discretion. During the February 1995 floor debate on US involvement in UN peace-keeping, Republican Congressman Jim Leach of Iowa declared: 'Congress simply can't be relied upon to share executive authority.'[98] During 1995, Republican support for Clinton in both House and Senate on foreign policy was about twice as high as on the domestic agenda.[99] The Republican leadership was also strongly committed to NATO expansion, a commitment which formed part of the 1994 Contract and of the ensuing 'National Security Restoration Act' which was extrapolated from the Contract. In 1996, Year Two of the 'Republican revolution', Clinton won eight out of 18 foreign/defence policy votes. He had his veto of the defence authorisation bill upheld and won approval for renewal of China's most-favoured nation trading status. In the same year, the White House won seven out of 12 such votes, including controversial arms control measures.[100]

The personification of the post-1994 Republican challenge to Clinton's foreign policy was Jesse Helms of North Carolina, who became chairman of the Senate Foreign Relations Committee in 1995. Helms, who had previously warned Clinton that, if the president were to venture into North Carolina, he had 'better have a bodyguard', appeared initially as a nemesis of Clintonite internationalism.[101] He trained his sights on all aspects of Clinton's foreign policy, criticising the invasion of Haiti, the 'betrayal' of Taiwan, the 'weak posture' in Iraq and the 'uncertain policy' in Somalia. Helms pressed for cuts in US financial support for the International Monetary Fund (IMF). Demanding 'serious and lasting' reform at the UN, Helms led the policy of refusing to pay America's dues to the organisation. The 'Helmsman's' rock-ribbed conservatism – fiercely nationalist, unilateralist and bordering on isolationist – embodied an almost visceral antipathy to foreign aid, even including aid to Israel.[102] He claimed never to have voted for a foreign aid bill and argued that Americans 'are tired of pouring hard-earned money down ... ratholes'.[103] Helms remained a major concern for the Clinton administration until the end of the presidency. He led the opposition to the CNTBT in 1999 and indulged in a variety of guerrilla tactics, most famously involving the refusal to approve several key ambassadorial nominations. Helms's blocking of the nomination of Massachusetts Republican Governor William Weld as Ambassador to Mexico became a long drawn-out *cause celebre*. (Helms objected to Weld's liberal record as well as to the apparent opening of the Massachusetts governorship to Joseph Kennedy.) Jesse Helms also trained his sights on the US Agency for International Development (AID), the US Information Agency (USIA) and the Arms Control and Disarmament Agency (ACDA), supporting the collapse of their residual functions into the State Department. Helms gave his support to various initiatives linked to conservative evangelical foreign policy agendas: notably the promotion of laws designed to apply sanctions to countries believed to be persecuting religious believers, and ending US involvement in aid programmes which included money for abortion or family planning.[104]

The initial White House reaction was squarely to meet the Helms challenge. Clinton vetoed Helms's first State Department reform plan and launched a campaign to 'save' AID, USIA and ACDA. Warren Christopher's strategy for the State Department was, to quote a commentator in the *Foreign Service Journal* in 1995 'to use a Mosada stand-or-die tactic', refusing to compromise while leaving the entire diplomatic budget 'equally vulnerable to congressional budget axes'.[105] State Department employees began to display buttons bearing the slogan, 'JUST ONE PER CENT' – a reminder of the actual proportion of federal tax dollars devoted to non-military foreign spending. Some 32 US embassies closed between 1993 and 1997. Brian Atwood, head of AID, defended his agency by appealing to both the moral force and the 'preventive diplomacy' arguments for a foreign aid policy that is 'tough-minded, relevant, and responsive to the forces that drive events and move governments'.[106]

Gradually the White House came to see the virtues of balancing confrontation with compromise. The administration accepted the formal incorporation of USIA and ACDA into the State Department in 1999. It developed a kind of 'good guy/bad guy' strategy, using fear of Helms to promote its own campaign for UN reform. Madeleine Albright pioneered this way of dealing with – 'co-opting' would be too strong a term – Helms while she was US Representative to the UN in 1995 and 1996. When Albright moved to State, she consciously wooed the North Carolinian Senator, appealing always to his patriotism and developing a kind of working relationship with him. She was famously photographed walking hand-in-hand with Helms in 1997. Jesse Helms also acted as kind of cover for administration-led efforts (some connected with Al Gore's 'reinventing government' programme) to reorganise the State Department. Senator Helms was an important political figure in these years, but he himself appreciated that he had weaknesses and that compromise was sometimes desirable. As a rather self-conscious relic of the Old South, his electoral base in North Carolina was far from completely secure. The prestige and authority of the Senate Foreign Relations Committee had also waned considerably since the days when Bill Clinton went to work there for Senator Fulbright. Several leading Republicans were frankly embarrassed by what they saw as the atavistic antics of Helms, especially regarding race and homosexuality. The administration was also able to reach out to internationalist Republicans on the Foreign Relations Committee, particularly Richard Lugar. Lugar's internationalism was evidenced in the fact that he considered that foreign policy under Clinton 'has been totally subordinated to domestic policy': almost precisely the reverse criticism to that being made by Helms.[107]

None of this is to suggest that the Republican takeover of Congress had no important impact on Clinton's foreign policy. It has already been argued that it was a major force in shaping and re-directing it. The Congress was a major factor in pushing Clinton towards unilateralist positions in the second term, and left its mark on both foreign and defence policy. At the very least, the takeover was an important factor in encouraging Clinton to re-prioritise foreign policy after 1994, from which time it became difficult to envisage much opportunity for achieving liberal domestic reform. Clinton won some important victories in Congress after 1994, such as the Senate's 74–26 approval, in 1997, of the Chemical Weapons Convention (CWC); but he also suffered major reversals, notably the rejection of the Comprehensive Test Ban Treaty (CTBT) in 1999. Yet the 'Republican revolution' in foreign policy – as in its constitutional and domestic dimensions – was more or less contained. In a sense, it actually re-energised the administration. In attacking the 'new isolationism', the administration found its foreign policy voice. Indeed, it could even be argued that, if America really did need a new identity-forming 'enemy' after the Cold War, it had now found it. 'America', for Clinton's second term foreign policy team, was itself re-defined in liberal internationalist garb, and pitted against the forces of darkness as represented by those who would undermine the global reach of the 'indispensable nation'.

3   The globalisation president

From the early days of the Clinton Presidency, commentators strained to discern the emergence of a new, integrating foreign policy doctrine to replace George Kennan's concept of anti-communist containment. President Bush's concept of the New World Order did not survive the 1992 election, and indeed was not emphasised greatly even by Bush himself during the campaign. In July 1993, *The Economist* announced that a 'Clinton Doctrine' was emerging along the lines of 'management' of economic globalisation (rather than complete surrender to it) and 'preventive diplomacy' (defusing potential crises, especially relating to nuclear proliferation in South Asia and the former Soviet Union).[1] No absolutely clear and unequivocal successor to containment actually did emerge, although – as we will see below – several candidates for the label of 'Clinton Doctrine' did present themselves. In 1998, Senator Joe Biden (Democrat of Delaware) noted that there was 'no consensus on the US role in the world'.[2]

This chapter opens with a discussion of the Clinton administration's effort to find integrating, and preferably one which could be succinctly and persuasively expressed and sold to the US public. It concludes that the Clinton team failed to find its own George Kennan. Yet it did find an integrating purpose in its commitment to the expansion of market democracy under conditions on accelerating globalisation. The chapter provides an account of the politics of free trade under Clinton, arguing that he should be remembered, for good or ill, as 'the globalisation president'.

The Kennan sweepstakes: searching for doctrine

Various candidates present themselves for the title, 'the Clinton Doctrine'. The Clinton administration itself embarked in its first two years on a self-conscious quest – labelled some of its participants 'the Kennan sweepstakes' – for a successor to anti-communist containment. At one level, this was simply a hunt for a sellable label to support post-Cold War internationalism. In January 1994, Clinton, in the context of remarks about policy towards Russia, referred to the need to find the right 'bumper-sticker' for the new era.[3] He frequently invoked the necessity to identify what he called 'the theory of the case': a new conceptual understanding, to guide both policy-makers and public.[4]

The key terms which emerged, both as bumper-sticker and sustaining concept, were 'engagement' and 'enlargement'. The former term figured prominently in Clinton's 1992 election rhetoric. William Safire traced it back to Gary Hart's 1988 campaign and the notion of 'enlightened engagement'.[5] 'Enlargement', or 'democratic enlargement', constituted the NSC staff's early entry into the sweepstakes. Coined by Tony Lake and Jeremy Rosner, 'enlargement' embodied the commitment to expanding free markets and to democracy-promotion. It bridged traditional Wilsonianism and the Kantian notion of the democratic peace, under which democracies are seen as unlikely to go to war with one another. Describing 'democratic enlargement' in September 1993, Lake outlined a neo-Jeffersonian unity of ideals and interests; the policy would 'combine our broad goals of fostering democracy and markets with our more traditional geopolitical interests'.[6] Strobe Talbott told an Oxford University audience in 1994 that democracy-promotion was 'in our best interests'.[7] The 1994 National Security Strategy of the United States, largely drawn up by Morton Halperin on the NSC staff, was subtitled 'Enlargement and Engagement'. It contained clear references to the democratic peace and to Washington's central role in shaping it: 'As the world's premier economic and military power, and its premier practitioner of democratic values, the US is indispensable to the forging of stable political relations and open trade.'[8] Administration spokesmen continually emphasised that 'enlargement' was no 'starry-eyed crusade' for global democracy, but rather 'a pragmatic commitment to see freedom take hold where that will help us most'.[9] The 'enlargement' side of the 'engagement and enlargement' partnership was less in evidence during the second term, probably in recognition of the fact that 'enlargement' in the broad sense outlined by Lake in September 1993 had become hopelessly confused in the public mind with the narrower (though linked) commitment to NATO enlargement. The failure to find a suitable post-Cold War 'bumper sticker' or 'theory of the case' was acknowledged in State Department transition memos delivered to Madeleine Albright in November 1996, and indeed in Clinton's own rhetoric in late 2000.[10] However, whatever its limitations, 'engagement and enlargement' essentially was Clinton's grand strategic concept.

Before offering some thoughts on 'engagement and enlargement', it is worth at least briefly considering the notion of a presidential 'doctrine'. Most widely recognised 'doctrines', in fact, were not grand strategies or 'visions' for America's role in the world at all; rather, they were unilateral warnings to enemies, often primarily designed to mobilise domestic American opinion. In this category falls, for example, the Eisenhower Doctrine (a 1957 warning to the Soviet Union in relation to the Middle East) and the Carter Doctrine (the 1980 declaration of US intent regarding Soviet ambitions in the Persian Gulf region).[11] Defined in these terms, the 'Clinton Doctrine' might reasonably be construed in terms of the 'dual containment' of Iran and Iraq, or even of Clinton's 1996 deployment of naval force in 1996 to protect Taiwan. The concept of 'rogue states' is possibly even more promising. Though harking back at least as far as the Carter administration, the 'rogue states' concept emerged under Clinton in connection with Iran–Iraq 'dual containment'. It also rapidly became bound up in the administration's concern about Weapons of Mass Destruction (WMD) and nuclear proliferation. Defense Secretary William Cohen moved in the summer of 1998 to place WMD clearly at the heart of American public strategic thinking. States such as Iraq must come to appreciate that even 'contemplation' of the use of 'weapons of mass destruction – chemical, biological, any other type – against our forces' would cause the US to 'deliver a response that's overwhelming and devastating'.[12] Clinton used the phrase, 'rogue states' in his 1999 State of the Union Address, in connection with WMD. Tony Lake in 1994 had called such countries as Iraq and North Korea 'backlash states': rogues existing beyond the pale of post-Cold War cooperation and democratisation.[13] The 'rogue states' concept actually proved of little use as a practical guide to policy. Lumping together Stalinist holdovers and Middle Eastern dictatorships made little sense. When India and Pakistan tested nuclear weapons in 1998, the US was faced with the problem of how to deal with 'rogue' behaviour by 'non-rogue' states. By 2000, the 'rogue states' terminology had been dropped in favour of the phrase, 'states of concern'.[14] However, especially if we reserve the use of the term, 'doctrine', for unilateral warnings to enemies, 'rogue states' has a good claim to be considered as 'the Clinton Doctrine'.

The key Clinton concept here, however, was 'engagement and enlargement' rather than 'rogue states'. Indeed the latter can plausibly be read as a sub-set of the former. At one level, thinking about 'rogue' or 'backlash' states seemed to contradict the Wilsonian, democracy-promotion aspect of Lake's original 'democratic enlargement' idea. It seemed to reflect judgements about *external* state behaviour – the acquisition of WMD, bullying of neighbours – rather than internal political factors. In many respects, 'rogue states' was a realist component of the administration's 'engagement': a means of justifying unilateral American action – typically economic sanctions, but also possibly military action – against regimes deemed to embody some kind of sustained threat to US interests. It had no basis in international law. Yet, certainly as codified by Lake, 'rogue states' was also linked into marketised democracy-promotion thinking. The 'rogues' were those states who stood out from what Lake called the 'family' of nations – the pariahs who resisted the logic of free markets, globalisation and political freedom and who stood outside the confines of the emerging post-Cold War democratic peace.

Moving on to a few observations about 'engagement and enlargement', it is the view of the current writer that the concept was a reasonable and sensible response to the demands of the times. 'Engagement and enlargement', however, was insufficiently slick to make a successful new era bumper sticker. It was insufficiently coherent to serve as a useful basis for clear conceptual thinking. In truth, 'engagement and enlargement' was little more than a reworking and re-branding of Bush41's New World Order: rather less menacing – 'New World Order' had provoked a host of popular cultural references to a new American imperialism – to those who feared American power; slightly more expansionist and optimistic about the prospects for a world of marketised democracy. To some extent, the failure of 'engagement and enlargement' is explicable in terms of the relatively short shelf-life of the 'post-Cold War order', which fell apart on 11 September 2001. The fundamental problem, however, was identified by none other than George Kennan himself, who made several public interventions in his own sweepstakes. According to Kennan, the post-Soviet world did not require 'a single grand strategy', no 'vast common denominator'. Indeed, the previous 'common denominator' – his own strategy of 'containment' – had led to damaging 'fixation' with the Soviet Union. Post-Cold War American leaders needed a flexibility rooted in the commitment to providing a democratic *example* in the United States itself.[15] General foreign policy concepts – especially if they are also likely to be pressed into service as bumper stickers – are subject to enervation over time, particularly if they are not linked to any commonly perceived specific external threat. The dominant view within the administration was that a successor to 'containment' had to be found. Sometimes, however, Clintonites sounded a minor key; as Maynard Glitman, arms control negotiator within the Clinton administration put it in 1995 – 'competent stewardship' rather than an integrating 'rallying cry' should be the real priority.[16] Warren Christopher would have agreed. Perhaps they (and Kennan), rather than Lake and Clinton, were correct.

'Engagement and enlargement' embraced Clinton's general commitment to post-Cold War democracy-promotion. Bill Clinton declared in his second Inaugural Address in 1997 that, for the first time in human history, more people were living under democracy than under dictatorship. His intention here was to associate his administration with the apparent onrush of democratising globalisation, reviving the democratic optimism of 1989. During the second term in particular, democracy-promotion became rhetorically entangled in the kind of 'assertive humanitarianism' which Clinton appeared to embrace in his June 1999 speech to NATO forces in Macedonia:

> Whether you live in Africa or Central Europe or any other place, if somebody comes after civilians and tries to kill them *en masse* because of their race, their ethnic background, or their religion, and it is within our power to stop it, we will stop it.[17]

In such rhetoric, Clinton was effectively putting the US forward as an international guardian of market democracy, but of universally defined human rights. While he referred to practical limits – intervention must be 'within our power' – the huge growth of relative US economic and military power in the later 1990s rather undercut this apparent expression of caution.

Two thoughts about this interlinking of 'enlargement', 'humanitarianism' and 'democracy-promotion' come to mind. First, the characteristic administration reaction to ringing declarations of democracy-promoting intent was a fairly rapid rowing back, always emphasising the potency of practical limits. In the early days of the administration, invocations of 'assertive multilateralism' were qualified by Undersecretary of State Peter Tarnoff, who declared in 1993 that human rights activism by the US would be based on 'a case by case decision to limit the amount of American engagement'. Christopher (of all people) in turn expressed the view that 'our need to lead ... is not constrained by our resources'.[18] The administration frequently tied itself up in rhetorical knots. Soon after Clinton's 1999 Macedonia address, Sandy Berger entered the declaratory fray: 'I don't think anybody ever articulated a doctrine which said that we ought to intervene whenever there's a humanitarian problem. That's not a doctrine, that's just a prescription for America to be all over the world and ineffective.'[19] Second, there is the question of how 'democracy' is to be defined. When Clinton made his claims about global democracy in the second Inaugural, the international democratising tide was no longer in full flood. Much of the massive academic and journalistic comment on his claim focussed on questions of the form and content of 'democracy' – for example, the phenomena of 'illiberal democracy' (legally elected governments pursuing the erosion or cancellation of human rights), and 'low intensity democracy' (polities geared to market penetration and outward democratic forms, rather than to sustained and comprehensive democratic development).[20] At the very least, Clinton's second Inaugural rhetoric dragged in states whose claim to be fully functioning and rights-respecting 'democracies' was rather questionable.

'Democratic enlargement' was always conceived within the Clinton administration as much in economic as in political terms. The clearest expression of the perceived interpenetration of markets, political democracy and American security was found in Lake's 1993 Johns Hopkins University address, 'From Containment to Enlargement'. Lake's goal was 'to help democracy and markets expand and survive' where 'we have the strongest security concerns and where we can make the greatest difference'.[21] Clinton in 1993 saluted the world-wide 'explosion of entrepreneurship and political liberalization'.[22] Economics adviser Gene Sperling commented: 'We either grow together or we will grow apart'; Al Gore expressed the same sentiment by saying that the time had come to implement the 'trade for peace' ideas of Cordell Hull, fellow Tennessean and Secretary of State in the Second World War.[23]

The globalisation president

On 21 September 1995, President Clinton gave an interview to talk-show host Larry King in a 'Larry King Radio Town Meeting' in Culver City, California. Asked what he was doing in California, Clinton admitted it was partly an early campaign trip. At the time he was facing the prospect of Colin Powell becoming Republican candidate in 1996. His immediate purpose, however, was to announce a new arrangement between the federal government and a group of local information technology firms 'to provide computer hook-ups for all the schools in California over the next couple of years, and challenging the rest of the country to follow the lead'. Clinton launched into a breathless panegyric for the new information age:

> people are going to be faxing us, they're going to be e-mailing us, they're going to be doing all this stuff on the Internet ... we don't have the Cold War anymore, with nation states organized in two different camps. We've

got instead a global economy. And the good news is you've got economic integration. The bad news is there's all this power for unsettling people's lives, whether it's people being less secure in their jobs, or working harder for less, or being subject to smaller fanatic groups who practice destruction like the sarin gas attack in the Tokyo subway, or the Oklahoma City bombing (19 April 1995), or a bus blowing up in Israel.[24]

Clinton's comments to King echoed his 1993 Inaugural Address, when he had linked the shrinking and integration of the globe to the onward march of democracy. Such themes – sometimes overwhelmingly positive in tone, sometimes (as in the Culver City references to economic dislocation and terrorism) more unsettling – became an almost obsessive feature of the presidential (and even more so of the vice-presidential) rhetoric. At one level, Clinton's response to globalisation and its challenges was expansively internationalist. The US must embrace the new era, delighting in its complexities and opportunities. At another level, however, it was nationalist, even mercantilist. The US was 'like a big corporation competing in the global marketplace'.[25] Clinton sometimes snared himself in rhetorical and conceptual tangles, rather reminiscent of those early twentieth-century Marxists who could not decide whether to wait for the logic of history to work itself out, or, like Lenin, to give history a shove. Clinton frequently used the term 'inexorable' to describe the process of globalisation. Inexorable or not, history also needed, in the world-view of the Clinton administration, to be given a shove – and a shove in America's direction. Right at the close of the Clinton presidency, Sandy Berger put the point thus:

> Globalization does have qualities that we can harness to advance our enduring objectives of democracy, shared prosperity and peace. ... Some of the world's most positive recent developments have occurred precisely because of how we chose to use that influence not because globalization preordained them.[26]

'Inexorable' the 'logic of globalisation' might be. Its practice, however, was threatened by an array of forces, from protectionism and 'isolationism' on Capitol Hill to terrorism and 'backlash states' abroad. Moreover, America was still a nation state and Clinton was its leader. On his watch, America would not be out-traded. For these reasons, Clinton never accepted the hyper-inexorability thesis of WTO Director Renato Ruggiero, who declared that reversing globalisation was 'tantamount to trying to stop the rotation of the earth'.[27] Though sometimes uncertain exactly how to respond to globalisation, Clinton was consistent at least in his insistence that his main task was somehow to put America 'in the stream of history': to grasp the opportunities of the new era; to avoid facile optimism; to reconcile national and universal interests.

By the early 1990s, it had become commonplace to think in terms of the post-Cold War world as the age of globalisation. In 1992, Roland Robertson pointed to 'the compression of the world and the intensification of the consciousness of the world as a whole' as the mark of the new era.[28] Numerous commentators hailed the computer revolution as the contemporary equivalent of the nineteenth-century railway revolution, or even of the Industrial Revolution itself. Many commentators also depicted the age as one of simultaneous integration and disintegration. Globalised markets encountered and stimulated local nationalisms; global civil society rubbed against ethnic fragmentation; 'MacWorld' peered across to 'jihad'.[29] These themes were the stuff of post-communist discourse in the 1990s. Hillary Clinton, for example, was impressed by a speech made along these lines by President Vaclav Havel when she visited the Czech Republic in 1996.[30]

American economic statistics in the 1990s tell a story of accelerating change, of prosperity and dislocation, and of international integration. In 1990, about one-third of American households owned stocks; by 2000, over a half owned them. The Dow Jones index climbed from 3,000 to 5,000 between 1991 and 1995. It rose to 10,193 in 1999. By the end of 1996, Federal Reserve chairman Alan Greenspan was warning of the markets' 'irrational exuberance'.[31] Four years later, all attention was on the bursting of the 'dot.com bubble'. By the mid-1990s, and especially with progress being made in eliminating the federal deficits inherited from the Reagan/Bush era, a new confidence in the American economic model was evident. As early as March 1994, Labor Secretary Robert Reich was proclaiming the end of the period when it seemed as if Japan 'had nothing to learn from and everything to teach the United States'. Now the US economy was the model for Japan and Europe.[32] Interest rates dropped from 7.32 in 1993 to 5.19 in 1999, and unemployment from 7.3 per cent in 1993 to 4.3 in 1999. During the entire Clinton period, foreign direct investment, measured in annual net inflows had risen from $49 billion to $275 billion. US exports as a percentage of America's GDP rose from 9.9 in 1992 to 12.1 in 2000: not an astronomically huge rise, but a significant departure from the traditional US focus on domestic demand. *Per capita* American GDP rose from $5,400 to $6,526 between 1992 and 2000, during which time American infant mortality (per 1,000 live births) fell from 8.6 to seven. Global exports as a percentage of global GDP rose from 19.2 to 23.3.[33] Commentators in the 1990s disagreed on the degree to which the world economy was an integrated whole, just as they disagreed on the desirability of any such integration.[34] It was also frequently pointed out that a combination of a global integrated economy and instant global communications made the job of national governments increasingly difficult. The 'end of geography' seemed nigh.[35] Looking back on the Clinton years, Benjamin Barber felt that the real problem for Clinton's foreign policy was a lack of control, linked to the primacy of global economics: 'actual sovereignty was passing from the political to the economic arena, from democratic states with public constituencies to private firms with private constituencies'. According to Barber, when Clinton criticised WTO and IMF policies in 1999, he sounded 'more like an irate citizen critic than a chief of state in a position to alter the positions he assailed'.[36]

In the policy environment of the 1990s, the NSC staff and the State Department often found themselves sidelined by key economic policy personnel, such as Robert Rubin (formerly of investment bankers Goldman Sachs and Treasury

Secretary from 1995 to 1999), Mickey Kantor (US Trade Representative from 1993 to 1996), and his successor Charlene Barshefsky. The NEC (originally chaired by Rubin, subsequently by Laura D'Andrea Tyson, and in the second term by Gene Sperling) was created by Clinton as a bureaucratic response to a policy environment centred on global economics. Its creation was linked to the perception that Bush41 had enjoyed excellent foreign policy, but poor foreign economic policy coordination. Rubin tended to lead the charge for free markets and deficit-reduction, usually assisted by Alice Rivlin (originally deputy to Leon Panetta, and then director of the Office of Management and Budget in the first term). The main opposition to Rubin's economic orthodoxy tended to come from Laura Tyson and from Secretary of Labor Robert Reich. From Rubin's point of view, although Reich's 'populism' embodied an admirable commitment to 'human capital' – education and training – it was 'sometimes unwise economically'.[37] Between 1995 and 1997, Joseph Stiglitz, as chair of the Council of Economic Advisers (CEA), tended to provide the internal opposition to the line being advocated by Rubin, and especially by Rubin's deputy, Larry Summers. At least during the first Clinton term, these economic policy divisions defined and structured the intra-administration foreign policy debate almost as much as the varying viewpoints of the State Department and the NSC staff.

The NEC was designed to factor economic considerations into all presidential decisions. Clinton later praised Robert Rubin for building the NEC into 'the most important innovation in White House policy making in decades'.[38] In addition to the NEC, economic advisers became formal members of the NSC committee structure. Within the administration, the Commerce Department (headed by Ron Brown until his death in 1996, then by Kantor and, from 1996 to 2000, by William Daley, son of former Chicago mayor Richard Daley) achieved new prominence. Its main early priority was to strengthen US involvement in ten 'emerging big markets' (China, India, Brazil, Indonesia, Mexico, Turkey, South Korea, South Africa, Poland and Argentina).

Clinton seemed squeezed between the impotence and the opportunity of globalisation. His commitments to the kinds of free trade and deficit-reduction policies being advocated by Robert Rubin were not made without a degree of self-doubt. Bob Woodward recorded the following *faux* sarcastic outburst by Clinton in front of Rubin and other economic advisers in April 1993: 'Where are all the Democrats? ... We're Eisenhower Republicans here, and we are fighting the Reagan Republicans. We stand for lower deficits and free trade and the bond market. Isn't that great?'[39] Robert Reich later described the Clinton administration as one of the most pro-business administrations in American history.[40]

During his presidency, Clinton's administration achieved around 500 bilateral and regional free trade or 'fair trade' deals, ranging from the NAFTA to ad hoc understandings about tariff relief on particular American products. Bill Clinton seemed to exemplify Fred Bergsten's 'bicycle theory', where free traders needed furiously to pedal forwards to reduce more and more trade barriers, because stopping this activity would cause them to fall off the bicycle and to succumb to the forces of protectionism.[41] Such hectic activity, of course, was not without its political costs. We have already encountered cross-party 'globosceptic' populism in the shape of figures such as Pat Buchanan and Jerry Brown. The American Federation of Labor–Congress of Industrial Organizations (AFL–CIO) had been broadly protectionist in its sympathies since the 1970s. Congressman Richard Gephardt of Missouri, leader of House Democrats during the Clinton years, was a focus for labour-inclined protectionist policies. Congressional majorities on free trade issues had to be assembled from cross-party coalitions. Both Clinton and many free trade commentators were exasperated by what they saw as the parochialism of many Members of Congress, both Democrat and Republican. Such putative parochialism, of course, reflected their long-standing – and constitutionally sanctioned – constituency-orientation, particularly of Members of the House of Representatives. It also reflected the very conditions which had brought Clinton himself, a critic of Bush's supposedly excessive preoccupation with global affairs, to the White House. The administration was nevertheless frequently incredulous, following the closing of free trade deals, when it found itself forced under legislative budget rules to find offsets for lost tariff revenue. Robert Paarlberg wrote in 1995 that Congress was 'coming full circle on tariffs', which 'were being treated, as they had been 200 years earlier, more or less as inward-looking revenue instruments than outward-looking foreign economic policy instruments'.[42]

If Clinton's credibility as a free trade leader was to some degree qualified by the difficulty of securing legislative majorities, it was also compromised by some internal contradictions. A relatively minor contradiction related to the administration's enthusiasm for regional free trade pacts. Did such agreements represent stepping-stones to more complete global economic integration, or were these pacts essentially a way of *resisting* more thoroughgoing integration? The answer presumably is that not all signatories to regional free trade deals understood their objectives in the same way. Another contradiction arose over the agency involved in free trade success. After all, US global economic competitiveness was more a responsibility of private business than of the federal government. Washington could encourage and help create the conditions for free trade but success depended on private innovation. Especially in the first term, the Clinton team seemed to be sending the message that economic competitiveness, rather than traditionally defined 'security' was the central concern of Washington. As Michael Oppenheimer argued in 1998, this encouraged a view that 'the returns to foreign policy need to be proximate and easily demonstrated in terms of job creation, growth, and export market shares'.[43] It was also by no means clear that trade expansion really could be separated from security commitments. As the British in India had discovered, trade and security were not easily kept apart. From an economist's perspective, Paul Krugman wrote in 1994 that it was actually misleading to argue that the US could or should compete with foreign countries in the way that Coca-Cola competed with Pepsi; for one thing, 'Coca-Cola does not sell the majority of its product to its own workers'.[44]

A coterie of 'economics firsters' emerged soon after Clinton's 1992 victory. These included Theodore Moran at State, Laura Tyson at the CEA (before her move to the NEC), and Jeffrey Garten at the Commerce Department. Some of

50 The globalisation president

their pronouncements were rather extraordinary. Their starting point was that American trade-promotion would no longer be restrained by security considerations inherited from the Cold War. Garten announced the administration's intention to 'put other nations on notice that America will no longer make trade concessions in deference to the NATO or US–Japanese security relationship'.[45] Lloyd Bentsen, Clinton's first Treasury Secretary, declared in September 1993: 'I'm tired of a level playing field. We should tilt the playing field for US business. We should have done it 20 years ago.'[46] According to *Business Week*, US ambassadors in 1993 'became unabashed peddlers in pinstripes, vigorously lobbying local officials on behalf of corporate America'.[47] A particularly aggressive weapon in the hands of economic nationalists – in the executive as well as in Congress – was the 'super 301' provision of US trade law, originally legislated in 1988 but extended by executive order in 1994. By-passing the GATT/WTO system, it required the president to retaliate against vaguely defined 'unfair' trade practices. 'Super 301' was widely invoked as an 'anti-dumping' measure and was used in trade disputes with Japan, especially in the first Clinton administration.

The pugnacity of this early 'economics firstism' declined as the Clinton administration found its feet. The apparent revival of American mercantilism reflected, at least at one level, the populist view that America had paid a price for its Cold War victory, and that other nations should no longer be allowed to free-ride on US benevolence. As the years went by, early economic battles with Japan and Europe became superseded by the globalised security (rather than the globalised economic) agenda. The 'economics firsters' still managed, however, to make their presence felt. Mickey Kantor, for example, in 1996 questioned the propriety of a 'playing field' on which US companies were forbidden (under the 1977 Corrupt Foreign Practices Act) to bribe foreign officials to win contracts.[48] The 'economic nationalist' strand within Clinton's economic foreign policy was neither sufficiently strong nor sufficiently sustained to undermine the administration's commitment to cooperative free trade, even if it did lend policy a rather ad hoc quality.[49] As Martin Walker noted in 1996, Clinton's strategy was an 'elegant' one. The Asia-Pacific, Latin America and Europe should 'all have one thing in common: Clinton's America was locking itself into the heart of each'. Bill Clinton, according to Walker, was likely to be remembered, if his trade pact strategy worked out as planned, 'as the true architect of the post-Cold War world'.[50]

The NAFTA

Congressional passage of the NAFTA was the first test of Clinton's emerging reputation as 'the globalisation president'. NAFTA passage became a test of strength for the new president, and indeed for his rapidly developing strategy of locking the US into the centre of an emerging and overlapping set of free trade networks. The attendant political debates and passions were clearly, in retrospect, out of proportion to any likely short- to medium-term impact on the American economy of the trade deal with Mexico and Canada. Throughout the debates, however, there was the perception that NAFTA would prove to be just the start of a new liberal global economic order.

The proposal for a North American trade pact was hardly novel. The US and Canada reached their own agreement in 1988, the year after Mexico began reducing its import tariffs. Mexican President Carlos Salinas formally suggested a US–Mexican trade deal in 1990. Congressional opposition was slow in emerging, though by 1991 the AFL–CIO was arguing that such a pact would threaten American jobs. Prospects for the deal depended on Congress agreeing, in 1991, to 'fast-track' extension: essentially an undertaking by legislators that the trade deal enabling legislation would be expedited, and not made subject to endless amendments designed to protect sectional interests. Once fast-track authority had been secured, the US, Mexico and Canada, in August 1992, were able to conclude the agreement to create a free trade zone. The agreement provided for a 15-year period to phase out tariffs and for the removal of obstacles to inward foreign direct investment. Clinton, following some prevarication, endorsed NAFTA during the 1992 campaign. In response to criticisms of the pact from important Democratic Party constituencies, he undertook to negotiate two side agreements, designed to ensure the enforcement of labour and environmental standards in Mexico, before submitting the substantive NAFTA agreement to Capitol Hill. These agreements were completed by September 1993, by which time a $140 million retraining programme, designed to assist American workers who might be adversely affected by the agreement, had been incorporated into the legislation.

Bill Clinton noted that, since Mexico 'only comprises four to five per cent of the size of the American economy', the ability 'of the Mexicans in the near term to hurt the American economy ... is somewhat limited'.[51] The spectre, raised in Ross Perot's 1992 presidential election campaign, of a Gadarene rush of US corporations to move their operations south of the Rio Grande provoked the following response from a *NYT* leader writer: 'Some companies will relocate, but the numbers won't be large. Mexico might attract about $15 billion in extra investment. But that's a small fraction of the $500 billion invested in plant and equipment every year in the US.'[52]

Rational calculation of cost and benefit, however, was not a feature of the related public debate. Three academic commentators noted in 1996 that the debate 'was imbued with a level of nearly metaphysical importance seldom seen in foreign trade policy'.[53] Reporting on a televised discussion on NAFTA between Al Gore and Ross Perot, William Safire argued that the 'scrap' over the trade deal had little to do with global economics. Rather, it was 'the old grudge fight between the politics of hope against the politics of fear (as the free traders put it) or the cultural elite against the pee-pul (as the protectionists put it)'.[54]

The Clinton White House decided to align the NAFTA vote with the necessary embrace of globalisation itself. On 10 November, Clinton announced: 'It all begins with NAFTA.' The agreement would be the first step to 'real job growth' which 'will come when all the other Latin American democracies and free market economies also join in a great trade group with Mexico, Canada and the United States'.[55] Ratification of NAFTA would, argued Clinton, 'increase the leverage that

I ... will have to get an agreement on the world trade round, the GATT (General Agreement on Tariffs and Trade) Round, this year'. Other developed economic powers would say to themselves: 'Well, we want access to that big Latin American market, and the best way to do it is to adopt a world trade agreement.'[56] Shortly before the House of Representatives vote, Vice President Gore stated that failure to ratify would actually damage the administration's entire foreign policy credibility.[57]

The NAFTA debate brought forth some of Clinton's most messianic and high-flown statements about the brave new world of globalised economics. The president linked hemispheric free trade to the march of democracy. A democratic, marketised Mexico would set the standard for other Latin American nations. NAFTA passage would also be a 'big deal' for the US, with associated benefits for immigration and drug policies.[58] Clinton acknowledged the insecurities inherent in the new globalised order, but argued that these could only be ameliorated, not avoided altogether: 'the average 18-year-old is going to change work eight times in a lifetime, anyway, whatever we do'.[59] Accepting NAFTA would enable America at least to shape and arrange global change to its benefit – surrendering to the inevitable while retaining the ability to lead. Following the positive House vote, Clinton compared the choice 'we faced tonight' with the choices facing the US in 1918, 'whether to turn inward or turn outward'. Following the First World War, America chose isolation, protectionism and economic depression. Tonight, 'we showed ... we are ready together to compete and win to shape the world of the 21st century'.[60] David Rosenbaum in the *NYT* struck a similarly millenarian chord. NAFTA was 'like the 1957 Civil Rights Act – a necessary symbolic manifestation of glories to come'.[61]

All this symbolism was a lot for a fairly humble trade pact to bear. Apocalyptic language – taken up, of course, by NAFTA opponents as well as supporters – reflected the acute contemporary perception that a new global age really was on America's doorstep. The symbolic heightening of the debate also indicated and exemplified the fact that Clinton himself was now moving from economic nationalist to global free trader. His promise that NAFTA would be the lever which would eventually prise open global free trade was his answer to those critics who saw preference-led regionalisation as an obstacle to the GATT system.[62] Raising the rhetorical stakes and putting the presidency on the line also served the administration's political purposes, albeit in a rather high-risk fashion. What is interesting is that the extreme prioritisation of NAFTA occurred quite late in the day. On 8 September 1993, press secretary Dee Dee Myers was asked about administration priorities. She mentioned Al Gore's 'reinventing government' initiatives, and the 'roll out' of 'a major health care proposal', but did not present NAFTA as major priority, declaring: 'I'm not going to categorize what's more important than anything else.'[63] Over the next month, NAFTA emerged as *the* priority, presumably reflecting both Clinton's newly intense personal commitment to free trade, and possibly the perception that NAFTA ratification would be easier to achieve than medical reform. Yet, even though NAFTA ratification, unlike health reform, had a clear legislative timetable, the medical proposals were really a rather more obvious priority. The health plan was announced to a joint session of

Congress on 22 September, and Clinton may have seen a NAFTA victory as easing their path. His wife's verdict, however, was less positive: 'Once again, health care would have to wait.'[64]

Before examining the legislative battle, a word about the case against NAFTA. Ross Perot and Pat Buchanan vied in the extravagance of their condemnation. Perot warned that the 'big sucking sound' of jobs moving south would put 5.9 million Americans at risk of unemployment. For Buchanan, concern for US sovereignty trumped other considerations. NAFTA was 'the chosen field upon which the defiant forces of a new patriotism ... have elected to fight America's foreign policy elite for control of the national destiny'.[65] Perot and Buchanan were joined by leftists like Jesse Jackson and Ralph Nader. Absurd as they were, Perot's 'great sucking sounds' and Buchanan's patriotic defence were no more than the reverse side of the coin to Clinton's hyperbole. NAFTA did excite genuine ad rational fears. AFL–CIO leaders were correct to point out that the side deal on labour did not extend to industrial legislation regarding the right to organise and bargain collectively. Labour boss Lane Kirkland remarked: 'The side agreements would relegate worker rights and the environment to commissions with no real enforcement mechanisms, no power to impose trade sanctions and no effective remedies.'[66] On both the pro- and anti-side, sensible argument was drowned out by emotion. According to the WP, NAFTA opponents felt a 'sense of betrayal' due to Clinton's failure to follow some of the populist themes he had begun to develop on the 1992 campaign trail.[67]

The legislative vote on NAFTA, especially the House vote of 17 November, was one of the great set-piece Congressional occasions of modern times. Domestic TV and radio advertising, designed to bring public pressure on Members of Congress, cost around $10 million, while the Mexican government ploughed in around $40 million in lobbying funds.[68] The measure passed the House 234–200, with 102 Democrats and 132 Republicans voting in favour. The Senate vote on 20 November was 61–38. The White House position was opposed in the House both by the Majority (Democratic) Whip David Bonior of Michigan, and by the Majority Leader Richard Gephardt. The Clinton team organised a pro-NAFTA 'war room', revealingly described by Michael Waldman (a communications director for the administration) as 'a freestanding operation that would be removed from the indecision and infighting that plagued the rest of the White House'.[69] Clinton's NAFTA liaison operation was subtle, opportunistic and inspired. On the day preceding the House vote, a commitment was made to compensate tomato growers in Florida in the event of cheap Mexican tomatoes entering US markets. Congressman Tom Lewis (Republican of Florida) switched to support for NAFTA. Floyd Flake (Democrat, NY) was promised that a Small Business Administration pilot project would be transferred to his district if he switched sides, which he immediately did.[70]

The NAFTA voting reflected not only the Clinton carrots offered to wavering Congressmen but also mirrored the complexity of likely free trade impacts on different parts of the US.[71] Clinton's ad hoc Congressional coalition was widely hailed as a model for future bipartisan coalition-building for free trade votes.

The politics of free trade: 1993–2000

Clinton moved on from the NAFTA victory to attend the first Asia-Pacific Economic Cooperation (APEC) summit, held in Seattle; and to prepare the way for Congressional acceptance of the (now rapidly closing) Uruguay Round of world trade (GATT) negotiations. In Seattle, Clinton began to float ideas for a 'Pacific rim' free trade area. Regarding the Uruguay Round, Clinton argued that it would 'add as much as 100 billion to 200 billion dollars per year to our economy'.[72] He also pointed to the codification of patent law as a major benefit to the US. The deal was closed, following frantic exchanges and assurances from Leon Brittan, the main EU negotiator, that the EU actually could make the deal stick. The administration's victory in the Congressional voting on GATT again involved reliance on Republican support. Richard Gephardt later sent a note to Clinton, partly blaming the White House enthusiasm for GATT for the 1994 mid-term defeats.[73] Clinton also had to take on 'anti-world government' anxiety over the creation of the WTO, set up under the Uruguay Round to arbitrate international trading disagreements.[74]

Binding the entire Clinton foreign economic policy together was the figure of Robert Rubin, first from the NEC and then from the Treasury. Rubin became, in effect, Clinton's first minister for globalised markets. He argued strongly in 1993 for putting NAFTA ahead of medical health reform. Rubin's orientation towards international economic policy in general was that the logic of markets would triumph if left to work itself out. Regarding international exchange rates, for example, he believed that 'economic fundamentals determine exchange rate levels over time'.[75] Yet Rubin worked for a pragmatic president and was himself aware of the snares of dogmatism. Indeed, Rubin was actually able to use his pro-market credentials precisely to bolster those currency market interventions that the US Treasury did support, either unilaterally or, more frequently, through the G-7 mechanisms for international central bank and finance ministry cooperation. (In broad terms, the Clinton administration favoured dollar appreciation from 1994, and a policy of dollar stabilisation and yen appreciation from 1997.) On free trade debates in general, Rubin located himself somewhere in the middle of a spectrum which extended from 'more doctrinaire free traders' in the administration, to those who embraced a clearer commitment to economic nationalism. In the Far East, for example, Rubin supported 'strong efforts to pry open (*sic*) the Japanese markets'; he was not prepared to follow free trade logic and simply accept the US–Japan trade deficit, blaming it on low US savings rates and accepting the benefits of Japanese imports.[76]

In terms of its trade agreement agenda, the administration, guided by Clinton and Rubin, kept pedalling furiously on its bicycle. As Trade Representative, with cabinet status, Mickey Kantor concluded around 170 trade deals, while also conducting numerous disputes, notably over steel subsidies in the US and European subsidies to the Airbus project. The agreements included important auto and computer chip deals with Japan. In December 1996, Clinton achieved an agreement at the Miami Summit of the Americas to work for a Western hemispheric free trade area. Tentative moves towards TAFTA, a transatlantic free trade area, were begun. Charlene Barchefsky, Kantor's successor as Trade Representative, negotiated about 300 trade deals, including important market-opening initiatives with China. In 2000, she negotiated a WTO agreement relating to 'duty-free cyberspace' (disbarring the imposition of tariffs on internet electronic communication).

The Clinton strategy of placing the US at the head of these overlapping free trade circles ran into major difficulties, and seems unlikely ever to achieve realisation. The free trade agenda under Clinton made massive headway, but primarily through the bilateral deals made by Kantor and Barchefsky, rather than through the Amero-centric globalism that had been promised at the time of the NAFTA debates in Congress. In April 1998, Clinton actually offered an apology to Latin American leaders for his failure to make much progress on, as the *NYT* put it, 'creating a hemispheric duty free shop from the Yukon to Tierra del Fuego'. Speaking in Santiago, Chile, Clinton blamed protectionist forces in the US Congress, but insisted that obstacles to trans-American free trade would eventually be removed. He quoted Winston Churchill: 'The United States invariably does the right thing, after having exhausted every other alternative.'[77]

The problems associated with the global trade commitment in Clinton's second term were most obvious in the context of his loss of fast-track negotiating authority, and in connection with the 1999 'battle of Seattle' – the failure of the 1999 WTO ministerial meeting. Also significant, however, were the problems of America's trading allies. Clinton's January 1995 rescue of the Mexican *peso* was a success. *NYT* commentator Thomas Friedman called it 'the least popular, least understood, but most important foreign policy decision of the Clinton presidency'.[78] A consequence of the unrestrained free market policies of President Salinas, the *peso* collapse raised several potential problems for the US: the potential loss of its third-largest trading partner, the possibility of a new economic refugee crisis if the Mexican economy imploded, not to mention the impact on regional and global confidence if Mexico City were allowed to default. The crisis actually had the unexpected effect of isolating Speaker Newt Gingrich, who shared the administration's worries south of the border. The House Speaker faced a revolt from many of his more isolationist fellow Congressmen, and found his authority profoundly damaged. In a moment of delicious irony, Senator Jesse Helms took the opportunity to lecture Robert Rubin on the virtues of the free market: 'Someday the markets must be allowed to run their course ... Maybe it's time now to consider a dose of tough love for our neighbour to the south.'[79] Faced by Congressional, and indeed by widespread public, opposition, Clinton launched the rescue on his own authority, using $20 billion from the administration's currency stabilisation fund, as well as over $17 billion from the IMF. Sandy Berger warned the president that he might stand 'accused of pissing billions of dollars down a Mexican rathole'. As it turned out, Mexico City was able to repay the loans by early 1997. Robert Rubin, who devised the rescue with his deputy Lawrence Summers, later wrote that the episode put to rest some long-standing doubts about Clinton's leadership: 'Often, when I've heard criticism of Bill Clinton as indecisive or driven by politics rather than policy, I've remembered and cited that night (10 January 1995) as a response.'[80]

In a sense, Mexico, the direct neighbour of the US, was, and always is, a special case. The administration was keen to emphasise that globalised interdependence did not obligate the US to rescue currencies across the world. Success and special case the *peso* rescue may have been; nevertheless, the by-passing of Congress in January 1995 did have negative implications for second term trade policy prospects. Denial of fast-track authority was a kind of revenge. What was also not lost on Clinton's political opponents was the realisation that global economic intermeshing involved potentially very expensive American commitments if things went wrong.

The Asian financial crash – beginning in Thailand in 1997 and rapidly spreading to Japan and elsewhere in East Asia – was a partial re-run of the 1995 crisis. Robert Rubin fretted about the 'moral hazard' issue – the possibility of countries being encouraged to act irresponsibly due to the prospect of a US-led 'bail-out' in the event of economic failure. In the case of the Asian crisis, the US response came primarily in the form of the IMF rescue packages. Even indirect US assistance raised the prospect of rewarding irresponsibility: 'investors would escape the burden of problems they had helped create'.[81] The Thailand IMF rescue of 1997 involved significant clashes between the economic advisers on the one hand, and Clinton's foreign and defence team on the other. The latter wanted direct US assistance to Thailand, predicated on the record of strong Thai support for the US ever since the era of the Vietnam War. Clinton himself later recorded his regret at following the Rubin line and in this case not offering direct (economic stabilization fund) aid to Thailand.[82]

The Asian economic rescues involved the Clinton administration in some extraordinary unilateral interventions into global currency markets. In June 1998, for example, shortly before Clinton's state visit to China, the US Treasury led a $2 billion intervention on behalf of the Japanese yen. As the Asian crisis continued, however, Washington became more inclined to favour multilateral action. This involved an increase in US commitment to the IMF, which was inevitably difficult to sell to the Republican Congress. Appealing for extra US money for the IMF, some 90 major US companies took out an advertisement in major newspapers on 11 February 1998 under the title, 'The Asia Crisis Requires American Action Now'. Signatories to the advertisement included former presidents Jimmy Carter and Gerald Ford.[83] IMF funding issues also became embroiled in the Clinton administration's refusal to accept 'legislative blackmail' – Albright's phrase – over abortion funding. In 1997 and 1998, House Republicans managed to block both IMF and UN money in protest at US-funded foreign aid programmes which provided assistance for abortions in developing countries.[84] IMF funding also came under fire from some liberal Democrats who objected to the conditions imposed in return for assistance. David Bonior, for example, House Minority Whip, argued that IMF help for Indonesia was being made conditional on the adoption by President Suharto of market-oriented reforms, but included no requirement that Suharto released imprisoned labour leaders. A vivid indication of the extraordinary nature of the anti-IMF subset of the new anti-globalisation coalition came in January 1998, when independent socialist US Representative Bernard Saunders of Vermont joined conservative Republican Senator Lauch Faircloth of North Carolina to lead opposition to the US underwriting of IMF rescue programmes. Generally, however, the inclusion of reform requirements – aimed essentially at changing the Asian tradition of 'crony capitalism' in a market direction – was a major cause of the Congressional majority gradually becoming more inclined to support the IMF.[85]

The Asian travails constituted a major setback for Clinton's free trade bicycle. The 1998 trade bill was shelved in January 1998 in favour of the effort to persuade Congress to vote $18 billion in new IMF funding.[86] Plans for a Pacific Rim free trade zone were rapidly overtaken by events. Despite relative success in post-1997 IMF funding, the later Clinton years were beset with organised resistance to the free trade agenda. The battle for legislative approval for Chinese entry into the WTO was eventually won when Congress voted for normal trade relations with Beijing in September 2000. This administration victory was the culmination of a long inter-branch struggle, involving allegations that Beijing had improperly helped to fund Clinton's 1996 election campaign. In November 1999, AFL–CIO president John Sweeney cited the imprisonment of Chinese labour leaders as a reason for opposing Chinese entry into the WTO. So much, declared Sweeney, for Clinton's promise to 'put a human face on the global economy!'[87]

Squeezed between the anti-globalist nationalism of the Republican right and the anti-globalist 'human face' idealism of the American left, Clinton found it enormously difficult to sustain the rhetorical commitment to global free trade. His problems, and his skill in handling them, were apparent in an address he gave at the University of Chicago in June 1999. Clinton began his speech by revealing that he had signed a petition, presented to him by the Chicago students, demanding 'fair trade, not free trade'. He linked global commerce to global communications: 'Every single day a half-million airline passengers, 1.4 billion e-mail messages, and $1.5 trillion cross national borders.' Globalisation 'with a human face' could and should be achieved. The plight of those left behind, including much of sub-Saharan Africa, had to be alleviated. He demanded a global 'legal framework of mutual responsibility and social safety' as essential to the *success* of the market. He announced that Robert Rubin was putting forward a proposal to triple debt relief to the world's poorest nations. The US – 4.5 per cent of the world's population with 22 per cent of its income – 'cannot sustain our standard of living unless we sell some things to other people'. However, 'the global community cannot survive as a tale of two cities'. The Chicago students would have to work for the next two or three decades on the alleviation of global inequality, always of course within the commitment to globalisation, and to the aversion of global warming.[88]

The loss by Clinton of fast-track negotiating authority in 1997 was a blow to his free trade ambitions and really spelled the end of the first term strategy of interlocking trade zones. The White House was still able, after 1997, to proclaim free trade successes. Indeed fast-track authority, originally granted to the White

House during the Ford presidency, had actually lapsed in 1994. The many country-to-country agreements made since 1994 had not required changes to US law and did not go to Congress for approval. In September 1999, the Clinton White House was able to point to various achievements at the APEC summit in New Zealand: progress on US–China free trade pending Chinese entry into the WTO and APEC endorsement of the WTO trade round due to be launched in Seattle at the end of the year. Charlene Barshefsky continued to negotiate bilateral trade deals. The stress in the White House report on the APEC summit was now on political/foreign policy agreements: agreement with Indonesia to deploy an international peace-keeping force in East Timor, regional progress on the curtailment of North Korea's long-range missile programme.[89]

To proceed with regional trade deals, however, the administration needed fast-track authority. Previous GATT rounds had commenced without the president having this authority; yet the prospect of meeting at Seattle without it was very unattractive. Without fast-track, US negotiating positions simply lacked credibility. Clinton raised the rhetorical heat in a radio address on 8 November 1997, a few days before the scheduled House of Representatives vote on fast-track. Anticipating a major Democratic push opposition, Clinton emphasised that a 'yes vote' would give the president the opportunity credibly to negotiate labour rights and environmental protection. 'A yes vote means that America helps to write the rules for the new global economy.'[90] Al Gore weighed in: 'When we use this negotiating authority to tear down barriers overseas, it is always more to our advantage than to that of other countries.'[91] Within a week, the administration effectively admitted defeat in the face of opposition mobilised by Richard Gephardt. Technically, Speaker Gingrich, who supported fast-track, withdrew the measure when it became apparent that Gephardt, who was by this time being talked of as a possible Democratic presidential nominee for 2000, would prevail. The *NYT* explained the outcome in terms of continuing Democrat dissatisfaction with the operation of NAFTA, including the ineffectuality of the original labour and environment side deals, and to blunders made by the White House: including 'the President's accusation that Democrats who did not support the bill were in the pocket of union bosses, and a ... fire-sale atmosphere suggesting that the Administration would barter away almost anything for a vote favouring the legislation'. David Obey (Democrat, Wisconsin) described fast-track as 'a further walking away from the traditional values of the Democratic Party'.[92] A re-run occurred in September 1998, with fast-track being defeated in the House, 243–180; Democrat Congressmen split 171 to 29 against the bill.[93] By this time, fast-track was dead for the foreseeable future.

The Seattle WTO trade negotiations witnessed two intersecting battles, both of which resulted in considerable damage to the Clinton free trade bicycle. Anti-globalisation protests on the streets seemed to indicate the end of any kind of consensus about the virtues of globalised free trade. The administration initially took the position that, in the words of Charlene Barshefsky, 'the views of civil society' should be heard, and indeed 'integrated' into the WTO deal.[94] With violence increasing and Seattle police using tear gas against protesters, the event soon assumed the aspect of a disaster for the forces of free trade. Inside the negotiations, Clinton fought a parallel battle to achieve progress in the actual trade talks, appearing before the delegates of the 135 countries represented in Seattle to urge a consensual basis for moving ahead with the 'Clinton Round'. Commentators tended to agree that suspicion of American motives, particularly of Clinton's desire to use the occasion as a launching pad for Al Gore's 2000 campaign, played an important role in his failure. Clinton's desire to keep pedalling probably contributed to the hasty and under-prepared nature of the occasion. The root causes of the collapse, however, were complex and certainly extended beyond misjudgements made by the Clinton administration.[95] Arguing that the WTO needed to overcome the distrust emanating from the unnecessary secrecy of its procedures, Clinton pushed for the opening up of the WTO's judicial panels. Given the stance of his party and also his own developing commitment to the 'human face', Clinton was bound also to lobby for the clear insertion of labour and environmental standards as priorities for the new round. He encouraged the WTO to create a working group to consider child labour and other types of labour exploitation. Yet the president's interview with a Seattle newspaper, in which he indicated that he favoured real sanctions for violators of 'core labour standards', was frequently cited as confirming the suspicion of developing countries that the US wished to cancel their comparative advantage in wages.[96]

Despite the failures with fast-track and with the Seattle agenda, Clinton had one more free trade victory – one which was comparable with NAFTA ratification: the campaign in 2000 to secure congressional approval for permanent normal trading relations (PNTR) with China. The politics of Chinese free trade during the 1990s revolved around the annual congressional debate over extension of Most Favoured Nation (MFN) status, allowing Chinese goods into the US at non-discriminatory tariff rates. Especially in the first term, the debate centred on efforts to tie MFN status to improvement in China's human rights record. As the Clinton presidency progressed, it became more deeply entwined in legislative complaints about unfair Chinese trading practices, and in concern about the imbalances in US–Chinese trade. The early politics of the Chinese MFN process will be discussed further in Chapter 6, in the context of Washington's developing policy stance towards Beijing. By the second term, majorities in Congress were generally prepared to accept that global economic integration probably was the best way to deal with China's human rights behaviour. Set-piece contests between White House and Capitol Hill over Chinese MFN were resolved in favour of trade liberalisation. In May 1997, during that year's MFN debate, Representative Nancy Pelosi (California Democrat) declared it 'time to stop holding our policy hostage to the profits of a few exporting elites at the expense of most products made in America'. *Congressional Quarterly*, however, reported that the primary goal of many legislative opponents of the MFN was simply 'to register their outrage at the ballooning US trade deficit with China'.[97]

White House support for Chinese entry into the WTO raised fears – not only on Capitol Hill, but also in parts of the executive bureaucracy – that Clinton would fail, as the price of US support for China's application, to set tough market-opening conditions. Charlene Barshefsky (as Deputy Trade Representative) actually agreed the broad outlines of a liberalising 'road map' with Beijing as early as November 1995. Efforts to achieve a firm deal in April 1999 foundered, despite Clinton's own publicly voiced support for Beijing's WTO aspirations. Robert Rubin and Commerce Secretary William Daley opposed the April 1999 deal, arguing that China still seemed unlikely to open important economic sectors, including Chinese banking.[98] Though severely hindered by the nationalist backwash from the accidental bombing (during the 1999 US action over Kosovo) of the Chinese Embassy in Belgrade, Barshefsky finally negotiated the WTO entry deal in November 1999. Madeleine Albright later noted that this 'reflected a leap of faith on Beijing's part that China would be able to compete in the global marketplace while abiding by international rules'.[99] More pertinently to the US political debate, it also involved a leap of faith to the effect that Beijing indeed would abide by international rules.

As part of the American side of the deal, Clinton announced in January 2000 that, pending legislative approval, permanent normal trade relations to China would be established. The PNTR campaign soon assumed a symmetrical relationship to the 1993 NAFTA ratification campaign, with the political dynamics transformed by the passage of time. Bronwen Maddox wrote in the London *Times*: 'The only blessing of being a lame duck is that there is nothing left to lose. After Monica, there is no such thing as embarrassment for President Clinton, nor any political cost in picking a fight.'[100] Madeleine Albright embarked on a campaign to argue that it actually 'was possible to be vigorously pro-PNTR and pro-human rights at the same time'.[101] The final House vote in May 2000, at 237–197 in favour of PNTR, was almost a replay of NAFTA's 234–200. The tactics of 1993 reappeared. Two Texan Representatives achieved federal support for a new oil pipeline; Democrat Congressman Gregory Meeks of New York was treated to personal presidential attention on *Air Force One*.[102] The Senate approved the measure easily in September, with China being admitted to the WTO at the end of 2001.

Clinton's trade policy was in many respects hugely successful. The relative enervation of the later years could not completely cancel the energy and purpose which the promotion of globalised free trade had given to the administration's earlier foreign economic policy – indeed, in some respects, to its entire foreign policy. The trade agenda became derailed to some extent by the sheer difficulty of constructing global trading alliances in which the US was always to be the master player. It was also damaged more by the fears and anxieties of Clinton's fellow Democrats than by the prejudices of insular Republicans. Yet the global free trade vision, from 1993 to 2001, remained the heart of Clinton's foreign policy. Sandy Berger, in the pages of *Foreign Affairs* (FA) in late 2000, neatly juxtaposed Clinton's earliest and final free trade political successes, setting them in the context of the administration's search for a way to combine interests and ideals in the post-Soviet age: 'Just as NAFTA helped erode the economic base of the one-party rule in Mexico, participation in WTO ... can help promote change in China.'[103]

During the second term, there was an acceptance within the administration that the search for easy new Kennanisms had floundered. At her nomination hearing in 1997, Madeleine Albright announced that she was 'not going to use words any longer that have a lot of syllables and end in an "ism"'.[104] The key concept of the second term was that of America as an 'indispensable nation', a term developed as much in the context of Republican assaults on the foreign aid budget as in response to global events. Yet Clinton remained 'the globalisation president' until the end. His speeches on globalisation after 1998, compared with the first term effusions, tended to have a darker side. Globalisation was still inexorable and glorious, but American leadership was required to guide it in the required direction. Even more than in the first term, history needed to be given a shove in America's direction. In February 1999, he acknowledged the possibility that, without proper American leadership of global processes, 'former adversaries' – primarily Russia and China – 'will not succeed in their transition to freedom and free markets'.[105] In December 2000, he declared in true first term style: 'The train of globalization cannot be reversed'. However, the train had 'more than one possible destination'; only America could ensure that the 'right' destination was reached.[106] Economic nationalism and free trade, inexorable globalisation and shoving history in America's direction: Clinton's foreign economic policies were not without their internal tensions. Like Walt Whitman, Bill Clinton was confident that his philosophy of democratic optimism was strong enough to contain contradictions.

4 Making war, avoiding war
1993–96

Important as trade policy was, particularly to the first Clinton administration, *the* foreign policy debate of the 1990s was the debate over humanitarian intervention. On the one side stood the forces of realism, caution and the logic of the Westphalian tradition of state sovereignty; on the other, stood the 'liberal hawks' or 'compassion warriors'. In the realm of academic International Relations, the debate was framed as one between 'pluralists' (upholders of traditional notions of state sovereignty) and 'solidarists' (believers in human rights as ontologically prior to state sovereignty).[1] For US policy-makers, the debate brought together numerous strands of understanding of the possible and correct role for America to play in the post-Cold War order. Memories of Vietnam mingled with hopes for the 'democratic peace'. Awareness of the limits of American power clashed with the 'CNN effect' and the military's insistence that its job was to fight winnable wars, not to repair 'failed states' or run foreign countries. Despite his willingness to intervene militarily in the cause of democratic human rights, Tony Lake asserted in 1996: 'Neither we nor the international community have either the responsibility or the means to do whatever it takes for as long as it takes to rebuild nations.'[2]

This chapter deals with two interventions which had a humanitarian, even democracy-promoting, dimension: Somalia and Haiti. It then moves on to discuss Bosnia, setting American options there against more general considerations about humanitarian intervention in the post-Soviet context. Chapter 4 begins with an assessment of Clinton's peculiar relationship with the US military.

Defence policy, 1993–96: Clinton and the military

What should the US do with its military now that the Cold War was over? Conventional wisdom in the early 1990s held that policy drift, hoping that military capability would somehow adapt itself to the new world, was the worst possible way forward. As well as the perceived need for directed adaptation, policy was also driven by the rather vague anticipation of a post-Cold War 'peace dividend'. America's huge sword was unlikely to be converted rapidly into a gigantic ploughshare, but surely now really *was* the time to reinvest dollars into domestic renewal. Indeed, it could be argued that, as a 'domestic renewal' presidential candidate with no military background, Clinton had been elected precisely to reinvest in America's domestic fabric. This expectation survived into the mid-1990s, and even into the Clinton second term. In 1995, *The Bulletin of the Atomic Scientists* argued that it was 'common sense' to prepare for the unexpected. 'But should such preparations include the deployment of a new fleet of attack submarines? ... The maintenance of combat forces sufficient to fight two major wars more or less at the same time? How strong is strong?'[3] Three writers in the journal, *International Security*, in 1997 put the case for switching spending away from defence: 'Now that the Cold War is over, George McGovern is right.'[4]

By the time Clinton assumed office, President Bush had made significant inroads into the defence budget. Though the incoming Clinton team tended to assume that Bush had been able to work on the 'fat' in the defence budget, US military spending (in constant dollars) fell from $369 billion in fiscal 1989 to just over $300 billion in fiscal 1993. Pentagon procurement levels fell 20 per cent between 1987 and 1992. The Bush administration's understanding of American military needs was developed under its concept of the 'base force', including 12 active-duty army divisions and 13 aircraft carriers. The outgoing administration had also accepted, in outline at least, what was coming to be termed the 'revolution in military affairs' (RMA): the view that, to quote Stephen Cimbala, 'the kinds of force required for future multilateral or unilateral US military intervention will be ... more mobile, technically advanced and elitist'.[5]

A successful commander-in-chief for the 1990s needed to respond to many competing sets of demands. Calls for a 'peace dividend' continued, though the dynamics of US military acquisition did not suddenly become more susceptible to political control with the end of the Cold War. The key question, 'How strong is strong?', had to be answered in the context of global strategic uncertainty. Clinton's ability to meet the challenges facing a post-Cold War commander-in-chief was severely compromised by his difficult personal relations with American military leaders. Where even Jimmy Carter had a military background, Clinton appeared simply to offer charm and evasion.[6] Civilian sinuousness and subtlety met military angularity. Moreover, Clinton's fondness for informality in decision-making – perhaps even more his *reputation* as a disorganised leader – upset the military. The situation was exacerbated by the personal traits of Les Aspin, Clinton's first Defense Secretary. As Powell recalled, many military officers made unfavourable comparisons with Bush41's Defense Secretary: Aspin was 'as disjointed as (Richard) Cheney was well organized'.[7]

Clinton's Vietnam record – or rather, lack of it – was arguably at the root of much of the difficulty. Clinton himself had reason to feel aggrieved; after all, Dan Quayle, Reagan's Vice President, and Newt Gingrich – not to mention George W. Bush – were among the leading Republicans who had also found a way of evading direct service in Vietnam. Clinton had been in no position to exploit family connections to escape or delay service in Vietnam. Quayle, Gingrich and George W., of course, were manifestly on the 'right' side, from the military's viewpoint, of the culture wars. Examination of Clinton's draft experience revealed the extreme complexity of the experience of so many American males who had looked for ways out of service in a war they opposed. His career as a draftee was punctuated by technical changes in the selective service system, enabling him to finish his first year of study at Oxford University (1968–69) and eventually to avoid service altogether. Again, his sinuousness became an issue. His early biographer, David Maraniss, concluded that Bill Clinton had 'played the draft like a chess player'.[8]

Clinton pledged shortly before the 1992 election that, if he won, it would 'finally close the book on Vietnam'.[9] His wife's comment was nearer the truth: 'Bill carried with him into the White House the unresolved feelings of our country about that war.'[10] Senior military figures were not all hostile or unsympathetic to the dilemmas of draftees like Clinton. Colin Powell saw the whole draft system as 'class-ridden, undemocratic and unjust' and, at least as far as his memoirs illustrate, did not blame Clinton for trying to beat it.[11] Yet to many in the military, the coming of the Clintons to Washington looked less like catharsis, more like vengeance. When Powell introduced Clinton at the Vietnam memorial in Washington DC on Memorial Day (31 May) 1993, the president was heckled by veterans. Clinton acknowledged his anti-war past: 'Just as war is freedom's cost, disagreement is freedom's privilege.'[12]

Early blunders made a tricky situation even trickier. Clinton ordered a military pay freeze and gained the reputation for being unwilling to salute correctly. A vague campaign pledge to end the ban on homosexuals serving in the military was allowed to become a major rift between White House and Pentagon. Tony Lake later commented on the gays in the military issue: 'I wouldn't say he (Clinton) got dragged into something he didn't believe – he just got entrapped into something he hadn't thought through.'[13] The final, congressionally approved, compromise – 'don't ask, don't tell' – incited further protest from the Joint Chiefs of Staff (JCS), including Powell. Reviewing the dispute in July, 1993, when it had effectively been resolved (along slightly altered 'don't ask, don't tell' lines), Clinton still could not resist trying to have the last word. He pointed out to the National Defense University that Senator Barry Goldwater, 'patron saint of the conservative wing of the Republican Party', had opposed the military ban on homosexuals.[14] In 1993, Clinton nominated Shirley Widnall to be secretary of the air force. She was to be the highest ever female appointment at the Pentagon.

The 'bottom up review' was the Clinton–Aspin update of the Bush 'base force' strategy. Its completion in September 1993 fulfilled a campaign pledge to re-think military commitments and capabilities. It proposed ten active-duty army divisions and 12 aircraft carriers. Like the 'base force', it involved a commitment to fight two regional wars simultaneously. Aspin's early effort to convert this into 'win, hold' – committing to one major conflict alongside one holding action – was abandoned. The review seemed to most observers as favouring multilateral engagement, but also insisted that US forces be 'sized and structured to preserve the flexibility and the capability to act unilaterally'.[15]

Aspin's review stimulated lines of criticism which were to echo down the remainder of the decade. Several of these emanated from the 'How strong is strong?' question. Did America really need the new stealth bomber, whose mission – to breach Soviet air defences in order to assault hardened targets – was outdated? Aspin himself described the C-17 cargo plane as demonstrating 'the unwillingness on the part of some high-ranking acquisition professionals to acknowledge program difficulties'.[16] The administration, during 1993 and 1994, sought to protect the C-17 from legislative budget-cutters. Following the Republican takeover on Capitol Hill, funding for National Missile Defense (NMD), a revived version of President Reagan's Strategic Defense Initiative (SDI) and part of the GOP commitment in the 1994 Contract with America, became a battleground for inter-branch conflict. Clinton applied his veto to the legislative defence authorisation budget for fiscal 1996, resulting in a stepping-back by the Republicans from their proposals on NMD, as well as their efforts to exercise greater control over US involvement in UN peace-keeping. In 1996, the Congressional Republican majority added $325 million to Clinton's budget request for NMD, dubbed by Congressman Gene Ackerman (Democrat, NY) 'Star Wars II, The Sequel'.[17]

Liberal Democrats accused Aspin and Clinton of failing to resist the blandishments of the military-industrial complex. They also objected to the way that neo-mercantilism was affecting Washington's attitude to foreign arms sales, which began to sky-rocket in the early 1990s; the Pentagon was increasingly helping US arms manufacturers to close contracts.[18] The administration was seen by some defence experts, however, as lagging behind the technological advances which were transforming warfare. To many of Aspin's critics, the administration seemed simply to have slightly scaled down the size of the US military, but with no commensurate contraction of commitments. The General Accounting Office estimated the fiscal 1995–96 spending shortfall of the 'bottom up review' at $50 billions: the Congressional Budget Office put the figure at $150 billion.[19] According to many critics, the defence budget was still geared towards big/medium war fighting, when the future seemed likely to be one of small scale peace-keeping. Edward Luttwack commented: 'the current inventory of combat forces contains too many manpower-intensive grand units that are highly exposed to casualties and simply unavailable as instruments of foreign policy.'[20] The need was for constant 'battlefield awareness', made possible by investment in, and acquisition of, new technology.

The Clinton administration in its first term was committed to the Revolution in Military Affairs. Especially when William Perry took over at the Pentagon in 1994, organisational changes were put in place to speed up high-tech procurement. Yet difficulties proliferated. The RMA was, at least in the short term before significant manpower reductions had been achieved, extremely expensive. While generally regarded as more attuned to flexible fighting rather than 'big wars', the new technology of 'battlefield awareness' could also be applied to more traditional combat. Defence budgeting remained a precarious balancing act. Clinton, Aspin and Perry were attacked (as Connecticut Democratic Senator Joe Lieberman put it) by 'an odd-couple marriage between liberals who want to cut defence ... and conservatives intent on eliminating the deficit'.[21] Champagne corks probably popped in the Pentagon when the 1994 election results were announced, but the Republican Congressional victory did not immediately turn military famine into military feast. (The impact of the change of chair at the Senate Armed Services Committee was somewhat lessened by the fact that the new Republican chair, Strom Thurmond of South Carolina, was 92 years old.) In this post-Cold War environment generally, however, Members of Congress tended to become more intimately involved in the minutiae of defence planning.[22] Public opinion polling tended to demonstrate support for defence cutting per se.[23] The real problem for the administration was a rather brutal mismatch between America's continuing global reach and its willingness to pay.

At the heart of many of the defence debates of the early 1990s was the relationship between readiness, modernisation and force structure. Congress did not vote enough money to keep pace with America's peace-keeping commitments. The shortfall tended to be made up from the 'readiness' budget. William Perry told Congress in February 1995 that 'readiness' was the 'first priority' for a post-Cold War military.[24] Even as he presented the defence budget request for fiscal year 1996, with some $6.6 billion cut from Pentagon spending, Perry admitted that within a year the downward trend in military procurement would have to be reversed.[25] Senator John McCain (Republican of Arizona) rekindled memories of the 1970s by accusing Perry of presiding over a 'hollow' military.[26]

These were years of rapid change, as the military sought to come to terms with new forms of organisation, as well as flexible fighting doctrines. By the early 1990s, as a result of the 1986 Goldwater–Nichols reforms, power within the US military moved away from the Washington-based service chiefs and towards the regionally based joint commanders in chief (CINCs), frequently characterised, in imperial parlance, as America's 'proconsuls'.[27] Clinton inherited the post-Vietnam Weinberger and Powell Doctrines, which emphasised that the US military should not be expected to perform non-military, 'nation-building' tasks. In 1984, Defense Secretary Caspar Weinberger advocated new standards for military intervention, including indisputable national interest, public and legislative support, and clearly defined military objectives. Colin Powell emphasised the need for clear exit points and for overwhelming force.[28] Reinforced by the perceived lessons of the 1991 Gulf War, Weinberger–Powell thinking was codified in the *National Military Strategy of the United States*, published by the JCS in 1992.[29] When Clinton entered the White House, it was not clear how these inhibitions on military engagement would be applied in the context of post-Cold War humanitarian intervention. Warren Christopher, in the early days of the administration, offered what amounted to a re-statement of the Weinberger–Powell line.[30] For Les Aspin, on the other hand, the Weinberger and Powell approaches – the famous 'lessons of Vietnam' – simply amounted to a cripplingly restrictive doctrine of 'all or nothing'.[31] Against Christopher, Aspin declared in public his opposition to the post-Vietnam military mind-set which held that 'if you aren't willing to put the pedal to the floor, don't start the engine'.[32] The Secretary of Defense was voicing a view which was emerging from specialist think tanks in the early 1990s: the view that the consensus 'lesson of Vietnam' was wrong, or rather that there was no single lesson to be derived from a war which, after all, had ended nearly 20 years ago. In this line of thought, the US, especially in the post-Cold War era, was ideally placed to 'undertake micro-interventions', dipping into regional conflicts, doing enough to turn the tide decisively in a favoured direction, usually towards some version of democracy-promotion, and then withdrawing.[33] The test of all this came in relation to a strange African intervention begun by Bush41: an intervention which was the first directly to confront the post-Cold War problem of 'failed states' and one which was completely at odds with the 'lessons of Vietnam' as summarised in Bush's own *National Military Strategy*.

Somalia

The misery of US involvement in Somalia was encapsulated and magnified in the 'Black Hawk Down' incident in October 1993. The disaster was precipitated by the shooting down, by the forces of Somalian warlord Mohammad Farar Aideed, of two US helicopters. In the ensuing gun battle, 19 Americans died. Over 500 Somalis were killed, after which – as Clinton recorded it – Aideed's men 'dragged the body of the slain Black Hawk crew chief through the streets of Mogadishu'.[34]

The October gun fight was not the only occasion of significant US casualties. Four American servicemen had been killed in June 1993. Yet, by the standards of previous or later US regional engagements, the fatality rate was not high. In subsequent judgements on American involvement in this corner of Africa, positive voices were not entirely absent. Writing in 1995, Chester Crocker, who had been in charge of African affairs in Reagan's State Department, estimated that 'upwards of a quarter of a million Somali lives had been saved by the humanitarian intervention'.[35] Yet Crocker's view was a minority one. The impact of the Somali experience on the subsequent attitudes of the Clinton administration was very significant. Clinton himself compared it to JFK's Bay of Pigs invasion – a disastrous enterprise, traceable to commitments made under the preceding administration, and overshadowing all subsequent military decisions.[36]

Many contemporaries interpreted the Somalian intervention as marking a watershed in US–UN relations. For Nancy Soderberg: 'Never again would President Clinton allow US forces to take part in an enforcement operation under UN command.'[37] Neo-conservative commentator Joshua Muravchik saw the intervention as making clear the true state of America's relationship to the UN. Clinton had 'turned to the United Nations to reduce America's burdens, but the United Nations itself was dependent on America'.[38] Madeleine Albright later defended her part in broadening the Somalian operational remit at the UN in the spring of 1993, but admitted that the 'relationship between the United States and the UN was never clearly straightened out'.[39]

The impact of the events of October 1993 was also increased by the sheer operational chaos that was exposed. J. G. Ruggie recalled 'three distinct forces with three different missions and three separate command-and-control structures' being dropped simultaneously on the streets of Mogadishu.[40] The three forces comprised the UN peace-keeping force, geared towards humanitarian assistance; a US Quick Reaction force, under direct US command but temporarily assigned to the UN; and the US Army Rangers, working completely outside the ambit of the UN. Much of this disorder was attributable to the haphazard US–UN coordination admitted by Madeleine Albright. It also reflected official Washington's own poor understanding of the situation on the ground. In the case of Somalia, as elsewhere, the early foreign policy process did not work adequately.

The policy inheritance from Bush41 was difficult. Bush partisans tended to emphasise the limited nature of the 1992 commitment and the open-ended nature of the Clinton equivalent. John Bolton, for example, quoted Bush41's 4 December letter to UN Secretary General Boutros Boutros-Ghali: 'the mission of the coalition is limited and specific: to create conditions which will permit the feeding of the starving Somali people and allow the transfer of this security function to the UN peacekeeping force.' Clinton converted this limited intervention into 'a deliberate experiment in "assertive multilateralism"'.[41] Yet, the Bush41 decision was itself rather extraordinary, even 'experimental'. The 1992 *National Military Strategy* did not completely rule out limited regional engagements, and clearly indicated America's ability to mount them. The 1992 Somalia engagement was presumably conceived as a genuinely time- and scope-limited deployment, which somehow could be squared with the thinking of Bush's own JCS head, Colin Powell. Yet 'mission creep' began even before Clinton's inauguration, with US troops moving beyond the humanitarian remit to raid suspected arms depots and attempting to convert clan armies into a new national force.[42]

In many respects Bush left Clinton a geopolitical miracle – the end of the Cold War. Yet he also left a disintegrating Cold War *system*, global uncertainty, expectations of a 'peace dividend' and continuing world-wide military commitments. In defence of the Bush team, it is worth noting that some of its senior members were prepared to acknowledge the bitter-sweet nature of Clinton's inheritance. Outgoing Defense Secretary Richard Cheney was quoted in 1993 as follows:

> The Clinton administration faces more difficult problems than anything we dealt with over the past five years. The pace of change is accelerating rapidly, and rather than making the world safer, it is making things less stable and less predictable.[43]

Given this judgement, and also given the Bush41 team's general reputation for realist caution and prudence, it is reasonable to wonder why US troops *were* committed to Somalia in the post-election period at the end of 1992. At the time, much was made of the CNN effect: the ability of the new, quickly sensitive media, in conditions where the traditional anti-communist framing of priorities had collapsed, actually to set agendas. Lawrence Eagleburger, Secretary of State in 1992, clearly acknowledged the 'television pictures of these starving kids' as a key element in the decision to send troops to Somalia.[44] The immediate crisis was provoked by the ouster of the sometime US-backed dictator Syed Barre in 1991. A combination of drought, clan warfare and the availability of modern weaponry rapidly brought the already fractured country to a state of chaos. Bush informed the NSC on 25 November 1992 that 'we want to do something about it'.[45] On 4 December, he announced on television that 28,000 US troops would be deployed to Somalia as America's contribution to an international force. The UN authorising resolution recognised that the force would be under American command.

Bush's motivation seemed to lie in a mixture of genuine humanitarian concern, the CNN effect, and a desire to set interventionist precedents in the new global order. If the 1991 Gulf War had not consigned the Vietnam syndrome to history's dustbin, a humanitarian intervention in Somalia – a part of the world generally seen to be devoid of core US strategic interest – surely would.[46] The administration seems to have regarded Somalia (unlike Bosnia) as 'doable'; however, it is difficult to resist the view that this was the decision of a demob-happy presidential team. Democratic Congressman R. E. Atkins from New Jersey commented: 'if Bush had won the election, there would have been a lot more thought given to the long-term consequences.'[47] Clinton, as president-elect, was briefed on Somalia on a daily basis by Brent Scowcroft. The incoming president commended Bush 'for taking the lead in this important humanitarian effort'.[48] Yet, as the *NYT* editorialised in early December: 'Bill Clinton, who backs the mission but seems not to have been consulted, may well be stuck with a messy crash landing.'[49]

Warnings about 'messy crash landings' in the Horn of Africa were effectively drowned out in the noise and confusion of the transition and the early emergence of a Clinton foreign policy process. Nancy Soderberg, later instructed by Tony Lake to review how Somalia had been handled in this period, found a policy which 'had been left in the hands of midlevel officials'. The shift from a mission which was (at least in theory) geared to limited humanitarian relief had never been discussed at principals' level, and never subject to detailed presidential scrutiny.[50] Warnings had been given about the deteriorating security environment by the CIA. Dick Moose, an old Somali hand from the Carter years, warned Lake and Berger that the US could easily become bogged down, and argued that mission objectives were dangerously unclear. Aspin did try to develop something approaching an exit strategy, but it was striking that no senior Clinton people actually took the trouble to visit Somalia.[51]

During the early part of 1993, Washington quarrelled with the UN General Secretary over the handover of responsibility of the operation to the UN (UNOSOM 2). The disagreements reflected a complex array of mutual suspicion and distrust. The Pentagon's view was that the UN could not perform effectively on the ground and that the US military should not serve under foreign command. Boutros-Ghali saw America's commitment as unreliable and liable to be undermined by domestic considerations. Robert Oakley, the Bush and early Clinton representative in Mogadishu, became increasingly frustrated by what he saw as the insensitive recklessness of the UN leadership.[52] The product of these tensions was Security Council Resolution 814, adopted on 26 March in the face of an ultimatum from Madeleine Albright to the effect that 'US troops would leave whether the UN was prepared to take their place or not'. Albright commented at the time that the resolution aimed 'at nothing less than the restoration of an entire country', later characterising it as 'requiring the UN to do more than the United States had accomplished but with fewer and less potent forces'.[53]

The handover to UNOSOM 2, which took place in early May, involved the continued deployment of some 8,000 US troops, not counting the 1,000-strong Quick Reaction force. Somalia descended into newly intense clan warfare, with the Aideed faction emerging as the winner. Twenty-four Pakistani soldiers were killed in June. Jonathan Howe, a former Bush NSC staffer now working for the UN in Mogadishu, urged Washington to disarm Aideed and his warriors. Albright supported Howe, whose status as Washington insider turned UN envoy further muddied the waters. Around this time, shortly before his retirement as chair of the Joint Chiefs, Colin Powell recommended a direct US effort in opposition to Aideed. Clinton ordered the Rangers to capture the Somali warlord. This was the mission which climaxed in the Mogadishu battle of October. Even before 'Black Hawk Down', leading policy-makers, including Aspin, were calling for the redefinition of 'success' in Somalia, effectively arguing that the US should content itself with achieving some acceptable level of security, falling well short of the re-building of national institutions.[54] Lee Hamilton (Democrat of Indiana), chairman of the House Foreign Affairs Committee, denounced the folly of US 'nation-building' in September.[55] On 25 September, the White House issued a press statement, declaring Somalia, 'especially outside of Mogadishu, to be 'on the road to recovery'.[56]

Speaking directly after 'Black Hawk Down', Clinton promised that all troops, 'except for a few hundred support' personnel, would leave by 31 March 1994. An immediate exit was not desirable since that 'would send a message to terrorists and other potential adversaries around the world that they can change our policies by killing our people'. He defended the intervention as a limited humanitarian mission that 'saved approximately a million lives that were at risk of starvation'. The American purpose 'is not nor was it ever one of "nation building"'.[57] His assertion here conflicted clearly not only with various UN statements made by Albright, but also with his own remark of 2 July ('we have to have patience in nation-building').[58]

Congress, in the first such use of a military cut-off threat since the Vietnam War, moved to enforce Clinton's 1994 exit deadline. The Congressional debate following 'Black Hawk Down' focused on the (in truth spurious) issue of Americans serving under UN leadership. As Peter Tarnoff, deputy to Warren Christopher, told the Senate Foreign Relations Committee on October 19: 'the combat forces that have been in Mogadishu and in the region have never been under UN command.'[59] Several Members also raised the issue of the applicability of the 1973 War Powers Resolution to the Somalian deployments. Senator Russ Feingold (Democrat of Wisconsin) argued that 'the troops should not have been there past 90 days after President Bush sent American soldiers there without a congressional resolution of approval'. The adoption by the White House of the March deadline effectively undermined any attempt to invoke the 1973 Resolution. The administration, as in later deployments, stuck to the view of its Republican predecessor on war powers; Congress might be consulted, but it had no business challenging a troop deployment which had properly been ordered under the president's responsibilities as commander-in-chief.[60]

A UN analysis of 'what went wrong' (by Tom Farar) offered a cogent explanation of the debacle. Both UN and US policy had been based on a superficial understanding of Somalian clan politics. It was never clear that Aideed's death or imprisonment would solve very much. The best US/UN strategy was always to work for the basic provision of security to ordinary Somalis. Short of the achievement of some basic security – which negotiations with aid might have been able to provide – widespread disarmament was not feasible. The Australian forces seem to have made progress on disarmament via negotiation.[61] For Farar, the requests by General Tom Montgomery (the US military commander in Somalia) for heavy armour were not simple re-runs of General Westmoreland's Vietnam era shopping lists; they were sensible responses to the need to provide simple security. The Farar report criticised Aspin (and Clinton) for seeing Montgomery as an updated Westmoreland and refusing his September requests. (A later study for the Joint Chiefs nevertheless concluded that presence of heavy armour in Mogadishu would not necessarily have prevented the killing of the 19 Americans.[62]) Most fundamentally, Farar's report attacked the lack of central direction, either from the UN or from Washington. Disarray at the centre meant that 'tactical and operational decisions were increasingly being made on the ground'.[63] Aspin announced his resignation on 15 December.

Haiti

The invasion, or quasi-invasion, of Haiti in September 1994 raised major questions about the nature of post-Cold War foreign policy and policy-making; about the relationship between force and diplomacy in the new era; and about the competence and guiding philosophy of the Clinton administration. The restoring to power of the elected Haitian president, Jean Bertrand Aristide, was, as *Congressional Quarterly* put it, 'a rare foreign policy success' in a year which had seen the rather ignominious retreat from Somalia.[64] Success was achieved in an extraordinary policy-making context. Nancy Soderberg recalled: 'The Haiti crisis ... points to the growing role that nonstate actors – refugees, terrorists, gangsters, corporations, NGOs, and protesters – had begun to play in foreign policy.'[65] To Soderberg's list, we might add the new news media. Right up to the final moment, a congressional majority was opposed to the invasion. Clinton's eventual success was also the product of decisional risk-taking. William Cohen, then the Republican Senator from Maine, declared just prior to the invasion: 'If things go well, fine, he'll get the credit. If things go awry, it could do mortal damage to his presidency.'[66]

Aristide, a leftist ('liberation theology') Roman Catholic priest, was elected in 1990, only to be deposed by the Haitian military some eight months later. The Bush41 administration had imposed a trade embargo, but, in practical terms, accepted the reality of the military dictatorship of Raoul Cedras. The use of force against the Cedras regime was contemplated in October 1991 in the face of a large exodus of refugees from the island. Colin Powell, however, advised against precipitate action, recalling that the US invasion of 1915 had led to an American occupation of Haiti which lasted 19 years.[67]

During the 1992 campaign, Clinton had criticised the Bush policy of intercepting and returning Haitian refugees *en route* to the US. Encouraged by this, large numbers of Haitians were preparing to leave the island as inauguration day approached.[68] Clinton responded by announcing that he would continue, at least for the time being, the Bush interception policy. Clinton felt he had been wounded politically by the location in Arkansas – in his view to protect electorally sensitive Florida – of Cuban refugees in 1980.[69] He was not about to repeat the experience on a national plane.

The Clinton position in early 1993 was that refugee interception, backed up by swifter processing of legitimate asylum claims, actually prevented many Haitian deaths by drowning. This argument was plausible, though self-serving. Madeleine Albright later cited the case of the Haitian refugees as an exemplification of the dilemmas of ethical foreign policy. When Clinton relaxed a few months later, the 'result was an upward spike in the number of Haitians trying to flee their island in leaky rafts': inevitably many drowned.[70]

Leading Clintonites debated the possibility of intervention. Tony Lake was enthusiastic about restoring Aristide to power, but was opposed by the Pentagon and by Secretary Christopher. A principals' meeting of 13 March 1993 discussed and rejected the possibility of military action. Colin Powell, remaining for a time as chair of the Joint Chiefs, predictably warned against committing to 'nonstrategic' situations – a designation which applied to Bosnia as well as Haiti.[71] The CIA at this stage was adamantly anti-Aristide and leaked a 'psychological profile' of Haiti's leader-priest to Republicans on Capitol Hill. Jesse Helms accordingly denounced Aristide as a 'psychopath'.[72]

Following these deliberations, the administration committed itself to a diplomatic path, largely to be conducted through the UN. In July, an agreement was reached with Cedras, at a meeting in New York City, whereby Aristide would return to power by the end of October. Despite contradictory signals and rising violence on the island, Washington continued to treat this as a done deal. Such was the background to the *Harlan County* incident of early October (just one week after the Mogadishu killings). The US ship, *Harlan County*, carrying around 200 US and Canadian military engineers, was turned back from the harbour in Port-au-Prince by a crowd shouting 'Somalia! Somalia!' The president and close White House staff were informed of the situation. David Gergen recalled the case he made to Clinton for regarding discretion as the better part of valour: 'You either got to go in with force and take care of that unruly mob. ... Or you got to get the ship the hell out of there.'[73] Probably fearing another Mogadishu and realising that the *Harlan County* lacked adequate support, Clinton decided on the latter option. Lake was sympathetic to the former, but the military argument that the US should pick the terms of its fights was difficult to resist.[74] According to George Stephanopoulos, Clinton complained to Lake that 'the Reagan people were much better at the politics of foreign policy than we are'. Following the 1983 terrorist bombing of marine barracks in Lebanon, Reagan 'went into Grenada two days later and fixed it'.[75]

The administration continued to be divided over the possibility of intervention, the likely impact of the economic sanctions which were being applied to Haiti, and over the trustworthiness of Aristide. Beyond the administration, the case for intervention was now being made most forcefully by the Congressional Black Caucus, a body which, under Cold War conditions, had invariably condemned US military action in the Caribbean as imperialistic. The caucus, along with various other liberal Democrats (such as Representative Joseph Kennedy) demanded tougher sanctions and an end to refugee interceptions. In April 1994, Randall Robinson, director of the Transafrica organisation, began a hunger strike associated with these issues. Clinton modified the interception policy in May, promising now to divert refugees to asylum centres in third countries. Fearing a mass exodus from Haiti, Florida legislators took up the cause of intervention, and Robinson came off hunger strike.

Clinton was becoming more attracted to military action by this time, telling associates that he would not 'wimp out' as he had done in October 1993. General Jack Sheehan told Cedras that he (Sheridan) had two uniforms, 'my dress uniform and my combat one'. It was up to Cedras which one Sheridan was wearing when they next met.[76] The balance of elite American opinion had been altered by the apparent ineffectiveness of sanctions, and also by the replacement of Colin Powell as JCS head by General John Shalikashvili. At a meeting on 7 May, the new military chief advocated invasion by the US acting alone. Post-Somalia suspicion of the UN also affected Tony Lake, who in May 1994 urged that the US should avoid tying itself into the willingness and/or capability of the UN to take credible action either alongside or as a 'follow-on' to American action. Nancy Soderberg, who attended key meetings on Haiti as third-ranking official on the NSC staff, recalled the general disenchantment with the UN as a turning point. Lake and Shalikashvili 'realized the power of the lone superpower. When the United States acted, others would follow. This principle would guide much of the rest of Clinton's foreign policy.'[77]

Though the case for intervention, and indeed for unilateral intervention, was now making massive bureaucratic headway, there still remained the '1915 problem' – the possibility of invasion leading to prolonged occupation. Apart from anything else, how could an invasion, certainly one with no obvious 'exit point', be sold to Congress and to the public? Senator John Glenn (Ohio Democrat) put the point succinctly: 'We could prevail militarily, but then what do you do? How do you establish order? ... And how do you get out?'[78] Various 'sense of Congress' measures were passed to the effect that any invasion would require prior legislative approval.[79] Public support for an invasion was running at less than one-third prior to September 1994.[80]

The administration's public rhetoric reflected the replacement of Powell by Shalikashvili and the general progress being made by the interventionist case. In May, Clinton promised never to 'interfere in the affairs of another country to try to thwart the popular will there'; Haiti, he insisted, was 'a different case'.[81] At the end of July, the UN Security Council passed resolution 940, inviting member states to use 'all necessary means' to topple the military government in Port-au-Prince. The resolution was the result of sustained American pressure: not least pressure on Aristide, who was, only with difficulty, persuaded to endorse it.[82]

The passage of resolution 940 itself raised complex problems for Washington. UN backing per se would not necessarily defuse regional unease at this latest expression of Yankee militarism. Brazil, then sitting on the Security Council, abstained in the July vote and later joined Mexico in expressing its opposition to invasion. The US Senate itself adopted a resolution, designed to head off any attempt by Clinton to use the resolution as a way of ordering an invasion without prior, specific legislative approval. Judd Gregg (Republican, New Hampshire) denied any desire to be seen 'bashing the United Nations', but insisted that the UN must not be allowed to usurp the prerogatives of the US Congress.[83] In fact, Clinton was now asserting an inherent, constitutional right to commit troops to Haiti quite separate from the UN authorisation: 'like my predecessors of both parties, I have not agreed that I was constitutionally mandated' to obtain legislative approval before deploying troops.[84] Like his predecessors from Nixon onwards, Clinton was prepared to observe some of the outward forms of the 1973 War Powers Resolution – notably submitting reports on deployments to Congress – but to accept neither the constitutionality nor any mandatory effect of the measure. The 1994 UN resolution also threatened the scenario that Lake had foreseen in May: that of the US becoming hostage to future UN 'follow-on' action. Nevertheless, the history of US policy in the Caribbean indicated that the US would take action under the Monroe Doctrine of hemispheric domination more or less as it chose. Rather than compromising American independence, the achievement by the US of resolution 940 was a way of ameliorating potential public disquiet. It also raised the prospect of a post-invasion international force taking some of the heat out of the '1915 problem'. Though William Perry and the Pentagon generally continued to worry about exit strategies, the momentum was now with the war party, led by Albright, Lake and Strobe Talbott. Christopher and the State Department were sidelined, tasked now with producing a report on conditions on Haiti.

By early September, the administration hawks moved to place human rights at the top of the rationale for action. The State Department report painted a grim picture of the human rights violations committed by the Cedras regime, described as worse than under the old dictator, 'Papa Doc' Duvalier.[85] On 15 September, Clinton outlined the inhuman conditions on the island during a TV address. He followed the advice of Dick Morris, who urged the president to 'center his comments much more on moral outrages against Haitian women and children' than on the plight of the refugees.[86] Following the speech, public approval of Clinton's handling of the crisis immediately leapt from 35 to 53 per cent.[87]

Clinton's line in September 1994 was that the US was acting on behalf of the UN to achieve a variety of goals: first and most important to stop human rights abuses on the island, but also to restore Haiti's elected president, to prevent new refugee tragedies and to uphold America's international reputation as an upholder of democracy and human rights.[88] In the 15 September speech, Clinton emphasised the multilateral nature of the effort, with Strobe Talbott also announcing that Washington had gained the approval of CARICOM, the largely economic community of (anti-communist) Caribbean countries.[89] Into the evolving interventionist dynamic now stepped former president Jimmy Carter, who had delivered detailed memoranda on Haiti to the White House in October 1993 and May 1994. Carter's fraught relationship with the White House was the subject of major press coverage, focusing primarily on his activities in North Korea, but also regarding Haiti. Elaine Sciolino recorded the administration being divided over whether Carter 'was making peace or just making trouble'.[90]

Drawing on indications that Carter had some influence with Cedras, Clinton accepted Carter's mediation plan shortly before the 15 September television address. Working with his Latin American affairs adviser Robert Pastor, Carter suggested that he visit Cedras, accompanied by Colin Powell and Senator Sam Nunn. Powell recalled the president regarding his Democratic predecessor as 'sometimes a wild card'. Carter's efforts to negotiate in Somalia had foundered. However, Clinton 'took a chance with him in North Korea, and that didn't turn out too badly'.[91] The potential for difficulty was huge. Robert Pastor later wrote: the 'Carter–Nunn–Powell team ... intended to approach the Haitian military very differently than the Clinton administration preferred'. By this time the invasion plan – 20,000 infantry landing on Haiti, led by paratroopers flown in from Fort Bragg – was well advanced. Clinton was not thinking in terms of it being aborted, but rather of Cedras accepting the inevitable. Carter, however, insisted on some flexibility and rejected a NSC 'talking points' memo which, according to Pastor, was 'nothing more than insults and threats'.[92]

Nunn had recently opposed an invasion from the Senate floor, while both Carter and Powell were sceptical about the wisdom of military action. All three began negotiating on 17 September in ignorance of the fact that the invasion was set to go ahead only 36 hours later. Powell appealed to the junta's strategic sense: 'What military code calls for the senseless sacrifice of life?'[93] The team offered terms for the junta members to leave the island freely. With all parties following the coverage on CNN, Clinton, on the afternoon of 18 September, ordered the 82nd airborne to fly out of Fort Bragg. He activated a hostage rescue team in case the negotiating team was imprisoned. The Oval Office at this time resembled the floor of the NY stock exchange, with numerous 'aides and officials rushing in and out'.[94]

The Keystone Cops atmosphere was intensified by the fact that, besides the negotiations (that the White House did not actually acknowledge as negotiations) going on in Haiti, a parallel set of talks were going on in Washington with Aristide.[95] The possibility of Aristide undermining the whole enterprise was always present. Even more alarmingly, Haitian General Philippe Biamby announced at 4pm on 18 September that a 'source' at Fort Bragg had told him that the paratroopers were on their way. The implications for Carter, Nunn and Powell, whom Biamby denounced as attempting a diversionary tactic, were very grave. Nunn concluded that they had a 50/50 chance of escaping death or captivity.[96] Clinton hovered between ordering the team out immediately and opting for one last chance. That a deal, involving a comic opera adjudication by provisional Haitian president Emile Jonaissant, was achieved was partly due to luck, partly due to the skill of the negotiators. Carter seems to have managed to instil a sense of realism into the minds of the junta. US troops landed unopposed, while the junta prepared to leave by the newly agreed deadline of 15 October.

Looking back on the story of the invasion-that-wasn't, one is struck by the atmosphere of decisional chaos. Carter's team, which seemed more certain of their course than anyone in Washington, could easily have been killed. CNN kept intervening in extraordinary ways. When the 82nd Airborne left Fort Bragg, Tom Johnson, head of CNN, called the Pentagon to relay the view that it was now obvious what was happening, and asking when the paratroopers would land. Aristide was restored to power, although his conduct was almost entirely unpredictable and could only be directly influenced by Washington if US troops were to remain on the island indefinitely. The administration was determined not to be drawn into a re-run of 1915. Congress began efforts to enforce a leaving timetable, though no meaningful effort was made to assert legislative war powers either immediately prior to, or following, the invasion. The administration evaded the War Powers Resolution via a mixture of simple defiance and semantic invention.[97] A UN 'follow-on' force took up security duties, only to leave the island without making much impact on the violence and corruption which continued to characterise Haitian politics.

Why did Clinton decide that it was in the national interest to invade Haiti? His emphasis in *My Life* was on human rights.[98] It is tempting to join Dick Morris[99] in pooh-poohing this human rights motivation. After all, human rights were hardly likely to improve on the island, and actually did not improve, under Aristide. Nevertheless, Jean-Bertrand Aristide was internationally recognised as the properly elected president, and the US was committed to hemispheric democracy-promotion. In this regard, the end of the Cold War could be seen as operating in contradictory ways. On the one hand, the end of Soviet adventurism might have been expected to have limited Washington's concern with the politics of its neighbours, especially its particularly poor and strategically insignificant neighbours. On the other hand, the Soviet collapse had arguably removed the attraction for Washington of anti-communist strongmen. In these circumstances, it is not completely naive to read Clinton's support for the invasion as a signal of commitment to democratic change.

Beyond democracy-promotion and human rights, there were the questions of refugee crisis and of US credibility beyond the Caribbean. These worries were not hidden by the administration, and indeed were clearly expressed in Clinton's 15 September address. What is potentially damaging to Clinton's reputation is the implication of his remarks to Stephanopoulos at the time of the *Harlan County* fiasco. Did Clinton, humiliated in Mogadishu as well as Port-au-Prince, decide to act in Haiti as Reagan had acted in Grenada? The idea of Reagan ordering the invasion of Grenada in 1983 as a kind of wilful compensation for the Lebanon killings is not merely the stuff of leftist conspiracy theory. It was expressed by none other than Margaret Thatcher.[100] If we are to believe Stephanopoulos, Clinton also accepted the Lebanon–Grenada link. The notion of a parallel Somalia–Haiti link was in fact implicit in Clinton's televised remarks about the need to consider America's international reputation. Dante Caputo, UN envoy to Haiti, advised Secretary General Boutros-Ghali two months before the invasion that Clinton was seeking an invasion in order to exhibit 'firmness of purpose in international political matters'.[101]

The proximity of the invasion to the 1994 mid-term elections also did not go unnoticed by hostile commentators. Yet unnecessary wars are a risky business. The invasion manifestly did not help in the 1994 elections.[102] Rather than a 'rare foreign policy success', Haiti was – to use Colin Powell's description of the Grenada invasion of 1983 – 'a sloppy success'.[103]

Humanitarian intervention in the first term

The first two years of Clinton's presidency witnessed a fairly consistent retreat from the precepts of 'assertive humanitarianism'. Presidential Decision Directive (PDD) 25, issued in May 1994, specified conditions for US participation in UN peace-keeping operations. Detailing the need for clear objectives, acceptable risks, international and domestic consensus, PDD 25 represented a victory for anti-Aspin forces at the Pentagon and for UN sceptics generally.[104] It also reflected the president's peculiar vulnerability to criticism emanating from the US military. PDD 25 was, in effect, a restatement of the Weinberger Doctrine for the post-Cold War, post-Somalia, era. The directive, re-codified as PDD 56, was re-issued some three years later, with extra detail regarding formal bureaucratic procedures governing humanitarian intervention.[105] PDD 25 was not simply the product of Somalia. It derived from proposals in the Bush years to improve US–UN command and control, and also to expand America's 'rapid reaction' capabilities. The initiative had stalled between 1992 and 1994, due to military unease about peace-keeping per se, as well as resistance to the degree to which the enhanced 'rapid reaction' force would drain existing capacity.

PDD 25 did not disbar US involvement in humanitarian interventions. Indeed some Clintonites defended it as actually securing a future for US involvement in peace-keeping. Madeleine Albright described the purpose of PDD 25 as being to put

> America squarely on the side of the strengthening UN peacekeeping operations, with the understanding that we would henceforth make the chain of command clearer and insist that such missions be carefully planned, with a precise mandate, efficiently implemented, and preceded by a significant period of consultations with Congress.[106]

At the other extreme, David Obey, Democratic Congressman from Wisconsin, argued that PDD 25 evidenced a desire for 'zero degree of involvement, and zero degree of risk'.[107] The directive, however, certainly did not prevent Clinton deploying troops; indeed, he became increasingly attracted to troop deployments in a whole range of disparate conditions. Rather, it signalled a high degree of scepticism about cooperation with the UN – a scepticism which, of course, was increasingly led by the Republican Congress – as well as a propensity to defer to military judgements. Such judgements were not uniformly hostile to humanitarian intervention; the Marine Corps, for example, seems to have welcomed the Somalian engagement as a potential boost to its budget. The consensus military view, however, was encapsulated by the anonymous Pentagon official who advocated 'selective and effective peace operations', driven by 'self interest, not foggy idealism'.[108]

The intensity of Somalia's impact on subsequent US foreign policy is a little difficult to understand, especially when we appreciate that Somalia was primarily a US, not a UN operation. Leonie Murray is probably correct to argue that this was a case of an administration willingly giving up any pretension to humanitarian globalism.[109] Somalia was never Clinton's chosen territory for intervention, and this was, after all, an 'economics first', domestic-oriented administration. While the Clinton White House did gain the reputation of pursuing 'foreign policy as social work', Bill Clinton himself had precious little attraction towards any such concept; moreover, public and Congressional opinion were certainly not pointing him in the direction of multilateral and militarised altruism. For Warren Christopher, Somalia's shadow 'loomed large': William Perry and General Shalikashvili 'were careful to heed its lessons. ... As a result, the Rwanda mission was limited to those tasks for which we had unique capabilities, such as the air transportation of heavy equipment'.[110]

Rwanda was, in fact, the first regional crisis to be considered under the terms of PDD 25. From the very limited perspective of the spring of 1994 (when the Rwandan genocide began), the existence of the PDD 25/Weinberger Doctrine 'tests' was actually welcomed by the administration as a way of escaping over-exposure to the hazards of open-ended commitment.[111] In May 1994, describing the policy review which led to PDD 25, Tony Lake declared that peace-keeping was 'not the centrepiece' of American national security policy; the central commitment still was the ability to fight two major regional conflicts 'nearly simultaneously and to do so unilaterally when necessary'. Regarding humanitarian intervention, 'we have to make distinctions ... to ask hard questions about where and when we can intervene'.[112]

Tony Lake was right about the need to make distinctions. Yet his above remarks were delivered on 5 May 1994; the Rwandan massacres began on 6 April. Four years later, in a speech delivered in Kigali, Clinton made the following 'apology' to the people of Rwanda:

> We did not act quickly enough after the killings began. ... It may seem strange to you here, especially the many of you who lost members of your family, but all over the world, there were people like me sitting in offices, day after day, who did not fully appreciate the depth and the speed with which you were being engulfed by this unimaginable horror.[113]

Clinton's plea of ignorance was not entirely credible. It was decisively undermined by the release of documents to the National Security Archive in March 2004 under the Freedom of Information Act. CIA daily intelligence reports, circulating to Clinton, Gore and many senior officials, were using the term 'genocide' as early as 23 April.[114] However, warnings relayed via Romeo Dellaire, UN force commander in Rwanda, were ignored not just by the US, but by the whole international community. The unfolding disaster gave as much ammunition to opponents of the bureaucratised and timid UN system as it did to critics of Clinton. Washington's focus was on the Hutu–Tutsi peace process, following the murder of presidents Habyarimana (Hutu leader of Rwanda) and Ntaryamira (of Burundi) on 6 April. On 16 April, the *NYT* reported the murder of over 1,000 people at a Rwandan church. On 26 April, Tony Lake described the massacres of Tutsis as 'a warning of what can happen if African nations and all of us do too little to stop simmering conflicts before they boil over'. The Security Council, with US support, voted to draw down the UN force to a symbolic presence of 270 personnel on 21 April, pending the achievement of a cease-fire. As Nancy Soderberg recalled: 'no decision maker in the US proposed sending in US or other troops in the middle of the genocide.'[115] Madeleine Albright wrote that perhaps 'the only solution would have been a large and heavily armed coalition led by a major power, but because of Somalia, the US military wasn't going to undertake that'.[116] Daily interagency meetings on Rwanda threw up some suggestions for 'soft intervention' – jamming the anti-Tutsi 'hate radio' broadcasts, imposing an arms embargo – only to be thwarted by the Pentagon, which tended to interpret such action either as ineffective or as a 'slippery slope' towards troop commitment. Samantha Power commented: 'If Pentagon objections were to be overcome, the president, Secretary Christopher, Secretary Perry or Lake would have had to step forward to "own" the problem, which did not happen.'[117] Some US and French forces were deployed on 22 July to Kigali to help survivors.

A number of comments are in order. Albright's remark about the military in effect refusing to take action simply pushes the onus back on Clinton, the commander-in-chief. It is important not to be too wise after the event. Clinton's recollection of a kind of self-willed denial probably does capture an important truth about international community reactions. 'Soft interventions', such as an arms embargo, probably would have been ineffective. Most of the massacres were carried out with knives and various crude weapons. A Rwandan intervention would have been difficult to sell to Congress and the public, but part of the president's job is to lead and educate. Memories of Somalia were potent, yet – as indicated above – these often involved a distortion of what actually had occurred there. Congress did move to limit the small July deployment, so a bigger intervention in April would certainly have stimulated opposition. Minority Leader (this was still the Democratic-dominated Congress) Bob Dole commented on 10 April, following the evacuation of the US embassy in Kigali: 'The Americans are out, and as far as I'm concerned, in Rwanda, that ought to be the end of it.'[118] In some ways the real guilty secret was the 1948 UN Genocide Convention, ratified, with some reservations concerning national sovereignty, by the US Senate in 1986. If the Convention is to be taken seriously, intervention was not a 'war of choice' – where exceptionally restrictive standards for troop deployment *should* be applied – but an obligation under international law. Samantha Power records the studied efforts of official Washington to avoid public use of the word, 'genocide', in order to head off calls (in a phrase used in a 1 May discussion paper from the Office of the Secretary of Defense) 'to actually "do something"'.[119]

To some commentators in the 1990s, America's main foreign policy problem appeared to be a lack of integrated moral purpose. On the neo-conservative right, this view was summed up in the title of a 1996 book by Michael Ledeen: *Freedom Betrayed: How America Led a Global Democratic Revolution, Won the Cold War, and Walked Away*.[120] Some neo-conservatives were prepared to applaud Clinton's internationalism, but most saw him as conspiring in the loss of American messianic purpose. Clinton himself was concerned to retain and reinforce the exceptionalist tradition, and indeed tied humanitarian intervention into the narrative of American exceptionalism and special destiny. Globalised humanitarianism was arguably one avenue along which the US could seek a purpose now that communism had been defeated. Yet the dangers of such a course were also obvious. They included over-extension, loss of domestic consensus and inconsistency. To quote David Rieff, a leading 1990s 'liberal hawk': 'To say that one is guided by moral principles, and then make it plain that these moral principles will only be binding situationally is to risk losing moral as well as operational coherence.'[121]

Clinton administration personnel who sought to defend a version of 'assertive humanitarianism' – even one carefully attuned to interests, consensus and capabilities – had formidable logical and ideational obstacles to overcome. The realist tradition in International Relations taught that nation states which lost sight of core interests, frittering away resources on 'foreign policy as social work', would eventually be 'punished' according to the logic of the anarchic, international state system. By the same token, calibrating humanitarian intervention according to perceivedly 'rational' calculations of interests and capabilities – something virtually all Clintonites viewed as inescapable – exposed the US to charges of hypocrisy and neo-imperialism. Policy-makers often felt themselves to be damned if they did, and damned if they didn't: accused of shameful neglect if humanitarian disasters were ignored, accused of imperialism if the US intervened.

Some contemporary criticisms of Clinton's internationalism were little more than transposed Cold War invective, descending into simple anti-Americanism. Yet criticisms of the failure to act in the face of the Rwandan carnage, one of the greatest human disasters of modern times, were of a different order. The failure drove Anthony Lewis, key journalistic supporter of 'liberal hawkism', to the expression of despair: if the US, he wrote in July 1994, 'cannot use force to prevent disasters, then the world is truly condemned to chaos'.[122]

5 Ancient enmities
The Balkans and Northern Ireland

Bill Clinton's version of liberal internationalism was, as we saw in the previous chapter, assailed from a variety of standpoints. By turns, it was attacked as imperialist, cynically over-restrictive, foggily idealistic and expensively irrelevant to core American interests. Another line of critical argumentation relates particularly to the regional conflicts to be discussed in this chapter: Bosnia, Kosovo and Northern Ireland. Robert Kaplan in 1993 published a book entitled, *Balkans Ghosts*. Bill Clinton reportedly emerged from a reading of Kaplan's grim history with the words: 'They've been fighting each other for 500 years. ... We need to stay out of there.'[1]

The cause of liberal internationalism/interventionism, advanced during the 1990s in journals such as the *New York Review of Books* (*NYRB*) by writers such as Leon Wieseltier, confronted this logic of 'ancient enmities': the view that conflicts, whether in the Balkans, Ireland or the Middle East, were frequently intractable, mysterious – traps for well intentioned American internationalists. On occasion, the 'ancient enmities' perspective became allied with 'liberal dovish' warnings about the dangers of repeating the mistakes made in Vietnam. There were various escape routes for liberal internationalists to explore. One was the doctrine of 'ripeness', which had been developed during the Bush41 presidency.[2] Developed further under Clinton, especially in respect of Northern Ireland, this doctrine held that circumstances on the ground – generational change, economic growth, war weariness and so on – could shift to such an extent that US diplomatic (in the Irish case, of course, not military) intervention could open the way to peace. Another escape route was to maintain that intervention, in this case primarily of the military kind, for humanitarian reasons could be a form of self-defence. In *Slaughterhouse: Bosnia and the Future of the West*, David Rieff argued that the US, of all countries, had a direct interest in defending Bosnia's multicultural pluralism in the face of intolerance, racism and tribalism. During the 1990s, the slogan, 'never again' – never again should the racist slaughter be allowed to occur in Europe – was frequently offered as a counter to the 'ancient enmities' argument. Rieff mocked those who refused to draw the correct lessons from European history, interpreting 'never again' as meaning: 'Never again would Germans kill Jews in Europe in the 1940s.' For Rieff and other liberal interventionists, action was needed *now*.[3]

Those regional conflicts which form the subject of this chapter, represent contrasting and reverberative instantiations of the debates over liberal internationalism which consumed so much passion and energy in the 1990s. Neither in the Balkans nor in Ireland was there an easy and unequivocal argument relating to American interests. Neither region had oil or any great economic salience to the US. The Balkans, close to the Russian sphere of influence and also with religious links to the conflicts in the Middle East, had a degree of strategic salience. Northern Ireland, because of the Irish-American lobbies, had domestic American 'overspill'. But in neither case could it be incontrovertibly maintained that core economic or security interests were at stake. Nor was it entirely clear why it should be *America* who should take the lead in resolving either of the conflicts. Northern Ireland was a province within the territory of a close American ally. Resolution of the Balkans disputes was, at least arguably, the prime responsibility of an integrated Europe, rather than of a potentially over-extended United States. Secretary of State James Baker memorably recalled how the Bush41 administration had viewed the former Yugoslavia: 'It was up to the Europeans to step up to the plate and show that they could act as a unified power.'[4]

Similar in some respects, the Balkans and Northern Ireland were utterly distinct in the balance of risk for would-be American interveners. Failure in the former would be measured in blood, treasure and the inevitable anti-interventionist backlash. Activism in the latter would simply test the credibility of post-Cold War American diplomacy in a context where military action was unthinkable. The cost of failure in Northern Ireland would include the possibility of wasted time and effort, damage to the UK alliance, and to the administration's reputation. Let us look at these conflicts in more detail.

Bosnia

It is not easy to defend Clinton's Bosnian policy between 1993 and 1995. In place of the sometime Washington policy of 'lift' (the arms embargo on the Bosnian Muslims) and 'strike' (air raids on key Bosnian Serb positions), 'lift and drift' seemed rather more appropriate. Wayne Bert wrote in 1997, that, prior to 1995, there was no American 'policy towards Bosnia, or put differently, there was a different policy for every crisis'.[5] American hesitation and prevarication unquestionably encouraged Serb attacks on putatively safe areas. Brendan Simms, reserving his main criticism for London, was slightly more positive: 'however hard they tried, the Americans proved unable to internalize British arguments about civil wars, quagmires and moral equivalence: an obstinate sense of rationality and fair play prevented them'. 'Lift and strike' was unlikely ever to be enough to safeguard the lives and futures of the Bosnian Muslims, but, at least according to Simms, it was 'better than nothing'.[6]

Part of the explosive fallout from the end of the Cold War, Serb attacks on the Muslim population and government of Bosnia had been condemned by the Bush41 administration, which also supported UN sanctions against Belgrade. Yet Bush left nobody in any doubt that there would, as Democratic Senator Joe

Lieberman (Connecticut) put it, there would be no 'Operation Balkan Storm' – no repetition of the 1991 Gulf War.[7] While Serbian aggression inescapably violated the New World Order, Bush was clear that the US would not play global policeman, especially in the absence of key US interests or domestic pressure. Secretary of State James Baker famously spoke of the US as having 'no dog in this fight'.[8] As late as 1995, Baker was still making the same point, now criticising Clinton for arguing that America's global leadership role required some kind of troop deployment in the Balkans: 'It seems to me that the United States can lead without having to fight ... on the ground in Europe.'[9]

Clinton's 1992 election speeches were contradictory in their references to Bosnia. He told an audience in East St Louis: 'I think we'll have more people killed in America today than there are killed in Yugoslavia, or what used to be Yugoslavia, probably.' He did, however, in the same speech advocate the use of 'air power against the Serbs to try to restore the basic conditions of humanity'.[10] Richard Holbrooke, who had worked under Cyrus Vance in Jimmy Carter's State Department, advised candidate Clinton in August 1992: 'This is not a choice between Vietnam and doing nothing, as the Bush administration has portrayed it.' Doing nothing in Bosnia 'now risks far greater and more costly involvement later'.[11] The early days of the administration saw several rhetorical reformulations of the Bush view of the conflict. During his Senate confirmation hearings, Warren Christopher referred to the Balkans as a 'European situation'. On TV's *Face the Nation* in March 1993, the Secretary of State described the hatred between 'the Bosnians and the Serbs and the Croatians' as 'centuries old' – 'really a problem from hell'.[12]

Implicit in the administration's early line on Bosnia was the view that resolution of the conflict was primarily the responsibility of the European Community (EC) or of the UN – or, to put it another way, that either the West Europeans or the UN somehow had the ability or the will to settle the Balkans, allowing Washington to remain on the diplomatic and military sidelines. The Europeans were engaged in frenetic diplomacy, while UN deployments concentrated on humanitarian relief. The UN Protection Force (UNPROFOR), hampered by a weak mandate, was attempting to keep a non-existent peace. The EC plans for a Bosnian settlement, the Vance–Owen plan of January 1993 and the Vance–Stoltenberg plan later in the same year, foundered. Washington was torn between a desire to support European diplomacy and the recognition that complex division of Bosnian territory was both unlikely to be acceptable to parties on the ground, many of whom felt that more could be achieved by war than by diplomacy, a reward for Serb aggression. As for the UN, the Security Council was slow to recognise the centrality and brutality of Serb action. The 1991 arms embargo applied to all former Yugoslav territories, including the Bosnian Muslims.

Evidence of Serb-led human rights atrocities in Bosnia were certainly available to the Bush administration and surfaced in statements from the Clinton team. In February 1993, between his confirmation hearing and his *Face the Nation* appearance, Christopher described Serb ethnic cleansing: 'mass murders, systematic beatings, and the rape of Muslims and others, prolonged shelling of innocents in Sarajevo and elsewhere, forced displacements of entire villages, inhuman treatment of prisoners in detention camps.' He urged the world to say 'no' to all this, in the name of the American hope to 'promote the spread of freedom' and 'the emergence of peaceful ethnic democracies'.[13] Yet the implication still was that the EC and the UN would or could make the running, with the US presenting its good offices in an effort to broker regional deals. Pushed by Democratic Senator Dennis DeConcini (Arizona) on 30 March to declare that 'genocide' was occurring in Bosnia, Christopher responded: 'The technical definition is not perhaps what's important here, but what is important is that it is atrocious conduct.'[14]

The inconsistency and hesitation in Christopher's public rhetoric reflected more than his desire to avoid suggestions that the US should intervene under the UN Genocide Convention. It was also the product of severe tensions between the US and its NATO allies over 'lift and strike'; the European allies saw any lifting of the embargo as likely to increase the vulnerability of their own forces on the ground, serving as part of UNPROFOR. There were also major intra-administration tensions. Tony Lake, Al Gore and Madeleine Albright favoured a new activism, clearly backed by a realistic military option. Warren Christopher and Defense Secretary Perry stood opposed even to limited action, arguing, in Perry's words: 'At the bottom of that slope will be American troops in ground combat.'[15] The prevalent line was to waver, always, in this early stage of Bosnian policy, falling short of any possible commitment of ground troops in a hostile environment. Lake found himself estranged from his old colleague, friend and co-author Leslie Gelb, who was advocating a much tougher line in his *NYT* column.[16] Three junior State Department officials – Bosnian desk officer Marshall Harris, intelligence analyst Jon Western and Croatian desk officer Steven Walker – embarked on a campaign of bureaucratic protest, culminating in their resignation in August 1993. Lake had sympathy with the three, though felt that 'they were making it sound easier than it was to change course'. The Pentagon was even opposing the 'strike' side of 'lift and strike': 'When our senior military guys were saying, "This mission can't be done", it's hard to say. "Listen, you professionals, here's an amateur's view of how and why it can be done."'[17]

Blowing hot and cold on 'lift and strike', President Clinton reopened negotiations with the European allies on the issue in May 1993; Warren Christopher was left in no doubt that the allies were still firmly opposed. The administration concentrated on pressurising the UN: for the establishment and safeguarding of 'safe areas', for the delineation and enforcement of 'no fly zones', for anti-Serb economic sanctions and for the setting up of a war crimes tribunal for the former Yugoslavia. The US restated the warnings given by the Bush administration to President Slobodan Milosevic not to attack the separatist Serbian province of Kosovo. Clinton acknowledged also that he would be prepared to deploy US forces in the event of an acceptable regional peace deal.[18] The US agreed with France, the UK, Russia and Spain that Bosnian 'safe areas' would be protected; American troops were despatched to Macedonia to add weight to the UN force deployed there.

President Clinton himself did begin, during the early months of 1994, to acknowledge that perhaps America did have some kind of dog in that ancient fight. A year after Christopher's 'problem from hell' remark, Clinton accepted that the US 'has clear interests' in the Balkans: 'an interest in helping prevent the spread of a wider war in Europe, an interest in showing NATO remains a credible force for peace, an interest in helping to stem the terrible destabilizing flows of refugees', as well as 'the humanitarian interest we all share'.[19] The impetus for this shift in emphasis was the shelling of Sarajevo in February. Washington began to promote tougher policies in NATO, arguing that the future of the organisation depended on its ability to work effectively in Bosnia. Air strikes were threatened if the Serb forces did not remove their heavy weapons from the immediate environs of Sarajevo. Washington also managed finally to broker an anti-Serb alliance between Bosnian Muslims and Croats and to achieve NATO approval for limited air strikes: 'pinprick' bombings of Serb positions, designed to signal that the US was no longer on the sidelines. A Serb assault on the Goradze 'safe haven' (April 1994) threw Washington into renewed confusion, including the issuance of conflicting public statements.[20] The US conducted, through NATO, five air strikes against Serb positions between February and August 1994. In communications to Congress, Clinton described the raids as efforts to protect UN personnel, some of whom were actually taken hostage by Serb forces, and as entirely consonant with his constitutional authority as commander in chief.[21] Washington was also involved, at some distance, in former President Jimmy Carter's negotiation of a cease-fire in late 1994. Also in late 1994, Clinton decided that, should the situation deteriorate to such an extent that the UN had to leave, the US would participate in a NATO rescue force.[22]

As fighting broke out again in early 1995, more NATO air strikes were launched and large numbers of UNPROFOR soldiers, as London had warned, taken hostage. By this time, a real shift was occurring in Washington's view of the conflict. A Croatian offensive was beginning to alter conditions on the ground. However, as late as a 23 May principals' meeting, the only clearly agreed position seemed to be that US troops should not be deployed. Nelson Drew of the NSC staff argued that the US had no choice but somehow to try to keep the (by now largely superseded) UN military mission on the ground: 'US interests are best served by finding a way to restore credibility to the UNPROFOR mission in a manner that permits existing troop contributors to sustain their presence and the Bosnian government to agree to retain that presence.'[23] As the dangers to the UN forces became even more evident, attention turned to how exactly they could be extricated. Tony Lake recalled the general administration commitment to American troops being part of any UNPROFOR rescue force; this 'meant that we were going in the context of a defeat. And nobody wanted that'.[24] Clinton told an audience at the Air Force Academy on 31 May that 'we have obligations with our NATO allies ... and I do not believe we can leave them in the lurch'.[25] Complex negotiations continued between Washington, the Europeans and the UN.

A 20 June principals' meeting was presented with three options: taking the initiative with a major US-led troop deployment; somehow keeping UNPROFOR in the field while pursuing a diplomatic initiative; and accepting UN withdrawal (with the US assistance Clinton had promised in his Air Force Academy speech). The only near-acceptable option seemed to be the second – but the logic of this option really had to be that the US should at last take a strong diplomatic lead, something which was hardly possible without some credible threat of force. As CIA head John Deutch put it: 'We can't just flap around as a government without an end point.'[26] Flapping around was actually pretty much what Washington had been doing in regard to Bosnia, but a decisive change was now taking place.

To some extent the policy shift was linked to the possibilities opened by Croatia's anti-Serb offensive. It was also associated with Clinton's growing doubts about the advice being proffered by Warren Christopher.[27] The implications of the late 1994 decision to aid any UNPROFOR exit from Bosnia were also beginning to sink in; as late as mid-June, after the Air Force Academy speech, Clinton was apparently expressing surprise at the implications of this undertaking.[28] Behind the policy shift was the perception that the US must avoid committing troops in a deteriorating situation, simply as the agent of UN retreat. The new policy, very importantly for the developing trajectory of Clinton's foreign policy, actually involved a moving away from the UN. The NATO air strikes which began in August were agreed in general terms between Washington and the UN, but were, unlike the earlier strikes, operationally independent of the UN.[29] Policy change, which was evident at a London NATO conference on 21 July, was linked most obviously to the 'jolt of electricity' sent through the administration by the bloody fall of Srebenica in mid-July.[30]

By the summer of 1995, Clinton was manifestly concerned about the extent to which US governmental 'flapping around' over Bosnia was damaging the credibility of post-Cold War foreign policy. Nancy Soderberg recalled his irritation at the French President Jacques Chirac's virtual assertion, during a June visit to Washington, that the US was incapable of effective leadership. Chirac supported the deployment of a new French, Dutch and British rapid reaction force. Soderberg recollected Clinton as remarking: 'I'm getting creamed over Bosnia.'[31] The president was also concerned about NATO credibility: without resolution of the Bosnian crisis how could an expanded NATO move to a new post-Cold War mission and identity?[32] Bureaucratic rivalries and reconfigurations also had their place, most obviously in the developing eclipse of Christopher, but also in terms of the complex positioning of Lake, Berger, Albright and, increasingly, Richard Holbrooke. Lake had been reported as opposing Strobe Talbott's original proposal in 1994 to bring Holbrooke back to Washington in order to take charge of European affairs at State. Holbrooke's energy and sometimes rather brutal commitment to Bosnian activism were at the centre of unfolding events from the spring of 1995. Leslie Gelb remarked in September that there 'was no one else who was ready' to move things on in terms of US policy towards Bosnia: 'Dick is a man of gargantuan traits, who jumps into the biggest boiling pot, and does so with intelligence, ambition and a desire to make a difference.'[33] The key player, however, was Tony Lake. He developed the new strategy with Berger and the NSC staff, and recruited Clinton to the changed policy in July, before inviting other principals to present their views.

Defense Secretary Perry and John Shalikashvili, chairman of the Joint Chiefs, became, following the Srebenica massacre, less reflective of the caution which seemed to dominate the Pentagon.[34]

US domestic politics, both electoral and inter-branch, provided the vital context for policy change. The sight of the administration flapping around while Bosnia descended into more bloodshed and chaos would have been something of an open goal for the Republicans in 1996. In August 1995, Senate Majority Leader Bob Dole, already being spoken of as a likely candidate in 1996, wrote: 'The bottom line is that since the war in Bosnia began, America has been a follower, not a leader.' He was not arguing for US troop commitment, but for an end to the arms embargo on the Bosnian Moslems – the US should stand for the 'right of self-defense against aggression'.[35] However, 1996 was not the immediate priority. Post-Cold War elections were unlikely to be fought on foreign issues. Public opinion was not evidencing any great desire for more Bosnian activism; if such activism were to lead to heavy American casualties, that (rather than aimless 'flapping') might cost Clinton his second term. Rather than 1996, the principal domestic concern was the need to mount a credible response to the congressional challenge to the president's conduct of foreign policy. The House of Representatives voted 318 to 99 to lift the arms embargo on the Bosnian Moslems, while the Senate followed suit a month later (in July 1995), 69 to 29. Journalist Elizabeth Drew called the legislation 'the most intrusive legislation on foreign policy in history'.[36] (The House measure also contained major foreign aid and diplomatic budget cuts, making it something of an all-purpose vehicle for legislative foreign policy assertion.) Democratic Senator John Kerry of Massachusetts called the vote 'a significant repudiation of the president's policy and his lack of involvement'.[37] At one level, the policy shift was Clinton's response to the legislative challenge. Clinton applied the veto, while rapidly changing events soon overtook any prospect of the Republican Congress using its override powers effectively to set Balkans policy.

Richard Holbrooke's negotiating effort was a triumph. It was based on Lake's plan for recognition of Bosnia, Croatia and Yugoslavia, and on a division of Bosnia, with 51 per cent of the land going to the Croat–Moslem federation.[38] One important concern was to pressure the Bosnian government to expel foreign Islamic extremists. (It is worth recalling that two of the 9/11 hijackers actually fought in Bosnia.) Clinton remained concerned not to see US combat troops deployed in hostile conditions, but all sides understood that any agreement would (despite continuing opposition in Congress) be underwritten by American force. The final agreement, made in Dayton (Ohio) was inevitably imperfect: for one thing, it left two warring armed forces on the ground in Bosnia. In that respect, in a context in which American memories of Indochina were always near the surface, it resembled the 1973 Vietnam peace. Clinton was forced to place a (soon to be abandoned) time limit on post-Dayton troop deployments to Bosnia. In December, the House of Representatives came within nine votes of passing legislation to cut off funding to the Bosnian deployments. Yet, as the conditions on the ground improved, legislative opposition declined.[39] Over and above the prospect of peace it brought to Bosnia, the Dayton Agreement reinvigorated NATO, including doing much to reconcile Russia to an enlarged NATO. Forming a bridge between the first and second terms, Dayton also exemplified and strengthened the confidence which flowed from the new American hegemonism.

Northern Ireland

Like Dayton, the 1998 Good Friday (or Belfast) Agreement was an imperfect peace deal which eventually worked. Like Dayton, it was achieved in spite of the apparent hopelessness of a conflict rooted in 'ancient enmities' and 'fanatic hearts'.[40] Dayton owed far more to American diplomacy than did the Irish agreement, yet the 1998 deal was at least to some degree the product of intense engagement by the Clinton administration. Following an outline of events, we will address two questions. First, why did Clinton devote so much time and energy to the search for agreement in an area of the world that, at best, was of almost no strategic or economic interest to the US? Second, how important *was* Clinton's intervention in securing Irish peace?

Bill Clinton's interest in the divided politics of Northern Ireland dated from his Oxford days, when he, not unnaturally, tended to interpret Ulster in the light of his own experiences of the fight for civil rights in the American South. During his involvement in the affairs of the six counties, Clinton strove conscientiously to be even-handed. He, after all was a Protestant Southerner. An important part of his strategy was to reach out to Northern Ireland's loyalist leaders, or at least those considered to be relatively open to accommodation. Following the issuance of a visa to Gerry Adams (leader of Sinn Fein, the political wing of the Provisional Irish Republican Army (PIRA)) in 1994, Al Gore opened a dialogue to Official Unionist leader James Molyneaux, while David Trimble was invited to the White House soon after he succeeded Molyneaux.[41] However, Clinton could never entirely rid himself of the impression that he was essentially a friend of Irish republicanism. To some extent, this impression was the product of the behaviour and attitudes of some key implementers of his Northern Irish policy, such as Jean Kennedy Smith (sister of John Kennedy and Ambassador to Dublin during the Clinton years).[42] Loyalist worries about American involvement, however, went much deeper: to fear and suspicion of Irish America itself. It is also evident that, for all his even-handedness, Clinton did essentially see the future of the island of Ireland in the way that he had done when he first took an interest in Irish affairs, in the way that most interested Americans (and indeed probably most inhabitants of mainland Britain) do – as a place on the road to eventual unification.

Clinton's first serious brush with the politics of organised Irish America occurred during the 1992 campaign. As a Southerner eager to glean Northern urban votes, Clinton became involved with a business-oriented group of Irish-Americans, Americans for a New Irish Agenda, associated with figures such as former congressman (and FoB) Bruce Morrison and the editor of *The Irish Voice*, Niall O'Dowd. The orientation of the group was broadly constitutional nationalist, with its leaders keen to disassociate themselves from rougher and tougher bodies, notably from the Northern Irish Aid Committee (NORAID), the US support group for the PIRA.[43] As the Clinton presidency got into gear, the White House effectively formed a coalition, embracing the Morrison–O'Dowd people, the constitutional nationalism of Senator Edward Kennedy and contacts within the Dublin government of Tsaoiseach Albert Reynolds. Clinton dropped a campaign pledge to appoint a 'peace envoy' to the province, but in February 1994 approved the issuing of a temporary visa to Gerry Adams. The Adams visa proposal involved intense bureaucratic warfare. On the one side were the various forces of constitutional nationalism, seeing the visa as a way to educate the Irish Republican Army (IRA) in the ways of peace and open the road to a settlement. The pro-visa cause was supported by the NSC staff, including Lake and deputies Nancy Soderberg and James Steinberg. Soderberg later explained: 'We wanted to expose Adams to American opinion that is opposed to violence and try to reach out in favor of moving the peace process forward'; it was Sinn Fein's 'opportunity to come in from the cold'.[44] On the other side stood Raymond Seitz (US Ambassador to London), the CIA, and the State Department. To these bureaucratic actors, granting a visa to Adams was – as Christopher Meyer (British Prime Minister John Major's press secretary and later UK Ambassador to Washington) put it – 'a reward for terrorism and a boost to the funds of NORAID'.[45]

The Morrison–O'Dowd group, closely backed by the White House, were intimately involved in sustaining the dynamic whereby Sinn Fein might be allowed to come in from the cold: the implied link with the end of the Cold War was an appropriate one.[46] The IRA declared its cease-fire in August 1994. Bill Clinton's Belfast visit of 1995 was the moment when 'hope and history' rhymed: one of the rhetorical and emotional high-spots of an extraordinarily rhetorical and emotional presidency. Clinton made it clear that he favoured a 'twin track' approach to peace, starting direct talks while also working on the problem of decommissioning terrorist weapons.[47] Clinton's Irish team saw themselves as having moved beyond the familiar British invocation of 'ancient enmities' – the view attributed to by Clintonites that London saw Northern Ireland as 'a third world country' with 'impossible' people.[48] American 'can do' would succeed where Old World cynicism had failed. In February 1996, an international body was established to handle the decommissioning issue, led by George Mitchell, former Democratic leader in the Senate and, in effect, a part of Clinton's Irish team. Clinton's Commerce Department also announced investment plans, the keenly anticipated 'Irish peace dividend' which did so much to sustain the peace process.

The IRA's breaking of its cease-fire in February 1996 seemed temporarily to expose the Clinton initiatives as facile and ill-judged. Adams was now allowed into the US but not invited to the White House (Adams had met Lake and Gore at the White House in late 1994, and was treated to an unphotographed presidential handshake there on St Patrick's Day, 1995). The restoration of the IRA cease-fire in July 1997 was more the product of intra-nationalist politics than of US pressure, though the ability of the Sinn Fein leaders to point to the anticipated US 'peace dividend' greatly strengthened their position in republican circles. By this time also, Tony Blair had replaced John Major in Downing Street. Blair welcomed Clinton's activism as the best chance of securing peace and as a chance to reenergise the US–UK 'special relationship'. In the run-up to the Belfast talks between the various Northern Irish factions, journalist John Carlin wrote: 'Every public declaration made by Mr Clinton, Mr Ahern (the Irish Taoiseach) and Mo Mowlam (Blair's Northern Irish Secretary) appeared almost as if it had been carefully orchestrated and carefully rehearsed.'[49]

Around St Patrick's Day 1998 in Washington, Clinton met David Trimble, Gerry Adams, John Hume (of the Social Democratic and Unionist Party, and a long-time friend of Senator Kennedy), Lord Alderdice (of the Alliance Party) and Gary McMichael from the paramilitary linked Ulster Democratic Party. Clinton's power-sharing agenda was essentially an updating of the Sunningdale approach from the early 1970s. Committed to the marginalisation of the Paisleyite Democratic Unionists, this approach had long been advocated by Edward Kennedy, and had been favoured by President Jimmy Carter.[50] During the 1998 Stormont talks, chaired by George Mitchell, Clinton was in near-constant telephonic contact. As recorded in the diaries of Alastair Campbell (Tony Blair's press secretary), Clinton was – with Blair – at the centre of a kind of negotiatory web, which also included Bertie Ahern: 'Bill said there was nothing more important to me right now than this. Call me whenever, even if it means waking me up.'[51] As George Mitchell recalled, Clinton 'knew each of the negotiators so well that he called them all by their first names, and he was already aware of the issues'.[52] The president continued to support acceptance of the ensuing Good Friday Agreement, though he was apparently sensitive to loyalist warnings – probably conveyed to him via Downing Street – that too much American activism in trying to sell the deal could be counter-productive. Clinton visited Belfast again in September 1998, and was involved in the subsequent efforts to pressure the IRA and the loyalist paramilitaries into meaningful arms decommissioning.

Our first overarching question – Why did Clinton prioritise Irish issues? – has no straightforward answer. The simple response that he was trying to attract 'green' votes and appease Irish America is not very convincing. Electoral concerns were certainly present in 1992. However, by 1998, when he had no further direct electoral incentives, Clinton was manifestly driven by intense personal commitment. There really is no such thing as anything resembling a cohesive 'Irish vote'. By the 1990s, the population of Catholic Irish America was sociologically and economically disparate, concerned with a wide range of issues, quite above and beyond any simple concern for Clinton's policy towards the old country. Many of Clinton's policy stances, notably on the abortion issue seemed almost designed to alienate conservative Catholic opinion; the Ancient Order of Hibernians withdrew an invitation to Clinton to address its annual convention in 1996 because of the president's pro-choice line on abortion. Of course, Clinton was aware that, to some degree, the investment of energy in the cause of Irish peace might help compensate for such unpopular policy stances. However, the time and energy invested in Ireland simply outweighed any conceivable electoral advantage.[53]

As noted in the introduction to this chapter, Clinton was attracted to Ireland by the relatively risk-free opportunity to secure a foreign policy breakthrough. With considerable intelligent foresight, the Clinton team discerned a real opportunity for peace in transformed conditions of war-weariness, and an external environment where Dublin and London were at last showing signs of cooperation in the cause of a Northern Irish settlement. They embraced the doctrine of 'ripeness'. The end of the Cold War removed the geopolitical rationale – the need for UK cooperation in maintaining American air bases in the UK – for avoiding rows with London; the transfer of power to Tony Blair in 1997 made the situation easier still. The absence of risk extended beyond the unthinkability of troop commitment in this particular regional conflict. Activism on Ireland drew some domestic criticism. Senator John McCain (Republican, Arizona) attacked Clinton for becoming involved in a conflict that 'has never ... remotely, affected our security interest'.[54] Ex-Secretary of State James Baker criticised Clinton for endangering the US–UK 'special relationship' by interfering in the internal affairs of a sovereign ally.[55] However, American opinion was generally either indifferent to, or passionately in favour of, presidential activism in Ireland. Here was a chance for internationalist foreign policy success, at virtually no political or other cost.

How far should we credit Clinton with bringing peace to Ireland? Internal Irish factors, along with the Dublin–London dimension of peace process cooperation, go a long way to provide an explanation for the achievement of the Belfast Agreement.[56] When Clinton welcomed Sinn Fein in from the cold, he found a republican leadership which was more than ready to respond. As Henry Patterson puts it: 'Republican enthusiasm for the injection of an American dimension into the situation was a reflection of the leadership's calculation that Clinton's support might make it easier to sell a compromise to the more fundamentalist elements of the IRA.'[57] The Clintonites tried conscientiously to reach out to the loyalists; indeed it is difficult to suggest what more they could have done, given the intransigence in these years of Ian Paisley's Democratic Unionists, to be even-handed. Yet they did not succeed in convincing grass-roots loyalist opinion of the purity of their intentions. Paul Bew wrote that the 'choreography' of Clinton's Belfast visits, 'initially well-balanced, has veered off into a markedly Irish nationalist direction'.[58] Nancy Soderberg's later assertion that Clinton's bestowal of 'political legitimacy' on the Official Unionists increased David Trimble's 'political power at home' hardly increases confidence in the White House's mature understanding of loyalist politics.[59] Trimble's welcome to Clinton, and his call for 'a pluralist parliament for a pluralist people', was a political gamble and a recognition that the peace dynamic must not be allowed to stall.[60] Far from increasing Trimble's authority at home, it led directly to the eclipse of the Official Unionists and the extreme polarisation of electoral politics in the province.

To carp about the less-than-perfect nature of Clinton's Irish intervention is to miss the point. Bill Clinton played a central part in the coalition of forces which produced peace. His personal lobbying in 1998, his Belfast visits and his dangling of the 'peace dividend' were vital aspects of the peace dynamic. Perhaps above all, the direct entry on to the Irish stage of the leader of the world's only remaining superpower simply transformed the political conditions which attended the search for Irish peace.

Back to the Balkans: Kosovo, 1999

The achievement of the Dayton Accords and the subsequent US troop deployments changed US attitudes towards the Balkans. By mid-1998, Clinton was actually facing pressure from Congress to become more active in the defence of Kosovo, a mainly ethnic-Albanian province of Serbia. In June 1998, Trent Lott (Mississippi), Majority Leader in the Senate, urged Clinton to do 'something pretty quickly, stronger than we've done so far' to protect the population of Kosovo from attack by the forces of Yugoslav President Slobodan Milosevic.[61] Belgrade's version of events was that it was policing terrorist forces in the Kosovo Liberation Army (KLA). Within the administration, views on the Kosovo issue varied, with the State Department advocating a strong line and the Pentagon, generally backed by Sandy Berger and the NSC staff, warning against precipitate US action, which might (among other risks) sacrifice the cooperation with Russia which had been a feature of Bosnian policy.[62] Some important Washington actors, such as General Wesley Clark (Clinton's fellow Arkansan and soon to be appointed NATO military commander), had been dissatisfied with a Bosnian settlement which left war criminals unpunished. Despite this, the Milosevic government in Belgrade had survived the Bosnian war, and indeed could, from a pragmatic perspective, even be regarded as a force for regional stability.[63]

Kosovo, however, was not simply to be a re-run of Bosnia. Madeleine Albright's enthusiasm for intervention contrasted sharply with Warren Christopher's attitude in 1995. Her commitment to the Kosovan cause was highly personal.[64] Arguing against the doubts expressed by Secretary William Cohen and General Hugh Shelton (now chairman of the Joint Chiefs), Albright saw herself as battling not only the 'Vietnam syndrome' ('don't get involved in anything'), but also the 'Gulf War syndrome' ('don't do it unless you can deploy 500,000 marines').[65] Parallel plans to use the threat of air strikes to compel Milosevic to negotiate in good faith were drawn up at the State Department and in the office of Alexander Vershbow, US Ambassador to NATO.[66] The replacement of John Major in London by Tony Blair also shifted the conditions which applied to the earlier Bosnian crisis. As conflict in Kosovo erupted, Blair outlined his doctrine of liberal interventionism in Chicago.[67] Above all, memories of Bosnia coaxed the administration away from aimless 'flapping' and towards decisive action.

In the later part of 1998, Washington reiterated the warning to Belgrade which had been issued by Secretary of State Lawrence Eagleburger in December 1992. The Bosnian experience certainly emboldened official Washington. However, as the arguments mounted by Cohen and Shelton exemplified, this most certainly did not amount to any enthusiasm to use ground troops in a hostile environment. In June 1998, even Albright's statements on the crisis were surprisingly cautious and even-handed: 'We condemn acts of violence by all sides, including the Kosovo Liberation Army, but we must also oppose, as strongly and effectively as we can, the campaign of terror and depopulation being waged by Serb forces.'[68] The emerging consensus in the later part of 1998 was that NATO must again take the lead. Despite Russian equivocation, the UN applied sanctions. Defense Secretary Cohen, working closely with London, pressured the NATO allies to toughen its stance, making credible the threat of action. In late September, NATO communicated to Belgrade a direct threat of air strikes if the military action against Kosovo continued. Richard Holbrooke visited Belgrade, returning with (swiftly broken) promises of restraint. Discussions within NATO were made more difficult not only by internal divisions, but also by lack of confidence (not least in London) in Washington's willingness to commit ground troops. Following the Serb attack on Racak (January 1999), however, the American position hardened. On 27 January, Clinton publicly declared his willingness to use air power if Belgrade refused to negotiate, while also threatening to blockade Albania (to cut off support to the KLA) if the Kosovars would not participate in the upcoming peace conference.

In February 1999, the US and the European allies convened a conference at the castle of Rambouillet, near Paris. Belgrade was offered the option of accepting autonomy for the Kosovan Albanians and a force of peacekeepers, including 4,000 Americans, to be stationed in Serbia. Albright, aided by British Foreign Secretary Robin Cook, set the tone of the conference. Indeed, according to UK Liberal Democrat leader Paddy Ashdown, Blair regarded Albright as more committed than London to intervention. Blair told Ashdown on 22 February: 'We can't bomb Milosevic if he accepts the Rambouillet deal but the KLA don't. That is our firm view. But the Americans seem to think otherwise.'[69] The ultimatum given to Serbia at Rambouillet has been the subject of intense criticism. In one line of argument, Milosevic was offered a deal which he, as the leader of a sovereign nation, could not possibly accept.[70] Unlike Bosnia, Kosovo was part of Serbia, indeed the part of Serbia which was revered as the ancestral home of the Serbs. Albright really had little expectation that the Rambouillet deal would be accepted by Belgrade. Milosevic held the conference in contempt and did not even attend in person. The real purpose of Rambouillet, according to Daalder and O'Hanlon, was rather to 'create a consensus in Washington and among the NATO allies that force would have to be used'.[71] Expectations varied, however. Elaine Sciolino and Ethan Bronner of the *NYT* reported that the conference was conducted generally in good faith:

> The NATO allies hoped, even assumed, that they were dealing with the Milosevic who negotiated the peace at Dayton, Ohio, the man who lied and manipulated and ranted in all-night Scotch-laden negotiations and then cut a deal in the morning[72].

Enormous hope was certainly invested in Richard Holbrooke, whose Dayton success had given him something of a magical quality. Holbrooke was not a miracle worker; at Rambouillet, Belgrade simply called NATO's bluff.

The confused nature of expectations for Rambouillet was reflected in a lack of preparation in Washington for war. Clinton's lack of involvement rapidly became cited as an indication of how the Lewinsky scandal was damaging his control of policy-making in his own administration.[73] The Senate impeachment trial ended on 12 February 1999. The following day, Clinton gave a national radio address on the Kosovo crisis. He emphasised the rational calculus of costs, as well as the humanitarian dimension: 'In this volatile region, violence we fail to oppose leads to even greater violence we will have to oppose later at greater cost.'[74] As conflict loomed, the White House issued a list of reasons why the behaviour of the Serbs in Kosovo impinged on US national interests: 'Violence in Kosovo could spread, threatening the fragile stability of the entire region, including Bosnia, Macedonia and Albania. Greece and Turkey – both NATO members – could also be drawn into a conflict.'[75] On 20 March, Anthony Lewis, in his *NYT* column, accused Clinton of 'bluffing and delaying' and criticised Holbrooke for apparently accepting Milosevic's promise of restraint the previous October.[76] By this time, the Kosovar Albanians had at last signed up to the Rambouillet terms and Holbrooke began a final, final attempt to have Milosevic do the same. He failed. On 24 March, Clinton announced the start of the bombing of Serbia: 'We act to prevent a wider war; to defuse a powder keg at the heart of Europe that has exploded twice before in this century with catastrophic results.' Action was both 'a moral imperative' and 'important to America's national interest'. American troops would go in as part of a NATO peace-keeping force, but, declared Clinton, 'I do not intend to put our troops in Kosovo to fight a war.'[77] This undertaking reassured Congress, where majority opinion was reflective of public opinion at large in its opposition to ground deployment of troops in hostile conditions. The legislative branch seemed largely supportive of Clinton's action; after all, he was at last responding to the demands made by Trent Lott in June 1998. Congress effectively chose not to attempt to write restrictions on ground troop commitment into law. Many Members of Congress were nevertheless doubtful whether a war could be won from the air. Congressman Bill Young (Republican of Florida) remarked: 'They certainly had a plan on how to start it, but I do not see a plan on how to end it.'[78] Journalist Craig Whitney saw Milosevic as simply sitting back, taking his punishment and waiting for the inevitable fissures to develop in NATO.[79] European diplomats also made the point that any restraint on the Serb actions in Kosovo had now effectively been removed.[80]

Serbian moves against Kosovo were indeed intensified. A refugee crisis was the inevitable result. As the bombing wore on, with key decisions made to use cruise missiles, it became more evident that Russia might hold the key to success. During the various earlier Bosnian crises, the contact group of Russia, France, the UK, Germany and Italy had been brought formally into dialogue with the US (in Strobe Talbott's words) 'for the sole purpose of including Russia in a kind of steering committee otherwise made up of key NATO allies'. The contact group was reconvened in 1999 at Rambouillet, where Russian diplomats were concerned to minimise the NATO role in enforcing any settlement and 'discrediting the Kosovars as little better than terrorists'.[81] By this time, the new international confidence evident in Clinton's second administration worked in the direction of marginalising, rather than integrating, Russia. Torn by competing pressures, Boris Yeltsin stood back from the build-up to war, but registered strong protest once bombing began. By activating NATO as the agency of intervention, Clinton had in effect sidelined the UN Security Council, along with the Russian veto. The *NYT* reported on 31 March that the NATO alliance had 'been forced to beat back an attempt by the Russian Prime Minister, Yevgeny M. Primakov, to open negotiations on terms dictated by President Slobodan Milosevic of Yugoslavia'.[82] Moscow accused Washington, not unreasonably, of pursuing a policy of Serbian regime change rather than simple protection of Kosovo. Russian diplomacy concentrated on convincing the NATO allies that the US was being intransigent, and that a deal which clearly left Milosevic in power in Belgrade could be achieved.[83]

The apparent inability of air power to achieve a breakthrough exposed divisions in Washington. A 'senior officer' at the Pentagon was quoted as saying that no 'compelling argument' had been made to the effect that the action was in America's 'national interest'. Defense Department spokesman Kenneth Bacon referred obliquely to excessive State Department optimism about the quick efficacy of air power. Commenting on Milosevic's continuation of the campaign against Kosovo, Bacon declared: 'In the Pentagon, in this building, we were not surprised by what Milosevic has done.'[84] NATO decision-making became increasingly difficult. Disputes arose, for example, between General Wesley Clark and European capitals over the targeting of Serbian television stations, regarded by several of the NATO allies as inappropriate civilian targets. General Clark in turn annoyed his Pentagon superiors by his assertive style and his defence of NATO procedure. Clark simply did not share the Pentagon's impatience and disdain for the liberal hawks at State, with whom Clark maintained close contact.[85] On April 21, Clinton (with Berger, deputy national security adviser James Steinberg and Madeleine Albright) met Tony Blair in Washington to discuss the apparently faltering bombing campaign. According to Alastair Campbell, Clinton 'was talking both about Milosevic being indicted for war crimes, and at the same time about whether we could do a deal with him'. The president said 'we had to bomb like hell, be more creative diplomatically, maybe arm the Albanians, sort the presentation'. By this time, Blair was lobbying for a ground invasion, or at least for serving notice on Belgrade that such action was on the cards. Sandy Berger said 'there should not be a whisper about ground troops'. Clinton apparently said that the Republicans might actually support a decision to send ground troops 'because it might destroy me'.[86] The bombing campaign reached its nadir on 7 May, when American B-52 bombers, following instructions from NATO targeters, accidentally attacked the Chinese embassy in Belgrade. It was also reported that the Pentagon was actually running out of cruise missiles.[87] Former Defense Secretary Caspar Weinberger entered the fray by criticising Clinton for failing to define the terms of victory. The administration spoke, wrote Weinberger, of 'degrading' the Serbian military, but damaging military capability was 'a means, not an end'.[88]

The Chinese embassy bombing came close to scuttling what proved to be the key Russian channel, which alone seemed capable of settling the stalemate. The Gore–Chernomyrdin Commission – the institutionalised connection between the US Vice President and Russian Prime Minister Victor Chernomyrdin, created to provide a cooperative context for American support for the cause of reform in Russia – was important here. This connection provided cover for Russian complicity in the search for a resolution to the conflict which involved effective surrender on the part of Milosevic. Soon into the bombing campaign, Clinton, Gore and Strobe Talbott came to the conclusion that Russia simply could not be excluded from the endgame diplomacy. In an effort to increase the pressure on Belgrade in early April, Al Gore's office released the information that it was in contact with Moscow with a view to engineering a settlement.[89] Though prepared to acknowledge the need for Russian involvement, Washington continued nevertheless publicly to warn Moscow against providing military assistance to the Serbs.[90]

By late April, commentary centred on the credibility of ground troop commitment. Answering criticism on Capitol Hill, Clinton announced that he was still confident that NATO could prevail through air power alone: 'However, were I to change my policy with regard to the introduction of ground forces, I can assure you that I would fully consult with the Congress.'[91] On 28 April, the House voted 249–180 to make legislative approval for ground troop commitment mandatory. Republican criticism, however, was divided and uncertain. The much vaunted 'isolationist' wing of the party was balanced, or indeed drowned out, by proponents of interventionism. Neo-conservative commentators applauded the campaign as tough Wilsonianism in action.[92] Senator John McCain was described in the *NYT* as 'winning the talk-show war' on behalf of the interventionists; while George W. Bush –' the man with all the money and all the endorsements (for the 2000 election) and of just about everything except positions' – endorsed the bombing campaign, demanded Serbian 'unconditional surrender' and wondered simply if the bombing were being undertaken with 'enough ferocity'.[93]

In his search for a Russian-linked settlement, Talbott managed to persuade Moscow to drop a demand that some Serbian security forces could remain in Kosovo. A new plan was eventually endorsed and presented jointly by Talbott, Chernomyrdin and President Martti Ahtisaari of Finland. The plan, though it omitted standard requirements for countries hosting NATO forces,[94] was somewhat tougher than the Rambouillet ultimatum. The Serbian army was to withdraw entirely from Kosovo, to be replaced by a NATO force of 48,000, rather than 25,000 as in the Rambouillet plan. Milosevic seems to have come to the realisation that the best way to remain in power was to accept the deal, which he did on 3 June. The implications of losing the Russian commitment to keeping him in power were underlined by his 27 May indictment by the UN-authorised special tribunal on war crimes in the former Yugoslavia. The post-settlement arrangements, as understood in Washington, were set out by Madeleine Albright: Serb forces would quit Kosovo, to be replaced by the NATO force; the UN would endorse the peace-keeping force and take over the administration of Kosovo; the Europeans would supervise reconstruction, which would also involve the Organisation for Security and Cooperation in Europe (OSCE).[95] On 10 June, Clinton acknowledged that Russia 'played an important role in achieving this peace' and expressed his hope that Moscow 'will join us in securing the peace'.[96]

Milosevic's climb-down was, almost certainly, primarily the product of Russian pressure. Ivo Daalder and Michael O'Hanlon also pointed out, soon after the settlement, that de facto NATO-allied ground forces – the forces of the KLA – had also played a role. The KLA had links to the Central European fascist tradition and were rather less than salubrious allies, but their forces of around 2,000 men were de facto allies nonetheless.[97] (One side-effect of the Rambouillet process, and indeed of the entire war, was to grant a new legitimacy to the KLA.) It is also the case that Clinton, however cautiously, was beginning by early June to admit the possibility that ground troops could be sent in under war-fighting conditions. We have seen how he approached this in the context of the congressional worries about such commitment. On 21 May, nearly 50,000 NATO forces were deployed on the Kosovan border, with General Wesley Clark publicly acknowledging that an invasion was a possibility. Tony Blair's lobbying for an invasion was also a warning to Belgrade, as was the leaking to the *NYT* of discussions about military options between Defense Secretary William Cohen and the Europeans on 27 May.[98] Yet it is far from certain that Clinton *would* have countenanced an invasion. Tony Blair certainly had huge doubts about whether Washington would order an invasion under any circumstances, and feared that the conflict would be resolved in a deal between Washington and Serbia which left the United Kingdom and NATO on the sidelines.[99]

Madeleine Albright speculated that part of Milosevic's rationale for conditional surrender related to the 'cooking up' of a deal with the Russian military, whereby part of Kosovo would come under Russian control.[100] Suspicions such as these underlay the confrontation between NATO and Russian forces at Pristina airport in Kosovo on 11 June. Wesley Clark ordered British commander General Mike Jackson to secure the airfield before the arrival of a Russian army column. Mike Jackson, in his own account, came 'to the brink of refusing a direct order' from Clark, his superior.[101] Wesley Clark, according to Jackson, saw the situation as analogous 'with the race to Berlin' in 1945. He regarded the whole affair as indicative of America's reluctance to abandon Cold War conceptualisation of its relationship with Moscow, and indeed as potentially risking the outbreak of a new world war.[102] Mike Jackson was backed not only by the Ministry of Defence in London, but also by the Pentagon. The Department of Defense in Washington was already irritated by what it perceived as Clark's lack of institutional loyalty, and effectively withdrew its support from the American commander of NATO. Clinton saw the incident as a case of Yeltsin 'throwing a "temporary bone" to pro-Serbian nationalists in Russia'.[103] Defense Secretary Cohen soon agreed an arrangement, whereby Russia could participate, under UN auspices, in the NATO force in Kosovo.

Wesley Clark later interpreted the Kosovo war as an instance of Washington's failure of will. The Pentagon was 'obsessively oriented on fighting hypothetical conflicts in two other theaters'. The despatch of the aircraft carrier, *Theodore Roosevelt*, to the Persian Gulf and away from the Adriatic was, according to Clark, a sign of lack of resolve which Milosevic noticed.[104] The Clinton/Albright war in Kosovo was, nevertheless, a success. In an implicit reference to reports that the impeachment crisis had distracted Clinton from his duties of foreign policy leadership, Sandy Berger described the war as evidence of Clinton's 'steadiness'. Republican Majority House of Representatives whip Tom DeLay of Texas had dubbed the conflict, 'Clinton's war'; it was now, according to Berger, Clinton's victory.[105] It appeared even more of a success when Milosevic fell from power in October 2000. The conduct of the war, however, was far from assured; indeed, at some point it bordered on the farcical. Clinton's initial handling of the crisis was uncertain, and gave the lie to assertions that his capacity for clear thinking and effective leadership were not damaged by the impeachment.

An irony of what Clinton famously called 'the first ever humanitarian war'[106] was that the administration was constantly under pressure to answer the accusation that it was simply indulging in 'foreign policy as social work'. Albright was always clear: 'My primary motive ... was moral: I did not want to see innocent people murdered.' Yet the desirability of stability in the Balkans was emphasised even by Albright, albeit as a secondary motive.[107] For James Steinberg, Deputy NSA, the US and its allies had an interest in 'the unity and credibility of NATO' as well as in averting a conflict which would have had 'no natural boundaries'.[108] The US did have 'national interest' motives in Kosovo, though any threat to American security hardly amounted to a clear and present danger. The Kosovo conflict was a product of second term hegemonic confidence, as well as of the peculiar circumstances which surrounded the bureaucratic eminence of the State Department under Madeleine Albright in relation to Kosovo. These circumstances included Albright's effective self-projection in issues relating to freedom in Central Europe, as well as Clinton's own deference to his female Secretary of State in the months following his impeachment.[109] The winning of the Kosovo war was celebrated by liberal hawks and neo-conservatives alike as making the world safe for just wars. In the short run, the conflict enhanced the international standing of NATO, which was now carving out an expansive post-Cold War role. However, intra-NATO squabbling and operational calamities, such as the Chinese embassy bombing, actually reinforced the case for American unilateralism. The war also stimulated lines of criticism of the United States – as a power prepared to act outside international law – which were to reverberate and intensify in the years following Clinton's departure from the White House.

6 Beyond the Cold War
Dealing with old enemies

Bush41 left much Cold War business unfinished. A major issue was that of post-Soviet 'loose nukes': despite the arms reductions achieved by presidents Reagan and Bush, Russia alone possessed, at the beginning of Clinton's presidency, about 30,000 nuclear warheads. North Korean nuclearisation was a special problem. The administration worried about the need for new 'strategic partnerships' with both Russia and China. The achievement of a wider post-Cold War international settlement remained mired in the complex interweaving of democracy-promotion, stability-promotion and market expansion.[1] To some contemporaries, the trumpeting and encouragement of market democracy seemed the answer to all ills; to others, marginalisation of old enemies was the key.[2] In its dealings with former Cold War adversaries, the Clinton administration kept to its faith in the inexorable reach of globalising democratic capitalism. Worries, however, were never very far away. Would market opening inevitably lead to political democracy and geopolitical stability? What if democratic countries elected the 'wrong' rulers? As Richard Holbrooke mused before the September 1996 elections in Bosnia: 'Suppose the election was declared free and fair', and those elected are 'racists, fascists, separatists. ... That is the dilemma'.[3]

Russia

The prospect of 'illiberal' democracy – elections producing racists, fascists, separatists and ultra-nationalists – became an increasing preoccupation for the Clinton administration, and came to dominate approaches to Russian policy. Washington struggled to reconcile its interests in marginalising the old foe in the Kremlin, in averting spectacular Russian economic and social disintegration, and in heading-off the emergence of populist revanchism. The administration was constantly trying to second-guess how the new regime in Russia would shape itself, and to assess how and whether its development could be influenced from outside. As Zbigniew Brzezinski wrote in 1997, until the future trajectory of the government in Moscow became clear – indeed until it *had* a clear trajectory – strategic uncertainty would continue: 'In Eurasia's center, the area between an enlarging Europe and a regionally rising China will remain a political black hole until Russia firmly redefines itself as a postimperial state.'[4]

Clinton inherited from the Bush presidency a clear commitment to treating Russia as the undisputed regional hegemon and successor state to the old Soviet Union, especially in the matter of strategic nuclear forces. Russian president Boris Yeltsin confirmed in 1992 that the US and Russia were allies and that the CIS (the Commonwealth of Independent States, the umbrella body which partially succeeded the Soviet Union) no longer had its missiles targeted at the US. The new Strategic Arms Reduction Treaty (START II, encompassing joint US–Russian nuclear warhead reductions to below 4,000 on each side by 2001) was signed in January 1993. Bush throughout his presidency had shied away from the 'grand bargain' ideas promoted by Graham Allison and former president Richard Nixon – the proposed offering of massive financial aid to Russia as a way of guaranteeing Moscow's commitment to democracy. However, in October 1992 Congress passed the Freedom Support Act, authorising around $410 million for democracy-promotion in the CIS, with Russia's share of the money being made conditional on the withdrawal of Russian troops from the Baltic states of Latvia, Lithuania and Estonia.

Yeltsin's unpredictability – as Winston Churchill said of John Foster Dulles, the Russian leader seemed like a bull who carried around his own china shop – had long alarmed President Bush and reinforced his reserve about any 'grand bargain'.[5] Towards the end of the Bush presidency, Yeltsin was characteristically blowing hot and cold over the strategic alliance with the United States. In late 1992, he pointedly affirmed that Russia would not, in any new order, 'shy away from defending our own interests'.[6] However, Yeltsin initially seemed far more positively disposed towards Bush than towards Clinton. As Strobe Talbott recalled, the old Kremlin leaders had always tended to prefer Republicans to Democrats.[7] As their relationship developed, however, the Bill and Boris show became one of the great partnerships – simultaneously amusing, alarming, hilarious and brittle – of recent international politics. Clinton seems to have perceived Yeltsin as a microcosm of Russia itself – partly an atavistic reactionary, partly a democratic optimist. If Yeltsin could be shoved or assisted in the right direction, then Russia, at best a quasi-democracy, might follow. Michael Wines of the *NYT*'s Moscow bureau described the September 1998 Clinton–Yeltsin public appearance at their Moscow summit as 'teetering on the brink of self-parody', as the two politicians presented themselves as jovial partners standing in good-natured opposition to the jackals of the press.[8] President Clinton remarked to Strobe Talbott after the 1995 summit, held at the Roosevelt estate at Hyde Park, NY: 'We can't ever forget that Yeltsin drunk is better than most of the alternatives sober.'[9] Clinton was attracted by Yeltsin's rumbustiousness and welcomed his directness. (In an understatement worthy of the Wooster novels of P. G. Wodehouse, Warren Christopher told Clinton before the Hyde Park summit: 'You'll probably not find Yeltsin in a subtle mood.'[10]) Talbott mused that Clinton was attracted by Yeltsin's combination of 'natural leader and incurable screw-up'. Clinton recognised these qualities, found them easy to forgive, and 'wanted others to join him in forgiving'.[11] Washington's commitment to 'Yeltsin drunk or Yeltsin sober' – to Yeltsin the democrat, and to Yeltsin, the enemy of effective democratic transition – however, was not entirely the product of Clinton's personal perception of the Russian leader. Clinton was urged to take a pro-Yeltsin line by Richard Nixon, whose apparent closeness to the White House up until his death in 1994 confirmed the view of sceptical liberals that Clinton was about to betray the ideals of his generation. Indulgence towards Yeltsin, however, was not just a vice of Clinton that was encouraged by a Republican predecessor. As George Stephanopoulos recalled, there was a common view, one which was certainly shared by Strobe Talbott at least in the early Clinton years, that 'Yeltsin was the only horse the forces of reform had'.[12]

As Clinton struggled to develop a coherent foreign policy at the start of the first term, there was no doubt about the centrality of Russia. In his confirmation hearings, Warren Christopher identified Russia as *the* foreign policy priority for the incoming administration.[13] Talbott was initially offered the post of ambassador to Moscow, but finally accepted a post at State as coordinator of Russian policy. He worked closely with Larry Summers, who served as the Russian economics point-man at the Treasury Department before becoming Deputy Treasury Secretary in 1995 and then succeeding Robert Rubin as Secretary in 1999. Another vital strand in the development and operation of Clinton's Russian policy was the formalisation of cooperation between Al Gore and Russian Prime Minister Victor Chernomyrdin. The Gore–Chernomyrdin Commission, an unprecedented institutionalisation in east–west policy-making, had its origins in a 1993 meeting between Talbott and Russian Foreign Minister Andrei Kozyrev, who put the case for the connection as an instrument of reform and as a way of linking US economic aid to Russia with the wider, mutual strategic partnership. Kozyrev, who tended to portray himself (not Yeltsin) to the Americans as the authentic advocate of market reform, saw this as a way of circumventing, or at least camouflaging, the problem of his boss becoming seen in Russia as a puppet of Washington, in receipt of 'patronizing charity'.[14] The arrangement was solidified at the Clinton–Yeltsin summit in Vancouver in April 1993. With significant and rapid progress (especially) on space and commercial cooperation, the Gore–Chernomyrdin Commission gained in bureaucratic authority in Washington and emerged as a focus for reformers in Moscow. It deepened Washington's involvement with the 'shock therapy' circle of reform in the Russian government associated with Anatoly Chubais, as well as signalling a faith in the commitment and survivability of Chernomyrdin himself. (Yeltsin finally sacked Chernomyrdin in March 1998.) The Commission profoundly implicated Washington in the Moscow power struggles between market reformers, nationalists and security-oriented figures such as General Alexander Korzhakov – described by Talbott as 'notorious among Kremlin insiders for pouring Yeltsin drinks and stoking his suspicions about his enemies, foreign and domestic'.[15]

US–Russian relations impinged directly on foreign policy themes considered in Chapters 5 and 7: policy in the Balkans and towards NATO enlargement. Each of these policy areas also fed back into the internal dynamics of post-communist politics in Moscow. Washington was told by self-styled Russian reformers in the first term that US military action in Bosnia would ignite a nationalist fire in

Russia. Yeltsin encouraged the involvement of the Gore–Chernomyrdin Commission in Kosovo negotiations as a way (at least as he sold the idea to Clinton) of spiking the guns of those in his own military who wanted to intervene on the Serbian side.[16] As for NATO enlargement, *NYT* columnist Thomas Friedman in May 1995 approvingly quoted Yegor Gaidar, at that time the leader of the reformist Russia's Choice parliamentary group, to the effect that expansion 'creates the best possible argument for our opponents that there is a world plot against Russia'.[17]

The START II remained stalled for virtually the whole of Clinton's presidency. It was ratified by the US Senate – with Jesse Helms backing away from opposition at the last minute – in 1996, but not accepted by the entire Russian parliament until April 2000. Aside from its general antipathy towards Yeltsin, the majority in the Duma (the lower house of the Russian parliament) was especially concerned about the 'de-MIRVING' provisions of START II: the ban on multiple warheads on land-based missiles. This provision – an aspect of arms control which Al Gore had long advocated in the Senate – particularly affected the principally land-based Russian nuclear force. Clinton appreciated the irony of having the Washington–Moscow arms control dynamic halted by 'illiberal democracy' as represented in the Russian version of separated powers.[18] John Bolton, who was appointed as Undersecretary of State for Arms Control in 2001, gleefully pointed out in 2007 that Clinton had only been able to keep 'arms control theology' on 'life support' by 'devotion and prayer rather than by hard reality'.[19] At various points in their association, Clinton and Yeltsin agreed to push forward with START III, attempting to use the prospect of an advantageous new agreement as a lever to encourage Duma approval of its predecessor. The START III process could not, however, begin formally without acceptance of START II, especially since the US Senate in 1996 effectively made any US progress on arms reduction contingent on Russian acceptance of the 1993 treaty. With the arms reduction dynamic stalled, what became especially worrying to US defence analysts during the 1990s was the apparent disintegration of the Russian early warning nuclear command network. A US weather probe launched in Norway in January 1995 apparently activated a nuclear alert which travelled up the command chain to Yeltsin.[20] Nuclear war by accident had been a common Cold War fear; the internal uncertainties of post-Cold War Russia ensured that the fear continued in the new era. Negotiators turned to proposals, to be incorporated into a future START III process, for 'de-alerting' missiles and putting them into some form of 'escrow'.[21]

As the ratification of START II indicated, the Republican Congress did not drastically alter the Clinton line towards Russia. Nevertheless, Senate Majority Leader Bob Dole did attack Clinton in 1995, declaring: 'developments like (Russian) arms sales to Iran, violence in Chechnya and the UN veto on behalf of aggressors (in Bosnia) should not be excused, ignored or minimized.' The 'Russia-first' policy was turning into 'a Yeltsin-first policy'.[22] Jesse Helms promised to reduce Russian aid in direct retribution for Moscow's Iranian nuclear technology sales and Russian assistance to Cuba, but these threats came to little. Where congressional activity did directly impinge on US–Russia nuclear policy, however, was the second term revival of anti-missile defence. Discussed further in Chapter 7, the rebirth of Reagan's SDI had major implications for the future of the 1972 Anti-Ballistic Missile Treaty. In November 1999, Clinton emphasised during the OSCE summit in Istanbul, that the new defensive missiles were designed to intercept attacks from 'rogue states', not to give the US a first strike capability vis-à-vis Russia.[23] However, Vladimir Putin, who succeeded Yeltsin as Russian president in March 2000, called American NMD 'the plan to destroy the strategic balance in the world'.[24]

Despite the continuing debates about the need to 'de-alert' missiles, Clinton's major successes in nuclear policy towards the former Soviet Union related to various agreements on containing and controlling nuclear capability. At one level, the Clinton era saw the continuation of the cooperative threat reduction programme, deriving from the Bush years and associated with Senators Sam Nunn and Richard Lugar. This provided funding for the operation and verification of weapon dismantling, as well as the transfer of nuclear weapons from the various states of the former Soviet Union to Russia. The programme, which also embraced chemical and biological weaponry, had to compete for congressional funding in the difficult years of the later 1990s; however, the programme was a massive and successful one. Between 1992 and 2003, the US spent around $7 billion on the Nunn–Lugar programmes.[25] This was not simply a matter of passively accepting a policy dynamic inherited from the Bush years. The de-nuclearisation of, in particular, Ukraine, involved the US in complex three-way negotiations, 'sweetener' deals and efforts to establish a degree of mutual trust between Kyiv (Kiev) and Moscow.[26] Also of considerable significance was the US–Russian Highly Enriched Uranium Purchase Contract agreement, announced by Clinton and Yeltsin at the start of 1994. This agreement provided for a huge increase in Russian uranium exports to the US. Contradicting his own mercantilist leanings, Clinton weathered protest from nuclear fuel interests in America concerned at what they saw as Russian 'dumping'.[27] Again, these nuclear stabilisation measures continued to the end of the 1990s. In September 1998, at their Moscow summit, Clinton and Yeltsin announced a programme of mutual information sharing regarding missile launches, designed to avoid a repetition of the Norwegian incident of January 1995. They also announced an agreement 'to remove from each of our nuclear weapons programs approximately 50 tons of plutonium', converting it into a form which would prevent it from ever being used to make lethal weapons.[28]

Clinton's public rhetoric on Russia and its democratic prospects tended to be relentlessly upbeat. Rather extraordinarily, it apparently echoed a student essay he had composed at Oxford University, for his tutor Zbigniew Pelczynski, arguing that Russia could develop towards a multi-party democratic state.[29] In 1998, as part of a Bill and Boris press conference, he declared: 'a country that rebuffed Napoleon and Hitler can surely adjust to the realities of the global marketplace.'[30] When extended to positive treatment of Moscow's behaviour in the two wars in Chechnya (1994–96 and from 1999 to the end of Clinton's presidency), this presidential sunniness seemed less well-judged. In April 1996, towards the end of the first major conflict in this Russian Islamic republic, Clinton reminded his audience – again at a Bill and Boris press conference in Moscow – that Chechnya was part of Russia:

> we once had a civil war in our country in which we lost, on a per-capita basis, far more people than we lost in any of the wars of the 20th century over the proposition that Abraham Lincoln gave his life for: that no state has a right to withdraw from our union.[31]

This is not to suggest that Russian military action in Chechnya was a matter of unconcern to Washington – merely that Clinton felt that there was little he could do about it, and that all problems would eventually be cured by the magic of globalising capitalist democracy. Russian military offensives in Chechnya sometimes seemed to be designed to cause Clinton maximum embarrassment, also allowing Yeltsin to use the putative anti-Western excitements of his generals as a lever with which to negotiate with Washington.[32] Following US action in Kosovo – a province that was as much a part of Serbia as Chechnya was part of Russia, or indeed the Confederate states part of the American Union – Clinton became much more critical of Russian policy towards the Chechens. In November 1999, he told Yeltsin (in words conveyed to the press by Sandy Berger) that 'the means that you're using will undermine your ends, and lead to a cycle of violence'.[33]

Washington was prepared to support Yeltsin in his many domestic crises, the most severe of which involved the military assault on the Russian parliament building in early October 1993, just as Clinton himself was struggling to come to terms with the disaster in Somalia. Backing for Yeltsin necessarily involved the administration in selective argumentation. Yeltsin was faced by a largely conservative/nationalist (or 'Red-Brown') majority in the Congress of People's Deputies, the pre-1994 parliamentary lower house. The Russian leader had not given any indication during the 1991 presidential election that he intended to embark on the 'shock therapy' programme of rapid economic marketisation. Yeltsin did win an important referendum on constitutional reform and socio-economic change in April 1993, but afterwards did not seriously attempt to negotiate with the oppositionists.[34] The advances made by the ultra-nationalist forces of Vladimir Zhirinovsky in the Duma elections of December 1993 seem merely to have confirmed Clinton and Talbott in the view that Yeltsin was essentially correct: the president and his entourage really did represent the only hope of preventing Russia's descent into the status of 'illiberal democracy', dominated by populist anti-Westerners. Following the December elections, and after exchanges with Chernomyrdin, Al Gore began to campaign for more generous IMF support for Russia, arguing that the stiff economic conditioning that had been attached to former loans had contributed to the conditions that had allowed Zhirinovsky to thrive. Larry Summers succeeded in securing a (generously conditioned) $1.5 billion IMF loan to ease the Russian economy.[35]

The IMF loan was one of many American and American-led financial initiatives designed to head-off extreme nationalism and to further integrate Russia into the global economy. The loans had to be fairly hefty if they were to counter nationalist accusations in Russia about Yeltsin and the reformers having become the creatures of Washington. The Clinton administration was also careful to balance dependent economic integration with symbolic recognition of Russian 'great power' status. Thus the invitation to Moscow to take an eighth seat at global G-7 meetings was as much a political as an economic gesture. (The initial Treasury opposition to the creation of a 'G-8' was overcome largely by this political argument; the first official G-8 meeting, with both Clinton and Yeltsin present, took place in Birmingham, England, in May 1998.) Assistance to Russia in the period 1993–94 amounted to something like the 'grand bargain' that had been recommended by Graham Allison and Richard Nixon. Clinton typically devoted considerable effort to winning congressional support for the various aid packages.[36] The Vancouver summit package of 1993 – explicitly designed to help Yeltsin in his referendum campaign – amounted to $1.6 billion, of which $48 million was to be for democracy-promotion per se and much of the rest in food credits (for the provision of US farm exports to Russia) Soon after, at the Tokyo G-7 meeting, another major aid package was agreed. As the 1990s progressed, congressional resistance became more pronounced, causing the administration to favour multilateral assistance over direct US loans. Responding to Republican pressure, as well as to the perceived need to expedite the regional nuclear agreements, aid after 1994 tended to be shared more equally between Russia and Ukraine. Democracy-promotion money found its way into local initiatives and general institution-building; the suspicion, however, was that much of it also fuelled corruption. Washington focused particularly on economic initiatives – the voucher schemes and 'loans-for-shares' privatisations, associated with Gaidar and Chubais.[37]

Clinton's policy towards Russia had numerous problematic features: the uncritical attachment to Yeltsin, the rather unconvincing reiteration that Yeltsin was the only possible reform leader in town, the inability to monitor how much of the assistance money was being used, the effective American complicity in the rise of the privatisation oligarchs. The very idea of the 'strategic partnership', as Zbigniew Brzezinski wrote in 1994, risked legitimising corruption, 'deferring to wounded pride' and becoming complicit in a new regional order in the former USSR almost by default.[38] The prospect of extreme nationalism was real, but it was also orchestrated by Russian reform elites to promote their own agendas. Whenever Yeltsin blew hot and cold over reform, sacking liberals and acting in an authoritarian manner, Washington began to suspect that perhaps it was being taken for a ride.[39] In retrospect, however, the development of Russian attitudes towards the West in the 1990s underwent a logical progression: from the pro-Western reformism of Andrei Kozyrev to the 'great power realism' of Yevgeny Primakov (Foreign Minister between 1996 and 1998). In 2000, Russia under Putin adopted a 'new foreign policy concept', geared to regional hegemony and (in effect) an attempt to advance multi-polarity as a counter to American international power.[40]

It could be argued that the Clinton administration succeeded in channelling and softening the reaction to the 1989–91 Russian geopolitical cataclysm. American aid arguably did help prevent complete Russian economic disarray; the forces of extreme reaction (nationalist and/or communist) were contained, or at least transposed into the social coalition which formed behind Putin in 2000. Picking winners in distant countries, however, is a difficult and often foolish enterprise. Rather than uncritically supporting Yeltsin and underwriting 'shock' economic reform, the Clinton administration might have been better advised to spend more effort in understanding the dynamic of Russian foreign policy development: the near-inevitable shift – not so much the product of political extremism as of the ineradicable dynamics of action and reaction – towards 'great power' suspicion of American global power. Clinton's Russia policy was not a disaster, but it did not realise the aspiration expressed by Warren Christopher in his March 1993 memo, 'A Strategic Alliance with Russian Reform': 'It should be US policy not just to prevent the worst but to nurture the best that might happen in the former Soviet Union.'[41]

Vietnam and Cuba

Clinton's election excited expectations of imminent normalisation of relations with two of America's most prominent, albeit relatively miniscule, Cold War enemies: Vietnam and Cuba. In a strange perspective on recent American history, normalisation of relations with Vietnam – a country which had defeated the US in a war which formed the international outlook of Clinton's generation – proved easier to achieve than it did with America's Caribbean neighbour.

As a vindication of his campaign pledge to 'close the book' on the Vietnam War, Bill Clinton announced in the first few days of his presidency that, although the 'deep wounds' of the Indochinese conflict had not healed, genuine progress towards a 'full accounting' of missing US service personnel in Vietnam had been made.[42] This declaration was Clinton's equivalent of President Jimmy Carter's announcement of the amnesty for Vietnam draft evaders, made directly after his 1977 inauguration. In February 1994, Clinton unilaterally ended the US trade embargo on Vietnam. A US liaison office was established in Ho Chi Minh City (formerly Saigon), paving the way for the nomination, in 1996, of a US Ambassador to the Socialist Republic of Vietnam (Florida Congressman Pete Peterson, a former Vietnamese prisoner-of-war). Normalisation was opposed by veterans' associations. Clinton's personal vulnerability on Vietnam-related issues was greatly eased by the support for normalisation in the Senate, led by two Vietvets (and two subsequent presidential candidates): John McCain of Arizona and John Kerry of Massachusetts. Against the position of his own Majority Leader in 1995, Bob Dole, McCain accepted that the Vietnamese were indeed cooperating on the issue of accounting for missing US personnel. Diplomatic normalisation with China, achieved during the Carter years, seemed to strengthen the case for a Democratic administration normalising with Vietnam. The process was eased by its compatibility with the narrative of inexorable economic globalisation. A Cititibank representative in Hanoi was quoted to the effect that US companies were eager to obtain access to Vietnamese infrastructure areas like petrochemicals and power generation.[43] In an instance of fearful symmetry, Clinton visited

Vietnam immediately after the 2000 US presidential elections; the former antiwar student protested at Communist Party leader Le Kha Phieu's description of American action in Indochina as 'an imperialist act'.[44]

Even allowing for the importance of veterans' lobbies in American politics, it was evident that the maintenance of hostile relations with Cuba was – far more than in the case of Vietnam – deeply embedded in American ethnic, regional and electoral politics. One consequence of the end of the Cold War was the removal of Cuba from the securitised agenda of executive branch-dominated 'high politics', and its immersion in the cross-currents of local and congressional political activity. Key actors here were the Cuban exile groups based in Miami, the government and electors of Florida, and various anti-communist Members of Congress (whose numbers included by the mid-1990s, three Cuban-Americans). The best known of the exile groups was the Cuban American National Foundation (CANF), led, up until his death in 1997, by Jorge Mas Canosa. Thriving on the expectations that foreign policy would become increasingly decentralised in post-Cold War conditions, several large US states developed something akin to their own 'foreign policy' positions, typically regarding trade and immigration. The *NYT* ran a story in May 1994 entitled, 'Foreign Policy: Florida Has One'. Governor Lawton Chiles of Florida was reported as trying to develop a Floridian foreign policy, primarily geared towards refugee issues connected to Haiti and Cuba, 'including the sorts of panels and policy wonks usually more characteristic of a sovereign nation'.[45] The influence of groups like the CANF at the state level was always liable to be diluted at the national level, precisely because of the regional basis of the Cuban lobbies and the 'national security' orientation of Washington decision-making processes. Within Florida, however, the exile groups clearly were very influential.[46] Moreover, Florida's national clout was always likely to be enhanced by that state's 'swing' electoral status, both at the presidential primary and the electoral college level. On Capitol Hill, Cuban issues – again, the island's descent from the realms of 'high politics' is relevant here – also assumed increasing importance, as congressional 'policy entrepreneurs' sought to make their legislative mark.[47]

Two such Cuba-oriented legislators, Democrats Robert Toricelli (New Jersey) in the House and Bob Graham (Florida) in the Senate, set the ball rolling in 1992 by achieving passage of the Cuban Democracy Act, endorsed by Clinton during his 1992 campaign. The Act provided for a toughening of economic pressure on Cuba, by expanding the trade embargo to cover foreign subsidiaries of American multinational firms and by preventing ships which had docked on the island from entering US ports. It also eased restrictions on contact with the island for refugees and exiles in the United States. Such loosening of contact restrictions tended to be very popular with Cuban-Americans, despite the tendency of some of their more conservative representatives to advocate complete isolation for the island. Clinton's attraction to the Toricelli–Graham measures was explained in an interview given to Walt Vanderbrush and Patrick Haney by an unnamed former Clinton administration official in 1998. The Clinton Latin Americanists liked the 'carrot and stick' aspect of Toricelli–Graham: 'get hard with the regime but open to the people and allow for freedom to change the embargo with political change in Cuba.'[48] Contact with civil society in Cuba was seen by most of the Clinton team as a way of defeating communism in Cuba, just as it had in Eastern Europe. Clinton lost Florida in 1992, but considerably increased the Democratic share of Cuban-American voting, the bulk of which had traditionally backed Republicans; Clinton won Florida in 1996.

Clinton's first skirmish with the Cuban-American lobby occurred over the appointment of Mario Baeza, a black Cuban-American, as Assistant Secretary of State for Inter-American Affairs. Baeza's appointment was dropped following opposition from Robert Toricelli, Mas Canosa and the CANF. In July and August 1994, there occurred one of the periodic exoduses of Cuban refugees, depicted by commentators as a potential re-run of the very 1980 Mariel boatlift which had caused problems for Clinton when he had been Governor of Arkansas. It was estimated that the Castro regime was effectively allowing around 30,000 refugees to take to the sea. On 18 August, Attorney General Janet Reno announced that rafting Cuban refugees would no longer be given automatic refuge in the United States. Vanderbrush and Haney suggest that Clinton's own involvement in the initial decision to suspend refugee rights was slight.[49] However, on 19 August, effectively reversing policy which had held since 1966, Clinton ordered rafter interceptions and the commitment of refugees either to the US Cuban base at Guantanamo or to a third country. (Only Panama actually accepted refugees, most of whom were returned to Guantanamo in 1995.) For Clinton, the crisis not only stirred memories of 1980, it also linked into contemporary problems associated with Haiti. The administration clearly acted in the face of what it considered to be a major crisis and in response to frenzied appeals from Governor Chiles. Canosa and the CANF were shocked by the policy reversal; they clearly were not controlling policy here, even at the level of the Floridian government. Clinton rapidly moved to make some concessions to the harder-line Cuban-American groups, announcing a tightening of restrictions on travel and on the sending of money remittances to families in Cuba. Again, it should be emphasised that such tightening pleased the conservative Cuban-American leadership far more than it pleased many ordinary Cuban-Americans; it also stretched the delegations of power to the president given under the Cuban Democracy Act.

The administration probably saw the crisis-management decisions of August 1994 as holding operations, pending direct negotiations with the Castro regime. Talks began with Cuban negotiator Ricardo Alarcon in September at the UN in New York. The US side offered to expand legal immigration from Cuba in return for a halt in rafter departures. Alarcon demanded an end to the trade embargo, which he blamed for creating the economic conditions which encouraged people to leave. An interim deal was agreed, however, largely along the lines favoured by the US; a more formal agreement in May 1995 (negotiated between Alarcon and Peter Tarnoff) included the provision that rafters would be intercepted and actually returned to Cuba. Clinton explained to a largely Cuban-American audience in June that he regretted the need to adopt the policy of interception and return. However, 'We cannot let people risk their lives on open seas in unseaworthy crafts. And we cannot sentence thousands of young men to live in limbo at Guantanamo.'[50]

With the refugee crisis shelved, the administration turned to its favoured tactic of engaging Cuban civil society. In October 1995, Clinton issued an executive order reversing the August 1994 concessions to CANF and expanding the 'carrot' side of the Toricelli–Graham strategy. Academic, charitable non-governmental organisations (NGOs), cultural and religious contact with the island would be encouraged. Money transfers and Cuban-American travel would become much easier. Western Union would set up a Cuban office to facilitate the transmission of money to visa-holding Cubans who wished to travel to the US. An anonymous State Department official was quoted in the *NYT*: 'We're trying to get more channels of communication open. We believe from what we saw in Eastern Europe that it helps to aerate the society.'[51] The problem with this 'aeration' strategy was not simply that it was opposed by those Cuban-American leaders (like Mas Canosa) who favoured isolation; rather, the policy was running counter to legislative initiatives sponsored by none less than the new chairman of the Senate Foreign Relations Committee.

The proposed Cuban Liberty and Solidarity Act, sponsored jointly by Jesse Helms and Representative Dan Burton (Republican of Indiana) represented a cobbling together of various anti-Castro measures (most famously the efforts of Florida Republican Connie Mack to strengthen the embargo) which had been pending on Capitol Hill ever since the collapse of the Berlin Wall had excited hopes about the imminence of the universal extinction of communism. Supported by Bob Dole, the Helms-Burton legislation was aimed directly and proudly at the goal of rapid regime change. It precluded negotiations with any post-Castro transitional regime. Most controversially, it embraced legal 'extraterritoriality', imposing penalties on foreign companies that invested in Cuba. Though this section was somewhat watered down in the final version, the legislation also allowed lawsuits to be taken out by Cuban-Americans to recover property confiscated by the Castro regime, even if such property were in non-American hands. Republican Representative Dana Rohrabacher described the measure as being aimed at 'the scum of the globe who cut deals ... to make money off tyranny'.[52] The law also hugely strengthened the legal foundation of the trade embargo, making it more or less impossible for any future president to lift it unilaterally, even pending legislative approval, as Clinton had done in relation to Vietnam.

Helms–Burton passed the House easily in September 1995. Warren Christopher, however, announced that a presidential veto could be expected. The White House mobilised significant corporate business opposition to the legislation and opened up a dialogue between Havana and Sturat Eizenstat, US Ambassador to the EU.[53] Clinton's executive order of early October was an attempt to seize the initiative before the Senate vote. The prospect of successful, veto-proof, passage of even a diluted version of the bill seemed poor at this stage, and progress on the legislation stalled. Clinton's executive order of October 1995, and subsequent 'aeration' and engagement activity with Cuba, was now setting the pace. However, on 24 February 1996, the Cuban air force shot down two US-registered

Cesna aircraft, piloted by members of the Brothers to the Rescue refugee assistance group. At the UN, Madeleine Albright, in her own words, 'delivered a statement that would never in a thousand years have been cleared by the State Department if submitted in advance': 'Frankly, this is not *cojones*. This is cowardice.'[54] Richard Nuccio, NSC staff adviser on Cuba, gave his opinion that Fidel Castro, in ordering the action which resulted in four deaths, 'created a veto-proof majority for the Helms–Burton Act'.[55] Clearly, if the shoot-down really had been ordered by Castro, this would have been done with the knowledge of its likely effect in Washington. Clinton later received a communication from Cuba to the effect that Castro had not ordered the action, but nonetheless wondered if the Cuban leader 'was trying to force us to maintain the embargo as an excuse for the economic failures of the regime'.[56]

After complex attempts to try to extract concessions on 'extraterritoriality', Helms–Burton was passed by the Senate and signed by President Clinton on 12 March 1996, the day of the Florida primary. Commentary on the legislation was generally hostile. For Stephen Lisio, its effect was to disrupt America's relations with its allies, while yielding severely diminishing returns in Cuba itself.[57] Canada and Mexico protested that the law violated the NAFTA. In July 1996, two UK businessmen with links to Cuba were refused admittance to the US.[58] In November 1997, a *NYT* editorial pointed out that the law showed no sign of undermining Castro: 'Despite the law, Cuba has attracted enough trade and investment to survive the loss of Soviet subsidies.' The embargo simply served to promote popular anti-Americanism.[59]

The legislation was controversial and open to challenge on any range of fronts. During the second term, in response to complaints from allies, the administration succeeded in weakening the 'extraterritoriality' provisions. Illustrating the ability of the executive branch to interpret legislation while implementing it, Clinton also claimed authority to waive claimant rights to sue for compensation under the act so as not – in his own words – 'to undermine our strong, broad-based and consistent commitment to open trade among nations'.[60] Enforcement of Title 3 of the law, relating to foreign 'traffic' in confiscated property, was waived; Title 4's measures to deter allied trade with Cuba were more or less ignored after 1996. White House spokesmen invoked the Helms–Burton executive 'licensing power' as virtually a *carte blanche* to ignore the law, while Congress itself became more pragmatic in its attitude once the symbolic gesture of passing Helms–Burton had been made. Farm state legislators, for example, campaigned successfully to lift some of the restraints on food sales.[61] Even in 1996, Clinton announced that some direct flights to the island would be allowed. In January 1999, he completely ignored the provisions and intent of Helms–Burton by unilaterally announcing yet another round of embargo liberalisation. This involved more charter flights to Cuba, further easing of cash remittance restrictions, and the allowing of food and agricultural sales to charities and privately owned farms.[62]

From 1996, administration policy towards Cuba became part of the battle with the Republican Congress – a battle which, despite the fact that the GOP was to remain in control of Capitol Hill until the elections of 2006, the president was winning. Policy was never driven by the CANF, as was widely alleged by Clinton critics. In fact, the administration was able to exploit clear divisions with Cuban-American opinion about how best to deal with Castro. Clinton's favoured approach, engagement with Cuban civil society, was clear and coherent. It was blown off course by the complex politics attending what had become, in the post-Cold War context, at best a middle-level foreign policy priority.

China

In his 1993 confirmation hearings as Assistant Secretary for East Asian and Pacific Affairs, Winston Lord averred that the US needed a 'nuanced policy' with China, one that 'condemned repression' yet encouraged 'links with progressive forces' in China.[63] Echoing Clinton campaign rhetoric on Bush's 'coddling' of dictators, Warren Christopher declared the US would seek 'a broad, peaceful evolution in China from communism to democracy'.[64] Winston Lord had worked for Republican administrations, but in effect straddled two Republican traditions on China: the pro-democracy, pro-Taiwan tradition deriving from the early Cold War, and the pragmatic 'opening to China' tradition associated with – and in the 1990s still advocated by – Henry Kissinger. Clinton's 1992 campaign stance made it inevitable that Kissinger's line, which (excepting arms sales to Taiwan) had generally been followed by Bush, would at least be temporarily abandoned. Arguing that China's big 1992 trade surplus with the US actually increased Washington's leverage over Beijing, Clinton promised to 'stick up for ourselves and for the things we believe in and how these people are treated in that country'.[65]

The policy debate over China in the 1990s has often been depicted as a conflict between advocates of 'integrating' China into global political and economic networks, and more hostile proponents of 'containment', with each side taking its cue from competing interpretations of the end of the Cold War.[66] Given the huge economic leaps achieved by China in the 1990s, it is more realistic, at least in terms of intra-administration thinking, to conceive the debate more in terms of differing versions of 'engagement': 'principled engagement', 'economic engagement' and 'defence engagement'.

Each version of Chinese engagement had its own bureaucratic and extra-administration base. 'Principled engagers' included Winston Lord and Tony Lake, who included China in his September 1993 designation of 'backlash states'.[67] 'Principled engagement' within the Clinton administration initially involved linking trade relations to improvement of China's human rights record. Conspicuous 'economic engagers' included Commerce Secretary Ron Brown, who in early 1994 defended unconditional US trade engagement as a branch of American 'economic security'.[68] With the Chinese economy showing annual growth rates of over 10 per cent, American business was overwhelmingly pro-integration by the early 1990s, with only organised labour left to argue the economic case for protection and Chinese isolation. When Warren Christopher visited China in March 1994, immediately following the arrest of high-profile dissidents, he was informed by the American Chamber of Commerce in Beijing that the US must not shut itself out of the world's fastest growing market.[69] Though situated primarily in the economic agencies, 'economic engagers' found an ally in Deputy NSA Sandy Berger. 'Economic engagers' also persuasively asserted that America's own allies showed precious little sign of being willing to curb their Chinese trade because of Beijing's refusal to democratise. The moral argument, of course, was that only integration *could* improve human rights in China. 'Defence engagers', led by William Perry (initially Deputy Secretary) at the Pentagon, argued the case for recruiting China to help in the North Korean nuclear dispute in particular, as well as more generally in arms sales and proliferation. China's primarily land-based, and America's primarily sea-based, regional military presences required constant negotiation and (usually tacit) re-negotiation in order to remain in balance. Within these cross-currents, Warren Christopher stood broadly with 'principled engagement'; he found the State Department increasingly sidelined by the economic agencies and by the Pentagon. On Capitol Hill, China policy cut across party affiliation and illustrated the fluid nature of post-Cold War congressional foreign policy. Alignments concerning the economic and geopolitical Chinese giant were more complex than in the case of Cuba. Human rights activism united liberal Democrats with anti-communist Republicans; 'economic engagement' pitted Republican and Democrat free-traders against Republican nationalists and Democrat protectionists. Clinton himself – the 'globalisation president' – was peculiarly attracted to the economic arguments, though aware of the political dangers inherent in being seen to be crudely trading-off human rights for geopolitical or economic advantage.

The initial policy debates focused on the annual legislative contest, inherited from the Bush years, over renewal of China's MFN trading status. Should free trade with Beijing be linked to internal human rights issues? The White House succeeded in persuading the sponsors of a bill, linking MFN status with human rights, to withdraw their measure in favour of an executive order issued by Clinton ostensibly to do the same thing. One of the sponsors, Democratic Representative Nancy Pelosi (representing a significant Chinese-American population in San Francisco), later recalled that Clinton 'was our new president. It never occurred to me, and frankly it never occurred to (fellow sponsors) George Mitchell or Richard Gephardt, that he wouldn't keep his word.'[70] Clinton's executive order was weaker than the proposed Pelosi–Mitchell measure, especially in regard to Chinese arms sales, and was much more easily revoked through unilateral presidential action.[71] The administration swiftly moved to establish high-level diplomatic contact with Beijing. Christopher was told in Beijing by Premier Li Peng that 'China will never accept the United States' concept of human rights'. Li Peng even cited recent police behaviour in Los Angeles (the Rodney King beating), and Christopher's own role in investigating it, as instances of American hypocrisy. Christopher was later asked when he realised the 1993 MFN executive order was doomed; he replied: 'On the way back from my trip.'[72] Clinton attempted some diplomatic nuancing of the consequent retreat. He tried, without success, to persuade Jimmy Carter to inaugurate a new commission on Chinese human rights. Approaches were made by Robert Rubin and Tony Lake to Chinese officials attending Richard Nixon's funeral in California. Clinton's 26 May 1994 announcement – in effect, that the executive order's human rights requirements had not been met, and that he was ending MFN/human rights linkage – represented the triumph of the 'economic engagers'. Reflecting the complex cross-cutting nature of legislative attitudes towards China, Clinton's position was supported 280–152 in a House vote taken in August 1994.

China had, in effect, called the American bluff and Clinton was either sufficiently alert or sufficiently sinuous to accept it. The president was chastened by the affair and characteristically bemoaned what he saw as an inevitable, but regrettable, retreat from principle. The *NYT* reported him as privately confiding his misgivings and anticipation of difficulties in the 1996 election campaign: 'I wish I was running *against* our China policy.'[73] The administration continued to think in terms of 'conditional engagement' and was soon to demonstrate sureness of purpose over Taiwan. However, the May 1994 *volte face* inevitably (as Nancy Tucker noted) 'undermined the credibility of future administration China policies'.[74]

Clinton's embarrassment over the MFN decision probably contributed to his eventual willingness to approve the entry into the United States, in June 1995, of President Lee Teng-hui of Taiwan to attend a graduate reunion at Cornell University. Lee's admittance ran counter to practice previously established under America's acceptance of the principle of 'one China', headed by Beijing. Clinton was aware of Lee's agenda. The Taiwanese leader was due to face direct elections in 1996 and was engaged in vigorous lobbying on Capitol Hill in support of Taiwan. The administration initially indicated its opposition to the visit, but was soon put under severe pressure by the new Congress. A non-binding resolution, supporting the Lee visa, passed the House, 398–0, and the Senate, where only the Louisiana Republican, Bennett Johnston – a Senator with strong Chinese business links – stood opposed. The State Department shifted its position almost immediately. Lee's visa would be forthcoming. Department spokesman Nicholas Burns stressed that 'Taiwan is a part of China', but freedom of travel was also an important principle.[75] Several Members of Congress argued that trade with Taiwan was just as important as trade with China. Clinton, who had visited Taiwan to promote trade as Governor of Arkansas, defended Lee's right to travel. There was also an interesting parallel: the 1993 visa issuance to Gerry Adams of Sinn Fein over London's opposition.

Beijing's belligerent response to the Lee visit took Washington by surprise. An invasion of the island was threatened if Taiwan proceeded towards a declaration of independence. The months between June and September 1995, when Hillary Clinton made her address to the International Womens' Conference in Beijing, were taken up with various attempts to limit the diplomatic damage. Congress seemed to back away from pro-Taiwan stances.[76] Warren Christopher, holding talks in Brunei with Chinese Foreign Minister Qian Qichen, conveyed a letter from Clinton to Premier Jiang Zemin. Clinton reiterated the 'one China' commitment, promising to spurn requests to support Taiwanese independence.[77]

Tension continued, however, into 1996, and was exacerbated by publicity surrounding Chinese arms sales to Iran, by (peaceful) US naval encounters with Chinese nuclear submarines, and by vague threats from Beijing that US support for Taiwan in the event of Chinese invasion could lead to nuclear war.[78] Clinton met Jiang Zemin unofficially in New York in October 1995, with the State Department indicating that an unofficial summit 'most appropriately reflects the current standing of US–China relations'.[79]

The March 1996 US–China confrontation over Taiwan was the most dangerous and intense interaction between the two powers since the Vietnam War. Prior to the elections in Taiwan, Beijing deployed around 150,000 troops on the mainland near the island. Missiles were fired into the Taiwan Strait. William Perry and Tony Lake delivered a warning to Beijing during a meeting in Washington with senior Chinese foreign ministry personnel. Following more missile launches, Clinton decided on 9 March to send two aircraft carriers to the seas just off Taiwan, though with orders not to enter the Taiwan Strait. Clinton's decision recalled President Johnson's order to the Sixth Fleet to turn around and sail to the eastern Mediterranean at the height of the 1967 Six Day War, following a telephonic argument with Soviet leader Aleksei Kosygin. The 1996 elections in Taiwan took place peacefully on 23 March, when Lee was re-elected. The operation had an element of gestural politics, but it still involved considerable risk. William Perry, leader of the 'defence engagers', presented the case for deploying the carriers.[80] In his realist analysis of the crisis, Robert Ross argued that the US did not see a Chinese invasion of Taiwan as imminent; Perry reportedly thought that Beijing would not countenance such a 'dumb thing'.[81] For Ross, the crucial factor was that the missile firings into the Taiwan Strait, challenging US credibility: Washington 'used deterrence diplomacy to communicate to both Chinese and regional leaders the credibility of its strategic commitments'.[82]

To the extent that the later 1990s saw the building of a new security order in the Far East, Clinton's carrier deployment may be judged as having done its job. Clinton's post-Taiwan crisis visit to Japan revitalised the US–Japanese mutual security alliance, including the promise to construct a regional (effectively anti-Chinese as well as anti-North Korean) missile system. Washington prioritised the building of a triadic alliance, bringing in South Korea along with Japan.[83] This security order of the later 1990s encompassed a degree of anti-Chinese military 'containment', attached to diplomatic and economic 'engagement'. In military affairs, Washington and Beijing became expert at avoiding each other. Jiang was invited to make a state visit to the US, while Beijing was reassured (notably during negotiations with Tony Lake in July 1966) that America recognised that China would occupy a central place in the emerging world order. A key symbol of the Clinton administration's commitment to 'defence engagement' was the visit of Chinese Defence Minister Chi Haotian, who had been directly involved in the Tiananmen Square killings of 1989, to the Pentagon's National War College in December 1996.[84]

China policy in the second term was led by Sandy Berger. Berger favoured 'a strong commitment to economic integration of China' including Chinese admission to the WTO. Here was another possible 'grand bargain': the achievement of a truly marketised Chinese economy as the price for admission to the WTO. Congressional opponents of Chinese integration, such as Richard Gephardt, foresaw Beijing being allowed far too generous a transition period to adapt to a market economy. Madeleine Albright in turn accused opponents of the administration line of pursuing 'containment', which would 'divide out Asian allies and encourage China to withdraw into narrow nationalism'.[85] Congress was also aware that support for China's WTO entry would entail an end to the annual wrangling over MFN status. The post-1996 election accusations of improper Chinese donations, associated particularly with the Taiwanese-American entrepreneur Johnny Chung, to the Democratic National Committee further muddied the waters. Republicans in Congress also protested the February 1998 presidential decision, apparently taken in spite of Justice, State and Defense Department opposition, to allow an American satellite-manufacturing firm a Chinese export licence. The decision was rendered yet more controversial by the fact that the head of the US company was yet another major contributor to the 1996 Clinton campaign.[86]

In the second term presidential rhetoric, China engagement became a special case of Clinton's general attack on congressional 'isolationism'. In June 1998, Clinton attacked those who would 'try to isolate and contain China'.[87] John Holum, arms controller at State, declared that huge progress was being made in 'bringing China into the community of countries working to impede the flow of weapons of mass destruction'.[88] As examples of 'effective engagement', the administration was able to point by this time to Beijing's signing of the CWC in 1993 and the CNTBT in 1996, its accession to a 1997 agreement on nuclear export controls and promises given in October 1997 to end its nuclear and cruise missile exports to Iran. Beijing appeared also to agree with Washington's push for regional arms control following the Pakistani and Indian nuclear tests in the spring of 1998. The problem, of course, was that many of Clinton's opponents in Congress not only opposed the very agreements (notably the CNTBT) that Beijing accepted, but also that they had no faith in Beijing's word. In February 1998, Clinton confirmed that China was now respecting the terms of the Nuclear Non-proliferation Treaty (NPT) which it had signed in 1992. A few weeks later, information was leaked to the effect that China was still exporting uranium-enriching chemicals to Iran.[89] By June 1998, the House of Representatives had passed eight separate bills which sought to punish China either for its human rights transgressions or its weapons proliferation. A special committee was set up, under Representative Christopher Cox (Republican, California) to investigate past, and indeed 'contemporary' accusations of Chinese spying at the Los Alamos nuclear research facility in New Mexico. Cox's 1999 report alleged a 'serial haemorrhage' of nuclear secrets to Beijing.[90]

Joseph Nye wrote in 1998 that the domestic American politics of China policy were 'a strange alliance of left and right against the centre'.[91] Against a background of both Republican and liberal scepticism about the wisdom and propriety of what Clinton had once referred to as 'coddling dictators', engagement with China in the second term took an increasingly personal turn. Visits to Beijing by

Al Gore, Sandy Berger and by key NSC staffer Sandra Kristoff prepared the way for the October 1997 state visit to the US by Jiang Zemin (who formally replaced party leader Deng Xiaoping after the latter's death in February 1997), and Clinton's reciprocal visit to Beijing in June 1998. Jiang's visit involved complex wrangles over US guarantees regarding Taiwan – the Chinese wanted Clinton to make his unequivocal commitment to 'one China' public – over Iranian technology transfers and Chinese accession to the WTO. Clinton deflected domestic criticism at the summit press conference by criticising Beijing's human rights record, and by stating that communist China was 'on the wrong side of history'.[92]

Clinton's Beijing visit was again accompanied by widespread suspicion that Clinton was becoming uncritical of Beijing. Richard Hornick in *Time* warned Clinton against agreeing to China's admittance into the WTO on terms which would not be extended to lesser nations.[93] Clinton's 'one China' commitment was seen by Carl Cannon as 'no longer a statement of calculated ambiguity', but as failing to 'take into account that Taiwan has become a democracy'.[94] Madeleine Albright recalled the embarrassment of having the welcoming ceremony in Tiananmen Square.[95] Clinton made a TV broadcast in Beijing, which was critical of China's human rights policy. Discussing Chinese policy in Tibet, Clinton 'got a laugh from the Chinese audience when' he said that he thought 'that if Jiang and the Dalai Lama did meet, they would like each other very much'.[96] In Shanghai, Clinton made his 'one China' position quite explicit – more explicit than had been publicly acknowledged at any time since the original 1972 US 'opening' to China.

Despite the opportunities taken by Clinton to speak out against the dark side of Chinese politics, the 1998 visit saw the continuation of cautious reciprocity between the world's superpower and the world's aspiring superpower: a mutual testing-out which was to continue well into the twenty-first century. China, engaged in what Albright called its 'balancing act' between fear of democracy and desire for economic integration, stepped up its persecution of dissidents following the presidential visit.[97] Testing-out on the American side took the form of enhanced military contact with Taiwan. The replacement of William Perry at the Pentagon by William Cohen signalled an important shift from the 'defence engagement' positions of the first term. In 1999 and 2000, the US sold fighter aircraft and an early-warning radar system to Taiwan. The sales stimulated a bureaucratic contest between the Pentagon on the one hand, and State and the economic agencies on the other. Foggy Bottom and the Commerce Department tended to see the arms sales as destabilising and as potentially destructive of America's wider engagement interests.[98] From Clinton's point of view, the sales to Taiwan were both a defensible part of the 'testing-out' of Beijing, and a covert warning that human rights violations by Beijing were not risk-free. Support for Taiwan also took some of the heat from Republican criticisms of administration policy, at a time when congressional investigation of the China-related campaign funding scandals was threatening to revive the agonies of Whitewater.

The key dynamic in US–China relations in the second term was provided by Beijing's eagerness to join the WTO. As discussed in Chapter 3, a deal with

China was actually rebuffed in April 1999, only to be revived in November 1999, when Charlene Barshefsky negotiated market-opening conditions for Chinese entry into the WTO in December 2001. The political expression of the November 1999 deal took the form of Clinton's successful battle for congressional approval of permanent normal trade relations status for China in 2000, again discussed in Chapter 3. By the last year of his presidency, there is no indication that Clinton wished, any longer, that he could run against his own China policy. The relative lack of progress on human rights, the Republican charges of corruption and high-level espionage, the bombing of the Chinese embassy in Belgrade, and howls from organised labour about the US–China trade deficit: these factors made China policy in the later 1990s exceedingly problematic for Clinton. In line with his general 'theory of the case', the president again put his faith in the march of economic globalisation. Clinton also seems to have appreciated the force of Joseph Nye's 1998 comment: 'If the United States treats China as an enemy now, it will guarantee an enemy in the future.'[99]

North Korea

The 1996 US–China confrontation over Taiwan was the second most internationally dangerous episode during Clinton's presidency. The most dangerous was the May 1994 near-confrontation with North Korea. An officer on the Pentagon's joint staff, interviewed by Don Oberdorfer, recalled a meeting of top military brass at this time: 'a real meeting of real war fighters to decide how they were going to fight a war.'[100] As James Hoare, British diplomat in the North Korean capital, Pyongyang, understood it, the US military 'believed it could win a war but that the costs in lives and destruction would be very high, especially given the closeness of the South Korean capital'.[101] The closeness of China was also, of course, a major consideration.

US relations with North Korea, especially in the first term, were linked directly to China policy and to Washington's hopes that Beijing could be encouraged to pressure Pyongyang into stepping back from its nuclear weapons programme. Beijing was prepared to help at the margins, especially by abstaining in anti-Pyongyang votes at the UN Security Council, but tended to emphasise the tenuousness of its leverage over North Korea.[102] China feared the consequences of a collapse of the Pyongyang regime even as it resented some of its deviations from the Beijing line on international relations. Partly as a result of the ambiguous nature of China's stance, Clinton's policy towards North Korea was itself frequently uncertain. Policy coherence was damaged by the lack of diplomatic experience in dealing with North Korea, as well as by the (understandably) nervous changes in direction exhibited by the South Korean government under Kim Young-sam. Nuclear proliferation was a major concern for the Clinton administration. The Joint Chiefs identified nuclear proliferation, including developments in North Korea, in January 1994 as the major military threat to American security.[103] However, nuclear diplomacy was dealt with formally at principals' committee level only on three occasions during the whole of 1993. Policy responsibility was devolved downwards, principally to Robert Gallucci, Assistant Secretary of State for Politico-Military Affairs. Policy coherence was compromised early on by Tony Lake's apparent reluctance to offer a clear direction. Assistant Defense Secretary Ashton Carter talked later of 'a dysfunctional NSC system' in relation to Korea.[104] Coherence was also hampered by emerging differences of perspective at the State Department and at the Pentagon. The former tended to concentrate on the integrity of the inspections regime and the free operation of 'special', random inspections of known nuclear sites. The Pentagon saw State as excessively oriented to possible past North Korean misbehaviour and advocated a sliding scale of measures to achieve an abrupt halt to the manufacture of new bombs. As Ashton Cater put it: 'Simply restoring North Korea' to the regime of international nuclear inspections was 'necessary but not sufficient'.[105]

The origins of the North Korean nuclear programme may be traced back to the 1950s. The programme was initially a combination of status symbol and coercive deterrence. Under pressure from Moscow, North Korea acceded to the NPT in 1985. By the closing years of the Cold War, however, its nuclear programme had developed (in the words of Robert Manning) into 'a political bargaining chip to achieve the key goal of regime survival'.[106] Between 1990 and 1992, the Bush administration developed a policy of offering Pyongyang various incentives (including the withdrawal of tactical nuclear weapons from South Korea) in return for compliance with the International Atomic Energy Agency (IAEA) inspection regime. By the first few months of the Clinton presidency, relations with the IAEA had effectively broken down, with Pyongyang announcing on 12 March 1993 its intention to quit the NPT. By this time, the main American worry was the possible reprocessing of spent fuel rods into plutonium, essential for the construction of nuclear bombs.

The US at last began serious preparations for negotiations with Pyongyang in April 1993. From then until the signing of the Agreed Framework in October 1994, there ensued complex interchanges between Pyongyang and Washington, recorded meticulously in the memoirs of Gallucci and two other officials who worked on North Korean issues for Clinton.[107] The dynamic of the negotiations, which began in a direct form in June 1993, seemed to lie in the emergence of a deal whereby Pyongyang would open up to 'special' inspections in return for a package of benefits, including US assistance with its civilian programme. In June 1993, in New York, a joint US–North Korean statement was issued to the effect that Pyongyang would suspend its withdrawal from the NPT; that mutual non-aggression assurances were given; and that each side agreed to the principles of 'peace and security in a nuclear-free Korean peninsula' and of 'support for the peaceful reunification of Korea'.[108] The US nevertheless, in the face of North Korean evasions of IAEA inspection, continued to combine coercive threat with diplomatic opening. The US increased its military presence in South Korea. US air strikes were considered at this time, but ruled out following military advice that destruction of nuclear facilities from the air could not be guaranteed. Air Force Chief of Staff Merrill McPeak declared: 'We can't find nuclear weapons now, except by going on a house to house search.'[109] For the rest of 1993, a complex cat-and-mouse game ensued. The US agreed in July to support North Korea's conversion to light-water reactors (for the civilian programme). The IAEA Board of Governors became increasingly frustrated by the North Korean evasions, while the UN Security Council issued its instructions for Pyongyang to cooperate. The US began to push for strong sanctions, which Pyongyang in turn declared that it would consider as 'an act of war'.[110] Tony Lake was reported as becoming increasingly sceptical about 'putting carrots out there where they could be eaten without getting anything in return'.[111] In December 1993, Washington persuaded Seoul to suspend a major military exercise, code-named *Team Spirit*. Neo-conservative commentator Charles Krauthammer characterised Clinton's policy as: 'Talk loudly and carry a big carrot.'[112]

Given the points already made about the possibility of military action – the threat to South Korea, the difficulty of targeting – it is tempting to conclude that such a course was never seriously considered in the first part of 1994. At one level, the threat of military strikes was an aspect of credible, coercive diplomacy. As Defense Secretary William Perry put it: 'The best way to avoid a war is to make sure they see our resolve.'[113] In February 1994, US forces were put on high alert for the first time since the Gulf War under Bush41. Anti-rocket Patriot missiles were shipped to South Korea. The Pentagon drew up war plans, including (as Clinton put it) 'a sobering estimate of the staggering losses both sides would suffer if war broke out'.[114] Yet Clinton was clearly frustrated and angry with the constant uncertainty of information coming from the IAEA. Echoing views which were to be expressed in Washington during the build-up to the 2003 Iraq invasion, Gallucci told Clinton that IAEA head Hans Blix '*meant* to mince words', as a way of undermining the possibility of US military action.[115] In December 1993, a CIA report, – in another pre-echo of the later Iraq crisis – though it acknowledged the lack of hard intelligence, estimated that North Korea probably did have one or two nuclear devices. Nancy Soderberg considered war in early 1994 'a real possibility', as did Madeleine Albright, who was viewing the escalating crisis from New York.[116]

Probably the closest move to war came in June, with discussion of a possible 'Osirak option' – a pre-emptive strike (similar to the 1981 Israeli raid on Iraq) on the Yongbyon nuclear facility. Such an option was floated publicly in the press by Brent Scowcroft, Bush's former National Security Adviser, and Arnold Kanter, Bush's chief negotiator with Pyongyang.[117] William Perry told Clinton that political leadership consisted of choices 'between what is disastrous and what is merely unpalatable'. The Defense Secretary was cautious but insisted that Washington could not entirely reject the possibility of war.[118] Gallucci and his associates later recorded some of the arguments against an immediate strike:

> Of course, there was no guarantee that the one or two bombs that North Korea may have already produced – each perhaps the size of a soda can as President Clinton would later describe it – were present at the reprocessing plant ... At best, the attack might delay the problem without eliminating it while risking a conventional war in Korea.[119]

Clinton decided to go for strong sanctions at the UN – itself a route that Pyongyang had indicated would lead to war. For Robert Gallucci, Joel Wit and Daniel Poneman, the crucial factor was the intervention of Jimmy Carter. Without the negotiations led by the former president (between June 15 and 18, as Clinton was considering and rejecting the 'Osirak option'), 'the North Koreans might have miscalculated by carrying through with their threats to expel international inspectors monitoring the unloaded fuel rods'. War might simply have broken out over the issue of sanctions. Without Carter, 'war would have been more likely', though Clinton would still have found military action very difficult, not least since it would almost certainly have been opposed by Seoul.[120]

Carter's deal with Pyongyang was one of the more extraordinary episodes in the history of diplomacy. Its major historical importance probably was to take the heat from the 1994 war-mongering and to act as the spur to intense American diplomatic re-engagement. Responding to earlier invitations to visit Pyongyang, Carter entered the fray with more than mere good intentions. A pre-trip conversation with Robert Gallucci seems to have confirmed Cater in his view that a deal was possible. Gallucci outlined the current divisions in the Clinton administration. Warren Christopher (uncertainly backed by Lake) held the view that the US would only signal weakness if it ignored past North Korean transgression of the IAEA regime. The Pentagon was prepared to consider war, but it also felt that a deal could be struck whereby past behaviour was discounted. This deal might prevent the sale of nuclear technology to other 'rogues' like Iraq and Libya. Gallucci quoted North Korean diplomat Kang Sok Chi: 'We can settle the future on nuclear and other matters, if the US drops its infatuation with the past.' Carter appreciated that negotiations were bedevilled by Washington having no direct line of communication to Kim Il Sung: what Gallucci described as the 'tube problem'. Stressing the importance of treating Kim Il Sung with courtesy, Carter was to supply that direct communication.[121]

Clinton's attitude towards Carter will be familiar from the account of the 1994 Haiti negotiations in Chapter 4. As Derek Chollet and James Goldgeier put it, the Clinton team (though many of course had worked for Carter) found the Georgian 'sanctimonious' and too inclined to freelancing.[122] Carter himself nursed grievances about the disinclination of the Clintonites formally to incorporate the Carter Center in Atlanta into its various environmental, human rights and diplomatic initiatives. Clinton was prepared to tolerate Carter's intervention, ensuring that Robert Gallucci and Tony Lake were in as much constant contact with the ex-president as the exigencies of negotiating in the North Korean 'hermit kingdom' allowed. When a White House meeting was interrupted by Carter reporting that he would announce an agreement to de-nuclearise the Korean peninsula on CNN (9:20 am, 16 June, Washington time), Clinton's response was apparently one of outrage and disbelief.[123] Tony Lake's telephonic imprecations to Carter to 'raise the ante' for any agreement were complicated by the realisation that the North Koreans were almost certainly listening in on their conversation.[124]

Carter's agreement included a promise by Pyongyang to allow IAEA inspectors and equipment to remain at Yongbyong – North Korea had formally withdrawn from the inspection regime on 13 June. The White House determined, as Al Gore put it, 'to make lemonade out of the lemon' of Carter's intervention.[125] Carter had, in the view of the White House, not secured proper commitments on reprocessing. However, kick-started by Carter, a new round of high-level talks began in August, with the final Agreed Framework being agreed in October (by which time Kim Il Sung had died, to be succeeded by his son, Kim Jong Il). The US agreed to provide light-water reactors to North Korea, while Pyongyang would remain committed to the NPT and to the freezing of its reprocessing programme. Rather predictably, the agreement was condemned as 'appeasement' by Republican Senator John McCain and also criticised by Senator William Cohen, the future Defense Secretary.[126]

The 1994 agreement had the virtue of supplying a degree of stability to the Korean peninsula and effectively capping the generation of plutonium. However, the regime accelerated its highly enriched uranium programme – a more straightforward route to a nuclear bomb than the plutonium technology which had been the main concern in 1994.[127] Robert Manning saw post-1994 Clinton policy towards North Korea as distorted into 'near paralysis' by pressure from the Republican Congress and from Seoul.[128] Extracting money from Congress to implement the Agreed Framework proved problematic; Kim Yung-sam in Seoul distrusted the agreement, which incorporated an important role for South Korea in supplying the reactors. Undercutting the common view that Washington was simply waiting for the Pyongyang regime to collapse, Clinton secured $8 million in food aid for North Korea in 1996, though unilateral trade sanctions remained. Contacts between Washington and Pyongyang – in relation to agreements regarding the retrieval of the remains of US soldiers killed in the Korean War, as well as to food aid and the reactor deal – were quite various and frequent, and usually conducted in a multi-party, regional security context. The election of Kim Dae Jung, and the emergence of his 'sunshine policy' in South Korea in 1998 also gave new impetus to developing US–North Korean relations.

During the second Clinton term, Madeleine Albright became convinced of the possibility of a real breakthrough. She was greatly impressed by the diplomatic path being followed by South Korean leader Kim Dae Jung, whom she compared to Vaclev Havel and Nelson Mandela.[129] Kim's 'sunshine' policy led to an unprecedented meeting in June 2000 between the leaders of North and South Korea. Pyongyang's stance, however, continued to be difficult to read. Ballistic missile testing by Pyongyang unnerved regional American allies. Worse, from 1998 stories began to appear in the US press that American intelligence was aware of new, clandestine nuclear sites.[130] The stage of the 1994 agreement, where North Korea was supposed to dispose safely and openly of its fuel rods, was never achieved. Speaking in November 1998, NSC Asian affairs specialist Jack Pritchard explained that a suspected underground site was 'not at this point' a violation of the Agreed Framework, and emphasised that the 1994 deal did not include missile testing.[131] The congressional pressure which followed the press disclosures led directly to Clinton's announcement, also in November 1998, of a new policy review, to be directed by former Defense Secretary William Perry, now a faculty member at Stanford University.

The unclassified version of Perry's report referred to Washington's 'serious concerns' about the nuclear and ballistic missile programmes. The report described a situation of 'stable deterrence' on the peninsula, a situation which nonetheless was threatened by North Korea's behaviour. Perry's 'big carrot' was the prospect of 'a step-by-step' reduction in behaviour that Pyongyang saw as threatening. Implicit in the report, one of whose intended readers of course was Kim Jong Il himself, was the recognition that the North Korean regime was not on the verge of collapse.[132] The regime was in many respects appalling: weirdly isolationist, much more of an atavistic holdover than its ambiguous sponsor in Beijing. However, like the communist government in China, and in defiance of many ill-informed Western press reports, it was not about to 'melt away'.[133] Complex negotiations continued into the last days of the administration, with the visit to Washington in October 2000 of Vice Marshall Jo Myong Rok, a close associate of the North Korean leader, to Washington. Later in the same month, Madeleine Albright visited Pyongyang to meet Kim Jong Il – easily the highest level US–North Korean interchange since the Korean War. Albright was convinced by Kim Jong Il that his main priority was normalisation with the US.[134] A proposal for Clinton to visit Pyongyang right at the close of his presidency was simply lost in the scramble to achieve the Israel–Palestine peace settlement.

The 1994 Agreed Framework was indisputably flawed, but it involved engagement rather than appeasement.[135] As in so many other areas, Clinton's policy towards North Korea frequently faltered. Leadership in this area, particularly in 1993, was sometimes weak, and the policy was adversely affected by internal American bureaucratic politics. Clinton, the wielder of Krauthammer's 'big carrot' was not naive about North Korea; evidence of North Korean cheating on the 1994 agreement can hardly have been a surprise. Given the proximity of China, a policy of regime change towards North Korea was not a good option. What alternative was there to a policy of dynamic engagement? Judgements about Clinton's policy decisions rest largely on the extent to which he was indeed prepared to go to war in 1994, only to be rescued by the Carter intervention. The judgement of insiders – that there was a serious risk of war – must be taken seriously, though it is difficult to believe either that Clinton would have gone ahead, given the dangers, or that Pyongyang would have gone to war over UN sanctions. The key problematic was that of misperception, misjudgement and misreading of anticipated reactions, especially in the context of the US–North Korean 'tube problem'. Calibrating the threat of force to the achievement of a credible diplomacy is inherently difficult: the more so in a strategic environment where the US depended so much on other regional actors. Perry's report was sensible and potentially productive. Clinton handed on to Bush an improving situation on the Korean peninsula – a truth recognised in Secretary of State Colin Powell's early undertaking not substantially to veer away from the Clinton legacy.[136]

7 Alliance politics and borderless threats

As we saw in Chapter 2, Clinton's foreign policy had a distinct arc of development: broadly, from the 'assertive humanitarianism' of the first term, to the remilitarisation and greater unilateralism of the second term. The post-1994 impact of the Republican Congress, the administration's growing international confidence and the Balkans learning curve were the main catalysts for change and development. In some ways, the Clinton trajectory mirrored that experienced during the Carter years: the move from the early Carter human rights phase to the post-1978 return of Cold War anti-Sovietism as the guiding principle of foreign policy.

Carter's policy shift was associated with intense bureaucratic politics (victories for national security adviser Zbigniew Brzezinski) and with overreaction to the 1979 Soviet invasion of Afghanistan.[1] It is tempting to interpret the Carter and the Clinton experiences as, in Harvey Sicherman's phrase, 'the revenge of geopolitics': the reassertion (in line with the International Relations theory of neo-classical realism) of the logic of the international system, following early presidential efforts to evade it. In this understanding of the Clinton years, the administration's 'plant-eaters' (advocates of 'assertive humanitarianism' and progressive international cooperation) had yielded to the logic of the 'meat-eaters' (advocates of a more traditional security-oriented agenda).[2]

We shall return to questions of Clinton's developmental trajectory – and the apparent parallel with Carter's – in the final chapter. The current chapter provides much of the empirical backdrop for an assessment of the cross-currents within the Clinton administration, as well as of the important issues of trajectory and development. Clinton's handling of alliance politics indicated both the extent of his administration's commitment to multilateralism, and his ability (especially in regard to NATO enlargement) to adapt Cold War alliance patterns to the needs of the post-Soviet era. The 'borderless threats' agenda incorporated both the concerns of meat-eaters (notably the threat of international terrorism) and of plant-eaters (notably regarding environmental issues). The chapter concludes with discussion of second term remilitarisation.

NATO enlargement

Any assessment of Clinton's record in enlarging and adapting the NATO must begin with an appreciation of the existential crisis faced by NATO in the early 1990s. As an anti-Soviet defence organisation, NATO seemed to many commentators (as Republican Congressman John Lander of Georgia put it in 1996) to have 'expired in 1989'.[3] Neo-conservative intellectual Irving Kristol described NATO in 1995 as an 'organization without a mission, a relic of the Cold War'.[4]

The 1990s debate over NATO was inextricably entangled with the policy towards Russia, discussed in Chapter 6. Moscow's attitudes towards the possible expansion of NATO were usually presumed to be very hostile, but were actually quite difficult to read. Boris Yeltsin in August 1993 publicly accepted Poland's right one day to join the alliance. Strobe Talbott mused that perhaps the Russian leader 'simply didn't share other Russians' visceral opposition to the idea of Central Europeans joining the alliance'. In September 1994, Yeltsin seemed to accept President Clinton's promise to frame US policy towards NATO in terms of 'no surprises, no rush and no exclusion' of Russia itself. Yet, only three months later in Budapest, Yeltsin gave very public voice to his view that Washington's handling of NATO expansion was indeed harming Russian security, threatening to plunge post-Cold War Europe into 'cold peace'.[5]

Clinton's commitment to expanding NATO raised major risks. The dangers of over-hasty expansion were graphically described by none other than George Kennan. The father of containment described NATO enlargement in November 1996 as a 'strategic blunder of potentially epic proportions'. Clinton himself had doubts, according to Strobe Talbott, not about the desirability of expansion, but about 'the feasibility of reconciling it with the integration of Russia'.[6] It will be useful here to illustrate the arguments for and against expansion.

The case for proceeding swiftly with NATO expansion was made at the start of the Clinton administration by Lynn Davis and Sam Lewis (respectively, Undersecretary for International Security and Policy Planning Chief at the State Department). They advised Warren Christopher in August 1993 that delay would reinforce 'the growing perception that the Alliance is only marginally involved in addressing Europe's new security problems'. Prevarication would stimulate disillusionment with democracy in East and Central Europe: 'This mood could trigger new instability ... with dangerous ripple effects across the continent.'[7] These arguments were elaborated in an influential 1993 *Foreign Affairs* piece, co-authored by Ronald Asmus.[8] (Asmus, NATO specialist at the California-based RAND think-tank, emerged as a key bureaucratic player; he was appointed as consultant to Talbott in 1996, prior to his formal move to the State Department.) For Al Gore, speaking in January 1994, shortly after the nationalist advances in Russian elections, the 'security of the states that lie between Western Europe and Russia affects the security of America'. These states must not 'again be rendered pieces of a buffer zone prize to be argued over by others'.[9] Strobe Talbott later recorded his sympathy for Czech, Polish and Hungarian arguments that NATO had *already* expanded to embrace East Germany. Central Europeans had suffered in the Cold

War as much as East Germans: 'To exclude them from NATO on the grounds that Moscow would object' would amount to 'grotesque double jeopardy'.[10] Tony Lake declared in 1996: 'NATO can do for Europe's East what it did 50 years ago for Europe's West: prevent a return to local rivalries, strengthen democracy ... and provide the conditions in which market economies can flourish.'[11] For Talbott in 1997, commitment to expansion was a natural corollary of Clinton's acceptance that NATO would survive the end of the Cold War. NATO simply *had* to adapt. It was 'the anchor' of America's commitment to Europe. Adaptation of what already existed was 'easier and cheaper' – as well as more rational – than attempting to build new structures.[12] Madeleine Albright argued in 1998 that neither Moscow nor Washington should treat 'European politics as a zero-sum game'.[13] Denial of 'NATO protection' would leave Central Europe in 'political limbo', encouraging unpredictable alliances and political violence.[14] Above all, as Clinton emphasised in his 1997 West Point graduation address, enlargement would 'help secure the historic gains of democracy', erasing 'the artificial line in Europe that Stalin drew'.[15]

The anti-expansion case focused, of course, on Russia. In May 1995, some 15 retired diplomats lobbied Warren Christopher, arguing that Russia would become convinced 'that the United States is attempting to isolate, encircle and subordinate them'.[16] In this analysis, expansion would simply encourage extreme Russian nationalism. Expansion would be costly and would spread the alliance too thinly. A *NYT* editorial in May 1995 argued that NATO extension 'would unwisely commit American troops in advance to defend countries, with nuclear weapons if necessary, where no vital American security interests may be involved'.[17] Opposition was evident across the political spectrum. From the libertarian right, Amos Perlmutter and Ted Carpenter quoted congressional, RAND Corporation and Pentagon forecasts to drive home the enormous anticipated monetary cost of expansion. The new security commitments amounted to a bluff which Russia 'might someday be tempted to call'.[18] For Alvin Rubinstein, the whole enterprise was linked to nothing more high-minded than Clinton's 'bid for votes' in American states 'with strong cultural, ethnic, and religious ties to Central and Eastern Europe', in the context of the 1996 presidential election.[19] Several anti-expansionists made the point that moving NATO eastwards would make arms control much harder. Russian ratification of START III would become that much more remote. Some commentators argued that Moscow had a right to feel betrayed by the breaking of the informal assurances given by the Bush41 team on NATO expansion.[20] Democrat Senator Patrick Leahy of Vermont foresaw young Americans being sent to war 'to protect a couple of countries most Americans haven't heard of'.[21] The cost of expansion would endanger the post-Cold War 'peace dividend'. Anti-expansionists also pointed to divisions between the US and its Western European allies over the issue. Was it really worth endangering the cooperative basis of the world's most successful alliance – all for the prospect of unrealistic continental defence commitments?

The extended public debates over NATO expansion involved defenders of the policy in efforts to rebut these various fears. During the 1997–98 congressional debates, for example, the administration challenged the costings provided by the Congressional Budget Office and RAND, and revised downwards Pentagon estimates. By mid-1997, the administration was estimating the cost of admitting three new NATO members at $35 billion by 2010, compared to the 61 billion estimated by the Congressional Budget Office, and the 42 billion RAND figure.[22] The White House also challenged the common view that budget-cutting Western Europeans would manage to avoid paying their due share. Regarding the wider issues of the 'Russia problem' and of American over-commitment, the administration fell back on the argument that boldness would overcome fear. Russian reform was portrayed as a complex process, whose vagaries and uncertainties should not be allowed to impede the necessity of NATO expansion.[23] Far from inviting the Western Europeans to shirk their spending commitments, demonstration of the US commitment would put their governments on the spot. Warren Christopher argued in 1994: 'Fortifying the European pillar of the alliance contributes to European stability and to transatlantic burden-sharing.'[24]

Let us briefly consider the convoluted history of the expansion proposals under Clinton. The Bush41 legacy in this area was confused. The six Warsaw Pact countries – Bulgaria, Czechoslovakia, Hungary, Poland, Romania, and the Soviet Union (as it still was) – were invited to open regular diplomatic contacts with NATO at the London summit of 1990. By 1992, Defense Secretary Richard Cheney was being reported as favouring the expansion of NATO to Russia's borders. During Clinton's first year, as we have seen, elements within the State Department promoted the cause enthusiastically, while the Pentagon remained profoundly sceptical. Among the allies, London expressed concern about diluting NATO; while Paris favoured the pursuit of enhanced European security through revived European, rather than transatlantic, institutions. Germany made no secret of its desire to have Poland, rather than itself, as NATO's easternmost extension.[25]

Washington's preparation for the January 1994 NATO summit in Brussels saw the emergence of the 'Partnership for Peace' (PfP) proposal, essentially a compromise between State and the Pentagon. PfP involved the cooperation of Russia and several Central European and Central Asian states in NATO activities, though without membership or security guarantees. When PfP was launched in Brussels, Polish leader Lech Walesa dubbed it the 'programme for prevarication'. Clinton announced that enlargement was not a 'whether', but a 'when' question.[26] By mid-1994, Clinton was making it clear that PfP was part of the enlargement agenda, rather than an end in itself.

September 1994 saw the appointment of Richard Holbrooke as European policy chief at State. Holbrooke drew on arguments made by Helmut Kohl, the German Chancellor, in favour of enlargement. Holbrooke, according to James Goldgeier, was now expansion's 'enforcer'.[27] In the White House, Tony Lake was now strongly in favour of the policy, as was Al Gore. Talbott had initial doubts, but was developing a pro-expansionist case by early 1995. NSC staffers such as Alexander Vershbow worked in earnest to further the agenda. On Capitol Hill, the Republican upsurge actually worked in their favour. In February 1995, the House of Representatives passed, 241–81, the NATO Expansion Act. Part of the Contract with America, the Act directed Clinton to recommend the admittance of Poland, Hungary, Slovakia and the Czech Republic. Meanwhile, Defense Secretary William Perry laid out the Pentagon's conditions for eligibility. These became the 'Perry principles', involving commitments to democracy and market economies, secure borders, civilian control of the military, and moves towards doctrinal and operational defence compatibility with NATO. These principles were, in effect, adopted by NATO in September 1995, four months after Russia's dramatic accession to the PfP.

Clinton, now irrevocably committed to enlargement, was also very concerned about the domestic pressures on Yeltsin, conveying his worries to British Prime Minister John Major. As for the Western Europeans: 'They're probably sympathetic to some of the arguments they're hearing from the Russians.' They were concerned that 'I'm being driven by the Polish-American vote in 1996 and the Republicans just aggravate that calculus'.[28] Pressure from the US pro-expansionist ethnic lobbies was certainly part of the evolving dynamic. The Polish American Congress issued a statement in October 1995 to the effect that its supporters – the 19 million or so Americans with roots in Central Europe – would not tolerate endless dithering over the expansion issue.[29] Many of Clinton's most enthusiastic pro-expansion speeches were delivered in cities with large Polish- or Hungarian-American populations. By the same token, as Newt Gingrich later acknowledged, NATO expansion was included in the Republicans' Contract with America for 'political' as well as for 'foreign policy and ideological reasons'.[30] The pro-expansionist ethnic constituency was strong in Midwest 'battleground' states, as well as among swinging 'Reagan Democrats'. The GOP, as well as Clinton, had every reason to woo both groups. Republican attitudes towards NATO expansion were actually extremely complex, illustrating the extraordinarily febrile nature of post-Cold War domestic position-taking on foreign policy. Senior Republicans such as Brent Scowcroft tended to accept at least elements of the Kennan case against enlargement. NATO widening was also opposed by the neo-isolationist wing of the party, led by Pat Buchanan. For the Gingrichite GOP revolutionaries, however, expansion was a key part of their call to arms. Clinton's steadily solid support for the cause was also, at least at one level, part of his complex response to the Republican challenge.

Yeltsin continued to deliver public denunciations of the Clinton policy on NATO. Compromises by NATO in 1996–97, particularly in setting new country-by-country ceilings for NATO tank and troop deployment, went some way to meeting Russian demands. NATO leaders also denied any intention to deploy nuclear weapons on the territory of any new member. The thrust of this compromise strategy had its origin in a June 1996 paper, 'NATO Enlargement Game Plan', written by Tony Lake. Central to this initiative, which was aimed at Western European capitals almost as much as at Moscow, was the idea of selling enlargement as 'adaptation'. Lake saw the Western Europeans as concerned particularly with NATO mission clarification, an important aspect of his adaptation theme. 'Adaptation' as a selling theme would also, it was hoped, take 'some of the sting' from Russia's hostility, by demonstrating 'that NATO has indeed been transformed from its Cold War structure and is, in fact, becoming increasingly "European" and focused on new missions such as peacekeeping and crisis management'.[31]

Madeleine Albright's appointment as Secretary of State gave new prominence to a convinced pro-expansionist, albeit one who was initially portrayed in Moscow as an inveterate Cold Warrior. Also affecting the international climate in 1996–97 was the backwash from the Dayton Agreement on Bosnia. When Clinton and Yeltsin met in Helsinki in March 1997, the former cited Dayton and US–Russian cooperation in the Balkans as part of the case for Moscow accepting a package which included a new NATO–Russia joint council, as well as alliance enlargement. Bosnia, argued Clinton, was the worst conflict in Europe since 1945, and one which Europeans alone could not solve. What if a new crisis emerged?[32] Warren Christopher later recalled his pre-1995 efforts to 'delink Bosnia from NATO'. After Dayton, however, Bosnia became 'a vital factor' in Russian acceptance of NATO expansion and of the NATO–Russia Founding Act, setting up the joint council.[33] At Helsinki, Yeltsin declared his willingness to support the Founding Act as a way to 'minimize the negative consequences for Russia' of enlargement.[34] Clinton attended the Helsinki meeting on crutches and in a wheelchair, having injured himself in a fall at the house of golfer Greg Norman. The president's condition evoked memories of Franklin Roosevelt: ironic memories in view of the Central Europeans' often articulated worry that the US might abandon the push for enlargement and settle for 'another Yalta'. As it was, Russia even failed to achieve a guarantee in the Founding Act that nuclear weapons would not be placed on the territory of the new members. Clinton seems to have made it very clear to Yeltsin that the Baltic states of Estonia, Latvia and Lithuania would certainly not be in the first batch of new members.[35] Clinton's spectacular Helsinki success greatly strengthened his hand, both with the US Senate in the context of the forthcoming ratification debate, and with the Western Europeans. Among the latter, only the UK and Germany clearly supported America's view that membership invitations should first be sent out to Hungary, Poland and the Czech Republic. After Helsinki, the US preference proved impossible to resist[36].

The ratification debate in the Senate stalled to some extent before the Madrid NATO meeting in July 1997. Nevertheless, Jeremy Rosner, who maintained that failure to ratify would equal Woodrow Wilson's humiliation in 1919 over the Treaty of Versailles, had already set up a very effective liaison operation to push for Senate votes. Rosner saw Jesse Helms as the Henry Cabot Lodge of 1997, and set out to sell ratification to the chair of the Senate Foreign Relations Committee as a way to contain Russia. Concern for Senate support, in fact, had been built into the administration's negotiating strategy since 1994. A Senate NATO Observers Group (SNOG) included leading Republicans; it attended the crucial negotiating sessions, including the Helsinki meeting.[37]

The Madrid summit confirmed the accession arrangements for the three candidate members, drawing on a revised version of the Perry principles. Following Madrid, Rosner refined his liaison strategy, first consolidating support among 'internationalist' Democrats and Republicans, and then moving out to the anti-expansion extremes. The final Senate majority (80–19, on 30 April 1998, with 45 Republicans and 35 Democrats supporting expansion) was an historic victory for Clinton, even more convincing than the 1993 NAFTA ratification. However, the victory margin did not reflect the heat of the legislative battle. The denoument was complicated by two wrecking amendments. One, from Senator John Warner (Virginia Republican), would have significantly delayed the accessions; the other, from Senator John Ashcroft (Missouri Republican), sought to limit any future out-of-area action. Both amendments were defeated, though Warner's only by a 59–41 margin. Secretary Albright reassured Democratic Senators immediately before the vote that wider US–Russian problems, notably regarding prospects for arms control, could not be laid at the door of NATO enlargement: 'That's like blaming everything on El Nino.'[38]

The formal welcoming of the three new NATO members at the Washington summit in 1999 was rather overshadowed by debates about who was next in line. The Clinton administration was sensitive to the charge that, in admitting Hungary, Poland and the Czech Republic, NATO was creating new divisions, new exclusions. Washington made it clear that membership was a possibility for all countries in Europe. The particular issue of possible Russian membership was clearly a nettle to be grasped by future leaders; Clinton and Sandy Berger, however, lost no opportunity to point out that the 'open door' policy applied to the former USSR. Negotiations with Ukraine began in 1997. In July 1997, Berger declared: 'The first shall not be the last.'[39] Six months later, he announced that his forebears came from Riga, and that he was the first Baltic-American NSA. A Baltic–US charter was signed in January 1998, with Clinton promising that he would work towards the day when the Baltic states could 'walk through' NATO's door.[40] Such a statement virtually amounted to a public affirmation of Russia's geopolitical weakness.

The final phase of Clinton's presidency saw little formal movement on NATO's 'open doors', beyond the adoption at the 1999 Washington summit of a new membership action plan, designed to assist candidates to meet the requirements of the updated Perry principles. The 2000 'Community of Democracies' conference, organised by Madeleine Albright and held in Warsaw, was designed firmly to tie in NATO enlargement to wider democratisation agendas, and even to set the ball rolling for new global alliance patterns. Nevertheless, after 1997, despite developments in the Balkans, Clinton actually tended to emphasise NATO mission continuity as much as change and even adaptation. Shortly before the ratification vote, for example, he announced, with some disingenuousness: 'NATO's core mission will remain the same – the defense of the territory of its members.'[41] As well as looking to the Senate, Clinton was, in effect, celebrating one of the great achievements of his presidential leadership: the re-making of the European Cold War alliance.

Alliance politics

NATO enlargement was a positive achievement for Clinton's handling of alliance politics. As we saw in Chapter 2, elsewhere the second term witnessed a moving away from cooperative multilateralism: not a rejection of international cooperation and stable alliances, but an enhanced willingness – in a climate set by the Republican Congress and by undisputed American hegemonism – to go it alone. This was seen most obviously in Kosovo, where the confusions of the air campaign confirmed the preference of sections of the US military for (as far as possible) working without allies,[42] and in the attacks on Iraq, Sudan and Afghanistan. Even in the first term, the commitment to multilateralism was by no means absolute. In 1993, Warren Christopher described multilateralism as 'one of the many tools at our disposal'.[43] The administration was certainly always prepared to take unilateral action in trade policy, notably in imposing sanctions on Japan in market access disputes. Clinton's final signing (hours before the 31 December 2000 deadline) of the treaty to set up the new International Criminal Court (ICC) illustrated some of the complexity of his second term stance on international cooperation.

The White House originally supported the ICC treaty, drafted in 1998 in order to replace the temporary tribunals which dealt with genocidal crime in the Balkans and Rwanda. The US, however, objected to the court's proposed independence from the UN Security Council where, of course, the US had the power of veto. The American case was that, as the world's last-resort guarantor of security, the US could not be subject to the same conditions as other nations. The Pentagon regarded the treaty as incompatible with US participation in UN peace-keeping. Clinton's signing of the treaty excited the condemnation of Jesse Helms, who committed himself to opposing the ICC, thereby 'protecting American men and women in uniform from the jurisdiction of this kangaroo court'.[44] Yet Clinton's own signing statement made it clear that he was 'not abandoning our concerns about significant flaws in the Treaty'.[45] Signing the treaty, on the one hand, kept the ICC alive as a credible institution; it also, however, allowed the US to influence its development – notably towards the incorporation of an exemption for states that had not ratified the treaty. As *The Economist* noted, the prospects of ratification in the foreseeable future were zero; although, to be fair to Clinton, the dóor to eventual ratification was kept open.[46]

As with the ICC, so with the UN. Just a few weeks before Clinton left the White House, Richard Holbrooke (appointed as Ambassador to the UN in 1999) worked out a deal with Jesse Helms to commence repayment of America's $1 billion back-dues in return for reform of the UN organisational structure. Holbrooke promised Helms that he would continue to push for significant reductions in America's share of the UN budget, particularly in regard to peace-keeping (in the latter case, from 31 to 25 per cent). Part of the wooing of Helms involved arranging for him to speak directly to the Security Council. Joe Biden, ranking Democrat on Helms' Foreign Relations Committee was reported as saying: 'Just as only Nixon could go to China, only Helms could fix the UN.'[47] Clinton joked that making a deal with Helms 'took Dick longer than making peace in Bosnia'.[48]

Holbrooke's eleventh-hour peace of New York could not extinguish the tensions of the 1990s, nor (as with Clinton's signing of the ICC treaty) disguise the fact that a rough road for US–UN relations lay ahead under the incoming Bush43 administration. Difficulties in America's relationship with the organisation to which it played host were evident, as we have seen, in the peace-keeping operations of the first term. PDD 25 continued, during the second term, to be described by the administration as simple 'common sense': in the words of Karl Inderfurth (deputy to Bill Richardson, Clinton's ambassador to the UN between 1996 and 1999), PDD 25 merely recognised that the Security Council 'had to be far more rigorous in its analysis and examination of which missions it could undertake and what it had to know before authorizing them'.[49] The US continued to participate in peace-keeping operations, though scarcely in huge numbers. A State Department survey of April 1997 recorded the largest deployment of US military personnel directly under the aegis of the UN as the 498 troops in Macedonia.[50] The issue of the back-dues was a running sore. Richardson, whose authority as UN ambassador was severely undercut by his difficult relationship with Albright, blamed America's loss of 'leverage on issues important to us' on the refusal of the Republican Congress to pay the dues.[51] Boutros Boutros-Ghali (UN Secretary General, whose bid for a second term was vetoed by the US in 1996) recalled Clinton as telling him of 'his strong belief that the United States should pay its bills to the United Nations in full and on time'.[52] The problem was that the pre-1995 Democratic Congress had also been reluctant to pay. Clinton fairly consistently bemoaned this state of national indebtedness, but was clearly also keen (to use Al Gore's phrase) to squeeze lemonade from the lemon of Republican intransigence. Much nationalist GOP hostility to the UN was little more than grandstanding prejudice. That the organisation suffered from incoherence, corruption and risible self-righteousness, however, could scarcely be denied. The Republican complaints of over-assessment were not entirely wide of the mark. In 1999, Joseph Connor, UN Undersecretary for Management, compared the UN to Los Angeles, 'a collection of suburbs pretending to be a city'. The UN was 'a collection of funds and programs pretending to be an organization'.[53] Clinton's own commitment to the UN was not always convincing. To many at the UN, his attitude seemed menacing. One anonymous UN diplomat remarked at the time of the Boutros-Ghali veto: 'We remember what happened to the League of Nations without the Americans.'[54] Even Joseph Connor, who effectively owed his UN appointment to Warren Christopher, argued that Boutros-Ghali was actually a friend of reform.[55] Kofi Annan, Boutros Boutros-Ghali's successor as Secretary General, complained of the 'constant harassment of reform, reform, reform'.[56] Yet Clinton's goal of combining a return to financial rectitude with the securing of organisational reform was, in the circumstances, a reasonable one. The US under Clinton was prominent, at least in 1999–2000, in promoting the issue of HIV/AIDS funding in Africa and even secured a measure of reform, notably in the establishment of the UN Office of Internal Oversight.[57]

In all its alliance commitments, especially in Clinton's second term, the US struggled to reconcile the impulses of hegemony with the duties of a cooperative ally. The truth was that, by the beginning of the second term, the sheer power differential between the US and all its various individual allies was so clear and obvious that tensions became inevitable. Against this background, the administration can be credited with the forging of a new security relationship in the Far East. Relations with Japan were often tricky. In 1998, former Japanese Prime Minister Morihiro Hosokawa complained in the pages of FA that Americans tended to see 'the presence of US troops in Japan as a gracious favour meant to underpin Japan's security'.[58] The continued presence of 47,000 US troops in Okinawa, was endangered by the rape of a Japanese girl by American soldiers in 1995. Tensions over Japan's trade surplus, and, in the second term, over Tokyo's stubbornness (from the American viewpoint) in reforming its banking system were also apparent. During a radio address in May 1995, Clinton announced that 'when it comes to selling cars and auto parts to Japan, we are hitting a brick wall'.[59] Despite all this, a significant second term achievement for the administration was the creation of a new regional security order, based on US–Japanese–South Korean cooperation. The transcendence of economic issues by security ones was emblematic of the second term, though it derived from first term dialogue between Tony Lake and Japanese Foreign Minister Ikeda Yukihiko, and was cemented during Clinton's Japanese visit of April 1996. The triangular alliance between Washington, Seoul and Tokyo rested on America's military leverage and pressure to forget old rivalries in the (largely unstated) mutual interest of containing China.[60] The Clinton years also saw a new closeness to Australia, an alliance which was to grow in significance under Bush43. In line with the spirit of the 1997 PDD 56 on humanitarian intervention (essentially an updated version of PDD 25), the US gave logistical support to the Australian-led 1999 peace-keeping effort in East Timor, following the Indonesian invasion.

In South Asia, the administration seemed, prior to the 1998 Pakistani and Indian nuclear tests, keen to build a parallel three-way security relationship, similarly aimed at transcending old enmities and balancing China. Visiting Islamabad in 1995, William Perry advocated new US–Pakistan security cooperation, effectively departing from the Bush41 legacy of distrust regarding Pakistan's relationship with China, as well as Islamabad's nuclear ambitions and involvement in the Kashmir dispute with India.[61] In India also, the governments of the 1990s, recognising the shift in international conditions, sought good relations with the US, in the process backing away from the Nehru non-alignment tradition. The US also saw India, whose trade balance with the US changed dramatically in the 1990s, as a rising economic power. The 1998 tests saw the imposition of sanctions on both countries, followed by a swift American coming to terms with the new realities. Indian Prime Minister Atal Bahari Vajpayee declared at the UN, following the tests, that India and the US were 'natural allies'.[62] Some observers felt that the Indian test had actually cleared the air in terms of the bilateral Washington–New Delhi relationship. In the last year of his presidency, Clinton seemed firmly to lean to an alliance with democratic and economically emergent India, rather than with Pakistan, which suffered a military coup in 1999. On a trip to South Asia in March 2000, Clinton spent five days in India and five hours in Pakistan, a destination which the US secret service considered too dangerous for an American president to visit. Reflecting what had become the dominant US regional preoccupation by this time, Clinton warned General Parvez Musharraf to rein in terrorist groups in Kashmir and to cooperate with the US over al Qaeda.[63]

In Latin America, the end of the Cold War had (despite the continuation of the Cuban regime) removed the anti-communist purpose from the US-led regional organisation, the Organization of American States (OAS). In a sense, the OAS was experiencing an existential crisis parallel to NATO's. Clinton's attempt to fill the existential void with talk of institutionalised hemispheric free trade was rather undercut by the stalling of credible efforts to extend NAFTA southwards. The 'Washington consensus' – the free market recipe for Latin America's future – still held. However, the Clinton priorities shifted increasingly towards issues of drug production. Countries from Mexico to Colombia were subjected to an annual 'certification' process by Congress: the issuing of a bill-of-health on drug trafficking, giving the president authority to impose sanctions on miscreants. The process had more than a whiff of extraterritoriality, involving demands for change in areas such as extradition and domestic criminal codes. *The Economist* commented in 1997: 'That a big country can arm-twist small ones is a fact of life; codified, public display of it ought not to be.'[64] In 1993, the Pentagon announced a shift in approach to illegal drug importation: away from interception, and towards direct aid for Latin American countries in policing drug trafficking.[65] By far the most controversial aspect of this policy related to Colombia, a country identified by Secretary Albright (along with Nigeria, Indonesia and Ukraine) as especially deserving of American support: 'Nothing would do more for the health of democracy in Latin America ... than the restoration of stability in Colombia, a country ravaged by ruthless guerrillas, and drug traffickers.'[66] Between 1998 and 2000, Clinton successfully requested more than $1 billion from Congress to aid President Andres Pastrana in his operations against the guerrilla forces who controlled about one-third of Colombian territory. In 1999, in a UN speech, Pastrana asked for $3.5 billion over the next three years, the bulk of which would inevitably come from the US; yet he also distanced himself from what journalist Tim Golden described as 'the American perception that the most serious new turn in Colombia's troubles is the growing alliance between drug producers in the south and the leftist guerrillas there who tax the producers' crops or protect their laboratories or fields.'[67] Despite efforts led by Democratic Senator Patrick Leahy to have human rights standards written into the legislation, the majority of the US 'Plan Colombia' aid went to the Colombian military with few conditions attached.[68]

Even the briefest catalogue of US–Western European tensions and differences during the 1990s gives an impression of a transatlantic alliance in flux, if not in extreme crisis. Bosnian policy famously stimulated transatlantic splits on the scale of the Suez crisis.[69] Disputes over who exactly should join the newly expanding NATO – various Western European capitals favoured Romania and Slovenia – erupted at summit meetings.[70] In June 1997, French President Jacques Chirac announced that Washington was displaying 'a certain tendency towards hegemony' within NATO.[71] The French Foreign Minister Hubert Vedrine's term, 'hyperpuissance' – perhaps best translated as 'America is too powerful by half' – became common European currency even before the election of George W. Bush.[72] Trade disputes between the US and the EU continued their rising dynamic from the 1980s; a detailed study of 1996 concluded that most of them were 'rooted not in aggressive nationalist behaviour ... but in different approaches to economic, industrial, agricultural, social and trade policies that are as old as the US–EC relationship itself'.[73] President Clinton and Warren Christopher repeatedly insisted that they supported European integration more firmly than any US administration since that of John Kennedy. The Cold War American preoccupation with the supremacy of NATO's integrated structure seemed in the mid-1990s to have disappeared, with the Clintonites more ready than the Bush41 team to accept the concept of the 'European defence identity'.[74] In December 1995, France announced that it wished to move to rejoin NATO's military structure. Yet, especially towards the end of Clinton's presidency, tensions over European defence integration seemed to point in a contrary direction. In December 2000, Defense Secretary William Cohen warned against 'any element of using the (EU) force structure to simply set up a competing headquarters ... then NATO could become a relic'.[75] Several years on from the end of the Cold War, proposals for new transatlantic 'architecture' still proliferated.[76] The US–UK 'special relationship' in some respects (such as London's support for actions against Iraq) seemed to thrive. Yet it also stuttered badly, at least in the first Clinton term, over Irish and Balkans issues.[77]

Even as American diplomats affirmed that America was a European power, their European equivalents voiced the view that the US was becoming primarily a Pacific-oriented nation that would, at least in the medium-term, quit Europe.[78] Perhaps, above all – and rather extraordinarily, given Clinton's subsequent popularity as the anti-Bush president who 'spoke European' – it often appeared in the 1990s that Americans and Western Europeans actually did not like each other very much. Martin Walker wrote in 2000 (again, it must be emphasised *before* the election of George W.) that Western Europe was 'a place where more and more people live and work and eat and dress and relax like Americans, while exercising considerable ingenuity in finding new complaints about the United States'.[79] These various tensions were linked by commentators to the end of the Soviet threat and to the 'new nationalist' American mood that Clinton apparently despised, but also to some degree reflected.[80] The simultaneous charges laid at America's door – that Washington was both imperialist *and* uncommitted to Europe – were contradictory. They amounted to little more than the scarcely deniable assertion that Washington wanted European engagement on terms favourable to Washington. The upshot of the 1990s, of course, was that the transatlantic alliance continued in the revived form of an enlarged NATO. Clinton's efforts to sustain the transatlantic alliance, in an era of muted and ambiguous external threat, broadly succeeded in achieving a relationship of bickering rather than divorce.[81] With the award of the Charlemagne Prize in 2000, Clinton even began his second life as an honorary European.

Following the Somalian intervention and the issuance of PDD 25, the Clinton administration looked to regional organisations on the continent (under the general auspices of the UN) to take on the peace-keeping burden.[82] The commitment to American allies in sub-Saharan Africa was also diminished in the post-1994 legislative drive to cut foreign aid. Senator Patrick Leahy pointed out in 1998 that the whole of sub-Saharan Africa received less in American aid than either Egypt or Israel.[83] Clinton's second term, however, did see some African re-engagement, much of it associated with Susan Rice, who had replaced George Moose as the leading Africanist at State. Rice, formerly on the NSC, argued for re-engagement on the grounds that Africa was being strangely left out of the administration's vision for globalised capitalist democracy, and that there must be no more standing aside from regional genocide.[84] The second term saw a more sustained US attempt to work with allies, such as Malawi and Senegal, to defuse conflict. There was a rather botched effort, involving Jesse Jackson, to intervene diplomatically in the conflict in Sierra Leone. PDD 25 still set the parameters, however, and civil wars in Angola, the Democratic Republic of the Congo – as well as the war between Ethiopia and Eritrea, both US allies – continued with little prospect of even limited US intervention. (This, of course, at the very time of the intervention in Kosovo.)[85]

In March 1998, the Clintons visited sub-Saharan Africa. Hillary rhetorically invited Africa into the world of capitalist democracy, declaring in Kampala that 'democracies, free market economies and civil societies are all taking root'.[86] Bill spoke in Cape Town, where he said that the US and South Africa were united in their vision of 'real multi-racial democracy'.[87] Nelson Mandela, for his part, apparently criticised Clinton for his policies towards Cuba, Iran and Libya.[88] Following his African visit, Bill Clinton submitted substantial requests for African AIDS relief to Congress, and in 2000 gained passage of the Africa Growth and Opportunity Act, which significantly stimulated African trade.[89]

Borderless threats: international terrorism

The notion that Clinton was a president who ignored the threat of international terrorism is absurd. One of the tasks of the staff of the 9/11 Commission, set up in 2002 to investigate the circumstances of the 11 September 2001 terrorist attacks, was to compare the public addresses of Clinton on the terrorist threat (primarily from al Qaeda) with those of Bush43. They found numerous instances of Clinton discussing the threat publicly, while Bush referred to it less frequently (in the months leading up to 9/11), and then usually in the context of direct state terrorism and the need to act against North Korea, Iran and Iraq. According to journalist Philip Shenon, evidence of this Clinton–Bush imbalance was removed from the final report at the insistence of Philip Zelikow, executive director of the Commission staff, on the grounds that Bush had not had time to pronounce on terrorism. Staffer Alexis Albion did manage to smuggle in a reference to Clinton's terrorism warnings in a footnote to chapter six of the Commission report.[90]

Terrorism of various kinds, of course, was forced on the national agenda by (among many other events) the 1993 World Trade Center bombing, the 1995 Oklahoma City bombing (undertaken by American anti-federal government fanatic Timothy McVeigh), the 1996 Khobar attack (a huge explosion outside US military facilities in Saudi Arabia), the bombing in 1998 of US embassies in Kenya and Tanzania, and the October 2000 attack on the USS *Cole* in waters off Yemen. (The *Cole* had been involved in cruise missile attacks on an al Qaeda base in Afghanistan in 1998.) The assassination of Israeli leader Yitzhak Rabin in November 1995 also reminded America of the deadly and destabilising nature of terror in the Middle East.

Clinton referred to the international terrorist threat in every one of his State of the Union addresses. Following the 1995 State of the Union address, Clinton introduced an omnibus counterterrorism measure, creating new federal jurisdictions in regard to matters such as terrorist funding. He declared a state of national emergency in regard to 'foreign organizations that threaten to use violence to disrupt the Middle East peace process', with consequent enhancement of federal authority. On the 5 August 1996, the president spoke at George Washington University in DC, where he detailed various foiled terrorist plots. On the second anniversary, in March 1997, of the sarin gas attack on the Tokyo subway, he enlarged on international terrorist dangers, urging the US Senate to ratify the CWC. In July 1998, the president issued PDD 67 on 'counterterrorism and the protection of the homeland'. The directive announced: 'Because of our military superiority, potential enemies, be they nations or terrorist groups ... are increasingly likely to attack us in unconventional ways ... to exploit vulnerabilities against civilians.' In March 1999, Clinton and Gore unveiled new measures 'to provide firefighters and other "first responders" with the tools they need to defend the American people against terrorist attacks using chemical and biological weapons'. In June 1999, Clinton nominated Michael Sheehan as 'Co-ordinator for Counterterrorism' with ambassadorial rank. Five months later, Clinton identified in a Third Way summit speech, delivered in Italy, 'the biggest problems to our security' as coming from 'the enemies of the nation-state, from terrorists and drug runners and organized criminals' who were now able to exploit the machinery of globalisation, including the internet. In October 2000, he submitted to the Senate a new international convention on the financing of terrorism. In February 1999, CIA chief George Tenet told the Senate Armed Services Committee in open testimony that 'we are concerned that one or more of bin Laden's attacks could occur at any time'.[91]

The Clinton administration was very aware of the terrorist threat, including the developing threat from al Qaeda. President Clinton gave very frequent public expression to his fears, began the federal commitment to homeland security and attempted (admittedly without much apparent success) to coordinate anti-terrorist purpose in the Federal Bureau of Investigation (FBI) and the CIA. Richard Clarke, NSC counterterrorism specialist at this time, concluded that President Clinton 'identified terrorism as the major post-Cold War threat' and acted to improve counterterrorism. He also 'quelled anti-American terrorism by Iraq and Iran and defeated an al Qaeda attempt to dominate Bosnia'. Yet Clinton 'weakened by continued political attack, could not get the CIA, the Pentagon, and the FBI to act sufficiently'. According to Clarke, Clinton 'approved every (anti-terrorist) snatch' that he was asked to review.⁹² Though initially dismissed as a 'Gucci terrorist' with more money than menace, Osama bin Laden was, by the time of the 1993 World Trade Center bombing, being taken very seriously. CIA operatives followed his efforts to buy a Russian nuclear warhead on the black market. In late 1995, Clinton issued an order, approved by the congressional intelligence committees, for the CIA to begin covert operations against bin Laden's network. Clinton repeatedly supported the mounting of anti-terror special forces operations, though he found the Pentagon very sceptical about their efficacy. The CIA also began its 'rendition' programmes, the transfer of foreign terrorist suspects to third countries, during the later 1990s: the post-9/11 War on Terror built on the Clinton experience. The 9/11 Commission recorded a meeting in December 2000 between Clinton and George W. Bush, the incoming president. Clinton informed the commission that he had told Bush: 'I think you will find that by far your biggest threat is Bin Laden and the al Qaeda.' Bush responded that 'he felt sure President Clinton had mentioned terrorism, but did not remember much being said about al Qaeda'. The final report concluded:

> Before 9/11, al Qaeda and its affiliates had killed fewer than 50 Americans, including the East Africa embassy bombings and the *Cole* attack. The US government took the threat seriously, but not in the sense of mustering anything like the kind of effort that would be gathered to confront an enemy of the first, second, or even third rank. The modest national effort exerted to contain Serbia and its depredations in the Balkans between 1995 and 1999, for example, was orders of magnitude larger than that devoted to al Qaeda.⁹³

The idea that Clinton was soft on terrorism is to some degree traceable to partisan politics – the view that this was an administration of counter-culturalist 'plant-eaters'. Clinton also told the 9/11 Commission that he deliberately used the name of Osama bin Laden rarely, precisely in order to avoid giving notoriety to the leader of al Qaeda. Sandy Berger's later attempt to steal documents from the National Archives dramatically illustrated the continuing concern of the Clintonites about accusations that they were sleeping on anti-terrorist duty; (Philip Shenon interpreted Berger's theft as an attempt to remove a 2000 report by Richard Clarke, whose views were liable to be misconstrued).⁹⁴ In Britain, negative views of Clinton's anti-terror policies are also linked to perceptions of his attitude towards the IRA. The important question, of course, is: how *effective* was Clinton's anti-terrorism?

Clinton clearly was not able, despite the programme of action instituted in June 1995 under PDD 39, adequately to coordinate foreign intelligence-gathering, homeland security and counterterrorism. The FBI and CIA did not work well together; a joint CIA–FBI intelligence team, set up on the 'zero line' of the Pakistan–Afghan border in 1998 floundered. Khalid al-Mihdhar, one of the 9/11 hijackers, was identified by the CIA following a January 2000 al Qaeda meeting in Malaysia; yet al-Mihdhar was not placed on the State Department's watch list of people denied entry to the US until 23 August 2001. Louis Freeh, head of the FBI, effectively refused to work with NSC staff in relation to the al Qaeda threat. Freeh's growing distrust of the White House reached huge and deeply counter-productive proportions; it was a problem which Clinton – largely because of his vulnerability to corruption and other charges – simply allowed to fester. Freeh was, nevertheless, correct to complain that the US alliance with the Gulf oil monarchies obstructed effective investigation of the Khobar Towers bombing and other terrorist activity emanating from Saudi Arabia. The CIA itself was in a condition of chronic existential crisis during the 1990s. Clinton's directives on terrorism tended merely to multiply and confuse the CIA's priorities, rather than clarify them. As George Tenet himself recalled, the Agency had no coordinated or viable anti-terror plan.[95]

Islamic terrorism was a phenomenon which operated on a bewildering array of fronts: Afghanistan, Bosnia, Chechnya, Egypt, Kashmir, Somalia, Sudan, among many others. Washington was often caught between the Scylla of ascribing too much organisational coherence to al Qaeda, and the Charybdis of ascribing too little. Clinton's view of bin Laden was clear: as he told the 9/11 investigators, 'I wanted to see him dead.'[96] However, the way to either 'snatch' or assassinate the al Qaeda leader seemed, at least after his move to Afghanistan (probably in early 1996), to lie either via the Afghanistan's Taliban or via Pakistan. A better mixture of diplomacy and coercive threat could probably have been applied to the Taliban. As we have seen, efforts were made to treat Pakistan as an ally; however, its intelligence services, which had effectively created the Taliban regime, were looking the other way.[97]

A 1998 memo from CIA chief George Tenet announced, 'We are at war'.[98] The most obvious expression of this war was the military action taken against Afghanistan and Sudan in August of the same year. When the Afghan attack failed to kill bin Laden, Clinton announced the doctrine that was to be taken up later by Bush43: 'Countries that persistently host terrorists have no right to be safe havens.' The US would take pre-emptive action against al Qaeda, particularly to prevent it acquiring 'chemical weapons and other dangerous weapons'.[99] The action against Afghanistan and Sudan was unilateral, but Clinton was punctilious in consulting Congress in preparation for the action. Sensitive intelligence was shared with Newt Gingrich, while both Gingrich and Trent Lott, Republican Leader in the Senate, were briefed by Sandy Berger on the evening preceding the strikes. Speaker Gingrich judged that they had been carried out 'in a methodical and professional way'.[100] Clinton's sharing of information – in stark contrast to Reagan's 1986 attack on Libya – was not only proper; it was designed to defuse accusations of using military action as a way of deflecting attention from the Lewinsky affair, to which Clinton had confessed only three days previously. The attacks drew forth some of the purplist of purple prose from British journalist Christopher Hitchens: 'Did then a dirtied blue dress from the Gap cause widows and orphans to set up grieving howls in the passes of Afghanistan, the outer precincts of Khartoum, and the wastes of Mesopotamia?'[101] Around 40 per cent of Americans suspected some connection between the scandal and the air strikes, yet Republicans in Congress more or less refrained from making this accusation.[102]

The Afghanistan assault seems to have been a rationally based, intelligence-led attack on a clear terrorist target. The Sudan attack, on a pharmaceutical plant believed to have been connected to bin Laden's pursuit of chemical weapons, was a disaster. As General Anthony Zinni put it, 'all we did was spread aspirin all over Khartoum'.[103] The failure of the 1998 attacks effectively took further military action, at least in the absence of a degree of intelligence accuracy which the Clinton administration simply did not have, off the agenda.

Borderless threats: the global environment

As in the case of international terrorism, Clinton cannot realistically be accused of ignoring or rhetorically downplaying the environmental issue. By the early 1990s, eco-awareness was an important part of the Democratic Party's spectrum of ideas. In his 1992 Earth Day address (delivered on 21 April), candidate Clinton had promised to follow an active environmental agenda, and be especially engaged on the subject of global warming. President Bush Senior's pretensions to be the 'environmental president' were ridiculed. It was not long, however, before the American press was reporting disagreements between Vice President Gore and Secretaries Lloyd Bentsen (Treasury) and Hazel O'Leary (Energy) over the former's support for environmental initiatives. Gore was apparently overruled on the proposed shutting down of a toxic waste incinerator in Ohio, while Interior Secretary Bruce Babbitt faced opposition from the White House to some of his conservationist stances on public land management. The *NYT* speculated about just how far Gore and Babbitt could 'steer the onetime friend of polluters in the Arkansas chicken industry to new heights of global stewardship'.[104] Ouch!

Clinton's 1993 Earth Day speech was widely interpreted as a victory for Gore. Clinton promised to sign the Convention on Biological Diversity, rejected by Bush. Clinton committed the US to 'reducing our emissions of greenhouse gasses to their 1990 levels by the year 2000'.[105] Clinton also made significant pro-environmental bureaucratic changes. Bush's Council on Competitiveness was abolished; (under the chairmanship of Vice President Dan Quayle, the Council had gained a reputation for pro-business conservatism on environmental issues). In June 1993, Al Gore addressed the UN Commission on Sustainable Development in New York, arguing for a new global determination to address problems ranging from ozone depletion to the destruction of the earth's forests: the latter were 'being destroyed at the rate of one football field's worth every second'.[106] In his 1994 State of the Union address, Clinton committed himself to new clean water legislation and to reforming the 'superfund'. A public/private initiative to improve polluted areas in the US, the superfund was indeed reborn. Clinton noted in his memoirs that he and Gore had succeeded in cleaning up 'three times as many Superfund sites as the Reagan and Bush (Senior) administrations combined'.[107]

Clinton's pledge to reduce emissions to 1990 levels by 2000 was, by international standards, quite modest, but was nevertheless a clear victory for Gore. It should also be borne in mind that the battle for emissions-reduction in the US, the world's leading economy and emitter of about one-quarter of global carbon dioxide emissions, was an inherently extremely difficult one for elected leaders to pursue. Clinton wooed the American biotech industry on behalf of the biological diversity convention, but failed to win ratification in the Senate.[108] Congress similarly rejected the presidential proposal for a new tax on the heat content of energy, effectively the main means whereby the emissions reduction target could be achieved. The Democratic Congress scrapped the energy tax as proposed in Clinton's first budget, replacing it with spending cuts and a rise in gasoline tax.

Early in 1997, and with one eye on the global warming negotiations due to begin in Kyoto in December, Clinton proposed a new emission-reduction plan. He now supported 'carbon trading', the buying up of 'credits' from industries that cut emissions even lower than required. His plan also allowed companies to accumulate credits by assisting developing economies to reduce emissions. Congratulating Clinton on his initiative, Gregg Easterbrook nevertheless noted that Clinton's plan 'would not have teeth until 2010', long after Clinton – and even a putative President Gore – had left office. Easterbrook proposed a new tax on the burning of fossil fuels, with other corporate taxes being reduced to offset the congressional backlash.[109] The US role at Kyoto was actually dramatic and, in some ways, hugely successful. The opening American bid was predictably lower than the EU's stated goal of a 15 per cent reduction, on 1990 levels, by 2010. The main difficulty for the US delegates was their commitment, deriving from legislative action in the Senate, to opposition to any deal which did not impose restrictions on developing countries. As talks deadlocked, Al Gore intervened to assist the chief American negotiator, Stuart Eizenstat. The ensuing agreement involved a US commitment to cut emissions by 7 per cent (from 1990 levels) by 2012, with only a fudged compromise on participation by China and India.[110]

Clinton defended the treaty as 'environmentally and economically sound' and as a valuable expression of the global will.[111] The January 1998 State of the Union address proposed new tax incentives for energy efficiency; later in 1998, Clinton devoted a national radio address to global warming.[112] Following the Kyoto agreement, the *NYT* reported that there were reasonable prospects for ratification, pointing out that Republican Senators like Olympia Snowe of Maine and John Chafee of Rhode Island were likely to back it.[113] Clinton linked the Kyoto agreement to his other pro-environment policies, such as (the successfully passed) clean water legislation. With Gingrich calling Kyoto an 'outrage', Clinton ridiculed those Republicans who declared that 'the sky is falling':

> Every time we've tried to improve the American environment in the last 25 or 30 years, somebody has predicted it would wreck the economy. And the air is cleaner, the water is cleaner, the food supply is safer, there are fewer toxic waste dumps. And the last time I checked, we had the lowest unemployment rate in 24 years.

Gore promised to work for 'meaningful participation' by China and India. The Republican leadership continued to condemn a treaty where, to quote Gingrich, 'approximately 134 countries were allowed to vote on a treaty by which they will not be bound'.[114] In the event, 'meaningful participation' by China and India was not secured, and the treaty never reached the Senate.

It is too easy to relate the history of Clinton's environmentalism as a tale simply of empty rhetoric and lost opportunities. Clinton could have fought harder for Kyoto ratification, but it is doubtful whether he could ever have succeeded. His failure to sign the 2000 Cartagena Protocol on Biosafety evidenced the unilateral turn in second term foreign policy attitudes. The Clinton administration, however, did go a way down the road towards at least environmental awareness. Speeches by Clinton and Gore – even, in the first term, by Warren Christopher – began to define environmentalism in post-Cold War 'collective security', rather than 'do good', language. And, of course, in the person of the Vice President, the administration had probably the most effective publicist in the history of the environmental movement.

Defence issues in the second term

The various defence debates discussed in Chapter 4 – especially regarding readiness and the balance between capabilities and commitments – continued into the second term. Reviews of America's post-Cold War posture continued to proliferate. The tendency was for these reviews to emphasise problems, new commitments and more claims on the defence budget, rather than new opportunities for savings. The Pentagon's Quadrennial Defense Review, for example, released in May 1997, outlined a strategy of 'selective engagement', with particular emphasis on the need to deter potential rivals at the regional level. Assistant Defense Secretary Edward Warner explained: 'When we looked at the nature of the future, we saw a messy, troubled, uncertain world that includes regional hegemons who will threaten US interests.'[115] This was language which recalled the 1992 Defense Planning Guidance under Bush41 – the document which was later seen as foreshadowing the neo-conservative defence philosophy of Bush43.[116] John Hillen, a conservative defence analyst writing in *Foreign Affairs* in 1999, discerned 'an American foreign policy that is growing more imperial by the day'.[117]

The key problem, of course, was the dialectic of capability and commitment. William Odom in 1997 saw current budget levels as leading to 'de facto disengagement', with spending on aircraft carriers and amphibious forces necessarily putting pressure on ground troops. Odom suggested that the 'emerging force structure may result in the incremental withdrawal of the United States from key alliances in Europe and northeast Asia'.[118] By 1998, the US Army was 40 per cent smaller than 15 years previously, but was stretched over more overseas deployments. To some defence analysts, the answer was technological – the Revolution in Military Affairs. Other voices called for clearer regional prioritisation and the re-thinking of the Pentagon's goal of readiness to fight two simultaneous regional wars. Linguistic changes suggested a degree of imperialisation of military thinking. The Quadrennial Defense Review referred to 'two major theaters of war' – in the context of 'shaping' the international environment – rather than, as formerly, of 'two major regional contingencies'. Coalitions would be sought where feasible, but the US must always be prepared to fight unilaterally.[119] These debates about the scope and purpose of US military engagement, of course, dragged on, in greatly intensified form, into the era of Bush43 and the War on Terror.

Clinton's second term was an era of remilitarisation. Republican budget-balancing in the mid-1990s seemed to put spending hikes in jeopardy, but the achievement of budget surpluses in the later Clinton years actually gave significant scope for increases. The president, in a formal communication to Defense Secretary Cohen and JCS chairman Hugh Shelton in 1998, wrote: 'Readiness is a perishable commodity and requires our serious attention.'[120] In 1999, Clinton proposed an increase in military spending of $112 billion over the next six years. A fact sheet issued by the White House as Clinton left office in January 2001 rebutted accusations that Clinton had left a 'hollow' and weakened military. It pointed out that, by 2001, the US was spending 22 per cent more on operations and maintenance than it did in 1993 (in current dollars). Military pay had increased dramatically. The military science and technology budget for fiscal 2001 exceeded that of the rest of the world entirely.[121] By this time, the US had about 1.4 million active duty service personnel. The US Navy had twice as many principal combat ships as the combined total for China and Russia.[122]

Clinton left a military which was indeed imperial in scope, though one which was also vulnerable to overstretch in the face of rather vague strategic prioritisation. The unilateralist tone of the second term was evident also in the triumph of NMD. As we saw in Chapter 4, NMD proposals were prominent in provoking Clinton's veto of legislative defence authorisation in 1995. Battles continued into the late 1990s over the extent to which NMD contravened the Anti-Ballistic Missile Treaty of 1972. For arms control liberals like Spurgeon Keeny, who had worked on these issues for presidents Johnson and Carter, NMD merely risked restarting a global arms race at a time when the US was no longer in danger of a nuclear attack.[123] NMD was variously opposed on the grounds of the possible damage it would cause to alliances – Western Europe had long seen NMD as part of America's 'decoupling' from Europe – its huge cost and the fact that, at best, it held out an illusion of security from incoming missile attack. Even the Joint Chiefs seemed lukewarm, worried about NMD diverting money from more vital budgets.[124] Between 1994 and 1998, the NMD debate tended to divide along partisan lines, with a majority of Democrats insisting that no decision should be made without agreement with Russia on the Anti-Ballistic Missile Treaty. During 1998, however, Clinton reversed his position, moving to a co-option strategy on missile defence. Clinton committed himself to support for NMD technology development, and indicating that a decision on deployment feasibility would be made by 2000. In March 1999, Clinton signed a measure which provided $10.5 billion for the programme of testing interceptor defences. In September 2000, he announced that the system was 'sufficiently promising and affordable' to stay with the programme, though a hard and fast deployment decision could not yet be made.[125]

The September 2000 announcement essentially constituted Clinton's NMD legacy to George W. Bush, a strong enthusiast for anti-missile defence. Clinton's motivation for switching sides was attributed by some commentators to a desire to help Gore in the 2000 election. Zbigniew Brzezinski suggested that NMD was designed not just to shield the US from attack, but also to shield Gore from accusations that he would be less keen than Bush on 'defending American families'.[126] Given the actual timing of Clinton's switch, a more plausible explanation relates to the exigencies of managing the Republican Senate, and avoiding any possibility of a veto override, while staying in control of key NMD decisions, at least until January 2001. Defense Secretary Cohen, though not a straightforward defence hawk – he had a record, for example, of opposing the B-1 bomber – was generally regarded as a supporter of NMD.[127] Particularly crucial, of course, was the administration's developing perception of rogue threats, nuclear proliferation, and reports of Chinese progress on nuclear missile technology (at the time linked to American press reports of thefts from the US national laboratory at Los Alamos). The Washington climate on missile defence was transformed by the issuing of a report in 1998 by a commission, set up by the Republican Congress and chaired by Donald Rumsfeld. This commission, whose membership included Paul Wolfowitz, directly attacked CIA assessments of the threat from 'rogue' missiles. Its warnings were given almost immediate credence by North Korean missile tests.[128]

During the scandal-hit summer of 1998, and indeed from 1998 until the end of his presidency, Clinton was unable to ignore the missile panic. General Ronald Kadish, NMD specialist at the Pentagon, estimated in 2000 that 20 or more states possessed some effective missile capacity, while maybe two dozen had, or were close to having, WMD capacity. The administration seemed confident about the possibility of negotiating a way around the problem posed by the 1972 Anti-Ballistic Missile Treaty; Moscow had actually agreed to changes in the treaty in 1996. The relatively limited NMD system being developed in the late 1990s – limited at least in comparison with Reagan's Star Wars programme – would not have given the US the ability to attack Russia at will.[129] Speaking at Georgetown University, Clinton said that an anti-missile system, 'if it worked properly, could give us an extra dimension of insurance in a world where proliferation has complicated the task of preserving the peace'. In an upbeat commentary on NMD, Clinton referred to a test which seemed to show it was 'possible to hit a bullet with a bullet'.[130]

Second term defence issues tended to merge with anti-terrorism. The policies on WMD were aimed both at states and at non-state terrorist groups. The Pentagon issued a 1997 report (the so-called 'Chemical and Biological 2010 Study') which concluded that 'massive battlefield use of chemical and biological weapons ... is no longer the most likely threat'. 'Limited, localized' assaults, including attacks by terror groups, were perceived as more menacing.[131] Clinton himself became especially active on the issue of biological weapons and bio-terrorism; he let it be known that he had read *The Cobra Event*, a novel about bio-terrorism by Richard Preston.[132] In May 1998, Clinton announced both new anti-bio-terrorism precautions in US cities (under the Nunn–Lugar–Domenici programme), and urged further strengthening of the international Biological Weapons Convention.[133] In

April 1997, the Senate ratified the CWC. Clinton marked the occasion by inviting to a press event in the White House Roosevelt Room a First World War veteran, George Clark, who had survived a chemical attack in 1916.[134]

Anti-nuclear proliferation policies were dealt a huge blow by the Indian and Pakistani tests. To emphasise that not all was in ruins, the White House produced publicity material to detail such anti-proliferation successes as the Ukraine agreement, and the 1995 extension of the NPT.[135] By 1998, however, a series of events – the South Asian tests, the Rumsfeld Commission reports, press stories about poor security at the Los Alamos laboratories, the North Korean missile tests, worries about Iran and China – had severely raised the temperature surrounding WMD issues. Although the Senate did accept the CWC, the mood in Congress was conspicuously unilateralist and distrustful of official intelligence. Under pressure from Congress and to the dismay of allies such as the UK, the Pentagon strengthened its controls on the export of military technology. The Joint Chiefs and legislative pressure also persuaded Clinton against signing an international treaty banning land mines. Clinton's retreat here was embarrassing since he had in May 1996 declared his 'horror at the devastations that land mines cause' and launched an international effort to ban them.[136] He ordered a unilateral ban in 1997 on those land mines which 'remain active and dangerous long after soldiers have left the scene', but yielded to the Pentagon view that a total ban would compromise the defence of South Korea.[137]

The test of the national mood on WMD was tested in the White House campaign to secure ratification, in the autumn of 1999, of the CTBT. Clinton had signed the CTBT at the UN in September 1996. As the treaty came up for Senate vote in October 1999, Clinton portrayed the measure as part of the campaign against WMD, especially the miniaturisation of weaponry[138]. The treaty would both prevent many countries from acquiring nuclear weapons and (through monitoring stations and on-site inspection) 'enhance our ability to detect suspicious activities by other nations'.[139] Though the treaty was aimed at underground testing – atmospheric testing was already banned – it would chime in with the administration's commitment to environmentalism. The debate over the CTBT was conducted against the background of the upcoming 2000 presidential campaign, and was widely analysed in terms of what it had to say about the likely conduct of any incoming Republican administration.

The test ban treaty, which the Clintonites looked upon as a major legislative priority, was defeated 48–51, well short of the two-thirds necessary for ratification. By 1999, of the 44 nations with some kind of nuclear capacity, 26 had signed. When in 2000, the Russian parliament ratified the treaty, Clinton noted that 'even the Russian Duma was more progressive on arms control than the US Senate'.[140] What many commentators noted, however, was that White House lobbying for CTBT ratification was less than intense, and contrasted sharply with Jeremy Rosner's efforts on behalf of ratification for NATO expansion, or even with the committed bargaining process with Jesse Helms which had preceded the Senate's acceptance of the CWC. Senator Richard Lugar declared that Clinton had 'declined to initiate the type of advocacy campaign that should accompany a treaty of this magnitude'.[141]

The Senate certainly seemed to miss a 'defence Democrat' of the stature of Sam Nunn of Georgia, who might have brokered a deal. The vote was surrounded by intense partisanship, though Lugar, who finally opposed the measure, put a strong substantive case. According to Lugar, and to former Defense Secretary James Schlesinger, 'virtual' computer-based testing (under the 'stockpile stewardship' programme) was not yet sufficiently developed to be an adequate substitute for underground testing. For Lugar, the treaty had no enforcement teeth: 'Arms control advocates need to reflect on the possible damage to the concept of arms control if we embrace a treaty that comes to be perceived as ineffectual.'[142] The counter-argument was that, without US ratification, the test ban effort would simply expire and an important prospect of limiting proliferation would be lost. Writing in *The Bulletin of the Atomic Scientists*, Stephen Schwartz traced the ratification failure, and the administration's lack of leadership, to highly complex post-impeachment partisan politics. In such an analysis, the White House might actually welcome the emergence of an isolationist Republican bugaboo as the presidential election loomed. Al Gore's first 2000 campaign broadcast was aired just after the Senate vote and declared, in the context of the CTBT, that 'there is no more important challenge than stopping the spread of nuclear weapons'.[143] A boost for Gore's line was achieved in May 2000, when all five 'traditional' nuclear powers – the US, Russia, China, the UK and France (not Israel, India nor Pakistan) – declared their willingness via the UN to eliminate nuclear weapons.

The CTBT vote opened up some revealing and portentous fissures in the GOP. Senator John McCain condemned what he saw as 'a growing isolationism' in his party. Herbert Bateman of Virginia, chairman of the House Armed Services Military Readiness Subcommittee distanced himself from the '"Get out of the United Nations" crowd'.[144] From the neo-conservative flank, Jeanne Kirkpatrick (US Representative to the UN under President Reagan) opposed the test ban treaty on the grounds that 'not all cultures put the same emphasis on keeping their word'.[145] James Kitfield in the *National Journal* (NJ) sniffed 'a return to isolationism', linked to 'a generational change within the Republican Party between an aging cadre of Cold War warriors and a new, younger generation of Republicans committed to shrinking the size and scope of government – including the role of the United States overseas'.[146] In fact, both the NMD and the CTBT debates were vital in mobilising the various strands within the Republican Party – broadly, narrow nationalist (Kitfield's 'new, younger generation', though also including Helms); cooperative internationalist (the Cold War, and indeed the Second World War, generation exemplified by former Bush41 and many of his inner circle); democracy-promoting neo-conservative and/or offensive realist. These battles would be fought out during the presidency of the younger Bush, who intervened in the CTBT debate by invoking 'a world of terrorists, madmen and missiles'[147].

8 The Middle East

It has become commonplace to point out that the prospects for some successful settlement of the tensions and conflicts in the Middle East were generally very positive when Clinton assumed power in 1993. Radical Arab nationalism seemed to be on the decline. President Carter's Camp David agreement between Egypt and Israel had achieved stability. The end of the Cold War had lowered the international temperature of the region's fissures. The Bush41 administration had led an international coalition against an expansionist Iraq. The US–Israel alliance was close, but many commentators saw it as developing towards a condition of greater 'normalcy' in post-Cold War conditions.[1] The October 1991 Madrid conference (and subsequent talks in Washington) between Israel, Syria, Lebanon and a joint Jordanian–Palestinian delegation made little progress. The fact, however, that the Madrid meeting had George H. W. Bush and Mikhail Gorbachev as joint presidents indicated how much had changed. The Israeli coalition government led by Yitzhak Rabin seemed committed to a peace process which embraced Palestinian autonomy.

The implication of assertions that conditions for regional settlement were favourable in 1993, of course, is that opportunities were squandered by Washington. Clinton's stance towards the region was initially quite relaxed, reflecting the retreat of geopolitical immediacy under post-Cold War conditions. An overarching regional strategy of 'dual containment' of Iraq and Iran was developed, partly to protect opportunities for Arab–Israeli peace, partly to further strategic order objectives in the Persian Gulf.[2] As the years went by, it became increasingly evident to Washington that peace and stability would not be achieved without diplomatic activism on the scale of President Carter in 1978–79. In 1998, regime-change in Iraq was adopted as an explicit goal of US policy. Cold War tensions were replaced by concerns about WMD proliferation and the rise of terroristic Islamic extremism.

By the last year of his presidency, Bill Clinton was more and more preoccupied with the prospect of Arab–Israeli peace. The issue dominated his last year in office and constituted the heart of his attempt to leave a positive foreign policy legacy. Martin Indyk, who worked on Middle Eastern issues at the White House and at State (as well as being Ambassador to Israel in 1995–97, and again in 2000) recalled that Clinton eventually 'became almost a desk officer' on

Arab–Israeli negotiations, becoming 'too involved in the details'.[3] Bearing in mind the need to strike a balance between policy detail and the bigger picture, this penultimate chapter will attempt to provide the evidence for an evaluation of Clinton's policies in the Middle East.

From Oslo to the Wye River

Policy-making towards the Arab–Israeli conflict in the Clinton years was concentrated at the State Department in the office of Dennis Ross, special Middle East coordinator. Ross and staffers such as his deputy Aaron Miller (who, like Ross had worked as a policy planner at State under Bush41), Gamal Helal (Egyptian-born and leading Arabic interpreter) and Nicholas Rasmussen constituted a fairly tight, exclusive policy circle. As Aaron Miller later wrote, they reported direct to Clinton and to the Secretary of State, often not even fully briefing the State Department Near East Affairs Bureau nor the relevant ambassadors. Bob Pelletreau, appointed Assistant Secretary for the Near East Bureau in 1994, described the operation as being run out of Dennis Ross's 'hip pocket'.[4]

As inherited by Clinton, the peace process was moving along two negotiating paths: one between Israel and Syria, one between Israel and the Palestinians. The administration, encouraged by Rabin, initially concentrated on the Syrian track. It rapidly became apparent, however, that the Israeli–Palestinian path was somewhat more promising. The catalyst here was the government of Norway, which originally made fruitful contact with the Palestinian Liberation Organisation (PLO) via a research project headed by Terje Roed-Larsen, an ex-Norwegian government minister. In late August 1993, Yitzhak Rabin alerted Warren Christopher to the existence of the secret Norwegian channel to the Palestinians. Norwegian Foreign Minister Johan Holst produced a Declaration of Principles – in effect, a draft agreement between the PLO and Tel Aviv. Dennis Ross recalled his own reaction: 'The Israeli government had made a choice to try to settle the conflict with the Palestinians, and to recognize that peace with the Palestinians would offer the best guarantee of security.'[5] The Oslo Accords were signed by Rabin and PLO leader Yasser Arafat on the White House lawn in September 1993, with Clinton famously encouraging the reluctant Israeli leader to shake Arafat's hand.

Under the Accords, an agreed plan for an 'interim period' of not more than five years was accepted. Israel would pull back from West Bank and other lands occupied since 1967, beginning with Gaza (apart from the Israeli settlements) and Jericho. Authority there would fall to a Palestinian Authority with, under the 'Oslo 2' agreement signed in Washington in September 1994, varying degrees of internal autonomy in various parts of Israeli-vacated land. The PLO would recognise Israel as a legitimate state and foreswear terrorism, while Israel would recognise the PLO as the legitimate representative of the Palestinian people. The Accords continued the gradualist, trust-building dynamic that had been a central aim of US diplomacy since the early 1970s. 'Final status' settlement would come in due course, once trust had been built and once peace agreements between Israel and all of its potentially or actually hostile neighbours had been achieved.

The following four years saw the breaking down of the Oslo process. Some reasons for failure were inherent in the 1993 deal, which had been negotiated by the exiled PLO leadership, rather than by Palestinians actually living in the occupied territories. According to former President Jimmy Carter, Arafat agreed to the Oslo Accords as 'an assurance of organizing a form of Palestinian government and staying in power so that he could administer Palestinian affairs in the West Bank and Gaza'. Existing Jewish settlements would be unaffected, while the Israeli authorities (including the military) would be relieved of onerous policing duties within the occupied territories.[6] Hamas, the Islamic Resistance Movement, gaining strength in the occupied lands – especially in Gaza – opposed Arafat's more secularist Fatah group; Hamas actually killed three Israeli soldiers in Gaza on the day before the signing of the Accords. The Likud party in Israel cited such action as proof of the foolishness of making concessions which endangered Israeli security. The 1993 agreement was also in many respects alarmingly and intentionally vague, for example, in the matters of defining the dimensions of Jericho, in a rather ambiguous Israeli commitment to cease establishing new settlements in occupied land, and regarding the nature of Israeli/Palestinian Authority border controls. According to Dennis Ross, the Oslo agreement collapsed primarily because of the mutual Palestinian–Israeli failure to take risks for peace. Each side's leaders, facing huge internal opposition to any concession-making, at best simply went through the motions. The process became overwhelmed by cynicism: 'neither side succeeded in transforming itself.'[7]

The Oslo Accords, both their actual signing as well as their breakdown, raised fundamental questions about the feasible and proper role for Washington in achieving a Middle Eastern peace. In 1993–94, it seemed that perhaps the best way for America to deal with this particular 'ancient enmities' dispute was actually to stand back from it. The good offices of Norway had been enough to broker the 1993 deal. Clinton was criticised for trying to muscle in on Norway's achievement. Jimmy Carter was 'surprised and embarrassed' to see that Johan Holst and Terje Roed-Larsen were not in the front row of spectators at the 1993 signing ceremony.[8] A peace treaty between Israel and Jordan was signed in October 1994 without huge American involvement; a dialogue between Tel Aviv and King Hussein of Jordan, who had now dropped any claim to Jerusalem and the West Bank, had been proceeding since well before Clinton assumed office.[9] Yet all sides appreciated the need to secure American approval of all Arab–Israeli agreements, along with Washington's help in implementation. Arguments were eventually forthcoming to the effect that Clinton's relatively low level of involvement in the 1993–94 agreements and accords encouraged an excessively relaxed attitude in Washington in respect of the need for close American attention to the details of implementation. Aaron Miller later criticised the relaxed wishful thinking of the post-1993 period, concluding that one 'of the most important lessons to emerge from the Oslo years is that ignoring bad behaviour on either side dooms any chance of serious and successful negotiations'.[10]

Linked to the question of the need for intense American involvement per se were the problems of gradualist processes and of American good faith. By 1996, it was commonly being argued that gradualism was leading to a reification of process: that keeping the peace dynamic going had become almost an end in itself, almost to the extent that the process was making a comprehensive settlement less likely. Interested parties on both sides were acclimatising themselves to detailed trust-building which, far from building substantial trust, was becoming a way of postponing more difficult decisions. Henry Kissinger entered the fray by insisting that the time had come to address two 'unmentionables': Palestinian statehood, defining the Israeli borders, agreeing the status and future of Jewish settlement as well as the future of Jerusalem.[11] The desire to keep the process moving was analogous to the bicycle metaphor for Clinton's free trade deals. In the Middle East, it worked, but also underlay the problem of ignoring bad behaviour. American pressure to keep contacts, meetings and local agreements going often resulted in the negotiations becoming divorced from experience on the ground. As Denis Ross recalled an important lesson of Oslo: 'no negotiation is likely to succeed if there is one environment at the negotiating table and another one on the street.'[12] According to Robert Malley of Clinton's NSC, Ross would often 'seek to bridge differences by resorting to constructive ambiguity, papering over deep disagreements with skilful formulations, allowing Israelis and Palestinians to believe they got what they wanted, even as the things they wanted were irreconcilable'.[13]

The question of American good faith and even-handedness has been raised by both Robert Malley and Aaron Miller. For Malley, at least after 1993, the Clinton administration became *too* engaged, too concerned to maintain American ownership of the process. Given that Washington's premier dialogue was with Tel Aviv, this led to the ascendancy of a US–Israeli peace dynamic which shut out the Palestinians (and indeed the Europeans) from much in the way of a constructive stake in the development of the process: 'Failure to give Arab states a genuine role in the process relieved them of any responsibility for its success.'[14] Miller recalls a large degree of American 'groupthink': 'not a single senior-level official involved with the negotiations was willing or able to present, let alone fight for, the Arab or Palestinian perspective.' In Miller's view at least two policy dissenters, Rob Malley and Dan Kurtzer, should have been incorporated into Ross's inner group.[15] Kurtzer left his position in the Near Eastern Affairs Bureau in 1994 in protest at being shut out of policy-making. Later appointed as US Ambassador to Egypt, he criticised the lack of understanding in Ross's circle of what exactly was happening in the Arab world. According to Kurtzer, the Clinton administration was simply too slow to see 'that radical Islam was replacing secular nationalism as the most powerful political ideology in the region'.[16]

This failure of even-handedness was not the result of conspiracy, but rather of a combination of reversible policy structure and the accretion of past ways of understanding and approaching issues relating to the Middle East. It had an obvious parallel in Northern Ireland, where for similar reasons the administration – despite the huge success of 1998 – failed entirely to shake off its inclinations (real and perceived) to the nationalist side. In the Middle East, the American practice was invariably to start either with Israeli proposals, or with American proposals that

Washington felt that the Israeli government could accept, and *then* try to sell the proposals to the Arab side.[17] These problems with even-handedness were often understandable, and were to some extent derived from the nature of regional politics in the Middle East. The central Israel–US dynamic was sustained by the fact that Israel, unlike the Palestinians, had a credible, democratically elected leadership. On many occasions, Washington became angry and exasperated by Israel. Following the narrow election victory of Likud leader Benjamin Netanyahu in 1996, anger and exasperation were a regular condition.[18]

As with the Irish peace process, it is tempting to trace problems with even-handedness to the domestic US ethnic lobbies. John Mearsheimer and Stephen Walt argue that 'the Clinton administration's Middle East policy was heavily shaped by officials with close ties to Israel or to prominent pro-Israel organizations'. Martin Indyk was a former deputy research director at the American Israeli Public Affairs Committee (AIPAC, the main pro-Israel lobbying organisation in the US); in 1995, he became the first Jewish US Ambassador to Israel. Dennis Ross joined the Washington Institute for Near East Policy (a generally pro-Israel think tank founded by Indyk) in 2001. Mearsheimer and Walt acknowledge that Ross and Indyk supported the creation of a Palestinian state, and encountered condemnation from Likud for so doing, but 'they did so only within the limits of what would be acceptable to Israeli leaders'.[19] During the Clinton years, AIPAC was unquestionably the premier ethnically-based foreign policy lobby in Washington. Although the PLO was, at least for most of the 1990s, allowed to maintain a lobbying office in Washington, pro-Israeli lobbies were incomparably more powerful. It can also be argued that the end of the Cold War opened up the policy-making environment in a way that favoured domestic lobbies such as AIPAC. However, the specialist literature tends to overstate the foreign policy impact of the ethnic lobbies, which tend to be more geared towards Capitol Hill (and, in AIPAC's case, the ongoing Israeli foreign aid budget) than towards elite diplomacy in the executive branch.[20] The Jewish origins of Ross, Indyk and Miller certainly gave ammunition to paranoid anti-Americanism in the Middle East. On the other hand, Ross and Indyk were credible allies to Israeli peaceniks. They broadly opposed the increasing pro-Likud orientation of AIPAC that had increased since the early Reagan period. As Lawrence Freedman puts it:

> The important point about Ross and Indyk (and (Thomas) Friedman in his influential columns for the *New York Times*) was not that they were Israeli agents in the American system but that they were in many respects partisans in the Israeli debate, and to an extent American agents, for they could shape American intervention.

The price of their position was suspicion on the Arab side, righteous anger from Israeli hard-liners, and a presumption on the part of Israeli Labor leaders that *their* transgressions of the peace process would be infinitely tolerated.[21]

Between 1993 and 1996, Warren Christopher led a fruitless quest for a Syrian agreement. Syrian President Hafez al-Assad required Israeli withdrawal from the

Golan Heights, including the dismantling of settlements established there by Israelis since 1967, as well as a deal with Israel over influence in Lebanon. Movement on these issues did occur, with Rabin apparently offering to quit the Golan. Clinton publicly interpreted Assad as being in favour of full normalisation – rather to the apparent chagrin of the Syrian leader himself – during a joint press conference in Geneva in January 1994. Prospects for a Syrian deal disappeared as the Oslo Accords disintegrated amid a succession of events that may be briefly summarised.

Violence erupted, including the attack by a Jewish gunman on a mosque at Hebron in February 1994, and suicide and car bomb attacks associated with radical Islamists in the occupied territories. Yitzhak Rabin was assassinated in November 1995, an event which visibly shook Clinton, setting the US leader (in Warren Christopher's recollection) to reflect upon his own mortality.[22] Rabin was succeeded initially by his foreign minister, Shimon Peres, an author of the Oslo Accords. Peres worked with Washington to keep open the chance of a Syrian deal. The subsequent Likud-led coalition initially presided over a virtual collapse of hopes for peace. Ross regarded Netanyahu – educated at a Philadelphia high school and at the Massachusetts Institute of Technology – as 'overcome by hubris', determined to show America how to treat the Palestinians.[23] Following a meeting with the new Israeli leader in Washington, Clinton remarked: 'He thinks he is the superpower and we are here to do whatever he requires.'[24] Netanyahu developed links with Republican politicians, building on a developed pro-Likud American outreach network.[25] However, prodded by Washington and assured by Christopher that the US was completely committed to Israeli security, Netanyahu eventually agreed to a deal on withdrawal from Hebron in January 1997. By mid-1997, Netanyahu was supporting the emergence of some kind of Palestinian 'entity', to be established behind buffer zones (designed to provide Israel with 'security in depth'). Both Israel and Washington were also coming to the view that gradualism, an approach which was now primarily identified with the PLO, was achieving little. In August 1997, Secretary Albright raised the prospect of accelerated 'final status' talks, during a speech at the National Press Club in Washington, where she also declared that there was no 'moral equivalence' between terrorism and Jewish settlement in Gaza and the West Bank – 'between killing innocent people and building houses'.[26]

Visiting Israel and the occupied territories in 1997, Albright expressed an emotional frustration with the apparent inability of either side to build trust and negotiate in good faith. Washington began to prepare for a summit that would attempt both to revive the Oslo process and move to 'final status' negotiations. Albright brought Netanyahu and Arafat together at the UN General Assembly session in New York in September 1997. The summit – which included Arafat, Netanyahu, Ariel Sharon (the new Israeli Foreign Minister and 'final status' coordinator), and a dying King Hussein of Jordan – met at the Wye River Conference Center in Maryland in October. On 28 September, Clinton responded with uncharacteristic bluntness to press references to remarks made by the First Lady to the effect that Palestinian statehood was an objective of the negotiations: 'she's not the president and she's not trying to manage this peace process.'[27]

The nine-day long Wye negotiations were predictably complex, with protracted wrangling over the status of Jonathan Pollard, an Israeli spy held by the US. In a clash with Sandy Berger, CIA chief George Tenet threatened to resign if Pollard was released. Aaron Miller recalled a 'brilliant' Clinton performance and an unexpected agreement on Israeli troop redeployments and Israeli–Palestinian security cooperation.[28] Netanyahu seems to have been squeezed by an agenda set by Israeli oppositionists (such as Yossi Beilin, former Deputy Foreign Minister under Shimon Peres), by leading Palestinians such as Saeb Erekat, and by the Americans.[29] Even the Israeli leader, however, appreciated Clinton's energy and dedication: 'I mean, he doesn't stop. He has this ability to maintain a tireless pace and to nudge and prod and suggest and use a nimble and flexible mind.'[30] A Likud leader had been cajoled into making an agreement with Arafat. Netanyahu did not succeed in having Pollard released, but could plausibly claim to have achieved more safeguards for Israeli security than had been won by the Israeli Labor leaders. Albright summed up the Wye River division of the spoils: the Palestinians acquired 'more land' – actually about 40 per cent of the West Bank – 'an airport, a seaport, safe passage between the West Bank and Gaza, a prisoner release, a commitment to restrain Israeli settlement activity, and a fresh influx of economic aid'; while Netanyahu 'would get unprecedented security cooperation, the jailing of wanted Palestinians, repudiation of offensive language in the Palestinian Covenant, and a quick start to final status talks'.[31] In truth, however, as Ross realised, the deal was still hostage to Israeli domestic politics.[32] Clinton visited Gaza in December during the impeachment crisis. His public appearance with Arafat, who presided over the symbolic erasure from the Palestinian National Covenant of the section calling for the extinction of Israel, seemed to presage a concerted push for a Palestinian state. Under attack from the right and the left, however, Netanyahu's domestic position failed to hold, and Israeli elections were called for May 1999.

Iraq and Iran

The policy of 'dual containment' of Iraq and Iran, announced by Martin Indyk in May 1993, was far from entirely novel. Its roots could be traced back to the Carter years. The Bush41 administration had pursued both containment and regime change in Iraq. Bush authorised a covert CIA operation to topple Saddam Hussein shortly after the conclusion of the 1991 Gulf War.[33] Major American, British and French air strikes were launched against Iraq just a week before Clinton's January 1993 inauguration. Saddam was the object of an intense programme of UN sanctions and demands, mostly relating to his putative WMD development, but also regarding his internal repression of the Kurdish and Shia populations. The UN had imposed 'no-fly' zones, enforced by US and allied aircraft, to protect at-risk Kurds and Shia in the north and south of the country, respectively. During the election campaign, Al Gore in particular had attacked Bush's pre-Gulf War record on Iraq, and (again in terms which were critical of the Bush41 line) had denounced Saddam's evasions of UN weapons inspections. Clinton declared there was 'no difference' between his policy on Iraq and that of his predecessor (following an earlier interview in which he appeared to suggest that, were Saddam to moderate his behaviour, the US and Iraq might move to a normalisation of their relationship).[34]

Martin Indyk in May 1993 outlined what was in most respects a continuation of the Bush policies towards Iraq. Economic pressure on the regime, via UN sanctions, would be combined with military threat and military policing (of the 'no-fly' zones) to keep Saddam's behaviour within broadly acceptable limits. The implication was also that sanctions might force Saddam from power; 'containment' of Iraq also did not necessarily mean that covert regime-change operations were off the agenda. 'Dual containment' was devised more in regard to Iran than to Iraq. The administration was worried that action against Iraq might increase the regional sway of Iran, especially in the context of Persian Gulf security.[35] While containment of Iraq would be primarily multilateral, the US would commit itself to containing Iran unilaterally, with the aim of modifying Tehran's behaviour on the external sponsorship of terrorism, destabilisation activities in the Gulf and Africa, interference in the Arab–Israeli peace process, and WMD development. Tony Lake explained in 1994: 'the Clinton administration does not oppose Islamic government, nor does it seek the (Iranian) regime's overthrow.' For the Clintonites, 'dual containment' was only new in so far as it recognised the military eminence of the US in the Middle East, and the possibility which this raised for dispensing with a reliance on an Iran/Iraq balance of power. Lake declared that the administration did 'not accept the argument that we should continue the old balance of power game, building up one to balance the other'. The US was sufficiently powerful not to 'need to rely on one to balance the other'. Policy would be predicated on 'a clear-headed assessment of the antagonism that both regimes harbor towards the United States and its allies in the region' (including Israel and the Gulf allies).[36] Contradicting Lake, and emphasising the shift in policy which accompanied her ascendancy at Foggy Bottom, Madeleine Albright described the first term 'dual containment' policy as 'essentially equating Iran with Iraq'. Both were 'rogue regimes': 'Our policy was to isolate them and deny them the capacity to develop advanced arms.'[37]

In June 1993, Clinton ordered the first air strikes on Iraq to be undertaken on his watch. This was primarily an attack on the Iraqi Intelligence Service command and control complex in Baghdad, the facility which, according to Clinton, 'planned the failed attempt to assassinate former President Bush during his visit to Kuwait', in April 1993.[38] Clinton, by his own account, was dissuaded from a wider assault by Colin Powell, who advised that such attacks 'would have been unlikely to kill Saddam Hussein and almost certain to kill more innocent people'. As it was, the death of eight civilians in Baghdad was 'a stark reminder' of the unintended consequences of military action.[39] Evidence for the plot against President Bush derived from 'materials' in the possession of a dozen people (apparently whisky smugglers) arrested in Kuwait on the day before Bush's scheduled visit there. Bush's son famously remarked of Saddam in 2002: 'After all, this is a guy who tried to kill my dad at one time.'[40] The evidence for the plot was circumstantial, and Pentagon researchers found no mention of the plot (nor indeed of any Iraqi link to the February 1993 World Trade Center bombing) in 600,000 pages of intelligence documentation seized following the 2003 invasion.[41]

Cat-and-mouse interactions between Washington and Baghdad continued between 1994 and 1996. Deployments of Iraqi troops along the Kuwait border were answered by American force increases, both within Kuwait itself and in the Persian Gulf region. Deployments in Saudi Arabia rapidly became a particular object of venom for Osama bin Laden. In September 1996, Clinton ordered cruise missile strikes on Iraqi air capabilities in the south of the country, along with an extension of the southern 'no-fly' zone. This action was in direct response to Saddam's seizure of the Kurdish city of Irbil. Clinton emphasised the limited objectives of such action: 'to make Saddam pay a price for the latest act of brutality, reducing his ability to threaten his neighbours and America's interests.' He cited UN Security Council condemnations of Saddam's repressions as justification for the US action. The justification included the fact that Irbil was an aid distribution centre under the UN-sanctioned policy of allowing Iraq to sell oil in return for food and medicine. Despite the multilateral framework for the missile attack, Clinton found it difficult to explain to journalists why only Britain was directly involved: 'I believe that we will be able to go forward with this mission, and I think others feel that at this time there may be, for their own domestic purposes, some limits on how much they can do.'[42]

The September 1996 crisis was directly linked to efforts to dethrone Saddam. As we have seen, direct promotion of regime-change in Iraq was not ruled out in the version of 'dual containment' articulated by Indyk and Lake.[43] However, as the first term wore on, Clintonites became increasingly concerned about the prospect of continuing limited, tit-for-tat skirmishing. State Department memoranda, prepared for Albright's takeover from Warren Christopher, put the case for a major policy re-think: 'we need to determine whether there is more to do to accelerate Saddam's departure, whether more can be done to consolidate the coalition, or whether we can envisage beginning Iraq's rehabilitation.'[44] The regime-change track during Clinton's first term was associated primarily with Ahmed Chalabi and the Iraqi National Congress (INC), the organisation which was to be supported by Pentagon regime-changers under Bush43.

Chalabi was extremely successful in establishing contacts among American neo-conservatives, notably Paul Wolfowitz and the organisers of the Project for the New American Century launched in 1997. Among the Clintonites, however, he encountered caution and a general suspicion about being dragged into complex anti-Saddam escapades, which were seen by the administration as potentially foolish, counter-productive and beset by factionalism. Martin Indyk publicly endorsed the INC, commending its embrace of Kurdish, Shia and Sunni oppositionists. Indyk described the INC as 'committed, as are we, to maintaining the territorial integrity of Iraq'.[45] Al Gore promised Chalabi in August 1993 that the US would 'do whatever it can to assist you, to overthrow Saddam and establish democracy in Iraq'.[46] US intelligence, however, was sceptical, both about the INC's oppositionist strength and its ability to form a stable, non-factional regime after the ousting of Saddam.⁴⁷ The Clinton administration, unlike its successor, did not parlay imperfect and sceptical intelligence into a justification for reckless action. Chalabi offered a plan for a revolution to be spearheaded by Kurdish insurgents in the north of Iraq. Tony Lake's opposition to the scheme, intended to peak in March 1995, seems to have been crucial.⁴⁸ Saddam's seizure of Irbil in 1996 was part of a strike from Baghdad against Kurdish fighters, as well as against both the INC and the Iraqi National Accord (INA; a group primarily of dissident ex-regime officers, who were supported by British intelligence). Baghdad's action was also a strike against the CIA, which had a small operation centred near Ibril.⁴⁹ Clinton's September 1996 attacks were his response.

Both the INC and the INA received CIA backing, but Clinton was not prepared to intervene more directly. Washington remained a sponsor of the INA which, despite constant problems of Iraqi intelligence penetration, after 1995 was preferred to the INC. Yet, despite the now open US commitment to Iraqi regime-change, Washington was unwilling to become potentially hostage to the schemes of fractious Iraqi governments in exile. Though broadly committed to regime-change, the administration was nevertheless sensitive to the implications of peremptory deposition of Saddam. As *The Economist* noted in 1997, a fallen Saddam might have become 'at least briefly a martyr for anti-Americans in the Middle East; his successor, while unlikely to have been as bad, might have been no great improvement; and the chaos after his removal might have strengthened the bad-guy faction in next-door Iran'.⁵⁰ US military caution was expressed publicly in 1998 by General Anthony Zinni, head of CENTCOM, the US Military Central Command, under whose aegis a proxy war (or actual invasion) would have been conducted. Zinni upset Defense Secretary Cohen by calling, during a Senate hearing, an Iraqi intervention a potential 'Bay of Goats': a damaging sequel to President Kennedy's Cuban intervention of 1961.⁵¹ Zinni wrote a piece in *Foreign Affairs* in 1999 describing the INC's proposed insurrection as 'militarily ludicrous' and likely to result in 'either direct American intervention or a massive bloodbath'.⁵²

The US contented itself with trying to reconcile the contending Kurdish factions in the hope of a meaningful military challenge in the north. Sanctions were also a possible, if rather unlikely, route to regime-change. Madeleine Albright (by her own admission, very foolishly) declared in 1996 that sanctions, now bringing severe hardship to the Iraqi people, were a price worth paying in terms of the possibly terminal damage to Saddam.⁵³ Regarding WMD, the administration broadly had confidence in the UN inspections regime, at least until the defection from Baghdad of General Hussein Kamal. In 1995, Kamal relayed tales of Iraqi evasion and defiance of the inspections mandated under the terms of the 1991 Gulf War peace. He also raised the prospect of Saddam's capacity to produce new weapons, effectively beyond the practical remit of the UN inspectors. In his January 1998 State of the Union Address, Clinton threatened the Iraqi leader directly: 'You have used weapons of mass destruction before. We are determined to deny you the capacity to use them again.'⁵⁴ The address was followed by a campaign by Clinton, strongly backed by Al Gore, to alert the allies and the American public to the threat of Saddam's weapons development. With UN Secretary General Kofi Annan trying to broker a deal via Moscow, Clinton still insisted that his aims were limited: 'Would the Iraqi people be better off if there were a change in leadership? I certainly think they would be. But that is not what the United Nations has authorized us to do.'[55] Clinton publicly denied any policy to promote Saddam's assassination (something which would actually have been inadmissible under US law). Russia, France and China, however, left no doubt about their opposition to a sustained US military attack.[56] The US Congress also began to raise doubts about the propriety of a wide enabling resolution on Iraq; Democratic Senator Max Cleland of Georgia compared such a measure to the 1964 Gulf of Tonkin Resolution, with its virtually unrestricted grant of power to President Johnson in Vietnam.[57] Clinton declared that US 'soldiers, our ships, our planes' would stay in the Persian Gulf until 'we are satisfied that ... Iraq is complying with its commitments'.[58]

Opinion in Congress began to coalesce towards the view that administration policy towards Iraq was confused, and that Saddam was in effect taking the US for a ride. Jesse Helms and Trent Lott accused Clinton of 'appeasement'. At the other end of the scale, Madeleine Albright, Sandy Berger and William Cohen faced a difficult and hostile, anti-war audience at a televised session at Ohio State University. At this stage, Clinton in some journalistic accounts seemed almost to have retreated into the White House, unwilling to participate in 'town hall' or question-and-answer events while the Lewinsky scandal was progressing.[59] In October 1998, Congress eventually passed, and Clinton signed, the Iraq Liberation Act, authorizing (as the *NYT* put it) 'the Pentagon and the State Department to transfer up to $97 million in US military equipment to Iraq's unreliable opposition groups in the hope that they can somehow overthrow the Iraqi dictator and replace him with a democratic government'.[60] Regime-change was now written into law. Clinton incorporated the goal of unseating Saddam into his narrative of globalising democratisation. A post-Saddam Iraq would be welcomed into the 'family of nations'.[61]

Yet another demonstration of Baghdad brinkmanship in early November 1998 – Saddam expelled UN inspectors only to make concessions almost immediately after – raised more doubts about US credibility. Sandy Berger was at the public centre of the controversy over Iraqi 'cheat and retreat' tactics, sprinting (as *Time* reported) 'back and forth between his West Wing desk to the Oval Office and even to the President's putting green to muster all the pieces for a strong strike against Saddam'. Saddam's concessionary letter, according to Berger, had 'more holes than Swiss cheese'.[62] Three permanent members of the UN Security Council – Russia, China and France – were still, however, refusing to be mustered by Berger. Gore and Albright emerged to present the case for America going ahead anyway. Secretary Albright was quoted as remarking: 'Up to now, we've had diplomacy backed by force. Now we need to shift to force backed up by diplomacy.'[63]

The ensuing operation, Desert Fox – sustained air attacks for four days by US and UK forces – marked a significant shift away from multilateralism. The immediate occasion of the attacks was a report on Iraqi inspection evasions from

Richard Butler, head of the UN team. Clinton and Tony Blair insisted that their goal was still to force Saddam to comply with UN requirements, but there was no explicit UN Security Council endorsement of the attacks. Yet there was still no real prospect even of this intense bombing and missile action actually unseating Saddam. The key targets were elite military and intelligence facilities. Secretary Cohen talked of weakening Saddam's 'personal support structure and sowing unrest within the Iraqi military'.[64] Tony Blair commented upon the conclusion of Desert Fox: 'What we have done is to put (Saddam) back securely and firmly in his cage.'[65]

It is very difficult to assess how the impeachment crisis affected Clinton's decision. Not to act after the November build-up would certainly have occasioned charges of domestic weakness translating into international irresolution. Clinton never seriously considered the use of ground troops in Iraq, and certainly not at the height of the impeachment crisis. The four-day bombardment was a kind of middle way between damaging inaction and overreaching recklessness. The operation nevertheless had elements of the kind of back-to-the-wall desperation which Clinton probably felt. Unlike the August 1998 Sudan and Afghanistan strikes, Desert Fox was not preceded by any meaningful consultation with legislative leaders. It was conducted, as Ryan Hendrickson writes, with 'scant attention' to the War Powers Resolution.[66] It was as if Clinton was declaring his own, temporary personal liberation from the restraints of the American system, appealing (as he was implicitly in the impeachment crisis itself) over the heads of Congress to the US people. The White House web site announced on 17 December: 'if we turn our backs on Saddam's defiance, the credibility of US power as a check against him will be destroyed.'[67] The public backed Clinton, with 67 per cent in a *Time*/CNN poll rejecting suggestions that the attacks were linked to the impeachment.[68] A majority in Congress also backed the president, yet there was now, four months after the anti-al Qaeda attacks, little Republican reluctance to link military strikes with the domestic crisis. Jesse Helms backed Clinton. However, Trent Lott declared that 'both the timing and the policy are subject to question'. House Rules Committee chairman Gerald Solomon of New York told CNN: 'The president ought to know better. We should not be handling impeachment while bombing is going on, and that's exactly why he's doing it.'[69]

During 1999 and 2000, the US concentrated on sustaining sanctions at the UN, in the face of Russian and French proposals to lift them in response to Iraqi concessions. Most of the Iran Liberation Act money remained officially unspent, although, towards the end of 2000 Congress effectively forced the administration to increase its disbursements to oppositional groups. In Iraq, the Clinton administration managed to avoid a replay of John Kennedy's 'Bay of Pigs'. It displayed a healthy suspicion of grandiose schemes floated by exile groups. Yet the Iraq policy, floating as it did between containment and regime-change, was confused and unsatisfactory. Washington was sorely provoked by Saddam's 'cheat and retreat' tactics – tactics which were pursued by an Iraqi leadership which was aware of Clinton's domestic problems. Trent Lott and Gerald Solomon were wrong to ascribe the decision to launch the Desert Fox programme to the exigencies of impeachment. Nevertheless, the rather peculiar handling of the Iraq crisis at the end of 1998 cannot entirely be divorced from the unique domestic political circumstances which surrounded it.

The other half of 'double containment' – Clinton's policy towards Iran – was somewhat more straightforward. Robert Pelletreau told the House Foreign Affairs Committee in 1994 that the administration's objective was to bring about a change in Iranian behaviour, regarding weapon development, promotion of terrorism, meddling in the Arab–Israeli peace process, domestic human rights and threat to neighbouring countries.[70] Policy towards Iran in the first term centred on sanctions, with the Republican Congress passing (and Clinton eventually signing) the 1996 Iran–Libya Sanctions Act. This legislation, sponsored by Senator Alphonse D'Amato (Republican, NY), had been pending in Congress since 1994. (D'Amato was an important figure in the congressional investigations into the Clintons' financial affairs – a denizen of what Bill Clinton was coming to call 'Whitewater World'.) Objecting principally to the extraterritoriality of the 'D'Amato bill' – the penalties to be applied, as in the Helms–Burton legislation on Cuba – Clinton made several efforts to pre-empt it. In March and May 1995, he issued executive orders which effectively amounted to a unilateral US trade embargo on Iran, minus the extraterritoriality sought by D'Amato. The president, wearing a *yarmulke*, announced the policy to the World Jewish Congress in May 1995. Principally affected was the US Conoco corporation, a DuPont subsidiary which had recently been offered the opportunity to develop two offshore oilfields by Iranian leader Hashemi Rafsanjani.[71] The WP reported, in September, a battle over the D'Amato legislation between the Clinton administration, Iran, European oil companies and Congress, with AIPAC strongly supporting the legislation. A US oil industry spokesman was quoted as saying that D'Amato's proposals, which were significantly stronger than Clinton's pre-emptive version, made for 'political appeal', but 'not a lot of sound economics'.[72] Clinton eventually signed D'Amato's anti-Iranian law, complete with extraterritoriality. The legislation included sanctions on Libya – added by Senator Edward Kennedy – as a way of pressurising President Mu'ammar Qadhafi to extradite suspects in the 1988 bombing of Pan Am Flight 103 over Lockerbie in Scotland.[73] Ensuing rows with European allies were defused by an agreement whereby the US suspended extraterritoriality in return for tougher EU policies on terrorism. Special arrangements were also negotiated for US companies who wanted to transport oil from Central Asia via Iran.[74]

Some of the competing pressures in containment of Iran were exposed in May 1996 when, on the very same day, Warren Christopher criticised European companies for trading with Tehran, and Richard Holbrooke admitted to Congress that the administration had permitted (even encouraged) Iran to ship arms via Croatia to the Bosnian Muslims.[75] Rafsanjani's public welcoming of the Rabin assassination outraged Clinton, who certainly contemplated a shift to a clearer CIA-oriented regime-change strategy regarding Iran in 1995–96. Overt military action against Iran was seriously contemplated following the Saudi (Khobar Towers) bombing of June 1996; the weight of evidence for the attack, however, pointed to al Qaeda rather than to Tehran.[76] At the FBI, Louis Freeh became convinced that the White House was soft on Iran.[77]

The election of reformist President Muhammad Khatami in December 1997 set the agenda for Clinton's second term. With Saudi Arabia acting as a potential broker between Washington and Tehran and Khatami proclaiming the need for 'thoughtful dialogue with the US', relations thawed.[78] By early 2000, with more and more breaches appearing in the sanctions regime, *The Economist* was reporting the containment policy towards Iran as 'long gone'.[79] Forces for relaxing anti-Iranian containment included the oil corporations, some elements at State, and also Democrats in Congress who were anxious to provide a counter to the Republican charge on foreign policy. Archie Duncan, head of Conoco, urged Clinton to 'get on the dance floor' with Khatami. Lee Hamilton of Indiana, ranking Democrat on the (newly re-named) House International Relations Committee, urged a 'new policy of engagement'.[80] The State Department and White House drew back from imposing sanctions on French, Russian and Malaysian oil companies engaged in trade with Iran. In June 1998, Madeleine Albright spoke of the possibility of finding a 'road map' that would lead to 'normal relations'.[81]

Yet evidence of Iranian involvement in sponsorship of terrorism tugged the other way. In 1998, the State Department declared that Iran was the 'most active state sponsor of terrorism'.[82] FBI head Louis Freeh personally travelled to Argentina to investigate possible Iranian complicity in anti-Jewish bombings in Buenos Aires.[83] When Iran and the US met in a World Cup soccer match in June 1998, the press began to speculate about 'soccer diplomacy' as an equivalent to the US–Chinese 'ping-pong diplomacy' of the early 1970s. The spell was rather broken by Ayatollah Ali Khamenei, still Iranian supreme leader, who declared: 'Tonight again the strong and arrogant opponents felt the bitter taste of defeat at your hands.'[84] Martin Indyk, now Assistant Secretary at State for Near Eastern Affairs, opposed Albright's olive branch. He told the Senate Foreign Relations Committee in May 1998 that America's 'basic purpose' was to 'persuade Iran that it cannot have it both ways': any move away from containment would occur only in response to *consistent* evidence of positive changes in Iranian behaviour.[85] Indyk became increasingly concerned to publicise Iranian weapons development. Iranian ballistic missile tests in July 1998 caused Inyk to condemn Tehran's 'clandestine nuclear program', which he described as threatening, despite actual acquisition of nuclear weapons being 'many years off'.[86] In 2000, Clinton signed a measure aimed at curbing Russian military and technological aid to Iran. The legislation incorporated the possibility of presidential waivers of retaliatory action against Russia; but it also indicated the degree to which a combination of Iranian inconsistency and US suspicion of, in particular, Tehran's weapons programme had incinerated Albright's olive branch.[87] Indyk offered the following commentary on 'dual containment' as it applied both to Iran and to Iraq at the close of the Clinton administration: 'on the Iraqi side it's containment plus regime change, ... on the Iranian side it's containment until they are ready for engagement.'[88]

Camp David, 2000

The Wye River Agreement, though it rapidly froze as in anticipation of the May 1999 Israeli elections, was an important achievement for Clinton's personal diplomacy. The year of 1998, however, contained many signs that, the more things changed in the Middle East, the more they remained the same. At the beginning of the year, even as Washington pressured Netanyahu to move on peace concessions, new American long-range fighter-bombers were delivered to Israel.[89] Despite UN resolutions, Israel remained in both the West Bank and in South Lebanon, while the settler movement continued. From America's viewpoint, the election of Israeli Labor leader Ehud Barak appeared as a sign of hope. Barak joined Yasser Arafat, who had won Palestinian elections in 1996, as a leader who seemed committed to serious 'final status' negotiations. Barak was not especially keen on moving to implement the Wye River accords; as Clinton explained, 'the 180,000 Israeli settlers in the West Bank and Gaza were a formidable force' for Barak to oppose.[90] The Wye Agreement, or at least those sections of it that involved US (including CIA) security assistance, was also still bogged down in the process of US congressional approval. Believing Wye in its present form to be 'more than the Israeli public could handle', Barak engineered a renegotiation of its terms at Sharm el-Sheikh in Egypt in September 1999. Albright reassured Arafat that the US 'knows how destructive settlement activity has been to the pursuit of Palestinian–Israeli peace'. Mocked as 'an agreement to implement an agreement to implement an agreement', the renegotiation of the Wye accords nevertheless gave Albright the opportunity to schedule a 'final status' meeting for 2000.[91] Delivering the Yitzhak Rabin memorial lecture in Tel Aviv in November 1999, Hillary Clinton promised the US would do its part: 'by fighting terrorism and intimidation; by helping the parties, not by imposing decisions upon them; by fighting for the foreign aid that helps guarantee Israelis' security and brings prosperity to the West Bank and Gaza.'[92]

American disillusionment with Barak began during the Israeli–Syrian negotiations held in Shepherdstown, West Virginia, in January 2000. Agreement on an Israeli retreat to the pre-1967 war was not achieved. A subsequent meeting between Barak and President Assad in Geneva (March 2000), by which time Israel had announced its intention to withdraw from South Lebanon, became, in Dennis Ross's words, 'a high-visibility failure'.[93] Though Barak had agreed to a withdrawal from the Golan Heights, he would not agree to retreat fully to the pre-Six Day War line. The Americans saw Barak, with an eye on his domestic audience, as having indulged in devious manipulation of the US. The Israeli leader failed to keep Washington informed of his negotiating position, even though Clinton had agreed personally to communicate Barak's territorial offer to Assad. To quote Aaron Miller: 'Not only did Barak's offer have zero chance of working, it wasted valuable time and again eroded American credibility.'[94] President Assad's death in June effectively closed off the Syrian track.

Though content to blame Barak (as well as Assad) for the failure at Shepherdstown and Geneva, Clinton and Albright had not been immune from a degree of wishful thinking, even naivety, in handling the Israeli–Syria negotiations. Clinton's presentation of himself as a well-intentioned American, committed to make up for in energy and good-natured enthusiasm what he lacked in un-American guile, of course, was also something of a ploy. It drew on a long diplomatic tradition of American self-presentation towards the devious Europeans. Yet this was essentially the mode in which Clinton agreed with Barak to convene an Israeli–Palestinian summit at Camp David in July 2000. Back-channel Israeli–Palestinian contacts and an upsurge in violence contributed to Clinton's decision to proceed. This was to be Clinton's great effort to secure the prize of peace in the Middle East. It was something of a gamble on the scale of Jimmy Carter's 1978 Camp David summit. To the extent that Clinton, unlike Carter in 1978, was not facing re-election, it was perhaps less courageously foolhardy. However, there was little doubt that Clinton's Camp David – the parallel with 1978 raised the stakes even higher – would constitute his ultimate bid to move from impeached leader to historic peace-maker. Clinton brought all his usual intelligence, charm and energy to the task.

At the summit, Clinton outlined his view of a plausible settlement. It would include a reversion to pre-1967 borders, but with special arrangements and transfers for existing Jewish settlements; an autonomous Palestinian state would be established; the status of Jerusalem, 'a practical, a holy and a political city', would have to recognise its particular importance to Jews, Muslims and Christians; some arrangements for the return of refugees, certainly to Palestine and at least some to Israel, would have to be agreed. (The problem with refugee returns to Israel, of course, was their implication for the future of the Jewish state.) Clinton noted that 'the Palestinians believed in compensation for modifications' – special arrangements regarding the Israeli settlements – 'made to accommodate Israeli needs'. On refugees, Clinton outlined his 'parameter' – 'the Palestinians needed the right' to return, but 'Israel must have the sovereign right to determine who should be admitted to their land'.[95] The US promised financial assistance for a settlement. Barak responded with a territorial offer for a Palestinian state, including around 90 per cent of the West Bank, complex shared sovereignty arrangements on Jerusalem, but no refugee returns to Israel. On day eight of the discussions, Clinton, due to leave for a G-8 summit in Okinawa, outlined to Arafat what he thought was practical: '91 per cent of the West Bank, plus at least a symbolic swap of land near Gaza and the West Bank; a capital in East Jerusalem' and complex administrative sharing over disputed areas of Jerusalem, including the holy sites. When Arafat refused, Clinton tried to exert pressure via other Arab leaders, King Abdullah of Jordan and President Ben Ali of Tunisia. On his return from the G-8 meeting, Clinton began again, finally 'giving up when effective control over the Temple Mount and all East Jerusalem was not enough for Arafat without the word "sovereignty"'. Arafat rejected a last, last attempt to start a renegotiation with Barak over Jerusalem.[96]

Clinton had not given up hope. The summit had failed, but perhaps a Camp David 'process' could be made to produce results before Clinton's time ran out. While a result in the Middle East before presidential election day would have been an optimal conclusion, the real deadline was not July, nor September (the first goal set after the July summit), nor even November, 2000, but January 2001. Clinton felt that Arafat was always unlikely to make a deal until the last minute. The possibility of eventual success was certainly receding. Arafat would doubtless be calculating his chances of winning a deal under either a Republican or Democratic successor to Clinton. Nevertheless, Arafat might still make a dramatically timed acceptance of Barak's conditions (on territory and refugees, as well as on Jerusalem). Clinton just hoped that 'Arafat's watch kept good time'.[97] He urged the Israelis and Palestinians to 'avoid any unilateral actions that would only make the hard task ahead more difficult', to 'bridge the gaps' in the months ahead, since 'the alternative is unthinkable'.[98] Dennis Ross was actually encouraged by the fact that the 'taboos on serious discussion of the core issues like Jerusalem, borders, and refugees had been broken'. Yet this was the third high-visibility failure in a row, following Shepherdstown and Geneva. The American temptation was simply to blame Arafat. The 'real question' for Ross was: 'Was the summit transforming for Yasser Arafat?'[99]

Ross's team continued to develop proposals for a deal. Aaron Miller and Rob Malley tended to focus on notions of 'fairness', with Ross himself arguing for proposals which were geared to 'what each side needed' in practicable and political terms, 'not what they wanted and not what they felt they were entitled to'.[100] Negotiations continued in September between Ross and both Israeli and Palestinian representatives in Washington. Progress was made, with Ross suggesting new arrangements for Palestinian sovereignty in Jerusalem's Arab neighbourhoods. Barak actually invited Ross to his home on 25 September, where they both spoke to President Clinton on the telephone. Tension mounted, however, on the news that Likud leader Ariel Sharon was to visit Haram Al-Sharif (Temple Mount) in Jerusalem on 28 September. The visit was, in effect, a demonstration against any Israeli concessions on Jerusalem, and seemed sure to provoke violence. Ross attempted to intercede with Shlomo Ben-Ami, Acting Foreign Minister and Minister for Internal Security, but it seemed that neither he nor Ehud Barak had much influence over Sharon. The incident sparked the extended violence associated with the 'al Aqsa Intifada' or second major Palestinian uprising against the Israelis. The violence set the increasingly frenetic context for Clinton's final efforts to save the peace deal.

Ross now arranged a meeting in Paris with Barak, Albright, George Tenet, and Arafat. This was designed to give the Palestinian leader 'an excuse to reassert control and step back from the violence'.[101] On 16 October, the show shifted to Sharm al-Sheikh for a summit chaired by Clinton and Egyptian President Hosni Mubarak, and then to Washington. In Paris and at Sharm al-Sheikh, Arafat pushed successfully for an American-led commission of enquiry into the violence following Sharon's Temple Mount trip. Refusing actually to sign a cease-fire deal, Arafat was treated to an expression of anger from President Mubarak: 'Come on man, what more do you want, this guy (Clinton) came all the way from Washington, we've been hammering away trying to get a deal, and now you want to revisit it?'[102] On 9 November at the White House, Arafat appeared to accept the 'parameters' outlined by Clinton.[103] Ross went on to meet Arafat in Rabat

(Morocco). He told the PLO leader that, although the 2000 US election was still disputed, it was likely that George W. Bush would win. The new administration 'was unlikely to invest much in Middle East peace – particularly if President Clinton, after all his efforts, failed to achieve an agreement'.[104] Arafat seemed impressed by this, and the negotiations rolled on to Bolling Air Force Base, just outside Washington, on 19 December 2000.

Out of this diplomatic maelstrom emerged the 'Clinton ideas'. These were presented to Israeli and Palestinian negotiators on 23 December at the White House. They were presented in an informal way, designed to counter Arafat's 'style of pocketing any advance and treating it as a point of departure and not the culmination'.[105] Jerusalem would again be subject to complex division, with Palestinian sovereignty over the Temple Mount, and Israeli sovereignty over the Western Wall and its associated 'holy place'. There would be a demilitarised Palestinian state, in receipt of international security and financial assistance, notably for refugee resettlement. There would be guaranteed refugee returns only in the West Bank and Gaza. Clinton's new 'parameter' included a land swap and a guarantee that 80 per cent of the Israeli settlers would remain. From the Palestinian point of view, this was an improvement on the deal available at the July summit. As Jimmy Carter later wrote, however, the various concessions to Israeli security concerns – such as roads, 'life arteries' for the settlements, and emergency arrangements for Israeli troop deployments – did make the deal difficult for Arafat, faced as he was by violent extremist challenges to the ascendancy of his al-Fatah organisation, to accept. In Carter's words, the Clinton ideas divided 'the West Bank into at least two non-contiguous areas and multiple fragments', while Israeli 'control of the Jordan River Valley' denied the Palestinians direct access to Jordan.[106]

In developing his 'ideas', Clinton, of course, was aware that Barak too was under enormous pressure at home. Likud, led by Ariel Sharon, won a landslide victory over Barak in the February 2001 Israeli general election. On 7 January 2001, Clinton announced that both Barak and Arafat 'have now accepted these parameters as a basis for further efforts, though both have expressed some reservations'.[107] Negotiations carried on at Taba in Egypt into the new American presidency, but without much further progress. This final round of talks was actually broken off by Barak rather than Arafat. Nevertheless, Clinton, Albright and Ross later laid the blame squarely on the Palestinian's shoulders.[108] In retrospect, it appears the outbreak of the second intifada produced conditions in which any meaningful, enforceable agreement was unlikely to emerge. The best chance of peace was at the July summit, and it was a pity that Arafat did not, there, choose the path of more positive commitment, if not of actual and final acceptance. Joe Lockhart, Clinton's press secretary recalled Arafat's behaviour at Camp David in the following way:

> I think he was at the point in his life where this sense of willingness to take huge risks was gone, and he looked at his legacy, and it was almost as if he became a smaller person. He sat there and in his mind, he was saying, 'I'm not the Arab who is going to give up Jerusalem.'[109]

Despite the exchanges at Rabat, Arafat was apparently not especially impressed by the arguments relating to the American electoral timetable. To quote Robert Malley: 'he contemplated a rushed deadline from a departing US president and a departing – and despised – Israeli prime minister to accept an interesting but imperfect deal.'[110] His instincts and sense of self-preservation told him that other deals would be available in the future. Indeed, the whole idea of being summoned to Camp David to dance to the election-led American tune seemed to several members of the Palestinian delegation simply a manifestation of neo-colonialism.[111] Arafat does deserve a degree of blame; yet there were still important weaknesses in the American conduct of the summit. Clinton's team did not seem fully to appreciate the pressures on, and divisions within, the Palestinian delegation.[112] The summit was under-prepared. As Aaron Miller recalled, Clinton 'never developed or asked for either a strategy to maximise the chance for success, or a backup plan to minimize the impact of failure; nor, I might add, did we give him one'.[113] In particular, the failure to line up neighbouring Arab states to pressurise Arafat at Camp David was a chance lost. The staff work at Camp David was greatly inferior to that available to Carter in 1978. The ever-present parallels between 2000 and 1978 were also rather unhelpful; Joe Lockhart was driven in exasperation to tell the press, 'this is not 1978'.[114] Tensions between State Department and NSC personnel at Camp David were evident.[115] Clinton's 'innocent American' ploy was not without its strengths, but it tended to weaken his hard negotiating edge. Miller saw Clinton at Camp David as lacking 'Kissinger's deviousness, Carter's missionary focus, and (James) Baker's unsentimental toughness'.[116] Clinton's subsequent blaming of Arafat revealed a desire to avoid tough examination of his own conduct, including the American tendency to work out from proposals likely to be acceptable to Israel. Despite all this, Clinton's efforts in 2000 to achieve an Arab–Israeli settlement were extraordinary in their intensity and intelligent integrity. They emerge with credit from comparison with any diplomatic initiative mounted by any previous US president.

9 Bill Clinton's foreign policy

Let us remind ourselves of the key points raised in Chapter 1 concerning the assessment of presidential leadership in foreign policy. While recognising acute problems of subjectivism, and of structure and agency, it was concluded that there are at least some general pointers to guide us in judging presidential foreign policy performance.

A good foreign policy president will build on, and not squander, any positive inheritance from his predecessor. He will possess 'contextual intelligence': the ability to calibrate decisions in the light of understanding of both the domestic and international contexts in which his decisions are made.[1] A good foreign policy president will at least aspire to rationality – defined in terms of the conscious weighing of options and their likely costs and benefits – in decision-making. He will understand that good policy involves value trade-offs, and will approach the issue of value complexity in a spirit of measured rationality. A good president is at least cognisant of the potentially destructive power of intra-administration rivalries. He will not be able to abolish bureaucratic politics, but will nonetheless work consciously and conscientiously to mitigate their impact. A good foreign policy president will have an understanding of his own cognitive style, and indeed of his own emotional needs, and will strive to integrate these into an ordered, and possibly compensatory, decisional structure. He will recognise the virtues of multiple advocacy in his advisory process. He will be able to adapt and re-think. A good foreign policy leader will choose able people for his administration, and will not hesitate to remove individuals who are somehow undermining administration efficiency and purpose. A successful president will have some kind of integrating foreign policy purpose beyond a generalised commitment to advancing material American interests and security. He will appreciate the complex nature of international power relations, but will not allow this appreciation to paralyse him into a state of nervous inaction. He will communicate his foreign policy purpose to his administration and to Congress. He will find a culturally appropriate means of 'selling' it to the US public. He will avoid egregious and calamitous sins of commission. He will at least try conscientiously to respect domestic and international law, and will also recognise the value of stable alliance structures.

Bill Clinton, as we saw in Chapter 1, is conventionally seen as falling short of many of these judgemental standards. He is judged by many commentators as a leader who detested making hard choices, who often let policy drift, and who failed, ultimately, to put America on a clear post-Cold War foreign policy path. Hal Brands suggests that, by the end of the second term, Clinton had actually lost control of his own foreign policy.[2]

My general conclusions about Clinton are considerably more positive than this received, critical view. However, most of the common criticisms do have a degree of accuracy. Clinton was often a decisional ditherer. He was capable of swift decision-making, as in the cases of the Mexican *peso* rescue and the 1996 confrontation over Taiwan. His natural decisional style, however, was flexible to the point of prevarication. To quote Warren Christopher: 'When it comes down to the wire, Clinton likes to keep several names or options in play until the decision absolutely must be made.'[3] Clinton's decisional style recalls a famous description of how Lyndon Johnson 'did not reveal – indeed, he did not fully determine in his own mind – what his position would be until the last possible moment, when the conditions of battle were fully known to him'.[4] The style did not serve Johnson well in his foreign policy. It was less disastrous for Clinton, but in some policy areas, notably Bosnia in the first term, it caused serious harm. Another common criticism of Clinton, his early personal neglect of foreign policy, also has Johnsonian echoes. Again the early self-image of being primarily a domestic rather than a foreign policy president was more harmful for LBJ than it was for Clinton. Nevertheless, President Clinton's early reluctance to situate himself at the centre of the foreign policy process was damaging, and in relation to Somalia had negative implications for the entire course of his presidency. It is also appropriate here to acknowledge an important criticism of Clinton which does emerge from the preceding pages: the way in which the impeachment crisis negatively affected the coherence and integrity of foreign policy. There is no suggestion here that Clinton took military action in Iraq, Sudan or Afghanistan as part of an effort to divert attention from the Lewinsky scandal. Such a course of action would have been not only uncharacteristically unsubtle, but also entirely counter-productive. Rather, the finding in this book is that, although Clinton handled his impeachment crisis better than Richard Nixon during his Watergate agonies, President Clinton's second term foreign policy was far from 'business as usual'. We have seen how Bill Clinton's personal and political vulnerabilities during the impeachment crisis fed into his foreign policy in numerous ways: from his inept handling of the FBI (with implications for the battle against international terrorism), to the dynamics of military action in Kosovo.

This final chapter, in offering a broadly positive judgement of Clinton's foreign policy leadership, will consider the following: process and procedural integrity and efficiency; the existence and articulation of integrating purpose; policy development and adaptation; questions of continuity and discontinuity with the two Bushes; and, lastly, issues relating to Clinton's 'contextual intelligence' and character. First, however, a brief judgemental summary of the policy areas covered in the previous chapters.

Clinton's free trade initiatives gave purpose and integration to foreign policy. They were not uniformly successful, but (despite second term battles with

Congress over 'fast-track' and despite the wreckage in Seattle) they did broadly remain on track. In Somalia, Clinton faced a difficult inheritance from the elder Bush. Yet Clinton's own policy ran out of control, while an excessive reaction to Somalian failure constituted a kind of double jeopardy. Effective action in Rwanda would have been very difficult to accomplish, but was not even given serious consideration. The quasi-invasion of Haiti in 1994 was a sloppy success. Clinton struggled throughout his presidency to establish a reasonable working relationship with the US military. Bosnia was the site of acute presidential failure before Clinton bit the leadership bullet in 1995. Clinton's role in the Northern Irish peace process was historic, vitally important, and a lasting testament to creative American diplomacy. The Kosovo action was successful in narrow terms, but raised doubts about the ability of Washington to develop a responsible policy of measured internationalism under conditions of undisputed global US hegemony. Regarding relations with old communist enemies, Clinton enjoyed some clear successes: these included the de-nuclearisation of Ukraine and normalisation with Vietnam. Policy toward Russia, Cuba, China and North Korea was frequently blown off course. In some instances, such as the early near-confrontation with Pyonyang, it involved episodes of considerable international danger. In general terms, Clinton's policies towards the old enemies at least avoided calamitous disaster and exhibited some of the characteristics of a more or less defensible muddling through. NATO enlargement was a major Clinton success. Alliance relationships were sometimes unnecessarily fraught, though again some real successes – such as the newly invigorated security relationships hinging on Japan, South Korea and Australia in the second term – may be identified. The nuclearisation of Pakistan and India was an obvious Clinton foreign policy failure. President Clinton did not ignore international terrorism, though the 1999 attack on Sudan was a major blunder. Second term remilitarisation was a joint product of the Republican Congress and of Clinton's acceptance of global American commitments. Whatever its origins, this remilitarisation undermined the familiar accusation that Clinton bequeathed a hollow and denuded military to President George W. Bush (Bush43). Policy towards Iraq was muddled and the quest for Israeli–Palestinian peace was affected by misjudgement, as well as by a failure to demonstrate thoroughgoing American even-handedness. Nevertheless, the final diplomatic effort to secure a Middle East peace deal was a Clintonian *tour de force*.

With regard to decision-making process, we have seen numerous examples of intra-administration rivalry, and negative bureaucratic politics. Clashes between State Department and Pentagon were frequent, though they were as much the result of inherent differences of perspective as of any easily rectifiable bureaucratic or personnel problem. In assessing Clinton's foreign policy process, it is also important to appreciate the extraordinarily fluid nature of the post-Cold War policy-making context. This was a decisional world which frequently confounded expectation. It was a world in which liberals in Congress urged Clinton to take military action; a world in which Democratic liberals and Republican conservatives united to attack pragmatic policies towards China; and a world in which a post-Vietnam War, post-Cold War Pentagon was often far more cautious about military action than (particularly in the second term) was the State Department. Under Clinton, and in the face of bewildering shifts in expectations of the policy process, the almost ontological rivalry between the White House and the State Department was held more or less in check. There was no replay of the public battles between NSA and Secretary of State that had so damaged the Carter Presidency. Indeed, the second term partnership of Madeleine Albright and Sandy Berger was a model of successful transcendence of 'natural' bureaucratic rivalry. Criticisms have been raised concerning many of the key players in Clinton's foreign policy hierarchy: concerning Les Aspin's lack of personal organisation, about Tony Lake's stressful overwork, about Warren Christopher's lack of forcefulness, about Madeleine Albright's tendency towards excessive self-certainty, about Richard Holbrooke's apparently weak commitment to mutuality in teamwork, and so on. The preceding chapters offer detailed commentary regarding these, and many other Clinton appointees. In retrospect, however, Clinton's key players seem at least the equal to any recent administration in terms of ability and conscientious commitment. By the same token, while perhaps not quite achieving the ideal of multiple advocacy, a foreign policy team which included Aspin, Cohen, Christopher, Albright, Lake and Holbrooke straddled pretty much the entire range of post-Cold War policy opinion. With some important exceptions (such as Louis Freeh at the FBI), Clinton was not afraid to remove ineffective or disloyal personnel. There were instances of 'groupthink', as in the collective reluctance to come to terms with what was happening in Rwanda, but again Clinton's multiple advocacy record does bear comparison with that of other administrations. As already indicated, Clinton's personal difficulty with hard choices did have an enervating effect on the administration. What perhaps needs to be emphasised, however, is Clinton's great capacity for hard work, his acute intelligence and his willingness (as his abandonment of the early foreign policy disengagement) to learn and adapt.

In terms of integrating purpose, it will come as no surprise to find this identified once again as the presidential commitment to an intertwining political and economic globalisation. Expressed with translucent clarity in the February 1993 American University address, Clinton's commitment to 'the imperative of American leadership in the face of global change', to 'constant innovation', to the understanding that 'there is no such thing as purely domestic policy', and to riding the 'bucking bronco' of globalisation remained the central focus of the administration. These commitments were articulated with intensity and flair right up until the close of the second term. Crucial here was the theory of the democratic peace, a notion which also received canonical expression in the American University address: 'Just as neighbours who raise each others' barns are less likely to become arsonists, people who raise each others' living standards through commerce are less likely to become combatants.'[5] Expressions of hope for democratic peace became a little darker in the second term, as the administration became preoccupied with international terrorism and a little less confident about the trajectory of development in Russia and China. However, the foundational, optimistic commitment to democratising globalisation remained. The commitment represented Clinton's reworking of the American dialectic of ideals and interests. It drew on strands in the history of US foreign policy deriving from Thomas Jefferson, Alexander Hamilton and Woodrow Wilson. As we noted in Chapter 3, it embraced contradictions. Bill Clinton, as a pro-business, pro-global free trade president, may come to be remembered as a leader who surrendered to the market. He may come to be remembered as a president whose faith in the interweaving of free trade and political democracy was either naive or self-serving. He should not be remembered as a president who lacked an integrating foreign policy purpose.

In relation to foreign policy dynamics, the arc of development sketched out in Chapter 2 was designed to counter the accusation that everything about the 42nd President of the United States was random and haphazard. There was a logic of development, with key influences identified as the need to adapt to the Republican congressional challenge, the new confidence surrounding America's post-1994 international position, and the realisation that action must replace drift in the Balkans. There was a whiff of the 'revenge of geopolitics' about this arc of development, with some parallels with the experience of the administration of Jimmy Carter. Carter's human rights initiatives of 1977–78 gave way to more traditional security concerns in response to the Iranian revolution and the Soviet invasion of Afghanistan.[6] Clinton's second term – like the second part of Carter's single term – saw a move away from self-consciously 'humanitarian' foreign policy. Yet, as has just been indicated, Clinton certainly did not abandon the commitment to economic and political globalisation, and to democratic peace. The choice of an economics-centred advocate of free trade as his second term NSA was indicative of Clinton's concern to avoid defining his foreign policy in traditional 'security' terms. Clinton no more saw himself as abandoning humanitarianism in foreign policy than Jimmy Carter saw himself as abandoning human rights. The action in Kosovo, described by Clinton as the first-ever humanitarian war, took place in his penultimate presidential year. It is also noteworthy that the main security concern after 1996 related to non-state international terrorism, hardly the kind of traditional security concern taken up by Carter following the Soviet assault on Afghanistan. Rather than exemplifying 'the revenge of geopolitics', Clinton's foreign policy developed in a logical way, in response to changing post-Cold War domestic and international conditions.

There were high degrees of continuity between Clinton and the two Bushes. Between 1989 and 2001, America found itself in a world without a clearly defined strategic enemy. Against this background, Clinton articulated a world view which was more domestically and economically oriented than Bush41's New World Order, but which also shared many of its characteristics: the concern to avoid global over-exposure, the battle against a putatively resurgent domestic isolationism, the generalised commitment to American leadership and to world order. The chosen enemies of Both Bush41 and of President Bill Clinton were rogue states and domestic isolationists. If both presidents tended to exaggerate the dangers mounted by such enemies in order to strengthen foreign policy integration, at least both of them kept a sense of proportion. Even taking into account his accelerating preoccupation with international terrorism, Clinton did not in any sense seek to install a new national enemy to take the place of Soviet communism.

Clinton's continuity with the younger Bush is more problematic. The second term Clinton movements, under pressure from the Republican Congress, in the direction of unilateralism certainly constituted one such element of continuity. Regarding international terrorism, Clinton in his second term was actually far more focused on al Qaeda than was George W. Bush in the months preceding 9/11. Kosovo was a controversial war of choice, waged without UN sanction, which did have important implications for the future direction of US foreign policy. However, there was no parallel under Clinton to Bush43's reckless search for monsters to destroy which culminated in the 2003 invasion of Iraq. Clinton was committed to regime-change in Baghdad, but consciously decided against the course of action which his successor adopted. The 2001 disengagement from the Middle East peace process was another important strand of Clinton/George W. Bush discontinuity. The post-9/11 push for greater and more unaccountable presidential authority did have pre-echoes in the Clinton years. We have noted on many occasions the considerable extent to which Clinton was prepared, even as he adapted policy in the face of congressional pressure, to ride fairly roughshod over legislative war powers. The growth of presidential power after 9/11, however, represented a step change from that experienced in the 1990s. After all, for most of his presidency, Bill Clinton was actually and primarily engaged in a straightforward battle with Capitol Hill for control of foreign policy. Clinton fought the battle with a skilled and successful mixture of compromise, evasion and confrontation. The programme of presidential aggrandisement followed by George W. Bush, however, was simply beyond Clinton's reach.[7] Faced with shifting political coalitions at home, Clinton also generally eschewed the intensely partisan political strategies favoured by his Republican successor. Neither Bush41 nor Clinton were foreign policy dogmatists. The younger Bush's slogan – 'Anything But Clinton' – was an indication not only of Bush43's eagerness to reject the legacy of Clinton, but also encapsulated a move away from the pragmatic, cautious conservatism of his father.

We close with some observations about the intersection of character, policy context and leadership. In his novel, *America, America* (published in 2008), Ethan Canin introduces the flawed liberal Democratic Senator, and would-be president, Henry Bonwiller. Though most obviously modelled after Edward Kennedy, Bonwiller also has traces of Clinton. Describing Bonwiller's political rise, Canin's narrator argues that 'power first comes through character – that combination of station and forcefulness that produces not just intimidation, which is power's crudest form, but flattery too...' Bonwiller is described as a man on the cusp: a politician seeking to transcend the character-derived form of power and to grasp a new, less personally wilful, other-directed form of power: 'He must change his personal ambition into ambition for his country.'[8]

Clinton was not entirely successful in effecting this kind of transcendence. His leadership retained qualities of erratic wilfulness which would have been better left in Arkansas. However, it is a contention of this book that the erratic and wilful nature of Clinton's foreign policy leadership has been greatly exaggerated in most prior accounts of his presidency. Clinton was able to use his personal qualities of forcefulness and flattery to keep his foreign policy afloat in times of strategic uncertainty and domestic political challenge. His own political self-image was – as David Remnick put it in a review of Clinton's post-presidency – as 'an exemplary blend of idealist and political roughneck'.[9] Clinton is often seen as a lucky president who simply adopted the 1990s economic boom as his own unlikely creation. A narrator in another recent novel, Joseph O'Neill's *Netherland*, sees Clinton as having done 'little more than oversee the advent of a national fortunateness'.[10] Clinton did ride his luck, but he also developed a style of leadership which disguised his own hard work and keen contextual intelligence under a mask of optimistic facility. Clinton's style – forcefulness and flattery – was less the style of a heroic leader, more the style of a leader who recognised the complexity and uncertainty of the post-Cold War policy-making environment. Efforts to defend Clinton's flexible, inventive and pragmatic leadership as somehow authentically 'postmodern' already seem rather dated.[11] Yet Clinton's leadership was nevertheless a product both of his 'character' and of his contextual intelligence. Complex alignments on foreign policy at home required a complex, adaptable and pragmatic style of leadership. Writing in 1996, John Ikenberry hit the nail on the head. Today's leaders, argued Ikenberry, 'need to be good politicians who can balance domestic and international pressures, and who can cut deals, make compromises, and resolve disputes'. The post-Cold War era demanded 'not the ability to command troops and confront enemies, but the ability to bargain across many different issues and groups, build coalitions, and seize opportunities for agreement'.[12] At his best, Clinton provided exactly that type of leadership.

Bill Clinton did not lose control of his own foreign policy. He suffered big defeats in Congress, but was able, even in his final year in office, to win legislative support for Chinese entry into the WTO. As was argued in Chapter 2, the Republican challenge reinvigorated and refocused the foreign policy energies of the Clinton administration. Clinton actually defied the widespread expectation that presidents would, under post-Cold War conditions, cease to dominate the making of American foreign policy. Bill Clinton handed over to George W. Bush a strong foreign policy presidency. President Clinton also defeated the efforts of Newt Gingrich to smuggle into US government the constitutionally unrecognised office of 'Prime Minister'. It should not be forgotten that America's president 'between the Bushes' was only the second Chief Executive in US history to undergo a Senate impeachment trial. Despite this, Clinton deserves to be remembered as a president who, in real and unexpected ways, actually protected and defended the presidential office.

Notes

1 Perspectives on Clinton and his foreign policy

1 Michael Mandlebaum, 'Foreign Policy as Social Work', FA, 1996, vol. 75, pp. 16–32; Stephen Schlesinger, 'The End of Idealism', *World Policy Journal*, 1998–99, vol. 24, pp. 36–40; A. Z. Rubinstein, 'The New Moralists on a Road to Hell', *Orbis*, 1996, vol. 40, pp. 31–41; Richard N. Haass, 'Fatal Distraction: Bill Clinton's Foreign Policy', *Foreign Policy*, 1997, vol. 107, pp. 112–23; Garry Wills, 'Bully of the Free World', FA, 1999, vol. 79, pp. 50–9.
2 John C. Rielly, ed., *American Public Opinion and US Foreign Policy, 1999*, Chicago, Chicago Council on Foreign Relations, 1999, pp. 32–3.
3 12 January 1999 (cited by Emily O. Goldman and Larry Berman, 'Engaging the World: First Impressions of the Clinton Foreign Policy Legacy', in Colin Campbell and Bert A. Rockman, eds, *The Clinton Legacy*, New York, Chatham House Publishers, 2000, p. 227).
4 Todd S. Purdum, 'Striking Strengths, Glaring Failures', *NYT*, 24 December 2000.
5 Richard W. Stevenson, 'The Wisdom to Let the Good Times Roll', *NYT*, 25 December 2000.
6 David E. Sanger, 'Economic Engine for Foreign Policy', *NYT*, 28 December 2000.
7 Cited in Sally Bedell Smith, *For Love of Politics: The Clintons in the White House*, London, Aurum Press, 2007, p. 444.
8 Quoted in *The Economist*, 19 February 2000 ('It's the World, Stupid!').
9 Christopher Hitchens, *No One Left To Lie To: The Triangulation of William Jefferson Clinton*, London, Verso, 1999, p. 80.
10 William G. Hyland, *Clinton's World: Remaking American Foreign Policy*, Westport, Praeger, 1999, p. 203.
11 Goldman and Berman, 'Engaging the World', p. 252; see also James M. McCormick, 'Clinton and Foreign Policy: Some Lessons for a New Century', in Steven Schier, ed., *The Postmodern Presidency: Bill Clinton's Legacy in US Politics*, Pittsburgh, University of Pittsburgh Press, 2000.
12 As note 8.
13 Marc Landy and Sidney M. Milkis, *Presidential Greatness*, Lawrence, University Press of Kansas, 2000, p. 241.
14 For example, Warren Christopher, *Chances of a Lifetime*, New York, Scribner's, 2001; Madeleine K. Albright, *Madam Secretary: A Memoir*, London, Macmillan, 2003.
15 Stephen M. Walt, 'Two Cheers for Clinton's Foreign Policy', FA, 2000, vol. 79, pp. 63–79.
16 'Clinton's Foreign Policy', *Foreign Policy*, 2000, vol. 120, pp. 18–29, 26.
17 Sidney Blumenthal, *The Clinton Wars: An Insider's Account of the White House Years*, London, Viking, 2001, p. 776.

18 John F. Harris, *The Survivor: Bill Clinton in the White House*, New York, Random House, 2006, p. 435; Joe Klein (*The Natural: The Misunderstood Presidency of Bill Clinton*, London, Hodder and Stoughton, 2002) offered a self-consciously post-9/11 interpretation of Clinton's presidency. See also Todd G. Shields, Jeannie M. Whayne and Donald R. Kelley, eds, *The Clinton Riddle: Perspectives on the Forty-second President*, Fayetteville, University of Arkansas Press, 2004.
19 Michael Cox, 'Empire, Imperialism and the Bush Doctrine', *Review of International Studies*, 2004, vol. 30, pp. 585–609, 604.
20 Ivo H. Daalder and James M. Lindsay, *America Unbound: The Bush Revolution in Foreign Policy*, Washington DC, The Brookings Institution, 2003, p. 4; see also Stephen M. Walt, *Taming American Power: The Global Response to US Primacy*, New York, W. W. Norton, 2005, pp. 41–56.
21 See Robert E. Denton, *Moral Leadership and the American Presidency*, Lanham, Rowman and Littlefield, 2005.
22 George Stephanopoulos, *All Too Human: A Political Education*, London, Hutchinson, 1999.
23 *NYT* 19 June 2004 (Michiko Kakutani); Bill Clinton, *My Life*, London, Arrow Books, 2005.
24 Joe Klein, 'Citizen Clinton', *Time*, 28 June 2004; Anonymous, *Primary Colours: A Novel of Politics*, London, Vintage, 1996.
25 *Reviews in American History* (W. C. Berman), 2005, vol. 33, pp. 126–32, 127.
26 Garry Wills, 'The Tragedy of Bill Clinton', *NYRB*, 12 August 2004, p. 64.
27 Tim Hames, 'Clinton: Egotist and Wrecker', *The Times*, 21 June 2004.
28 Harris, *The Survivor*, p. 434.
29 Nigel Hamilton, *Bill Clinton: Mastering the Presidency*, London, Century, 2007. See also Nigel Hamilton, *Bill Clinton, An American Journey: Great Expectations*, New York, Random House, 2003.
30 D. T. Phillips, *The Clinton Charisma: A Legacy of Leadership*, New York, Palgrave Macmillan, 2007.
31 See Smith, *For Love of Politics*; J. Gerth and D. Van Natta, *Hillary Clinton: Her Way*, London, John Murray, 2007; Carl Bernstein, *A Woman in Charge: The Life of Hillary Rodham Clinton*, New York, Vintage, 2008.
32 Zbigniew Brzezinski, *Second Chance: Three Presidents and the Crisis of American Superpower*, New York, Basic Books, 2007, pp. 83–133, 132–3.
33 See, for example, the special issue of *White House Studies*, 2003, vol. 3; Robert K. Murray and Tim H. Blessing, *Greatness in the White House: Rating the Presidents*, University Park, The Pennsylvania State University Press, 1994; Richard Rose, 'Evaluating Presidents', in George C. Edwards, John H. Kessel and Bert A. Rockman, eds, *Researching the Presidency*, Pittsburgh, University of Pittsburgh Press, 1993; Michael Nelson, 'Evaluating the Presidency', in M. Nelson, ed., *The Presidency and the Political System*, Washington DC, CQ Press, 2003.
34 See Terry Eastland, *Energy in the Executive: The Case for the Strong Presidency*, New York, Free Press, 1992, p. 31.
35 Joseph S. Nye, *The Powers to Lead*, New York, Oxford University Press, 2008, p. 66.
36 Arthur M. Schlesinger, 'Rating the Presidents: Washington to Clinton', *Political Science Quarterly*, 1997, vol. 112, pp. 179–91, 187.
37 Ibid., p. 186.
38 Quoted in Stanley A. Renshon, 'The World According to George W. Bush', in S. A. Renshon and Deborah W. Larson, eds, *Good Judgement in Foreign Policy: Theory and Application*, Lanham, Rowman and Littlefield, 2003, p. 304.
39 Elizabeth Drew, *On The Edge: The Clinton Presidency*, New York, Simon and Schuster, 1994, p. 150.
40 Hillary R. Clinton, *Living History*, London, Headline, 2003, p. 289.

41 Michael J. Heale, *Twentieth-Century America: Politics and Power in the United States 1900–2000*, London, Arnold, 2004, p. 304.
42 Thomas E. Cronin and Michael A. Genovese, *The Paradoxes of the American Presidency*, New York, Oxford University Press, 2004, p. 374; see also Brian Newman, 'Bill Clinton's Approval Ratings: The More Things Change, the More they Stay the Same', *Political Science Quarterly*, 2002, vol. 117, pp. 789–804.
43 Erwin C. Hargrove, *The President as Leader: Appealing to the Better Angels of our Nature*, Lawrence, University Press of Kansas, 1998, pp. 49–75, 181–5.
44 Ronald Reagan, *An American Life*, New York, Simon and Schuster, 1990.
45 See Shirley Anne Warshaw, *The Clinton Years*, New York, Checkmark Books, 2005, p. 370.
46 See Kenneth Waltz, *Theory of International Politics*, New York, Madison-Wesley, 1979, p. 2.
47 Stephen Skowronek, *The Politics Presidents Make: Leadership from John Adams to Bill Clinton*, Cambridge MA, Harvard University Press, 1997, pp. 4, 409.
48 Nye, *The Powers to Lead*, p. 66.
49 Richard N. Haass, 'Why Foreign Policy is not Pornography', in Renshon and Larson, eds, *Good Judgement in Foreign Policy*, p. 252.
50 See C. W. Kegley and E. R. Wittkopf, *American Foreign Policy: Pattern and Process*, New York, St Martin's Press, 1996, pp. 466–99; J. W. Dumbrell, *The Making of US Foreign Policy*, Manchester, Manchester University Press, 1997, pp. 17–22.
51 Alexander L. George and Juliette L. George, *Presidential Personality and Performance*, Boulder, Westview, 1998, p. 2.
52 See Peter Suedfeld and Michael D. Wallace, 'President Clinton as a Cognitive Manager', in Stanley A. Renshon, ed., *The Clinton Presidency: Campaigning, Governing and the Psychology of Leadership*, Boulder, Westview, 1995, pp. 215–34.
53 See Deborah W. Larson, 'Good Judgement in Foreign Policy', in Renshon and Larson, eds, *Good Judgement in Foreign Policy*.
54 Irving L. Janis, *Groupthink*, Boston, Houghton Mifflin, 1982; A. L. George, 'The Case for Multiple Advocacy in Making Foreign Policy', *American Political Science Review*, 1972, vol. 66, pp. 751–85.
55 Richard E. Neustadt and Ernest R. May, *Thinking in Time: The Uses of History for Decision Makers*, New York, Free Press, 1986.
56 Hugh Sidey, *A Very Personal Presidency: Lyndon Johnson in the White House*, New York, Atheneum, 1968.
57 Gail Sheehy, *Hillary's Choice*, London, Simon and Schuster, 1999, p. 369.
58 Bedell Smith, *For Love of Politics*, pp. 56–7.
59 Benjamin R. Barber, *The Truth of Power: Intellectual Affairs in the Clinton White House*, New York, W. W. Norton, 2001, p. 495.
60 David Gallen, *Bill Clinton as They Knew Him: An Oral Biography*, New York, Gallen Publishing, 1994, pp. 152–3.
61 Steven J. Rubenzer and Thomas R. Faschingbauer, *Personality, Character, and Leadership in the White House*, Washington DC, Brassey's, 2004, p. 293.
62 Conor O'Clery, *America: A Place Called Hope?*, Dublin, O'Brien Press, 1993, p. 28.
63 Blumenthal, *The Clinton Wars*, p. 272.
64 Robert E. Rubin and Jacob Weisberg, *In an Uncertain World: Tough Choices from Wall Street to Washington*, New York, Texere, 2003, p. 133.
65 See M. Nelson, 'The Psychological Presidency', in Nelson, ed., *The Presidency and the Political System*; also, James D. Barber, *Presidential Character: Predicting Performance in the White House*, Englewood Cliffs, Prentice-Hall, 1985.
66 Robert B. Reich, *Locked in the Cabinet*, New York, Knopf, 1997, p. 64.
67 *Time*, 18 November 1996, p. 31.
68 Wills, 'The Tragedy of Bill Clinton', p. 61.

69 S. A. Smith, ed., *Preface to the Presidency: Selected Speeches of Bill Clinton, 1974–1992*, Fayetteville, University of Arkansas Press, 1996, p. 264.
70 Fred Greenstein, 'Political Style and Political Leadership: The Case of Bill Clinton', in Renshon, ed., *The Clinton Presidency*, p. 140.
71 Clinton, *My Life*, p. 94; see also, Randall B. Woods, 'Clinton, Fulbright and the Legacy of the Cold War', in Shields, Whayne and Kelley, eds, *The Clinton Riddle*.
72 Clinton, *My Life*, p. 109; see also David Marannis, *First In His Class: The Biography of Bill Clinton*, New York, Touchstone, 1996, pp. 86–8.
73 Clinton, *My Life*, p. 144.
74 Ibid., p. 137.
75 Michael Kelly, 'Where Clinton Stood on War in Iraq', *NYT*, 31 July 1992.
76 Blumenthal, *The Clinton Wars*, pp. 22–3.
77 See Daniel Wattenberg, 'The Lady Macbeth of Little Rock', *The American Spectator*, August 1992.
78 R. Emmett Tyrell, *Boy Clinton: The Political Biography*, Washington DC, Regnery, 1996, p. 197.
79 Bernstein, *A Woman in Charge*, p. 69.
80 Ibid., p. 81.
81 Ibid., pp. 81, 259.
82 Sheehy, *Hillary's Choice*, p. 427.
83 'Democratic candidates trade "Just Words" in Foreign Policy', http://rawstory.com//printstory.php?story=9639 (accessed 12 March 2008).
84 Clinton, *Living History*, p. 259.
85 See Barbara Burrell, *Public Opinion, the First Ladyship and Hillary Rodham Clinton*, New York, Routledge, 2001, pp. 130–1.
86 David Gergen, *Eyewitness to Power: The Essence of Leadership*, New York, Touchstone, 2000, p. 292.
87 See Gerth and Van Notta, *Hillary Clinton*, p. 123; Smith, *For Love of Politics*, p. 92.
88 Bill Turge, *Inventing Al Gore: A Biography*, Boston, Houghton Mifflin, 2000, p. 87; see also A. J. Badger, *New Deal, New South*, Fayetteville, University of Arkansas Press, 2007, pp. 181–201.
89 See Paul Kengor, *Wreath Layer or Policy Player? The Vice President's Role in Foreign Policy*, Lanham, Lexington Books, 2000, p. 133.
90 Turge, *Inventing Al Gore* p. 133; Kengor, *Wreath Layer or Policy Player?*, p. 213.
91 Al Gore, *Earth in the Balance: Ecology and the Human Spirit*, New York, Plume, 1993.
92 *Guardian*, 5 November 1992.
93 Remarks by the President at portrait unveiling, 30 March 1999, available on Clinton Presidential Library website (CPL).
94 Warren Christopher, *Chances of a Lifetime*, New York, Scribner's, 2001.
95 Albright, *Madam Secretary*, p. 132.
96 See David Halberstam, *War in a Time of Peace: Bush, Clinton and the Generals*, London, Bloomsbury, 2003, pp. 174–5.
97 Elaine Sciolino, 'Christopher Spreads the Limelight', *NYT*, 2 January 1994.
98 Raymond Seitz, *Over Here*, London, Weidenfeld and Nicolson, 1999, p. 106.
99 Elaine Sciolino, 'Madeleine Albright's Audition', *NYT*, 22 September 1996.
100 Albright, *Madam Secretary*, p. 219.
101 Thomas W. Lippmann, *Madeleine Albright and the New American Diplomacy*, Boulder, Westview, 2000, p. 89.
102 Strobe Talbott, *The Russia Hand: A Memoir of Presidential Diplomacy*, New York, Random House, 2003, p. 223.
103 Lippmann, *Madeleine Albright*, p. 335.
104 See Jason Deparle, 'The Man Inside Bill Clinton's Foreign Policy', *NYT*, 20 August 1995.

105 Anthony Lake, *Six Nightmares: Real Threats in a Dangerous World and How America Can Meet Them*, Boston, Little Brown, 2000, p. 269.
106 A. Lake, ed., *The Vietnam Legacy: The War, American Society and the Future of American Foreign Policy*, New York, Council on Foreign Relations, 1976, p. xxi.
107 A. Lake et al., *After The Wars: Reconstruction in Afghanistan, Indochina, Central America, Southern Africa and the Horn of Africa* New Brunswick, Transaction, 1990, pp. 3–4.
108 See I. M. Destler, Leslie Gelb and A. Lake, *Our Own Worst Enemy: The Unmaking of American Foreign Policy*, New York, Simon and Schuster, 1984, pp. 110–16.
109 See Hal Brands, *From Berlin to Baghdad: America's Search for Purpose in the Post-Cold War World*, Lexington, The University Press of Kentucky, 2008, pp. 200–1.
110 *NYT*, 25 August 1999 ('A 15-Hour Day and a Modest Ego').
111 See Philip Shenon, *The Commission: The Uncensored History of the 9/11 Investigation*, London, Little Brown, 2008, pp. 249–53, 413–14.
112 Tim Weiner, 'Clinton as a Military Leader', *NYT*, 28 October 1996.
113 Ibid. See also Dale R. Herspring, *The Pentagon and the Presidency: Civil-Military Relations from FDR to George W. Bush*, Lawrence, University Press of Kansas, 2005, pp. 337–8, 349–63.
114 Clinton, *My Life*, p. 737.
115 Halberstam, *War in a Time of Peace*, p. 243.
116 Gergen, *Eyewitness to Power*, p. 276.
117 See George Tenet, *At the Center of the Storm: My Years at the CIA*, New York, HarperCollins, 2007.
118 See Dennis Ross, *The Missing Peace: The Inside Story of the Fight for Middle East Peace*, New York, Farrar, Straus and Giroux, 2005, pp. 5–6.
119 Lake, ed., *The Vietnam Legacy*, p. xiii.

2 Foreign policy between the Bushes

1 Sandy Berger, 'A Foreign Policy Agenda for the Second Term', 27 March 1997, CPL.
2 *NYT*, 25 August 1996 ('A Friend of Bill's Who Never Left').
3 C. W. Kegley and E. R. Wittkopf, *World Politics: Trend and Transformation*, New York, St Martin's, 1995, p. 98.
4 George F. Kennan, *Around the Cragged Hill: A Personal Political Philosophy*, New York, W. W. Norton, 1993, p. 180.
5 Robert E. Hunter, 'Starting at Zero: US Foreign Policy for the 1990s', in Brad Roberts, ed., *US Foreign Policy after the Cold War*, Cambridge, MA, MIT Press, 1992, p. 3.
6 See James Petras and Morris Morley, *Empire or Republic? American Global Power and Domestic Decay*, New York, Routledge, 1995; S. P. Huntington, 'Why International Primacy Matters', *International Security*, 1993, vol. 17, pp. 68–83.
7 R. W. Tucker and D. C. Hendrickson, *The Imperial Temptation*, New York, Council on Foreign Relations, 1992.
8 Robert McNamara, *Out of the Cold*, New York, Pantheon, 1989.
9 C. Fred Bergsten, 'The Primacy of Economics', *Foreign Policy* 1992, vol. 87, pp. 3–24. See generally, G. T. Allison and G. F. Treverton, eds, *Rethinking American Security Beyond the Cold War to the New World Order*, New York, W. W. Norton, 1992.
10 See, for example, W. G. Hyland, 'America's New Course', FA, 1990, vol. 69, pp. 1–12; T. G. Carpenter, 'The New World Disorder', *Foreign Policy*, 1991, vol. 84, pp. 24–39; W. S. Lind, 'Defending Western Culture', *Foreign Policy*, 1991, vol. 84, pp. 40–50; Larry Diamond, 'Promoting Democracy', *Foreign Policy*, 1992, vol. 87, pp. 25–40; S. P. Huntington, 'The Clash of Civilizations', FA, 1993, vol. 72, pp. 22–49; Jessica T. Mathews, 'Preserving the Global Environment', in E. R. Wittkopf, ed., *The Future of American Foreign Policy*, New York, St Martin's, 1994.

11 Richard N. Gardner, 'Comeback of Liberal Internationalism', in Roberts, ed., *US Foreign Policy after the Cold War*, p. 357.
12 Michael Mandelbaum, 'The Bush Foreign Policy', FA, 1990–91, vol. 70, pp. 5–22, 5.
13 *Public Papers of the Presidents of the United States, George H. W. Bush, 1990*: Book 1, Washington DC, US Government Printing Office, 1991, p. 627 (4 May 1990).
14 Nelson Polsby, contribution to 'IGS Panel Assesses the Bush Administration', *Public Affairs*, September 1990, p. 31.
15 Richard N. Haass, 'Paradigm Lost', FA, 1995, vol. 74, pp. 43–58; see also, Robert J. Art, 'Geopolitics Updated: The Strategy of Selective Engagement', *International Security*, 1998–99, vol. 23, pp. 167–81.
16 G. H. W. Bush, 'Remarks to the Asia Society', 12 November 1991, available on the G. H. W. Bush Presidential Library website.
17 An exception was E. A. Nordlinger, *Isolationism Reconfigured*, Princeton, Princeton University Press, 1995.
18 Quoted in William Schneider, 'The New Isolationism', in R. J. Lieber, ed., *Eagle Adrift: American Foreign Policy at the End of the Century*, New York, Longman, 1997, p. 29.
19 Ronald Steel, 'The Domestic Core of Foreign Policy', *Atlantic Monthly*, June 1995, p. 87; also, S. Kull and I. M. Destler, *Misreading the Public: The Myth of a New Isolationism*, Washington DC, The Brookings Institution, 1999.
20 See S. Kull, 'What the Public Knows that Washington Doesn't', *Foreign Policy*, 1995–96, vol. 101, pp. 102–15.
21 Bruce W. Jentleson, 'The Pretty Prudent Public: Post-Vietnam American Opinion on the Use of Military Force', *International Studies Quarterly*, 1992, vol. 36, pp. 49–74.
22 John Dumbrell, *The Making of US Foreign Policy*, Manchester, Manchester University Press, 1997, chapters 6 and 7.
23 David Unger, 'Ferment in the Think tanks', *NYT*, 5 January 1991.
24 James M. Lindsay, *Congress and the Politics of US Foreign Policy*, Baltimore, Johns Hopkins University Press, 1994, p. 32; for opposing views, see Barbara Hinckley, *Less than Meets the Eye: Foreign Policymaking and the Myth of the Assertive Congress*, Chicago, University of Chicago Press, 1994; P. E. Peterson, ed., *The President, the Congress, and the Making of Foreign Policy*, Norman, University of Oklahoma Press, 1994.
25 Daniel Yankelovich and I. M. Destler, eds, *Beyond the Beltway: Engaging the Public in US Foreign Policy*, New York, W. W. Norton, 1994, p. 283.; see also D. A. Deese, ed., *The New Politics of American Foreign Policy*, New York, St Martin's, 1994.
26 George Stephanopoulos, *All Too Human*, London, Hutchinson, 1999, p. 30.
27 David Halberstam, *War in a Time of Peace*, London, Bloomsbury, p. 22.
28 See N. J. Ornstein, 'Foreign Policy and the 1992 Elections', FA, 1992, vol. 71, pp. 1–16.
29 Nancy Soderberg, *The Superpower Myth: The Use and Misuse of American Might*, Hoboken, John Wiley, 2005, p. 13.
30 See John Dumbrell, *The Carter Presidency: A Re-evaluation*, Manchester, Manchester University Press, 1995.
31 Bill Clinton, *My Life*, London, Arrow Books, 2005, p. 406.
32 Ibid., p. 341.
33 Martin Walker, *Clinton: The President They Deserve*, London, Fourth Estate, 1996, p. 147.
34 *NYT*, 11 December 1991 (Leslie Gelb).
35 Presidential debate in St Louis, 11 October 1992, available on G. H. W. Bush Presidential Library website.
36 Soderberg, *The Superpower Myth*, p. 14.
37 Ibid.

38 Clinton, *My Life*, p. 426.
39 Paul Kengor, *Wreath Layer or Policy Player?*, Lanham, Lexington Books, 2000, pp. 228–9.
40 Keith Schneiders, 'Book by Gore Could Become a Campaign issue', *NYT*, 27 July 1992.
41 Clinton, *My Life*, p. 401.
42 Soderberg, *The Superpower Myth*, p. 14.
43 R. W. Apple, 'Campaign Shifts', *NYT*, 29 July 1992.
44 Presidential Debate in East Lansing, 19 October 1992, available on G. H. W. Bush Presidential Library website.
45 Ibid.
46 *Time*, 16 November 1992, p. 18.
47 As note 43.
48 As note 34.
49 Thomas L. Friedman, 'Turning his Sights Overseas', *NYT*, 2 April 1992.
50 *NYT*, 14 August 1992.
51 *NYT*, 2 October 1992.
52 Presidential debate in St Louis, 11 October 1992, available on G. H. Bush Presidential Library website.
53 Bob Woodward, *The Agenda: Inside the Clinton White House*, New York, Simon and Schuster, 1994, p. 84.
54 Remarks by the president at American University centennial celebration, 26 February 1993, CPL.
55 Anthony Lake, *Six Nightmares*, Boston, Little Brown, 2000, pp. 143–4.
56 Richard Ullman, 'A Late Reckoning', *Foreign Policy*, 1995–96, vol. 101, pp. 76–80, 76–7, 79.
57 M. J. Heale, *Twentieth-Century America*, London, Arnold, 2004, p. 305.
58 Remarks by the President to the people of Detroit, 22 October 1996, CPL.
59 'Bill Clinton for President' (editorial), *NYT*, 27 October 1996.
60 R. W. Apple, 'A Once-Crucial Issue Now Languishes', *NYT*, 24 September 1996.
61 'Bob Dole's Centrist Foreign Policy' (editorial), *NYT*, 7 July 1996.
62 Elizabeth Drew, *On the Edge*, New York, Simon and Schuster, 1994, p. 138.
63 Dick Morris, *Behind the Oval Office: Winning the Presidency in the Nineties*, New York, Random House, 1997, p. 245.
64 Tim Weiner, 'Clinton as a Military Leader', *NYT*, 28 October 1996.
65 Elaine Sciolino, '3 Players Seek a Director', *NYT*, 8 November 1993.
66 R. E. Rubin and J. Weisberg, *In an Uncertain World*, New York, Texere, 2003, p. 114.
67 Bradley H. Patterson, *The White House Staff: Inside the West Wing and Beyond*, Washington DC, Brookings Institution, 2000, pp. 52–3.
68 Lexington, 'A Round of Applause', *The Economist*, 22 October 1994.
69 A. Devroy, 'Christopher's Job is Said Safe Until the End of the Year', WP, 3 July 1994; Drew, *On the Edge*, p. 144; Bob Woodward, *The Agenda*, New York, Simon and Schuster, 1994, p. 320.
70 Patterson, *The White House Staff*, pp. 74–5; Jason DeParle, 'The Man Inside Clinton's Foreign Policy', *NYT*, 20 August 1995.
71 Elaine Sciolino, 'The White House Turns Again', *NYT*, 28 June 1994.
72 D. Kirschten, 'One for the Books', NJ, 6 January 1996, p. 34.
73 Larry Reibstein, 'The Virtues of Being a Grown-Up in Washington', *Time*, 26 June 1995.
74 S. Erlanger, 'Albright, a Bold Voice Abroad', *NYT*, 1 September 1998.
75 Ibid.
76 Jane Perlez, 'An Embattled Albright', *NYT*, 9 April 1999.
77 As note 64.

78 Ibid.; see also Loch Johnson, *Secret Agencies: US Intelligence in a Hostile World*, New Haven, Yale University Press, 1996.
79 *Congressional Quarterly Weekly Report* (CQWR), 6 June 1998, p. 1543.
80 John Carlin, 'Spooked!', *The Independent on Sunday*, 23 March 1997.
81 Margaret G. Herman, 'Advice and Advisors in the Clinton Presidency', in S. A. Renshon, ed., *The Clinton Presidency*, Boulder, Westview, 1995, p. 161.
82 Ibid.; see also John F. Harris, *The Survivor*, New York, Random House, 2005, p. 159.
83 See A. W. Jewett and M. D. Turetzky, 'Stability and Change in President Clinton's Foreign Policy Beliefs', *Presidential Studies Quarterly,* 1998, vol. 28, pp. 638–65.
84 P. J. Haney, *Organizing for Foreign Policy Crisis*, Ann Arbor, University of Michigan Press, 1997.
85 Robert J. Lieber, 'Eagle without a Cause', in R. J. Lieber, ed., *Eagle Adrift: American Foreign Policy at the End of the Cold War*, New York, Longman, 1997, p. 3; also, Jeremy D. Rosner, *The New Tug of War: Congress, the Executive Branch, and National Security*, Washington DC, Carnegie Endowment, 1995.
86 Thomas E. Cronin and Michael Genovese, *The Paradoxes of the American Presidency*, New York, Oxford University Press, 2004, p. 169.
87 *Congressional Quarterly Almanac* (CQA) 1994, p. 451.
88 Morris, *Behind the Oval Office*, pp. 33–4.
89 CQWR, 3 February 1996, p. 309.
90 Elizabeth Drew, *Showdown: The Struggle between the Gingrich Congress and the Clinton White House*, New York, Simon and Schuster, 1996, p. 13; Charles Krauthammer, 'A Critique of Pure Newt', *The Weekly Standard*, 18 September 1995, p. 57.
91 USIA press release, 'Dole, Gingrich outline Views', 8 March 1995.
92 Ibid.; see also Lake, *Six Nightmares*, p. 255.
93 R. S. Greenberger, 'Dateline Capitol Hill', *Foreign Policy*, 1995–96, vol. 101, pp. 159–69, 166.
94 Christopher Layne, 'Dole: The Last Interventionist', *New Republic*, 3 July 1995, pp. 19–25.
95 Dissenting Views, Report of the Committee on Appropriations, *Department of Defense Appropriation Bill, 1996*, House of Representatives, 27 July 1995, p. 209.
96 CQWR, 27 May 1995, p. 1514.
97 See William Kristol and Robert Kagan, 'Toward a Neo-Reaganite Foreign Policy', FA, 1996, vol. 73, pp. 18–32; Joshua Muravchik, *The Imperative of American Leadership: A Challenge to Neo-Isolationism*, Washington DC, American Enterprise Institute, 1996.
98 *Congressional Record*, 16 February 1995, H1859; also, D. S. Cloud, 'Republicans Pushing the Envelope with Confrontational Approach', CQWR, 5 August 1995, pp. 2331–4.
99 J. R. Bond and R. Fleisher, 'Clinton and Congress: A First-Year Assessment', *American Politics Quarterly*, 1993, vol. 23, pp. 355–72.
100 CQWR, 21 December 1996, p. 3430; *US Foreign Policy Agenda* (USIA electronic journal), March 1997, p. 4.
101 S. A. Warshaw, *The Clinton Years*, New York, Checkmark, 2005, p. 158.
102 See Carroll Doherty, 'With Helms at the Helm', *Foreign Service Journal*, January 1995, pp. 42–47; Jesse Helms, *Here's Where I Stand*, New York, Random House, 2005.
103 See M. A. Pomper, 'The Religious Right's Revival', CQWR, 9 May 1998, pp. 1209–10.
104 Martin Walker, 'A New American Isolationism?', *International Journal*, 1997, vol. 52, pp. 391–410, 401.
105 Jim Anderson, 'Singing the Blues', *Foreign Service Journal*, September 1995, pp. 44–9, 45.

106 See James Kitfield, 'Jousting with Jesse', NJ, 27 September 1997, pp. 1886–9; 'Atwood Defends Foreign Aid', USIA press release, 26 September 1995.
107 See NJ, 27 May 1995, p. 1276.

3 The globalisation president

1. Lexington, 'Towards a Clinton Doctrine', *The Economist*, 17 July 1993.
2. Richard Cohen, 'Senate Stumbling on Foreign Policy', NJ, 14 March 1998, p. 585.
3. Graham Evans, 'The Vision Thing: In Search of the Clinton Doctrine', *The World Today*, August–September 1997, pp. 213–17, 214.
4. Derek Chollet and James Goldgeier, *America between the Wars: From 11/9 to 9/11*, New York, PublicAffairs, 2008, p. 99.
5. W. Safire, 'Engagement Party', *NYT*, 19 April 1992.
6. Anthony Lake, 'From Containment to Enlargement', in Alvin Rubinstein, Albina Shayevich and Boris Zlotnikov, eds, *The Clinton Foreign Policy Reader*, Armonk, Sharpe, 2001, pp. 14–22; see also, Bruce Russett, *Grasping the Democratic Peace*, Princeton, Princeton University Press, 1993.
7. S. Talbott, 'The New Geopolitics', *The World Today*, January 1995, pp. 7–10.
8. *National Security Strategy of the United States, 1994: Engagement and Enlargement*, Washington DC, US Government Printing Office, 1994, p. 4.
9. W. Christopher, 'America's Leadership, America's Opportunity', *Foreign Policy*, 1993, vol. 98, pp. 6–28, 15; Lake, 'From Containment to Enlargement'.
10. Chollet and Goldgeier, *America between the Wars*, p. 289.
11. Cecil V. Crabb, *The Doctrines of American Foreign Policy*, Baton Rouge, Louisiana State University Press, 1982.
12. William Cohen, 'Meeting the Threat of WMD', *US Foreign Policy Agenda* (USIA), July 1998, pp. 10–12.
13. Anthony Lake, 'Confronting Backlash States', FA, 1994, vol. 73, pp. 44–55.
14. See Robert S. Litwak, *Rogue States and US Foreign Policy: Containment after the Cold War*, Baltimore, Johns Hopkins University Press, 2000, pp. 242–3; Wyn Bowen, 'Rogues No More', *The World Today*, August–September, 2000, pp. 14–16.
15. George F. Kennan, 'The Failure in our Success', *NYT*, 14 March 1994.
16. M. Glitman, 'US Foreign Policy in the Post-Cold War World' (USIA), 26 September 1995.
17. Quoted in Jonathan Rauch, 'Two Cheers for the Clinton Doctrine (OK, Maybe Just One)', NJ, 27 May 2000, p. 314.
18. S. Brown, *The Faces of Power*, New York, Columbia University Press, 1994, p. 609.
19. Rauch, 'Two Cheers'.
20. See Fareed Zakaria, *The Future of Freedom: Illiberal Democracy at Home and Abroad*, New York, Norton paperback, 2004; S. Smith, 'US Democracy: Critical Questions', in M. Cox, G. J. Ikenberry and T. Inoguchi, eds, *American Democracy Promotion: Impulses, Strategies and Impacts*, Oxford, Oxford University Press, 2000, pp. 63–84.
21. Lake, 'From Containment to Enlargement' (see note 6), p. 16.
22. Address to 48th Session of UN General Assembly, 27 September 1993, CPL.
23. See Douglas Brinkley, 'Democratic Enlargement: The Clinton Doctrine', *Foreign Policy*, 1997, vol. 106, pp. 111–27, 116; Thomas L. Friedman, *The World is Flat: The Globalized World in the 21st Century*, Penguin, London, 2006, p. 284.
24. Larry King radio town meeting, Culver City, 21 September 1995, CPL.
25. Cited in Paul Krugman, 'Competitiveness: A Dangerous Obsession', FA, 1994, vol. 73, pp. 28–44, 29.
26. S. Berger, 'A Foreign Policy for a Global Age', FA, 2000, vol. 79, pp. 18–29, 24.
27. A. E. Eckes, 'A New Protectionism?', in R. L. Hutchings, ed., *At The End of the American Century*, Washington DC, The Woodrow Wilson Center, 1998, p. 175.

28 R. Robertson, *Globalization*, London, Sage, 1992, p. 48.
29 Benjamin R. Barber, *Jihad vs. McWorld: How Globalism and Tribalism are Reshaping the World*, New York, Times Books, 1995.
30 H. R. Clinton, *Living History*, London, Headline, 2003, p. 358.
31 See Haynes Johnson, *The Best of Times: The Clinton Years*, New York, Harcourt, 2001, pp. 471–2.
32 Barbara Noble, 'Must It Be No Pain, No Gain?', *NYT*, 8 May 1994.
33 'Clinton's Foreign Policy', *Foreign Policy*, 2000, vol. 120, pp. 18–29, 28.
34 See Paul Hirst and Graham Thompson, *Globalization in Question*, Oxford, polity, 1996; John Gray, *False Dawn: The Delusions of Global Capitalism*, London, Granta, 1998.
35 R. O'Brien, *Global Financial Integration: The End of Geography*, London, Routledge, 1992.
36 Benjamin R. Barber, *The Truth of Power*, New York, W. W. Norton, 2001, p. 64.
37 R. E. Rubin and J. Weisberg, *In an Uncertain World*, New York, Texere, 2003, pp. 114, 152.
38 Clinton, *My Life*, p. 636.
39 Bob Woodward, *The Agenda*, New York, Simon and Schuster, 1994, p. 165.
40 Robert Reich, *Supercapitalism*, New York, Icon Books, 2007, p. 133.
41 C. Fred Bergsten, 'Globalizing Free Trade', *FA*, 1996, vol. 75, pp. 105–20.
42 Robert C. Paarlberg, *Leadership Abroad Begins at Home*, Washington DC, The Brookings Institution, 1995, pp. 25–6.
43 M. F. Oppenheimer, 'The New Mercantilism', in Hutchings, ed., *At The End of the American Century*, p. 155; also, Philippe Legrain, *Open World: The Truth About Globalisation*, London, Abacus, 2003, p. 191.
44 Krugman, 'Competitiveness', p. 34.
45 J. Garten, 'Clinton's Emerging Trade Policy', *FA*, 1993, vol. 72, pp. 181–9, 183.
46 Paarlberg, *Leadership Abroad Begins at Home*, p. 28.
47 L. F. Kaplan, 'Dollar Diplomacy Returns', *Commentary*, 1998, vol. 105, pp. 52–4, 54.
48 Kirk Victor, 'Dirty Dealing', *NJ*, 20 April 1996, pp. 869–72.
49 Franklin Lavin, 'Clinton and Trade', *The National Interest*, 1993, vol. 32, pp. 29–34.
50 Martin Walker, *Clinton: The President They Deserve*, London, Fourth Estate, 1996, p. 286.
51 Press conference, 10 November 1993, CPL.
52 *NYT*, 14 November 1993.
53 Stephen D. Cohen, Joel R. Paul and Robert A. Blecker, *Fundamentals of US Foreign Trade Policy*, Boulder, Westview, 1996, p. 238.
54 W. Safire, 'Gore Flattens Perot', *NYT*, 14 November 1993.
55 As note 51.
56 Remarks by the President to NAFTA opinion leaders, 9 November 1993, CPL.
57 G. C. Edwards, 'Frustration and Folly: Bill Clinton and the Public Presidency', in Colin Campbell and Bert A. Rockman, eds, *The Clinton Presidency: First Appraisals*, Chatham NJ, Chatham House, 1996, p. 253.
58 As note 51.
59 As note 56.
60 Remarks after the NAFTA vote, 17 November 1993, CPL.
61 D. Rosenblum, 'Beyond a Trade Pact', *NYT*, 11 November 1993.
62 See J. Bhagwati, 'Beyond NAFTA: Clinton's Trading Choices', *Foreign Policy*, 1993, vol. 91, pp. 25–8.
63 Press briefing by Dee Dee Myers, 8 September 1993, CPL.
64 Clinton, *Living History*, p. 183.
65 Cohen *et al.*, *Fundamentals of US Foreign Trade Policy*, pp. 183, 245; Ross Perot and Pat Choate, *Save Your Job, Save Our Country: Why NAFTA Must Be Stopped*, New York, Hyperion, 1993.

66 CQA 1993, p. 173.
67 WP, 8 November 1993.
68 Cohen et al., *Fundamentals of US Foreign Trade Policy*, p. 255.
69 Michael Waldman, *POTUS: Finding the Words that Defined the Clinton Presidency*, New York, Simon and Schuster, 2000, p. 57.
70 CQA 1993, p. 179.
71 Paul Trubowitz, *Defining the National Interest: Conflict and Change in American Foreign Policy*, Chicago, University of Chicago Press, 1998, pp. 213–14.
72 CQA 1993, p. 182.
73 Walker, *Clinton: The President they Deserve*, p. 298.
74 On the origins of the WTO, see Rorden Wilkinson, *The WTO: Crisis and the Governance of Global Trade*, London, Routledge, 2006.
75 Rubin and Weisberg, *In an Uncertain World*, p. 182.
76 Ibid., p. 142; Andrew Baker, *The Group of Seven: Finance Ministers, Central Banks and Global Financial Governance*, Abingdon, Routledge, 2006, pp. 156–64.
77 *NYT*, 17 April 1998.
78 Clinton, *My Life*, p. 645.
79 CQA 1995, pp. 10–15.
80 Rubin and Weisberg, *In an Uncertain World*, p. 14.
81 Ibid., p. 219.
82 Clinton, *My Life*, p. 807.
83 CQWR, 14 February 1998, p. 379.
84 Ibid., p. 401.
85 See G. Franke-Ruta, 'The IMF Gets a Left and a Right', NJ, 17 April 1998, p. 914.
86 David Sanger, 'Clinton Shelving '98 Trade Bill', *NYT*, 28 January 1998.
87 Steven Greenhouse, 'Union Leaders, Sensing Betrayal', *NYT*, 17 November 1999.
88 Remarks by the President at the University of Chicago, 12 June 1999, CPL; see also G. Burtlers, R. Z. Lawrence, R. E. Liten and R. J. Shapiro, *Globophobia*, Washington DC, The Brookings Institution, 1998.
89 President Clinton: key achievements from the APEC Summit, 16 September 1999, CPL.
90 Radio Address to the Nation, 8 November 1997, CPL.
91 Remarks by the Vice President on fast track legislation, 6 November 1997, CPL.
92 K. Seelye, 'Gephardt Scores a Touchdown', *NYT*, 12 November 1997.
93 Eric Schmitt, 'House Rejects Expanded Trade Pact', *NYT*, 26 September 1998.
94 S. H. Verhovek, 'Trade Talks Start in Seattle', *NYT*, 30 November 1999.
95 See Wilkinson, *The WTO*, pp. 5–14, 112–18; also, John S. Odell, 'The Seattle Impasse and Its Implications for the WTO', in David Kennedy and James Southwick, eds, *The Political Economy of International Trade Law*, Cambridge, Cambridge University Press, 2002.
96 See 'The Collapse in Seattle' (editorial), *NYT*, 6 December 1999.
97 CQWR, 24 May 1997, p. 1205; CQWR, 14 June 1997, p. 1390.
98 Nancy B. Tucker, 'The Clinton Years: The Problem of Coherence', in R. H. Myers, M. C. Oksenberg and David Shambaugh, eds, *Making China Policy: Lessons From the Bush and Clinton Administrations*, Lanham, Rowman and Littlefield, 2001, p. 67.
99 M. K. Albright, *Madam Secretary*, London, Macmillan, 2003, p. 432.
100 Bronwen Maddox, 'President has Little to Lose', *The Times*, 25 May 2000.
101 Albright, *Madam Secretary*, p. 434.
102 B. Macintyre, 'Clinton Wins Vote', *The Times*, 25 May 2000.
103 Berger, 'A Foreign Policy for the Global Age', p. 29.
104 Cited in Hal Brands, *From Berlin to Baghdad*, Lexington, University Press of Kentucky, 2008, p. 203.
105 Clinton, 'On the Eve of the Millennium', San Francisco, 26 February 1999, CPL.
106 As note 104.

4 Making war, avoiding war: 1993–96

1. See A. J. Bellamy, 'Humanitarian Responsibilities and Interventionist Claims in International Society', *Review of International Studies*, 2003, vol. 29, pp. 321–40.
2. Quoted in Karin von Hippel, *Democracy by Force: US Military Interventions in the Post-Cold War World*, Cambridge, Cambridge University Press, 2000, p. 206.
3. Mike Moore, 'So Where's the Peace Dividend?', *Bulletin of the Atomic Scientists*, 1995, vol. 51, pp. 30–7, 31.
4. E. Gholz, D. Press and H. Sapolsky, 'Come Home America: The strategy of Restraint in the Face of Temptation', *International Security*, 1997, vol. 21, pp. 5–48, 6.
5. S. J. Cimbala, *US Military Strategy and the Cold War Endgame*, Ilford, Cass, 1995, p. 33.
6. D. R. Herspring, *The Pentagon and the Presidency*, Lawrence, University Press of Kansas, 2005, pp. 332–3.
7. Colin Powell, *A Soldier's Way*, London, Hutchinson, 1995, p. 578.
8. See David Maraniss, *First in his Class*, New York, Touchstone, 1996, p. 203.
9. *Time*, 16 November 1992, p. 50.
10. H. R. Clinton, *Living History*, London, Headline, 2003, p. 240.
11. Powell, *A Soldier's Way*, p. 581; Elizabeth Drew, *On The Edge*, New York, Simon and Schuster, 1994, p. 45.
12. Bill Clinton, *My Life*, London, Arrow Books, 2005, p. 522; Powell, *A Soldier's Way*, p. 582.
13. Nigel Hamilton, *Bill Clinton: Mastering the Presidency*, London, Century, 2007, p. 49.
14. Remarks at National Defense University, 19 July 1993, CPL; see also Powell, *A Soldier's Way*, pp. 573–5.
15. Les Aspin, *A Report on the Bottom Up Review*, Washington DC, Department of Defense, 1993, p. 11.
16. CQA 1993, p. 451.
17. David C. Morrison, 'Spar Wars', NJ, 4 March 1995, p. 540.
18. W. D. Hartung, 'Nixon's Children', *World Policy Journal*, 1995, vol. 12, pp. 25–35.
19. Moore, 'So Where's the Peace Dividend?', p. 36.
20. Edward Luttwak, 'Toward Post-Heroic Warfare', FA, May/June 1995 (online edition).
21. James Kitfield, 'Fit To Fight', NJ, 16 March 1996, pp. 582–6, 583.
22. Paul Stockton, 'Beyond Micromanagement: Congressional Budgeting for a Post-Cold War Military', *Political Science Quarterly*, 1995, vol. 110, pp. 233–44.
23. Kitfield, 'Fit to Fight', p. 583; D. C. Morrison, 'Defense Deadlock', NJ, 4 February 995, pp. 276–80.
24. D. C. Morrison, 'Ready for What?', NJ, 20 April 1995, pp. 1218–22, 1220.
25. CQA 1995, pp. 9–3.
26. As note 24.
27. Dana Priest, *The Mission: Waging War and Keeping the Peace with America's Military*, New York, W. W. Norton, 2003, p. 61.
28. Caspar Weinberger, *Fighting for Peace: Seven Critical Years at the Pentagon*, New York, Warner Books, 1990, pp. 433–45; Colin Powell, 'US Forces: Challenges Ahead', FA, 1992–93, vol. 72, pp. 32–41, 38.
29. Washington DC, US Government Printing Office, 1992.
30. Wayne Bert, *The Reluctant Superpower: United States Policy in Bosnia, 1991–95*, Basingstoke, Macmillan, 1997, pp. 17–18.
31. R. N. Haass, *Intervention: The Use of American Military Force in the Post-Cold War World*, Washington DC, Carnegie Institute, 1994, p. 183.
32. Bert, *The Reluctant Superpower*, p. 18.
33. Lexington, 'The Keys of the Pentagon', *The Economist*, 30 January 1993, p. 50.
34. Clinton, *My Life*, p. 551; Mark Bowden, *Black Hawk Down*, New York, Atlantic Monthly Press, 1999.

35 Chester A. Crocker, 'The Lessons of Somalia: Not Everything Went Wrong', FA, 1995, vol. 74, pp. 2–8, 3.
36 Clinton, *My Life*, p. 552.
37 Nancy Soderberg, *The Superpower Myth*, Hoboken, John Wiley, 2005, p. 40.
38 Joshua Muravchik, *The Imperative of American Leadership*, Washington DC, American Enterprise Institute, 1996, p. 74.
39 M. K. Albright, *Madam Secretary*, London, Macmillan, 2003, p. 46.
40 John G. Ruggie, *Winning the Peace: America and the World Order in the New Era*, New York, Columbia University Press, 1996, pp. 96–7.
41 John Bolton, 'Wrong Turn in Somalia', FA, 1993, vol. 73, pp. 56–66, 60, 66.
42 R. A. Melanson, *American Foreign Policy Since the Vietnam War*, London, M. E. Sharpe, 1996, p. 259.
43 As note 33.
44 Stephen Hess, *International News and Foreign Correspondents*, Washington DC, Brookings Institution, 1996, p. 1.
45 Dan Oberdorfer, 'The Road to Somalia', WP, weekly edn, 14–20 December 1992.
46 See John Dumbrell, *The Making of US Foreign Policy*, Manchester, Manchester University Press, 1997, pp. 197–203.
47 CQA 1992, p. 537.
48 Ibid., p. 536.
49 *NYT*, 5 December 1992.
50 Soderberg, *The Superpower Myth*, p. 36.
51 D. Halberstam, *War in a Time of Peace*, London, Bloomsbury, 2003, pp. 253–4.
52 See J. Hirsch and R. Oakley, *Somalia and Operation Restore Hope*, Washington DC, US Institute of Peace Press, 1995; also, J. L. Woods, 'US Government Decision-making Processes During Humanitarian Operations in Somalia', in Walter Clarke and Jeffrey Herbst, eds, *Learning from Somalia: The Lessons of Humanitarian Intervention*, Boulder, Westview, 1997, p. 166.
53 Bolton, 'Wrong Turn', p. 60.
54 Halberstam, *War in a Time of Peace*, pp. 260–1.
55 Louis Fisher, *Presidential War Power*, Lawrence, University Press of Kansas, 1995, p. 154.
56 Statement by the Press Secretary, 25 September 1993, CPL.
57 Office of the Press Secretary: To the Congress of the United States, 13 October 1993, CPL.
58 *Public Papers of the Presidents of the United States: William Jefferson Clinton: Book 1: 1993*, Washington DC, US Government Printing Office, 1994, p. 987; Linda Miller, 'The Clinton Years: Reinventing US Foreign Policy?', *International Affairs*, 1994, vol. 70, pp. 621–34.
59 Cited in Leonie Murray, 'Somalia and the "Body Bag Myth" in American Politics', *International Politics*, 2007, vol. 4, pp. 552–71, 562.
60 R. C. Hendrickson, *The Clinton Wars*, Nashville, Vanderbilt University Press, 2002, pp. 32, 35.
61 Peter Woodward, *US Foreign Policy and the Horn of Africa*, Aldershot, Ashgate, 2006, p. 66.
62 Herspring, *The Pentagon and the Presidency*, p. 348.
63 Louise Lief and B. B. Auster, 'What Went Wrong in Somalia?', *US News and World Report*, 18 October 1993, pp. 33–7.
64 CQA 1994, p. 449.
65 Soderberg, *The Superpower Myth*, p. 43.
66 CQA 1994, p. 451.
67 Powell, *A Soldier's Way*, p. 544.
68 Clinton, *My Life*, p. 463.
69 Dick Morris, *Behind the Oval Office*, New York, Random House, 1997, p. 5.

70　Madeleine Albright, *The Mighty and the Almighty: Reflections on Power, God, and World Affairs*, London, Macmillan, 2006, p. 54.
71　Soderberg, *The Superpower Myth*, p. 10.
72　CQA 1994, p. 450.
73　Nigel Hamilton, *Bill Clinton: Mastering the Presidency*, London, Century, 2007, p. 194.
74　Anthony Lake, *Six Nightmares*, Boston, Little Brown, 2000, p. 128.
75　G. Stephanopoulos, *All Too Human*, London, Hutchinson, 1999, p. 217.
76　Halberstam, *War in a Time of Peace*, pp. 273, 279.
77　Soderberg, *The Superpower Myth*, p. 48.
78　CQA 1994, p. 450.
79　Fisher, *Presidential War Power*, p. 156.
80　See J. M. McCormick, *American Foreign Policy and Process*, Belmont, Wadsworth, 2005, p. 520.
81　Fisher, *Presidential War Power*, p. 155.
82　Albright, *Madam Secretary*, pp. 158–9.
83　Hendrickson, *The Clinton Wars*, p. 55.
84　Fisher, *Presidential War Power*, p. 157.
85　Soderberg, *The Superpower Myth*, p. 50.
86　Morris, *Behind the Oval Office*, p. 65.
87　McCormick, *American Foreign Policy and Process*, p. 521.
88　CQA 1994, pp. 449–51.
89　Fisher, *Presidential War Power*, p. 157; Hendrickson, *The Clinton Wars*, p. 57.
90　Elaine Sciolino, 'For Carter, a Thrust Onto the Front Pages Again', *NYT*, 23 June 1994.
91　Powell, *A Soldier's Way*, p. 598.
92　Robert A. Pastor, 'More and Less than it Seemed: The Carter–Nunn–Powell Mediation in Haiti, 1994', in C. A. Crocker, F. O. Hampson and Pamela Aall, eds, *Herding Cats: Multiparty Mediation in a Complex World*, Washington DC, US Institute of Peace Press, 1999, p. 512.
93　Powell, *A Soldier's Way*, p. 599.
94　Soderberg, *The Superpower Myth*, p. 51.
95　Pastor, 'More and Less than it Seemed', p. 521.
96　Hamilton, *Bill Clinton*, p. 327.
97　Hendrickson, *The Clinton Wars*, pp. 64–7.
98　Clinton, *My Life*, pp. 617–18.
99　Morris, *Behind the Oval Office*, pp. 5–6.
100　Margaret Thatcher, *The Downing Street Years*, London, HarperCollins, 1993, p. 330.
101　*Congressional Record*, H6433, 28 July 1994.
102　Stephanopoulos, *All Too Human*, p. 315.
103　Powell, *A Soldier's Way*, p. 292.
104　For the text of PDD 25, see Michael G. MacKinnon, *The Evolution of US Peacekeeping Policy Under Clinton: A Fairweather Friend?*, London, Cass, 2000, pp. 124–39; see also, Richard Lock-Pullan, 'Learning the Limits of Virtue: Clinton, the Army and the Criteria for the Use of Military Force', *Contemporary Security Policy*, 2003, vol. 24, pp. 133–56; David S. Sorensen, 'The United States', in D. S. Sanderson and P. C. Wood, eds, *The Politics of Peacekeeping in the Post-Cold War Era*, London, Cass, 2005.
105　See Alton Frye, *Humanitarian Intervention: Crafting a Workable Doctrine*, New York, Council on Foreign Relations, 2000, at p. 77.
106　Albright, *Madam Secretary*, p. 147.
107　Samantha Power, *'A Problem from Hell': America and the Age of Genocide*, London, Flamingo Books, 2003, p. 342.
108　Sorensen, 'The United States', p. 127; Lock-Pullan, 'Learning the Limits of Virtue', p. 145.

186 Notes

109 Leonie Murray, *Clinton, Peacekeeping and Humanitarian Intervention*, London, Routledge, 2007; see also, Michael Hirsh, 'The Fall Guy', FA, 1999, vol. 78, pp. 5–10; Boutros Boutros-Ghali, *The Unvanquished: A US–UN Saga*, London, I. B. Tauris, 1999, p. 105.
110 Warren Christopher, *In the Stream of History*, Stanford, Stanford University Press, 1998, p. 468.
111 MacKinnon, *The Evolution of US Peacekeeping Policy Under Clinton*, pp. 105–10.
112 US State Department Dispatch, May 1994, pp. 318–19 (5 May); see also, Ivo H. Daalder, 'Knowing When to say No: The Development of US Peacekeeping', in William Durch, ed., *UN Peacekeeping, American Policy and the Uncivil Wars of the 1990s*, New York, St Martin's, 1996, p. 42.
113 R. C. DiPrizio, *Armed Humanitarians: US Interventions from Northern Iraq to Kosovo*, Baltimore, Johns Hopkins University Press, 2002, p. 84.
114 Rory Carroll, 'US Chose to Ignore Rwandan Genocide', *Guardian*, 31 March 2004; see also, Murray, *Clinton, Peacekeeping and Humanitarian Intervention*, p. 161.
115 Soderberg, *The Superpower Myth*, pp. 282–3. See also Romeo Dallaire, *Shake Hands with the Devil: The Failure of Humanity in Rwanda*, Toronto, Random House Canada, 2003.
116 Albright, *Madam Secretary*, p. 152.
117 Power, *'A Problem from Hell'*, p. 373.
118 David Remnick, 'The Wanderer', *The New Yorker*, 18 September 2006, p. 63.
119 Power, *'A Problem from Hell'*, p. 352; see also Scott R. Feil, *Genocide: How the Early Use of Force Might Have Succeeded in Rwanda*, New York, Carnegie Corporation, 1998.
120 Washington DC, American Enterprise Institute, 1996.
121 David Rieff, 'The Crusaders: Moral Principles, Strategic Interests, and Military Force', *World Policy Journal*, 2000, vol. 27, pp. 39–47, 46.
122 *NYT*, 15 July 1994.

5 Ancient enmities: the Balkans and Northern Ireland

1 See Paul Starobin, 'The Liberal Hawk Soars', NJ, 15 May 1999, pp. 1310–16, 1315; Robert Kaplan, *Balkan's Ghosts: A Journey Through History*, New York, St Martin's, 1993.
2 See Richard N. Haass, *Conflicts Unending: The United States and Regional Disputes*, New Haven, Yale University Press, 1990.
3 David Rieff, *Slaughterhouse: Bosnia and the Future of the West*, New York, Simon and Schuster, 1995, p. 27.
4 James A. Baker, *The Politics of Diplomacy: Revolution, War and Peace, 1989–1992*, New York, G. P. Putnam's Sons, 1995, p. 637.
5 Wayne Bert, *The Reluctant Superpower*, Basingstoke, Macmillan, 1997, p. 217.
6 Brendan Simms, *Unfinest Hour: Britain and the Destruction of Bosnia*, London, Allen Lane, 2001, pp. 91, 391.
7 CQA 1992, p. 534.
8 Simms, *Unfinest Hour*, p. 339.
9 CQWR, 14 October 1995, p. 3158.
10 CQA 1992, p. 533; Samantha Power, *'A Problem from Hell'*, London, Flamingo Books, 2003, p. 274.
11 Richard Holbrooke, *To End a War*, New York, The Modern Library, 1999, p. 42.
12 R. C. Hendrickson, *The Clinton Wars*, Nashville, Vanderbilt University Press, 2002, p. 73; Power, *'A Problem from Hell'*, p. xii.
13 Power, *'A Problem from Hell'*, p. 295.
14 Ibid., p. 298.
15 Ibid., p. 317.

16 D. Halberstam, *War in a Time of Peace*, London, Bloomsbury, 2003, p. 291.
17 Power, *'A Problem from Hell'*, p. 316.
18 R. C. DiPrizio, *Armed Humanitarians*, Baltimore, Johns Hopkins University Press, 2002, pp. 120–2; James Gow, *The Triumph of the Lack of Will: International Diplomacy and the Yugoslav War*, London, Hurst, 1997, pp. 240–50.
19 CQWR, 26 March 1994, p. 752.
20 Bert, *The Reluctant Superpower*, p. 76.
21 Hendrickson, *The Clinton Wars*, p. 76.
22 Derek Chollet, *The Road to the Dayton Accords: A Study of American Statecraft*, New York, Praeger, 2005, p. 9.
23 Ibid., p. 11.
24 Ibid., p. 9.
25 Ibid., p. 14.
26 Ibid., p. 18.
27 Soderberg, *The Superpower Myth*, p. 28.
28 Holbrooke, *To End a War*, p. 68.
29 Derek Chollet and James Goldgeier, *America Between the Wars*, New York, PublicAffairs, 2008, p. 128.
30 See Thomas Lippmann and Ann Devroy, 'Clinton's Policy Evolution', WP, 22 October 1995.
31 Soderberg, *The Superpower Myth*, p. 76.
32 Ivo H. Daalder, *Getting to Dayton: The Making of America's Bosnia Policy*, Washington DC, The Brookings Institution, 2000, p. 164.
33 See WP, 16 September 1995 ('Holbrooke Admired and Disliked').
34 Daalder, *Getting to Dayton*, pp. 170–2.
35 Bob Dole, 'Let Bosnia Control its own Future', *Newsweek*, 7 August 1995, p. 23.
36 Elizabeth Drew, *Showdown*, New York, Simon and Schuster, 1996, p. 249.
37 CQA 1995, pp. 10–12.
38 Holbrooke, *To End a War*, p. 74.
39 See R. C. Hendrickson, 'War Powers, Bosnia and the 104th Congress', *Political Science Quarterly*, 1998, vol. 113, pp. 241–62; C. P. David, '"At least 2001": US Security Policy and Exit Strategy in Bosnia', *European Security*, 2000, vol. 9, pp. 1–21.
40 W. B. Yeats, 'Remorse for Intemperate Speech' (1931), quoted in Jonathan Powell, *Great Hatred, Little Room: Making Peace in Northern Ireland*, London, The Bodley Head, 2008, p. vii.
41 John Dumbrell, *A Special Relationship: Anglo-American Relations from the Cold War to Iraq*, London, Palgrave, 2006, pp. 255–8.
42 Ibid., p. 257.
43 See John Dumbrell, 'The United States and the Northern Irish Conflict, 1969–1994: From Indifference to Intervention', *Irish Studies in International Affairs*, 1995, vol. 6, pp. 107–25; Niall O'Dowd, 'The Awakening: Irish America's Key Role in the Irish Peace Process', in Marianne Elliott, ed., *The Long Road to Peace in Northern Ireland*, Liverpool, Liverpool University Press, 2007.
44 Jimmy Burns, 'Blarney Before Bombs', *Financial Times*, 30 May 1994.
45 Christopher Meyer, *DC Confidential*, London, Weidenfeld and Nicolson, 2005, p. 108; see also, Timothy J. Lynch, *Turf War: The Clinton Administration and Northern Ireland*, Aldershot, Ashgate, 2004.
46 Michael Cox, 'The War that Came in from the Cold', *World Policy Journal*, 1999, vol. 16, pp. 59–67.
47 R. Wilson, 'Days Like These', *New Statesman*, 15 December 1995.
48 Conor O'Clery, *The Greening of the White House*, Dublin, Gill and Macmillan, 1996, p. 230.
49 *The Independent on Sunday*, 22 March 1998.

50 John Dumbrell, *The Carter Presidency: A Reevaluation*, Manchester, Manchester University Press, 1995, pp. 134–9.
51 Alastair Campbell and Richard Stott, eds, *The Blair Years: Extracts from the Alastair Campbell Diaries*, London, Hutchinson, 2007, p. 296 (10 April 1998).
52 George J. Mitchell, *Making Peace*, London, William Heinemann, 1999, p. 178; Powell, *Great Hatred, Little Room*, pp. 101, 104.
53 See M. J. Brady, 'Democratic Audit', *Fortnight*, 9 December 1995.
54 John McCain, 'Imagery or Purpose: The Choice in November', *Foreign Policy*, 1996, vol. 103, pp. 25–31, 28.
55 *The Times*, 16 August 1996.
56 See Paul Dixon, 'Rethinking the International: A Critique', in Michael Cox, Adrian Guelke and Fiona Stephen, *A Farewell to Arms? Beyond the Good Friday Agreement*, Manchester, Manchester University Press, 2006.
57 Henry Patterson, *Ireland since 1939: The Persistence of Conflict*, London, Penguin, 2007, pp. 323–4.
58 Paul Bew, *The Making and Remaking of the Good Friday Agreement*, Dublin, The Liffey Press, 2007, p. 87.
59 Soderberg, *The Superpower Myth* p. 72; Dean Godson, *Himself Alone: David Trimble and the Ordeal of Unionism*, London, Harper Perennial, 2005, pp. 566–90.
60 G. S. Walker, *A History of the Ulster Unionist Party*, Manchester, Manchester University Press, 2003, p. 261.
61 CQWR, 13 June 1998, p. 1628.
62 See Power, *'A Problem from Hell'*, p. 444.
63 See Peter Gowan, 'The NATO Powers and the Balkan Tragedy', *New Left Review*, 1999, vol. 234, pp. 81–102.
64 Jamie Rubin, 'A Very Personal War', *Financial Times*, 30 September 2000; Walter Isaacson, 'Madeleine's War', *Time*, 17 May 1999, p. 30.
65 Michael Dobbs, *Madeleine Albright: A Twentieth Century Odyssey*, New York, Henry Holt, 1999, p. 350.
66 M. K. Albright, *Madam Secretary*, London, Macmillan, 2003, pp. 394–5.
67 Tony Blair, 'Doctrine of the International Community', in I. Stelzer, ed., *Neoconservatism*, London, Atlantic Books, 2004.
68 Alexis Simendinger, 'Looking for Deeds to Match Words', NJ, 20 June 1998, p. 1448.
69 Paddy Ashdown, *The Ashdown Diaries, Volume 2, 1997–1999*, London, Penguin, 2002, p. 407.
70 See William Hagen, 'The Balkans' Lethal Nationalisms', FA, 1999, vol. 78, pp. 52–64; M. Weller, 'The Rambouillet Conference on Kosovo', *International Affairs*, 1999, vol. 75, pp. 211–52; Michael McGwire, 'Why Did We Bomb Belgrade?', *International Affairs*, 2000, vol. 76, pp. 1–23.
71 Ivo H. Daalder and Michael O'Hanlon, *Winning Ugly: NATO's War to Save Kosovo*, Washington DC, The Brookings Institution, 2000, p. 85.
72 Elaine Sciolino and Ethan Bronner, 'How the President, Distracted by Crisis, Entered Balkan War', *NYT*, 18 April 1999; see also, Aidan O'Hehir, 'The Impact of Analogical Reasoning in US Foreign Policy towards Kosovo', *Journal of Peace Research*, 2006, vol. 43, pp. 67–81.
73 'The Late March on Kosovo', *The Economist*, 27 March 1999; Sciolino and Bronner, *NYT*, 18 April 1999; Barton Gellman, 'The Path to Crisis: How the United States and its Allies Went to War', WP, 18 April 1999; David Sanger, 'Agony of Victory: America Finds it's Lonely at the Top', *NYT*, 18 July 1999.
74 Radio address by the President, 13 February 1999, CPL.
75 President Clinton: a commitment to peace in Kosovo, 19 March 1999, CPL.
76 Anthony Lewis, 'Incredibility Gulch', *NYT*, 20 March 1999.
77 Statement by the President to the nation, 24 March 1999, CPL.
78 M. A. Pomper, 'Members Rally Around', CQWR, 27 March 1999, pp. 763–4.

79 C. B. Whitney, 'Who Will Crack First?', *NYT*, 27 March 1999.
80 R. W. Apple, 'Bombs Fall', *NYT*, 28 March 1999.
81 Strobe Talbott, *The Russia Hand*, New York, Random House, 2003, pp. 123, 303.
82 M. R. Gordon and Eric Schmitt, 'US Sought Shift After Raids', *NYT*, 31 March 1999.
83 Talbott, *The Russia Hand*, p. 308.
84 Richard Norton-Taylor, 'Washington Split over Bombing Campaign', *Guardian*, 6 April 1999.
85 Chollet and Goldgeier, *America Between the Wars*, p. 226.
86 Campbell and Stott, eds, *The Blair Years*, pp. 381–2.
87 Lawrence Korb, 'Not Enough Missiles to Go Around?', *NYT*, 6 April 1999.
88 Caspar Weinberger, 'Losing Track of the Main Objectives of War', *NYT*, 12 April 1999.
89 Jane Perlez, 'Clinton Seeking Moscow's Help', *NYT*, 7 April 1999.
90 M. R. Gordon, 'US Warns Russia', *NYT*, 10 April 1999.
91 'In Clinton's Words', *NYT*, 29 April 1999.
92 Chollet and Goldgeier, *America Between the Wars*, p. 220.
93 Gail Collins, 'Who's Afraid of the Big Bad Balkans Quagmire?', *NYT*, 19 April 1999.
94 See Daalder and O'Hanlon, *Winning Ugly*, pp. 86–7.
95 Albright, *Madam Secretary*, p. 420.
96 Statement by the President, 16 June 1999, CPL.
97 Ivo H. Daalder and Michael O'Hanlon, 'Unlearning the Lessons of Kosovo', *Foreign Policy*, 1999, vol. 116, pp. 128–40, 131.
98 Ibid., p. 132; Daalder and O'Hanlon, *Winning Ugly*, pp. 104–10.
99 Anthony Seldon, *Blair*, London, The Free Press, 2004, p. 402.
100 Albright, *Madam Secretary*, p. 423.
101 Mike Jackson, *Soldier: The Autobiography*, London, Bantam Press, 2007, p. 275.
102 Ibid., p. 262; Wesley K. Clark, *Waging Modern War*, New York, PublicAffairs, 2001, pp. 394–5.
103 Bill Clinton, *My Life*, London, Arrow Books, 2005, p. 859.
104 Clark, *Waging Modern War*, p. 425.
105 'The Victors of Kosovo', *The Economist*, 10 June 1999.
106 DiPrizio, *Armed Humanitarians*, p. 130.
107 Madeleine Albright, *The Mighty and the Almighty*, London, Macmillan, 2006, pp. 59–60.
108 James B. Steinberg, 'A Perfect Polemic: Blind to Reality on Kosovo', FA, 1999, vol. 78, pp. 125–41.
109 For Albright's reaction to the Lewinsky affair, see *Madam Secretary*, pp. 357–8.

6 Beyond the Cold War: dealing with old enemies

1 See Michael Cox, G. J. Ikenberry and Takashi Inoguchi, eds, *American Democracy-Promotion: Impulses, Strategies and Impacts*, Oxford, Oxford University Press, 2000.
2 Graham T. Allison and Robert P. Berschel, 'Can the United States Promote Democracy?', *Political Science Quarterly*, 1992, vol. 107, pp. 81–98; Ian Clark, *The Post-Cold War Order: The Spoils of Peace*, Oxford, Oxford University Press, 2001.
3 Quoted in Fareed Zakaria, 'The Rise of Illiberal Democracy', FA, 1997, vol. 76, pp. 22–42, 22.
4 Zbigniew Brzezinski, 'A Geostrategy for Eurasia', FA, September/October 1997 (online edition).
5 M. R. Beschloss and Strobe Talbott, *At the Highest Levels: The Inside Story of the End of the Cold War*, Boston, Little, Brown, 1993, p. 471.
6 See H. Adomen, 'Russia as a "Great Power": Image and Reality', *International Affairs*, 1995, vol. 71, pp. 35–68, 45; see also Robert Levgold, 'Clinton Foreign Policy and the Revolution in the East', in T. G. Shields, J. M. Whayne and D. R.

Kelley, eds, *The Clinton Riddle*, Fayettville, The University of Arkansas Press, 2004, at p. 206.
7   Strobe Talbott, *The Russia Hand*, New York, Random House, 2003, p. 31.
8   'Bill Clinton's Shaken Friends', *NYT*, 2 September 1998.
9   Talbott, *The Russia Hand*, p. 185; see also, Boris Yeltsin, with Catherine A. Fitzgerald, *Midnight Diaries*, New York, PublicAffairs, 2000, pp. 211–25.
10 Talbott, *The Russia Hand*, p. 179.
11 Ibid., p. 186; see also, Yegor Gaidar, *Days of Defeat and Victory*, Seattle, University of Washington Press, 1999, p. 267.
12 G. Stephanopoulos, *All Too Human*, London, Hutchinson, 1999, p. 138; Richard Nixon, 'Clinton's Greatest Challenge', *NYT*, 5 May 1993.
13 Lee Marsden, *Lessons from Russia: Clinton and US Democracy Promotion*, Aldershot, Ashgate, 2005, p. 48.
14 Talbott, *The Russia Hand*, p. 59.
15 Ibid., p. 166; see also, Yeltsin, *Midnight Diaries*, p. 31.
16 Talbott, *The Russia Hand*, p. 95 (also pp. 73, 310–11).
17 T. L. Friedman, 'Eyes on the Prize', *NYT*, 10 May 1995.
18 Talbott, *The Russia Hand*, p. 376.
19 John Bolton, *Surrender is Not an Option: Defending America at the United Nations and Abroad*, New York, Simon and Schuster, 2007, p. 55.
20 James Kitfield, 'Don't Get MAD, Get De-Alerted', NJ, 3 April 1998, pp. 32–3.
21 See Stansfield Turner, *Caging the Nuclear Genie: A Workable Solution for Nuclear, Chemical, and Biological Weapons*, Boulder, Westview, 1999.
22 CQWR, 4 March 1995, p. 698.
23 Press briefing by Samuel Berger, 18 November 1999, CPL.
24 CQWR, 12 August 2000, p. 1973.
25 See George A. Maclean, *Clinton's Foreign Policy in Russia: From Deterrence and Isolation to Democratization and Engagement*, Aldershot, Ashgate, 2006, p. 115.
26 Talbott, *The Russia Hand*, pp. 107–10.
27 See Maclean, *Clinton's Foreign Policy in Russia*.
28 Press conference by President Clinton and President Yeltsin, Moscow, 2 September 1998, CPL.
29 Talbott, *The Russia Hand*, p. 13.
30 As note 28.
31 A. Mitchell, 'Clinton and Yeltsin Accentuate the Positive', *NYT*, 22 April 1996.
32 S. Greenhouse, 'US–Russian Intersection', *NYT*, 27 March 1995.
33 As note 23.
34 See Catherine Danks, *Russian Politics and Society*, Harlow, Pearson Longman, 2001, p. 89.
35 Talbott, *The Russia Hand*, p. 106; see also, James M. Goldgeier and Michael McFaul, *Power and Purpose: US Policy toward Russia after the Cold War*, Washington DC, The Brookings Institution, 2003, pp. 65–71.
36 James M. Goldgeier and Michael McFaul, *Power and Purpose: US Policy toward Russia after the Cold War*, Washington DC, The Brookings Institution, 2003, p. 93.
37 Marsden, *Lessons from Russia*, pp. 66–70, 74–6.
38 Zbigniew Brzezinski, 'The Premature Partnership', FA, March/April 1994 (online edition).
39 Talbott, *The Russia Hand*, p. 117.
40 See Danks, *Russian Politics and Society*, pp. 243–66.
41 Talbott, *The Russia Hand*, p. 52.
42 *Public Papers of the Presidents of the United States: William Jefferson Clinton: Book 1*, Washington DC, US Government Printing Office, 1994, pp. 990–1.
43 D. Cassata, 'Final Battle of the Vietnam War', CQWR, 3 June 1995; *The Guardian*, 4 February 1994.

44 Bill Clinton, *My Life*, London, Arrow Books, 2005, p. 930.
45 22 May 1994, by Larry Rohtermiami.
46 For various perspectives on the influence of the Cuban groups, see: Walt Vanderbrush and Patrick J. Haney, 'Policy Towards Cuba in the Clinton Administration', *Political Studies Quarterly*, 1999, vol. 114, pp. 387–408; Walter Russell Mead, 'Mutual Assured Stupidity: Washington's Cuba Policy is Made in Miami', *The New Yorker*, 11 March 1996; Patrick J. Kiger, *Squeeze Play: Cuba and the Helms-Burton Act*, Washington DC, Center for Public Integrity, 1997; J. C. Smith, 'Foreign Policy for Sale? Interest Group Influence on President Clinton's Cuba Policy', *Presidential Studies Quarterly*, 1998, vol. 28, pp. 201–11.
47 See Vanderbrush and Haney, 'Policy Towards Cuba in the Clinton Administration'.
48 Ibid., pp. 394–5.
49 Ibid., p. 396.
50 Ibid., p. 398; Robert A. Pastor, 'The Clinton Administration and the Americas: The Postwar Rhythm and Blues', *Journal of Interamerican Studies and World Affairs*, 1996, vol. 38, pp. 99–128, 111.
51 Paul Lewis, 'Cuban Talks Suspended', *NYT*, 8 September 1994; Vanderbrush and Haney, 'Policy Towards Cuba in the Clinton Administration', p. 400.
52 Kiger, *Squeeze Play*, p. 54; CQWR, 15 July 1995, p. 2085 and 23 September 1995, p. 2925.
53 S. Greenhouse, 'Clinton Signs Order', *NYT*, 6 October 1995; 'Eye on Congress', *US News and World Report*, 30 October 1995, p. 39; William M. Leogrande, 'Enemies Evermore: US Policy Towards Cuba After Helms-Burton', *Journal of Latin American Studies*, 1997, vol. 29, pp. 211–21.
54 M. K. Albright, *Madam Secretary*, London, Macmillan, 2003, p. 205.
55 CQWR, 2 March 1996, p. 565.
56 Clinton, *My Life*, p. 701.
57 Stephen A. Lisio, 'Helms-Burton and the Point of Diminishing Returns', *International Affairs*, 1996, vol. 72, pp. 691–711.
58 Ian Black, 'Britain Confronts US over Cuba Law', *The Guardian*, 12 July 1996.
59 'Turning a Page on Cuba', *NYT*, 25 November 1997.
60 Kiger, *Squeeze Play*, p. 59.
61 P. J. Haney and W. Vanderbrush, *The Cuban Embargo: The Domestic Politics of an American Foreign Policy*, Pittsburgh, University of Pittsburgh Press, 2005, pp. 116–19.
62 J. C. McKinley, 'Cuba Attacks as "Deceptive" Clinton's Easing of Embargo', *NYT*, 10 January 1999.
63 Quoted in Rosemary Foot, *The Practice of Power: US Relations with China*, Oxford, Clarendon Press, 1995, p. 255.
64 James Mann, *About Face: A History of America's Curious Relationship with China, from Nixon to Clinton*, New York, A. A. Knopf, 1999, p. 276.
65 Michael Schaller, *The United States and China: Into the Twenty-First Century*, New York, Oxford University Press, 2002, p. 212.
66 See, for example, C. J. Doherty, 'US Agonizes over China Policy: Engagement or Confrontation?', CQWR, 26 April 1997, pp. 967–72.
67 See Nancy B. Tucker, 'The Clinton Years: The Problem of Coherence', in R. H. Myers, M. O. Oksenberg and David Shambaugh, eds, *Making China Policy: Lessons from the Bush and Clinton Administrations*, Lanham, Rowman and Littlefield, 2001, p. 52.
68 Mann, *About Face*, p. 295.
69 Warren Christopher, *Chances of a Lifetime*, New York, Scribner's, 2001, p. 240.
70 Mann, *About Face*, p. 281; J. T. Dreyer, 'Clinton's China Policy', in Shields, Whayne and Kelley, eds, *The Clinton Riddle*, p. 164.
71 Kenneth Lieberthal, 'Domestic Forces and Sino-US Relations', in E. F. Vogel, ed., *Living with China*, New York, W. W. Norton, 1997.

72 Mann, *About Face*, pp. 301, 304; see also David Lampton, 'America's China Policy in the Age of the Finance Minister: Clinton Ends Linkage', *China Quarterly*, 1994, vol. 139, pp. 605–12.
73 Barton Gellman, 'US–China nearly came to Blows in 1996', *NYT*, 21 June 1998.
74 Tucker, 'The Clinton Years', p. 53; see also James Shinn, ed., *Weaving the Net: Conditional Engagement with China*, New York, Council on Foreign Relations, 1996.
75 CQA 1995, pp. 10–19.
76 Robert G. Sutter, 'The US Congress', in Myers, Oksenberg and Shambaugh, eds, *Making China Policy*, p. 101.
77 Mann, *About Face*, p. 330.
78 Ibid., pp. 332–4.
79 Robert S. Ross, 'Navigating the Taiwan Strait: Deterrence, Escalation, Dominance and US–China Relations', *International Security*, 2002, vol. 27, pp. 48–85, 63.
80 Mann, *About Face*, p. 312.
81 Ross, 'Navigating the Taiwan Strait', p. 80.
82 Ibid., pp. 50, 82.
83 See Schaller, *The United States and China*, p. 219; see also Ralph A. Cossa, ed., *US–Korea–Japan Relations: Building a 'Virtual Alliance'*, Washington DC, Center for Strategic and International Studies, 1999.
84 Mann, *About Face*, pp. 343, 346.
85 CQWR, 26 April 1997, pp. 968–72.
86 Ibid., p. 972; see also R. E. Cohen, 'GOP Breaking China over Clinton's Deals', *NJ*, 24 May 1998, pp. 1180–1.
87 Michael Kelly, 'Clinton's China Policy', *NJ*, 13 June 1998, pp. 1344–5.
88 James Kitfield, 'China's Long March', *NJ*, 25 April 1998, p. 926.
89 Ibid.
90 See Kelly, 'Clinton's China Policy'; Rhodri Jeffreys-Jones, *The FBI: A History*, New Haven, Yale University Press, 2008, p. 224; Wen Ho Lee, *My Country Versus Me*, New York, Hyperion, 2001.
91 J. S. Nye, 'As China Rises, Must Others Bow?', *The Economist*, 27 June 1998, pp. 23–5, 23.
92 See 'The China Summit', *NYT* (editorial), 30 October 1997.
93 Richard Hornick, 'How to Play the Summit', *Time*, 29 June 1998, p. 49.
94 Carl M. Cannon, 'What we did in China', *NJ*, 18 June 1998, pp. 1668–73, 1671.
95 Albright, *Madam Secretary*, p. 431.
96 Clinton, *My Life*, p. 993.
97 Albright, *Madam Secretary*, p. 431.
98 Tucker, 'The Clinton Years', pp. 63–6.
99 Nye, 'As China Rises', p. 25.
100 Don Oberdorfer, *The Two Koreas: A Contemporary History*, Reading, MA, Addison-Wesley, 1997, p. 315.
101 James Hoare, 'Talk is a Poor Gambit', *Times Higher*, 24 September 2004, p. 27.
102 Leon V. Sigal, *Disarming Strangers: Nuclear Diplomacy with North Korea*, Princeton, Princeton University Press, 1998, p. 58.
103 Michael Mazarr, 'Going Just a Little Nuclear: Nonproliferation Lessons from North Korea', *International Security*, 1995, vol. 20, pp. 92–122, 92.
104 Sigal, *Disarming Strangers*, p. 80.
105 Ibid., pp. 53–4, 60.
106 Robert A. Manning, 'United States–North Korean Relations', in Samuel S. Kim and Tai Hwan Lee, eds, *North Korea and Northeast Asia*, Lanham, Rowman and Littlefield, 2002, p. 65.
107 Joel S. Wit, Daniel B. Poneman and Robert L. Gallucci, *Going Critical: The First North Korean Nuclear Crisis*, Washington DC, The Brookings Institution, 2004.

108 Ibid., p. 419.
109 Sigal, *Disarming Strangers*, p. 76.
110 Manning, 'United States–North Korean Relations', p. 75.
111 Sigal, *Disarming Strangers*, p. 83.
112 Ibid., p. 85.
113 Nancy Soderberg, *The Superpower Myth*, Hoboken, John Wiley, 2005, p. 260.
114 Clinton, *My Life*, p. 603.
115 Soderberg, *The Superpower Myth*, p. 260.
116 Ibid., p. 261; Albright, *Madam Secretary*, p. 456.
117 Brent Scowcroft and Arnold Kanter, 'Korea: A Time for Action', WP, 15 June 1994.
118 See Soderberg, *The Superpower Myth*, p. 261; Ashton Carter and William Perry, *Preventive Defense: A New Security Strategy for America*, Washington DC, The Brookings Institution, 1999, p. 123.
119 Wit *et al.*, *Going Critical*, p. 211; see also S. J. Solarz, 'Next of Kim', *The New Republic*, 8 August 1994.
120 Wit *et al.*, *Going Critical*, pp. xvi, 245.
121 Marion Creekmore, *A Moment of Crisis: Jimmy Carter, the Power of a Peacemaker, and North Korea's Nuclear Ambitions*, New York, PublicAffairs, 2006, pp. 64–6.
122 D. Chollet and J. M. Goldgeier, *America Between the Wars*, New York, PublicAffairs, 2008, p. 94.
123 Creekmore, *A Moment of Crisis*, p. 176.
124 Ibid., p. 186.
125 Soderberg, *The Superpower Myth*, p. 265.
126 Chollet and Goldgeier, *America Between the Wars*, p. 95; Soderberg, *The Superpower Myth*, p. 267.
127 Wit *et al.*, *Going Critical*, p. 372.
128 Manning, 'United States–North Korean Relations', p. 177.
129 Albright, *Madam Secretary*, p. 457.
130 See Wit *et al.*, *Going Critical*, p. 374.
131 Press briefing by Jack Pritchard and Larry Summers, Tokyo, 20 November 1998, CPL.
132 Wit *et al.*, *Going Critical*, p. 375.
133 Readout to the pool: following the President's meeting with ROK President', Tokyo, 8 June 2000, CPL.
134 Albright, *Madam Secretary*, p. 467.
135 See Victor D. Cha and David C. Kang, *Nuclear North Korea: A Debate on Engagement Strategies*, New York, Columbia University Press, 2004.
136 Wit *et al.*, *Going Critical*, p. 377.

7 Alliance politics and borderless threats

1 See John Dumbrell, *The Carter Presidency: A Re-evaluation*, Manchester, Manchester University Press, 1995.
2 Harvey Sicherman, 'The Revenge of Geopolitics', *Orbis*, 1997, vol. 41, pp. 7–13.
3 CQWR, 3 February 1996, p. 306.
4 *Wall Street Journal*, 6 February 1995.
5 Strobe Talbott, *The Russia Hand*, New York, Random House, 2003, pp. 135–6, 141.
6 Ibid., pp. 220, 232.
7 Ronald D. Asmus, *Opening NATO's Door: How the Alliance Remade Itself for a New Era*, New York, Columbia University Press, 2002, pp. 36–7.
8 Ronald D. Asmus, Richard L. Kugler and F. Stephen Larrabee, 'Building a New NATO', FA, September/October 1993 (online edition).
9 Al Gore, remarks, Milwaukee, 6 January 1994, CPL.
10 Talbott, *The Russia Hand*, p. 93.

11 A. Lake, remarks to US–Russia Business Council, 'The Challenge of Change in Russia', 6 April 1996, CPL.
12 Strobe Talbott, 'Russia has Nothing to Fear', *NYT*, 18 February 1997.
13 M. K. Albright, 'NATO Enlargement: Build a Europe Whole and Free', *International Herald Tribune*, 30 April 1998.
14 M. K. Albright, *Madam Secretary*, London, Macmillan, 2003, p. 252.
15 Bill Clinton, West Point graduation remarks on NATO enlargement, 31 May 1997, CPL.
16 Asmus, *Opening NATO's Door*, p. 121.
17 Ibid., p. 122.
18 Amos Perlmutter and Ted G. Carpenter, 'NATO's Expensive Trip East', FA, 1998, vol. 77, pp. 2–6; see also T. G. Carpenter and Barbara Conry, eds, *NATO Enlargement: Illusions and Reality*, Washington DC, Cato Institute, 1998.
19 Alvin Z. Rubinstein, 'NATO Enlargement vs. American Interests', *Orbis*, 1998, vol. 42, pp. 37–49.
20 Roderic Braithwaite, *Across the Moscow River: The World Turned Upside Down*, New Haven, Yale University Press, 2002, p. 134.
21 See Bruce W. Nelson, 'Beyond Cool Borders', *Time*, 14 July 1997, pp. 22–9.
22 Ibid.
23 Robert D. Blackwill, R. Braithwaite and Akihiko Tanaka, *Engaging Russia: A Report to the Trilateral Commission*, New York, Trilateral Commission, 1995, p. 46.
24 Warren Christopher, *In the Stream of History: Shaping Foreign Policy for a New Era*, Stanford, Stanford University Press, 1998, p. 235.
25 David Halberstam, *War in a Time of Peace*, London, Bloomsbury, 2003, p. 344.
26 Asmus, *Opening NATO's Door*, p. 59; see also, James M. Goldgeier, 'NATO Expansion: Anatomy of a Decision', *The Washington Quarterly*, 1998, vol. 21, pp. 85–102; Frank Schimmelfennig, *The EU, NATO and the Integration of Europe: Rules and Rhetoric*, Cambridge, Cambridge University Press, 2003.
27 James M. Goldgeier, *Not Whether But When: The US Decision to Enlarge NATO*, Washington DC, The Brookings Institution, 1999, p. 11.
28 Asmus, *Opening NATO's Door*, p. 113.
29 See Gerald B. Solomon, *The NATO Enlargement Debate, 1990–1997*, New York, Praeger, 1998, p. 178; Schimmelfennig, *The EU, NATO and the Integration of Europe*, p. 251; George W. Grayson, *Strange Bedfellows: NATO Marches East*, Lanham, University Press of America, 1999, p. 147.
30 Asmus, *Opening NATO's Door*, p. 80; Goldgeier, *Not Whether But When*, p. 94.
31 Asmus, *Opening NATO's Door*, p. 165; Michael E. Brown, 'The United States, Western Europe and NATO Enlargement', in Frances G. Burwell and Ivo H. Daalder, eds, *The United States and Europe in the Global Arena*, Basingstoke, Macmillan, 1999, p. 29.
32 Asmus, *Opening NATO's Door*, p. 202.
33 Ibid.
34 Phil Reeves and Tony Barber, 'Russia cuts its Losses', *Independent*, 22 March 1997.
35 Asmus, *Opening NATO's Door*, p. 202.
36 See Brown, 'The United States, Western Europe and NATO Enlargement', p. 32.
37 Grayson, *Strange Bedfellows*, p. 125; see also, J. D. Rosner, 'The American Public, Congress and NATO Enlargement', *NATO Review*, 1997, vol. 45, pp. 12–14.
38 Asmus, *Opening NATO's Door*, p. 285.
39 Brown, 'The United States, Western Europe and NATO Enlargement', p. 33.
40 Asmus, *Opening NATO's Door*, p. 277.
41 Remarks by the President on the national interest for enlarging NATO, 20 March 1998, CPL; see also, D. S. Yost, *NATO Transformed: The Alliance's New Roles in International Security*, Washington DC, US Institute for Peace, 1998.

42 See John Dumbrell, 'Working with Allies', in John E. Owens and J. W. Dumbrell, eds, *America's "War on Terrorism": New Dimensions in US Government and National Security*, Lanham, Rowman and Littlefield, 2008.
43 Christopher, *In the Stream of History*, p. 89.
44 Quoted in Nancy Soderberg, *The Superpower Myth*, Hoboken, John Wiley, 2005, p. 125.
45 Statement by the President, 31 December 2000, CPL.
46 'Sign On, Opt Out', *The Economist*, 4 January 2001; see also J. G. Ralph, *Defending the Society of States: Why America Opposes the International Criminal Court and Its Vision of World Society*, Oxford, Oxford University Press, 2007.
47 See Derek Chollet and James M. Goldgeier, *America Between the Wars*, New York, PublicAffairs, 2008, p. 275.
48 Bill Clinton, *My Life*, London, Arrow Books, 2005, p. 876.
49 'The United States and the United Nations', *US Foreign Policy Agenda* (USIA electronic journal), May 1997, p. 11.
50 Ibid., pp. 29–30.
51 Ibid., p. 5.
52 Boutros Boutros-Ghali, *The Unvanquished: A US–UN Saga*, London, I. B. Tauris, 1999, p. 102; see also, Charles Hill, ed., *The Papers of United Nations Secretary General Boutros Boutros-Ghali*, New Haven, Yale University Press, 2003, Volume 3, p. 1903.
53 Miles Pomper, 'US Pays a Growing Price for UN Debt Impasse', CQWR, 16 January 1999, pp. 122–7, 123.
54 Barbara Crossette, 'Supporters of UN Chief in Disarray', *NYT*, 27 July 1996.
55 Barbara Crossette, 'Is the UN Inefficient?', *NYT*, 7 July 1996.
56 Pomper, 'US Pays a Growing Price', p. 122.
57 Office of the Press Secretary, 'US Support for the United Nations: Engagement, Innovation and Renewal', 6 September 2000, CPL.
58 Morihiro Hosokawa, 'Are US Troops in Japan Needed?', FA, 1998, vol. 77, pp. 2–5, 2.
59 Radio address by the President, 13 May 1995, CPL.
60 See remarks by President Clinton and President Kim Dae-Jung, Seoul, 21 November 1998, CPL; Morton L. Abramowitz, Funabashi Yoichi and Wang Jisi, *China–Japan–US: Managing the Trilateral Relationship*, Tokyo, Japan Center for International Exchange, 1998.
61 Dennis Kux, *The United States and Pakistan, 1947–2000*, Washington DC, Woodrow Wilson Center Press, 2001, p. 328.
62 See James Chiriyankandath, 'Realigning India: Indian Foreign Policy after the Cold War', *The Round Table*, 2004, vol. 93, pp. 199–211.
63 Kux, *The United States and Pakistan*, pp. 356–8; Clinton, *My Life*, pp. 900–3.
64 'Arm-twisting in Latin America', *The Economist*, 27 March 1997.
65 Joseph Treaster, 'Pentagon plans Shift in War on Drug Traffickers', *NYT*, 29 October 1993; see also, Peter H. Smith, *Talons of the Eagle: Dynamics of US–Latin American Relations*, New York, Oxford University Press, 1996.
66 M. K. Albright, *Madam Secretary*, London, Macmillan, 2003, p. 443.
67 Tim Golden, 'Colombia's Leader says US Won't be drawn into War', *NYT*, 21 September 1999.
68 See Douglas W. Stokes, *America's Other War: Terrorizing Colombia*, London, Zed Books, 2005, pp. 92–8.
69 See Lawrence S. Kaplan, 'NATO after the Cold War', in Jarrod Weiner, ed., *The Transatlantic Relationship*, Basingstoke, Macmillan, 1996; Pierre Martin and M. R. Brawley, eds, *Alliance Politics: Allied Force or Forced Allies?*, New York, Palgrave, 2000.
70 Asmus, *Opening NATO's Door*, p. 47; Goldgeier, *Not Whether But When*, p. 11.

71 Brown, 'The United States, Western Europe and NATO Enlargement', p. 32.
72 Francois Heisbourg, 'American Hegemony? Perceptions of the US Abroad', *Survival*, 1999/2000, vol. 41, pp. 5–19, 9.
73 Kevin Featherstone and Roy H. Ginsberg, *The United States and the European Union in the 1990s: Partners in Transition*, Basingstoke, Macmillan, 1996, p. 10.
74 John Peterson, 'Assessment of the Current State of EU–US Relations', in Christoph Bail, Wolfgang Reinicke and Reinhardt Rummel, eds, *EU–US Relations: Balancing the Partnership*, Baden Baden, Nomos Verlagsgesellschaft, 1997, p. 106; see also, Geir Lundestad, *"Empire" by Integration: The United States and European Integration, 1945–1997*, New York and Oxford, Oxford University Press, 1998, p. 118.
75 *The Independent*, 8 December 2000; see also, Paul Cornish and Geoffrey Edwards, 'Beyond the EU/US Dichotomy: The Beginnings of a European Strategic Culture', *International Affairs*, 2001, vol. 77, pp. 587–603; D. H. Dunn, 'European Security and Defence Policy in the American Security Policy Debate', *Defence Studies*, 2001, vol. 1, pp. 46–55.
76 See, for example, Richard Holbrooke, 'US Works to Build New European Security Architecture', USIA press release, 8 March 1995.
77 See John Dumbrell, 'The US–UK "Special Relationship" in a World Twice Transformed', *Cambridge Review of International Affairs*, 2004, vol. 17, pp. 437–50; John Dumbrell, *A Special Relationship: Anglo-American Relations from the Cold War to Iraq*, London, Palgrave, 2006.
78 Asmus, *Opening NATO's Door*, p. 47; Richard Holbrooke, 'America, a European Power', FA, March/April 1995 (online edition).
79 Martin Walker, 'What Europeans Think of America', *World Policy Journal*, 2000, vol. 27, pp. 26–38, 26.
80 See, for example, Charles A. Kupchan, 'Kosovo and the Future of US Engagement in Europe: Continued Hegemony or Impending Retrenchment?', in Martin and Brawley, eds, *Alliance Politics*.
81 See Robert J. Lieber, 'No Transatlantic Divorce in the Offing', *Orbis*, 2000, vol. 44, pp. 571–84; David Calleo, 'A Choice of Europes', *The National Interest*, 2001, vol. 63, pp. 5–16.
82 Robert G. Patman, 'US Foreign Policy in Africa', in M. E. Cox and D. W. Stokes, eds, *US Foreign Policy*, Oxford, Oxford University Press, 2008, p. 322.
83 Miles Pomper, 'Clinton's Promises to Africa', CQWR, 4 April 1998, pp. 896–7, 897.
84 Patman, 'US Foreign Policy in Africa', p. 323; E. J. Keller, 'Africa and the United States: Meeting the Challenge of Globalization', in D. Rothchild and E. J. Keller, eds, *Africa–US Relations: Strategic Encounters*, Boulder, Lynne Rienner, 2006.
85 Patman, 'US Foreign Policy in Africa', p. 324; Ryan Lizza, 'Where Angels Fear to Tread', *New Republic*, 24 July 2000.
86 Remarks by the First Lady at Makerere University, 25 March 1998, CPL.
87 Address by the President to the Parliament of South Africa, 26 March 1998, CPL.
88 'Happiness in the Bush', *The Economist*, 2 April 1998.
89 Patman, 'US Foreign Policy in Africa', p. 324.
90 Philip Shenon, *The Commission: The Uncensored History of the 9/11 Investigation*, London, Little Brown, 2008, pp. 396–7; *The 9/11 Commission Report: Final Report of the National Commission on the Terrorist Attacks on the United States*, New York, W. W. Norton, 204, p. 500; Richard A. Falkenrath, 'The 9/11 Commission Report; A Review Essay', *International Security*, 2004–05, vol. 29, pp. 170–90.
91 Fact sheet: Counterterrorism Act of 1995, 10 February 1995, CPL; Office of the Press Secretary, press release, 24 January 1995, CPL; remarks of the President at signing ceremony for Iran–Libya Sanctions Act of 1996, 5 August 1996, CPL; Derek Chollet and J. M. Goldgeier, *America Between the Wars*, New York, PublicAffairs, 2008,

p. 264; Statement by the President on the anniversary of the Tokyo subway attack, 20 March 1997, CPL; Richard A. Clarke, *Against All Enemies: Inside America's War on Terror*, London, Simon and Schuster, 2004, p. 170; Bill Clinton and Al Gore, 'Safeguarding Americans from the Threat of Terrorism', 15 March 1999, CPL; press release, 17 June 1999, CPL; Sidney Blumenthal, *The Clinton Wars*, London, Viking, 2001, p. 391; press release, 12 October 2000, CPL; Amy B. Zegart, 'September 11 and the Adaptation of the US Intelligence Agencies', *International Security*, 2005, vol. 29, pp. 78–111, 84.
92 Clarke, *Against All Enemies*, pp. xxiv, 145.
93 *9/11 Commission Report*, pp. 199, 340; Douglas Waller, 'Inside the Hunt for Osama', *Time*, 20 December 1998, pp. 42–5; Daniel Benjamin and Steven Simon, *The Age of Sacred Terror*, New York, Random House, 2002, pp. 317–20.
94 Shenon, *The Commission*, pp. 6, 396.
95 See *9/11 Commission Report*, pp. 88–92; George Tenet, *At the Center of the Storm: My Years at the CIA*, New York, HarperCollins, 2007, p. 16; Tim Weiner, *Legacy of Ashes: The History of the CIA*, New York, Doubleday, 2007, pp. 455–68; Amy B. Zegart, *Spying Blind: The CIA, the FBI, and the Origins of 9/11*, Princeton, Princeton University Press, 2007; Steve Coll, *Ghost Wars: The Secret History of the CIA, Afghanistan, and bin Laden from the Soviet Invasion to September 10, 2001*, New York, Penguin, 2004; Zegart, 'September 11 and the Adaptation of the US Intelligence Agencies', pp. 78, 106; Benjamin and Simon, *The Age of Sacred Terror*, pp. 302–4; Joe Klein, *The Natural*, London, Hodder and Stoughton, 2002, p. 191; Rhodri Jeffreys-Jones, *The FBI: A History*, New Haven, Yale University Press, 2008, pp. 222–3; Louis J. Freeh, *My FBI: Bringing Down the Mafia, Investigating Bill Clinton, and Fighting the War on Terror*, New York, St Martin's, 2005.
96 Shenon, *The Commission*, p. 305.
97 Lawrence Freedman, *A Choice of Enemies: America Confronts the Middle East*, London, Weidenfeld and Nicolson, 2008, pp. 366–70; Benjamin and Simon, *The Age of Sacred Terror*.
98 Chollet and Goldgeier, *America Between the Wars*, p. 267.
99 Soderberg, *The Superpower Myth*, p. 154.
100 Ryan C. Hendrickson, *The Clinton Wars: The Constitution, Congress and War Powers*, Nashville, Vanderbilt University Press, 2002, pp. 106–7; Chuck McCutcheon, 'Lawmakers Back Missile Strikes', CQWR, 22 August 1998, pp. 2289–90.
101 Christopher Hitchens, *No One Left to Lie To*, London, Verso, 1999, p. 89.
102 Hendrickson, *The Clinton Wars*, p. 107.
103 Chollet and Goldgeier, *America Between the Wars*, p. 268.
104 'Mr Clinton, Meet Mr Gore', *NYT* (editorial), 20 April 1993.
105 R. L. Berke, 'Clinton Declares New US Policies for Environment', *NYT*, 22 April 1993.
106 Keynote address, 14 June 1993, CPL.
107 Clinton, *My Life*, p. 576.
108 Robyn Eckersley, 'Global Environment', in Cox and Stokes, eds, *US Foreign Policy*, p. 381.
109 Gregg Easterbrook, 'Clinton is Waffling', *NYT*, 12 March 1997.
110 Clinton, *My Life*, p. 770; John McCormick, *The European Superpower*, Basingstoke, Palgrave, 2007, pp. 158–9; Norman J. Vig and Michael G. Faure, eds, *Green Giants: Environmental Policy of the United States and the European Union*, Cambridge, MA, MIT Press, 2004.
111 J. M. Broder, 'Clinton Adamant on 3rd World Role in Climate Accord', *NYT*, 12 December 1997.
112 Radio address, 25 July 1998, CPL.
113 'Facing up to Global Warming', *NYT* editorial, 22 December 1997.
114 As note 111.

115 James Kitfield, 'Strategic Muddle', NJ, 22 November 1997, pp. 2356–9, 2358.
116 See John Dumbrell, 'The Neoconservative Roots of the War in Iraq', in James P. Pfiffner and Mark Phythian, eds, *Intelligence and National Security Policymaking on Iraq: British and American Perspectives*, Manchester, Manchester University Press, 2008.
117 John Hillen, 'Defense's Death Spiral', FA, 1999, vol. 78, pp. 2–7, 7.
118 William E. Odom, 'Transforming the Military', FA, July/August 1997 (online edition); Pat Towell, 'Boots on the Ground', CQWR, 8 August 1998, pp. 2161–6, 2161.
119 Wesley R. Clarke, *Waging Modern War: Bosnia, Kosovo, and the Future of Combat*, New York, PublicAffairs, pp. 47, 71.
120 CQWR, 26 September 1998, p. 2598.
121 Fact sheet: Strengthening and Supporting the Military, 5 January 2001, CPL.
122 'Clinton's Foreign Policy', *Foreign Policy*, 2000, vol. 120, pp. 18–29, 26; W. J. Perry and John M. Shalikashvili, 'The US Military: Still the Best by Far', WP, 10 August 2000.
123 Spurgeon F. Keeney, 'The Arms Race is On', *NYT*, 12 September 1995.
124 See George C. Wilson, 'Joint Chiefs on Missile Defense: Yes, But', NJ, 8 July 2000, pp. 2222–3; Joseph Cirincione, 'Why the Right Lost the Missile Defense Debate', *Foreign Policy*, 1996, vol. 40, pp. 39–44.
125 See Chollet and Goldgeier, *America Between the Wars*, pp. 303–4.
126 See 'A Shield in Space', *The Economist*, 1 June 2000.
127 Pat Towell, 'Cohen's National Security Record', CQWR, 18 January 1997, pp. 181–3.
128 See Bradley Graham, *Hit to Kill: The New Battle over Shielding America from Missile Attack*, New York, PublicAffairs, 2001, pp. 30–50; James Mann, *Rise of the Vulcans: The History of Bush's War Cabinet*, New York, Penguin, 2004, pp. 240–2.
129 As note 126.
130 Remarks by the President on National Missile Defense, 1 September 2000, CPL.
131 Bruce W. Bennett and Richard A. Love, 'Consequence Management', in Barry R. Schneider and Jim A. Davis, eds, *Avoiding the Abyss: Progress, Shortfalls, and the Way Ahead in Combating the WMD Threat*, Westport, Praeger, 2006, at p. 177.
132 Sidney Blumenthal, *The Clinton Wars*, London, Viking, 2001, p. 657.
133 Fact sheet: Preparedness for a Biological Weapons Attack, 22 May 1998, CPL.
134 Remarks by the President on the CWC, 23 April 1997, CPL.
135 Office of the Press Secretary: 'Reducing the Nuclear Threat', 16 May 1998, CPL.
136 Statement by the President, 19 May 1996, CPL.
137 Remarks by the President on land mines, 17 September 1997, CPL.
138 Remarks by the President at CTBT event, 6 October 1999, CPL.
139 Statement by the President on the CTBT, 20 July 1999, CPL; see also, S. J. Freeberg, 'The Pentagon's Alphabet War', NJ, 12 September 1998, pp. 2110–11.
140 Clinton, *My Life*, p. 904.
141 Chuck McCutcheon, 'Senators Struggle to put Nuclear Treaty Back in Bottle', CQWR, 9 October 1999, pp. 2393–5, 2394.
142 Richard Lugar, 'Better Safe...', *The Bulletin of the Atomic Scientists*, 2000, vol. 56, pp. 44–6, 46.
143 Stephen I. Schwartz, 'Test Ban Debacle', *The Bulletin of the Atomic Scientists*, 2000, vol. 56, pp. 24–31, at p. 24.
144 James Kitfield, 'A Return to Isolationism', NJ, 9 October 1999, pp. 2872–7, 2873, 2874.
145 James Kitfield, 'The Senate's Blast Wave', NJ, 23 October 1999, pp. 3044–50, 3045.
146 Kitfield, 'A Return to Isolationism', p. 2874.
147 Kitfield, 'The Senate's Blast Wave', p. 3044; for further discussion of developing Republican Party factions, see Dumbrell, 'The Neoconservative Roots of the War in Iraq'.

8 The Middle East

1. See Adam Garfinkle, 'US–Israeli Relations after the Cold War', *Orbis*, 1996, vol. 40, pp. 557–75, 575; W. G. Hyland, *Clinton's World*, Westport, Praeger, 1999, p. 155; Aaron D. Miller, *The Much Too Promised Land: America's Elusive Search for Arab–Israeli Peace*, New York, Bantam Books, 2008, p. 237; William B. Quandt, *Peace Process: American Diplomacy and the Arab–Israeli Conflict since 1967*, Washington DC, The Brookings Institution, 2001, p. 321.
2. See Zbigniew Brzezinski, Brent Scowcroft and Richard Murphy, 'Differentiated Containment', FA, 1997, vol. 76, pp. 20–30.
3. 'Bush, Rice need to get more Involved', interview with Martin Indyk, 7 May 2008, Council on Foreign Relations website, accessed 12 August 2005.
4. Miller, *The Much Too Promised Land*, p. 240.
5. Dennis Ross, *The Missing Peace: The Inside Story of the Fight for Middle East Peace*, New York, Farrar, Straus and Giroux, 2005.
6. Jimmy Carter, *Palestine: Peace Not Apartheid*, London, Pocket Books, 2008, pp. 135, 137.
7. Ross, *The Missing Peace*, p. 764.
8. Carter, *Palestine*, p. 134.
9. Quandt, *Peace Process*, p. 333.
10. Miller, *The Much Too Promised Land*, pp. 374–5.
11. Henry Kissinger, 'The Mideast Deal', WP, 7 November 1996.
12. Ross, *The Missing Peace*, p. 769.
13. Robert Malley, 'Israel and the Arafat Question', *NYRB*, 7 October 2004, pp. 19–23, 20.
14. Ibid.
15. Miller, *The Much Too Promised Land*, pp. 243–4.
16. Daniel C. Kurtzer, 'Shortsighted Statecraft', FA, 2008, vol. 87, pp. 120–4, 123.
17. Malley, 'Israel and the Arafat question'.
18. Hyland, *Clinton's World*, p. 166.
19. John J. Mearsheimer and Stephen M. Walt, *The Israel Lobby and US Foreign Policy*, London, Penguin, 2008, p. 166.
20. G. Franke-Ruta, 'Arafat's Man in Washington', NJ, 1 August 1998, pp. 1822–3; John Dumbrell, *The Making of US Foreign Policy*, Manchester, Manchester University Press, 1995, pp. 158–9.
21. Lawrence Freedman, *A Choice of Enemies*, London, Weidenfeld and Nicolson, 2008, p. 316.
22. Warren Christopher, *Chances of a Lifetime*, New York, Scribner's, 2001, p. 208.
23. Ross, *The Missing Peace*, p. 260.
24. Ibid., p. 261.
25. Stephen S. Rosenfeld, 'Likud Reaches to Washington', WP, 15 September 1995.
26. M. K. Albright, *Madam Secretary*, London, Macmillan, 2003, p. 294.
27. Remarks by the President in photo opportunity with PM Netanyahu and Chairman Arafat, 28 September 1998, CPL.
28. Miller, *The Much Too Promised Land*, p. 275.
29. Ahron Bregman, *Elusive Peace: How the Holy Land Defeated America*, London, Penguin, 2005, p. xxvi.
30. John F. Harris, *The Survivor*, New York, Random House, 2006, p. 353; Clayton E. Swisher, *The Truth about Camp David: The Untold Story about the Collapse of the Middle East Peace Process*, New York, Nation Books, 2004, p. 8.
31. Albright, *Madam Secretary*, p. 317.
32. Ross, *The Missing Peace*, p. 459.
33. See Derek Chollet and J. M. Goldgeier, *America Between the Wars*, New York, PublicAffairs, 2008, p. 182; Kenneth Pollack, *The Threatening Storm: The Case for Invading Iraq*, New York, Random House, 2002, pp. 58–9.

34 Chollet and Goldgeier, *America Between the Wars*, p. 183; George Stephanopoulos, *All Too Human*, London, Hutchinson, 1999, pp. 156–9.
35 See Steven Wright, *The United States and Persian Gulf Security: The Foundations of the War on Terror*, Reading, Ithaca Press, 2007, p. 102.
36 A. Lake, 'Confronting Backlash States', FA, 1994, vol. 73, pp. 41–52, 48.
37 Albright, *Madam Secretary*, p. 320; F. G. Gause, 'The Illogic of Dual Containment', FA, 1994, vol. 73, pp. 52–61; Kenneth Pollack, *The Persian Puzzle: The Conflict Between Iran and America*, New York, Random House, 2004, pp. 260–5; Kenneth Pollack, 'Next Stop Baghdad?', FA, March/April 2002 (online edition); Sasan Fayazmanesh, *The United States and Iran: Sanctions, Wars and the Policy of Dual Containment*, London, Routledge, 2008; Sasan Fayazmanesh, 'The Politics of the US Economic Sanctions against Iran', *Review of Radical Political Economics*, 2003, vol. 35, pp. 221–40.
38 Text of letter from the President to the Speaker of the House of Representatives and the President Pro Tempore of the Senate, 28 June 1993, CPL.
39 Bill Clinton, *My Life*, London, Arrow Books, 2005, p. 526.
40 Michael Isikoff, 'Saddam's Files', *Newsweek*, 31 March 2008, p. 38.
41 Ibid.
42 Statement by the President, 3 September 1996, CPL.
43 See Wright, *The United States and Persian Gulf Security*, p. 135 (interview with Anthony Lake); Rhodri Jeffreys-Jones, *The FBI: A History*, New Haven, Yale University Press, 2008, p. 220.
44 Chollet and Goldgeier, *America Between the Wars*, p. 189.
45 Quoted by Wright, *The United States and Persian Gulf Security*, p. 136.
46 Freedman, *A Choice of Enemies*, p. 290.
47 See John Prados, *Safe for Democracy: The Secret Wars of the CIA*, Chicago, Ivan R. Dee, 2006, pp. 597–600; Scott Ritter, 'An Ineffective Policy Towards Baghdad', *International Herald Tribune*, 17 August 1999; Scott Ritter, *Iraq Confidential: The Untold Story of America's Intelligence Conspiracy*, London, I. B. Tauris, 2005; Jim Hoagland, 'How the CIA's Secret War on Saddam Collapsed', WP, 26 June 1997.
48 Freedman, *A Choice of Enemies*, p. 292; Robert Bauer, *See No Evil: The True Story of a Ground Soldier in the CIA's War on Terrorism*, New York, Crown, 2002, pp. 257–60.
49 See Wright, *The United States and Persian Gulf Security*, pp. 134–8; Andrew Cockburn and Patrick Cockburn, *Saddam Hussein: An American Obsession*, New York, Vintage, 2000.
50 'America's Demons', *The Economist*, 20 November 1997.
51 Tom Clancy, Tony Zinni and Tony Koltz, *Battle Ready*, New York, Putnam's Sons, 2004, p. 205; Brian Urquhart, 'The Good General', *NYRB*, 23 September 2004, pp. 28–33.
52 See ibid.; also, Daniel Byman, 'After the Storm: US Policy toward Iraq since 1991', *Political Science Quarterly*, 2000–01, vol. 115, pp. 493–516.
53 Albright, *Madam Secretary*, pp. 274–75; see also, Anthony H. Cordesman, *Iraq and the War of Sanctions: Conventional Threats and Weapons of Mass Destruction*, Westport, Praeger, 1999.
54 CQWR, 31 January 1998, p. 247.
55 CQWR, 7 February 1998, p. 327.
56 'The Days before Iraq's Storm Breaks', *The Economist*, 12 February 1998.
57 Donna Cassata, 'Cleland Warns Against Repeating Tonkin Gulf Mistake', CQWR, 31 January 1998, p. 247.
58 Remarks by the President on Iraq, 23 February 1998, CPL.
59 Bronwen Maddox, 'Angry Senators Accuse Albright of Appeasement', *The Times*, 27 February 1998.

60 'Fantasies about Iraq', *International Herald Tribune*, 20 October 1998 (reprint of *NYT* editorial).
61 Statement by the President, 31 October 1998, CPL.
62 Douglas Waller, 'The President's Triggerman', *Time*, 23 November 1996, p. 41.
63 William Dowell et al., 'The Whites of his Eyes', *Time*, 23 November 1996, p. 39.
64 Wright, *The United States and Persian Gulf Security*, p. 148.
65 Freedman, *A Choice of Enemies*, p. 297.
66 Ryan C. Hendrickson, *The Clinton Wars: The Constitution, Congress, and War Powers*, Knoxville, Vanderbilt University Press, 2002, p. 158.
67 The White House at Work: air strikes against Iraq, 17 December 1998, CPL.
68 Hendrickson, *Clinton's Wars*, p. 156.
69 Ibid., p. 155; also, Harris, *The Survivor*, p. 358.
70 Wright, *The United States and Persian Gulf Security*, p. 105.
71 Statement by the Press Secretary, 14 March 1995, CPL.
72 Daniel Southerland, 'Stiffer Trade Sanctions on Iran', WP, 15 September 1995.
73 Remarks by the President at signing ceremony for Iran–Libya Sanctions Act of 1996, 5 August 1996, CPL.
74 See CQWR, 30 June 1998, p. 1713; Freedman, *A Choice of Enemies*, p. 306.
75 Carroll Doherty, 'White House Walks Fine Line', CQWR, 25 May 1996, p. 1560.
76 Richard A. Clarke, *Against All Enemies*, London, Simon and Schuster, 2004, pp. 112–18, 127–9.
77 Daniel Benjamin and Steven Simon, *The Age of Sacred Terror*, New York, Random House, 2002, pp. 330–2.
78 'Khatami's Iran', *The Economist*, 18 December 1997.
79 'The Iranian Opportunity', *The Economist*, 24 February 2000.
80 Miles Pomper, 'Warmer US–Iranian Relations Get Cold Shoulder', CQWR, 16 May 1998, pp. 1321–3, 1322.
81 Christopher Ogden, 'Olive Branch Diplomacy', *Time*, 29 June 1998, p. 53.
82 Ibid.
83 'Meanwhile, there's Iran', *The Economist*, 27 June 1998, pp. 57–8.
84 'What to do about Iran', *The Economist*, 21 May 1998.
85 Pomper, 'Warmer US–Iranian Relations', p. 1322.
86 James Kitfield, 'Iran's Mushrooming Nuclear Ambitions', NJ, 1 August 1998, pp. 1820–1, 1820.
87 Statement by the President, 14 March 2000, CPL.
88 Freedman, *A Choice of Enemies*, p. 308.
89 'America's Old Alliance Subsides', *The Economist*, 22 January 1998.
90 Clinton, *My Life*, p. 911.
91 Swisher, *The Truth about Camp David*, pp. 51, 55, 54.
92 Rabin annual lecture: 'Building a Secure Peace', 11 November 1999, CPL.
93 Ross, *The Missing Peace*, p. 587.
94 Miller, *The Much Too Promised Land*, p. 287.
95 Ross, *The Missing Peace*, pp. 654–5.
96 Clinton, *My Life*, p. 915.
97 Ibid., p. 916.
98 Statement by the President on the Middle East peace talks, 25 July 2000, CPL.
99 Ross, *The Missing Peace*, p. 711.
100 Ibid., p. 726.
101 Ibid., p. 733.
102 Bregman, *Elusive Peace*, p. 138 (interview with Gamal Helal).
103 Ross, *The Missing Peace*, p. 744.
104 Ibid., p. 746.
105 Ibid., pp. 749–50.
106 Carter, *Palestine*, p. 151.

107 Remarks of President Clinton at the Israeli policy gala dinner, New York, 7 January 2001, CPL.
108 Clinton, *My Life*, p. 944; Albright, *Madam Secretary*, pp. 497–8; Ross, *The Missing Peace*, p. 776.
109 Swisher, *The Truth about Camp David*, p. 300.
110 Malley, 'Israel and the Arafat Question', p. 22.
111 Swisher, *The Truth about Camp David*, p. 304.
112 See Hussein Agha and Robert Malley, 'Camp David: The Tragedy of Errors', *NYRB*, 9 August 2001, pp. 15–22; Mearsheimer and Walt, *The Israel Lobby*, pp. 103–7; Jerome Slater, 'What Went Wrong? The Collapse of the Israeli–Palestinian Peace Process', *Political Science Quarterly*, 2001, vol. 116, pp. 171–99; Jeremy Pressman, 'Visions in Collision: What Happened at Camp David and Taba?', *International Security*, 2003, vol. 28, pp. 5–43; Shlomo Ben-Ami, *Scars of War, Wounds of Peace: The Israeli–Arab Tragedy*, Oxford, Oxford University Press, 2007; Charles Enderlin, *Shattered Dreams: The Failure of the Peace Process in the Middle East, 1995–2002*, New York, Other Press, 2002.
113 Miller, *The Much Too Promised Land*, p. 298.
114 Press briefing by Joe Lockhart, 12 July 2000, CPL.
115 Swisher, *The Truth about Camp David*, p. 302.
116 Miller, *The Much Too Promised Land*, p. 310.

9 Bill Clinton's foreign policy

1 See Joseph S. Nye, *The Powers to Lead*, New York, Oxford University Press, 2008.
2 Hal Brands, *From Berlin to Baghdad: America's Search for Purpose in the Post-Cold War World*, Lexington, The University Press of Kentucky, 2008, p. 261.
3 Warren Christopher, *Chances of a Lifetime*, New York, Scribner's, 2001, p. 154.
4 R. Evans and R. Novak, *Lyndon B. Johnson: The Exercise of Power*, New York, New American Library, 1966, p. 148.
5 Remarks by the President at the American University centennial celebration, 26 February 1993, CPL.
6 For differing views of the trajectory of Carter's foreign policy, see John Dumbrell, *The Carter Presidency: A Reevaluation*, Manchester, Manchester University Press, 1995; Scott Kaufman, *Plans Unraveled: The Foreign Policy of the Carter Administration*, DeKalb, Northern Illinois University Press, 2008. See also Harvey Sicherman, 'The Revenge of Geopolitics', *Orbis*, 1997, vol. 41, pp. 7–13.
7 See John E. Owens, 'Presidential Aggrandizement and Congressional Acquiescence in the "War on Terrorism": A New Constitutional Equilibrium?', in J. E. Owens and John Dumbrell, eds, *America's 'War on Terrorism': New Dimensions in US Government and National Security*, Lanham, Lexington Books, 2008.
8 Ethan Canin, *America, America*, London, Bloomsbury, 2008, pp. 297–8.
9 David Remnick, 'The Wanderer', *The New Yorker*, 18 September 2006, p. 53.
10 Joseph O'Neill, *Netherland*, London, Fourth Estate, 2008, p. 88.
11 See Steven E. Schier, 'American Politics after Clinton', in S. E. Schier, ed., *The Postmodern Presidency: Bill Clinton's Legacy in US Politics*, Pittsburgh, University of Pittsburgh Press, 2000.
12 G. John Ikenberry, 'The Future of International Leadership', *Political Science Quarterly*, 1996, vol. 111, pp. 385–401, 400–1.

Select bibliography

Books

Albright, Madeleine K., *Madam Secretary: A Memoir*, London, Macmillan, 2000.
Albright, Madeleine K., *The Mighty and the Almighty: Reflections on Power, God, and World Affairs*, London, Macmillan, 2006.
Asmus, Ronald D., *Opening NATO's Door: How the Alliance Remade Itself for a New Era*, New York, Columbia University Press, 2002.
Barber, Benjamin R., *The Truth of Power: Intellectual Affairs in the Clinton White House*, New York, W. W. Norton, 2001.
Bauer, Robert, *See No Evil: The True Story of a Ground Soldier in the CIA's War on Terrorism*, New York, Crown, 2002.
Benjamin, David and Steven Simon, *The Age of Sacred Terror*, New York, Random House, 2002.
Bernstein, Carl, *A Woman in Charge: The Life of Hillary Rodham Clinton*, New York, Vintage, 2008.
Bert, Wayne, *The Reluctant Superpower: United States Policy in Bosnia, 1991–95*, Basingstoke, Macmillan, 1997.
Bew, Paul, *The Making and Remaking of the Good Friday Agreement*, Dublin, The Liffey Press, 2007.
Blumenthal, Sidney, *The Clinton Wars: An Insider's Account of the White House Years*, London, Viking, 2001.
Boutros-Ghali, Boutros, *The Unvanquished: A US–UN Saga*, London, I. B. Tauris, 1999.
Bregman, Ahron, *Elusive Peace: How the Holy Land Defeated America*, London, Penguin, 2005.
Burrell, Barbara, *Public Opinion, the First Ladyship and Hillary Rodham Clinton*, New York, Routledge, 2001.
Campbell, Colin and Bert A. Rockman, eds, *The Clinton Legacy*, New York, Chatham House Publishers, 2000.
Carter, Ashton and William Perry, *Preventive Defense: A New Security Strategy for America*, Washington DC, The Brookings Institution, 1999.
Carter, Jimmy, *Palestine: Peace Not Apartheid*, London, Pocket Books, 2008.
Chollet, Derek, *The Road to the Dayton Accords: A Study of American Statecraft*, New York, Praeger, 2005.
Chollet, Derek and James Goldgeier, *America Between the Wars*, New York, PublicAffairs, 2008.
Christopher, Warren, *In The Stream of History*, Stanford, Stanford University Press, 1998.

Christopher, Warren, *Chances of a Lifetime*, New York, Scribner's, 2001.
Clark, Ian, *The Post-Cold War Order: The Spoils of Peace*, Oxford, Oxford University Press, 2001.
Clarke, Richard A., *Against All Enemies: Inside America's War on Terror*, London, Simon and Schuster, 2004.
Clarke, Walter and Jeffrey Herbst, eds, *Learning from Somalia: The Lessons of Humanitarian Intervention*, Boulder, Westview, 1997.
Clinton, Bill, *My Life*, London, Arrow Books, 2005.
Clinton, Hillary R., *Living History*, London, Headline, 2003.
Coll, Steve, *Ghost Wars: The Secret History of the CIA, Afghanistan, and bin Laden from the Soviet Invasion to September 10, 2001*, New York, Penguin, 2004.
Cox, Michael, Adrian Guelke and Fiona Stephen, eds, *A Farewell to Arms? From 'Long War' to Long Peace in Northern Ireland*, Manchester, Manchester University Press, 2000.
Cox, Michael, Adrian Guelke and Fiona Stephen, eds, *A Farewell to Arms? Beyond the Good Friday Agreement*, Manchester, Manchester University Press, 2006.
Cox, Michael, G. J. Ikenberry and T. Inoguchi, eds, *American Democracy Promotion: Impulses, Strategies and Impacts*, Oxford, Oxford University Press, 2000.
Crabb, C. V., L. S. Sarieddine and G. J. Antizzo, *Charting a New Diplomatic Course: Alternative Approaches to America's Post-Cold War Foreign Policy*, Baton Rouge, Louisiana State University Press, 2001.
Creekmore, Marion, *A Moment of Crisis: Jimmy Carter, the Power of a Peacemaker, and North Korea's Nuclear Ambitions*, New York, PublicAffairs, 2006.
Crocker, Chester A., F. O. Hampson and Pamela Aall, eds, *Herding Cats: Multiparty Mediation in a Complex World*, Washington DC, US Institute of Peace Press, 1999.
Daalder, Ivo H., *Getting to Dayton: The Making of America's Bosnia Policy*, Washington DC, The Brookings Institution, 2000.
Daalder, Ivo H. and Michael O'Hanlon, *Winning Ugly: NATO's War to Save Kosovo*, Washington DC, The Brookings Institution, 2000.
Deese, D. A., ed., *The New Politics of American Foreign Policy*, New York, St Martin's, 1994.
DiPrizio, R. C., *Armed Humanitarians: US Interventions from Northern Iraq to Kosovo*, Baltimore, Johns Hopkins University Press, 2002.
Dobbs, Michael, *Madeleine Albright: A Twentieth Century Odyssey*, New York, Henry Holt, 1999.
Drew, Elizabeth, *On the Edge: The Clinton Presidency*, New York, Simon and Schuster, 1994.
Drew, Elizabeth, *Showdown: The Struggle between the Gingrich Congress and the Clinton White House*, New York, Simon and Schuster, 1996.
Durch, William, ed., *UN Peacekeeping, American Policy and the Uncivil Wars of the 1990s*, New York, St Martin's, 1996.
Fayazmanesh, Sasan, *The United States, and Iran: Sanctions, Wars and the Policy of Dual Containment*, London, Routledge, 2008.
Featherstone, Kevin and Roy H. Ginsberg, *The United States and the European Union in the 1990s: Partners in Transition*, Basingstoke, Macmillan, 1996.
Fisher, Louis, *Presidential War Power*, Lawrence, University Press of Kansas, 1995.
Freedman, Lawrence, *A Choice of Enemies: America Confronts the Middle East*, London, Weidenfeld and Nicolson, 2008.
Freeh, Louis J., *My FBI: Bringing Down the Mafia, Investigating Bill Clinton, and Fighting the War on Terror*, New York, St Martin's, 2005.

Frye, Alton, *Humanitarian Intervention: Crafting a Workable Doctrine*, New York, Council on Foreign Relations, 2000.
Gallen, David, *Bill Clinton as They Knew Him: An Oral Biography*, New York, Gallen Publishing, 1994.
Gergen, David, *Eyewitness to Power: The Essence of Leadership*, New York, Touchstone, 2000.
Gerth, J. and D. Van Natta, *Hillary Clinton: Her Way*, London, Century, 2007.
Goldgeier, James, *Not Whether But When: The US Decision to Enlarge NATO*, Washington DC, The Brookings Institution, 1999.
Goldgeier, James and Michael McFaul, *Power and Purpose: US Policy Towards Russia After the Cold War*, Washington DC, The Brookings Institution, 2003.
Gore, Al, *Earth in the Balance: Ecology and the Human Spirit*, New York, Plume, 1993.
Gow, James, *The Triumph of the Lack of Will: International Diplomacy and the Yugoslav War*, London, Hurst, 1997.
Grayson, George W., *Strange Bedfellows: NATO Marches East*, Lanham, University Press of America, 1999.
Haass, Richard N., *The Reluctant Sheriff: The United States After the Cold War*, Washington DC, The Brookings Institution, 1998.
Halberstam, David, *War in a Time of Peace: Bush, Clinton and the Generals*, London, Bloomsbury, 2003.
Hamilton, Nigel, *Bill Clinton: An American Journey: Great Expectations*, New York, Random House, 2003.
Hamilton, Nigel, *Bill Clinton: Mastering the Presidency*, London, Century, 2007.
Haney, P. J. and W. Vanderbrush, *The Cuban Embargo: The Domestic Politics of an American Foreign Policy*, Pittsburgh, University of Pittsburgh Press, 2005.
Harris, John F., *The Survivor: Bill Clinton in the White House*, New York, Random House, 2006.
Hendrickson, Ryan C., *The Clinton Wars: The Constitution, Congress, and War Powers*, Nashville, Vanderbilt University Press, 2002.
Herspring, Dale R., *The Pentagon and the Presidency: Civil–Military Relations from FDR to George W. Bush*, Lawrence, University Press of Kansas, 2005.
Hippel, Karin von, *Democracy by Force: US Military Interventions in the Post-Cold War World*, Cambridge, Cambridge University Press, 2000.
Hirsch, J. and R. Oakley, *Somalia and Operation Restore Hope*, Washington DC, US Institute of Peace Press, 1995.
Hitchens, Christopher, *No One Left To Lie To: The Triangulations of William Jefferson Clinton*, London, Verso, 1999.
Hutchings, R. L., ed., *At the End of the American Century*, Washington DC, The Woodrow Wilson Center, 1998.
Hyland, William G., *Clinton's World: Remaking American Foreign Policy*, Westport, Praeger, 1999.
Johnson, Haynes, *The Best of Times: The Clinton Years*, New York, Harcourt, 2001.
Kiger, Patrick J., *Squeeze Play: Cuba and the Helms-Burton Act*, Washington DC, Center for Public Integrity, 1997.
Klein, J. *The Natural: The Misunderstood Presidency of Bill Clinton*, London, Hodder and Stoughton, 2002.
Kull, S. and I. M. Destler, *Misreading the Public: The Myth of a New Isolationism*, Washington DC, The Brookings Institution, 1999.

Select bibliography

Lake, Anthony, *Six Nightmares: Real Threats in a Dangerous World and How America Can Meet Them*, Boston, Little, Brown, 2000.

Lieber, R. J., ed., *Eagle Adrift: American Foreign Policy at the End of the Century*, New York, Longman, 1997.

Lippmann, Thomas W., *Madeleine Albright and the New American Diplomacy*, Boulder, Westview, 2000.

Lundestad, Geir, *'Empire' by Integration: The United States and European Integration, 1945–1997*, New York, Oxford University Press, 1998.

Lynch, Timothy J., *Turf War: The Clinton Administration and Northern Ireland*, Aldershot, Ashgate, 2004.

MacKinnon, Michael G., *The Evolution of US Peacekeeping Policy Under Clinton: A Fair-Weather Friend?*, London, Cass, 2000.

Maclean, George A., *Clinton's Foreign Policy in Russia: From Deterrence and Isolation to Democratization and Engagement*, Aldershot, Ashgate, 2006.

Mann, James, *About Face: A History of America's Curious Relationship with China, from Nixon to Clinton*, New York, A. A. Knopf, 1999.

Marannis, David, *First in his Class: The Biography of Bill Clinton*, New York, Touchstone, 1996.

Marsden, Lee, *Lessons from Russia: Clinton and US Democracy Promotion*, Aldershot, Ashgate, 2005.

Miller, Aaron D., *The Much Too Promised Land: America's Elusive Search for Arab–Israeli Peace*, New York, Bantam Books, 2008.

Mitchell, George J., *Making Peace: The Inside Story of the Good Friday Agreement*, London, Heinemann, 1999.

Morris, Dick, *Behind the Oval Office: Winning the Presidency in the Nineties*, New York, Random House, 1997.

Murray, Leonie, *Clinton, Peacekeeping and Humanitarian Intervention*, London, Routledge, 2007.

Myers, R. H., M. O. Oksenberg and David Shambaugh, eds, *Making China Policy: Lessons from the Bush and Clinton Administrations*, Lanham, Rowman and Littlefield, 2001.

Nye, Joseph S., *The Powers to Lead*, New York, Oxford University Press, 2008.

O'Clery, Conor, *The Greening of the White House*, Dublin, Gill and Macmillan, 1996.

Paarlberg, Robert C., *Leadership Abroad Begins at Home*, Washington DC, The Brookings Institution, 1995.

Phillips, D. T., *The Clinton Charisma: A Legacy of Leadership*, New York, Palgrave Macmillan, 2007.

Powell, Colin, *A Soldier's Way*, London, Hutchinson, 1995.

Powell, Jonathan, *Great Hatred, Little Room: Making Peace in Northern Ireland*, London, The Bodley Head, 2008.

Power, Samantha, *'A Problem From Hell': America and the Age of Genocide*, London, Flamingo Books, 2003.

Priest, Dana, *The Mission: Waging War and Keeping Peace with America's Military*, New York, W. W. Norton, 2003.

Quandt, William B., *Peace Process: American Diplomacy and the Arab–Israeli Conflict Since 1967*, Washington DC, The Brookings Institution, 2001.

Reich, Robert B., *Locked in the Cabinet*, New York, Knopf, 1997.

Renshon, Stanley A., ed., *The Clinton Presidency: Campaigning, Governing and the Psychology of Leadership*, Boulder, Westview, 1995.

Renshon, Stanley A. and Deborah W. Larson, eds, *Good Judgement in Foreign Policy: Theory and Application*, Lanham, Rowman and Littlefield, 2003.
Rieff, David, *Slaughterhouse: Bosnia and the Future of the West*, New York, Simon and Schuster, 1995.
Ritter, Scott, *Iraq Confidential: The Untold Story of America's Intelligence Conspiracy*, London, I. B. Tauris, 2005.
Rosner, Jeremy D., *The New Tug of War: Congress, the Executive Branch, and National Security*, Washington DC, Carnegie Endowment, 1995.
Ross, Dennis, *The Missing Peace: The Inside Story of the Fight for Middle East Peace*, New York, Farrar, Straus and Giroux, 2005.
Rubin, Robert E. and Jacob Weisberg, *In an Uncertain World: Tough Choices from Wall Street to Washington*, New York, Texere, 2003.
Rubinstein, Alvin Z., Albina Shayevich and Boris Zlotnikov, eds, *The Clinton Foreign Policy Reader*, Armonk, Sharpe, 2001.
Schier, Steven, ed., *The Postmodern Presidency: Bill Clinton's Legacy in US Politics*, Pittsburgh, University of Pittsburgh Press, 2000.
Sheehy, Gail, *Hillary's Choice*, London, Simon and Schuster, 1999.
Shields, Todd G., Jeannie M. Whayne and Donald R. Kelley, eds, *The Clinton Riddle: Perspectives on the Forty-second President*, Fayetteville, University of Arkansas Press.
Sigal, Leon V., *Disarming Strangers: Nuclear Diplomacy with North Korea*, Princeton, Princeton University Press, 1998.
Simms, Brendan, *Unfinest Hour: Britain and the Destruction of Bosnia*, London, Allen Lane, 2001.
Smith, Sally Bedell, *For Love of Politics: The Clintons in the White House*, London, Aurum Press, 2007.
Soderberg, Nancy, *The Superpower Myth: The Use and Misuse of American Might*, Hoboken, John Wiley, 2005.
Solomon, Gerald B., *The NATO Enlargement Debate, 1990–1997*, New York, Praeger, 1998.
Stephanopoulos, George, *All Too Human: A Political Education*, London, Hutchinson, 1999.
Stokes, Douglas W., *America's Other War: Terrorizing Colombia*, London, Zed Books, 2005.
Suettinger, Robert L., *Beyond Tiananmen: The Politics of US–China Relations: 1989–2000*, Washington DC, The Brookings Institution, 2003.
Swisher, Clayton E., *The Truth About Camp David: The Untold Story about the Collapse of the Middle East Peace Process*, New York, Nation Books, 2004.
Talbott, Strobe, *The Russia Hand: A Memoir of Presidential Diplomacy*, New York, Random House, 2003.
Tenet, George, *At the Center of the Storm: My Years at the CIA*, New York, HarperCollins, 2007.
Turge, Bill, *Inventing Al Gore: A Biography*, Boston, Houghton Mifflin, 2000.
Walker, Martin, *Clinton: The President They Deserve*, London, Fourth Estate, 1996.
Warshaw, Shirley Anne, *The Clinton Years*, New York, Checkmark Books, 2005.
Weiner, Tim, *Legacy of Ashes: The History of the CIA*, New York, Doubleday, 2007.
Wit, Joel S., Daniel B. Poneman and Robert L. Gallucci, *Going Critical: The First North Korean Nuclear Crisis*, Washington DC, The Brookings Institution, 2004.
Woodward, Bob, *The Agenda: Inside the Clinton White House*, New York, Simon and Schuster, 1994.

Wright, Steven, *The United States and Persian Gulf Security: The Foundations of the War on Terror*, Reading, Ithaca Press, 2007.
Yankelovich, Daniel and I. M. Destler, eds, *Beyond the Beltway: Engaging the Public in US Foreign Policy*, New York, W. W. Norton, 1994.
Yost, D. S., *NATO Transformed: The Alliance's New Roles in International Security*, Washington DC, US Institute for Peace, 1998.
Zegart, Amy, *Spying Blind: The CIA, the FBI, and the Origins of 9/11*, Princeton, Princeton University Press, 2007.

Articles

Art, Robert J., 'Geopolitics Updated: The Strategy of Selective Engagement', *International Security*, 1998–99, vol. 23, pp. 167–81.
Berger, Sandy, 'A Foreign Policy for a Global Age', FA, 2000, vol. 79, pp. 18–29.
Bhagwati, Jagdish, 'Beyond NAFTA: Clinton's Trading Choices', *Foreign Policy*, 1993, vol. 91, pp. 25–8.
Brinkley, Douglas, 'Democratic Enlargement: The Clinton Doctrine', *Foreign Policy*, 1997, vol. 106, pp. 111–27.
Byman, Daniel, 'After the Storm: US Policy Toward Iraq Since 1991', *Political Science Quarterly*, 2000–01, vol. 115, pp. 493–516.
Christopher, Warren, 'America's Leadership, America's Opportunity', *Foreign Policy*, 1993, vol. 98, pp. 6–28.
Cox, Michael, 'The War that Came in from the Cold', *World Policy Journal*, 1999, vol. 16, pp. 59–67.
Crocker, Chester A., 'The Lessons of Somalia: Not Everything Went Wrong', FA, 1995, vol. 74, pp. 2–8.
Dumbrell, John, 'The United States and the Northern Irish Conflict, 1969–1994: From Indifference to Intervention', *Irish Studies in International Affairs*, 1995, vol. 6, pp. 107–25.
Haass, Richard N., 'Fatal Distraction: Bill Clinton's Foreign Policy', *Foreign Policy*, 1997, vol. 107, pp. 50–9.
Haass, Richard N., 'Paradigm Lost', FA, 1995, vol. 74, pp. 43–58.
Hendrickson, Ryan C., 'War Powers, Bosnia and the 104th Congress', *Political Science Quarterly*, 1998, vol. 113, pp. 241–62.
Ikenberry, John G., 'The Future of International Leadership', *Political Science Quarterly*, 1996, vol. 111, pp. 385–401.
Jewett, A. W. and M. D. Turetzky, 'Stability and Change in President Clinton's Foreign Policy', *Presidential Studies Quarterly*, 1998, vol. 28, pp. 638–65.
Lake, Anthony, 'Confronting Backlash States', FA, 1994, vol. 73, pp. 41–52.
Lock-Pullan, Richard, 'Learning the Limits of Virtue: Clinton, the Army and the Criteria for the Use of Military Force', *Contemporary Security Policy*, 2003, vol. 24, pp. 133–56.
McGwire, Michael, 'Why Did We Bomb Belgrade?', *International Affairs*, 2000, vol. 76, pp. 1–23.
Malley, Robert, 'Israel and the Arafat Question', *NYRB*, 7 October 2004, pp. 19–23.
Mandlebaum, Michael, 'Foreign Policy as Social Work', FA, 1996, vol. 75, pp. 16–32.
Miller, Linda, 'The Clinton Years: Reinventing US Foreign Policy', *International Affairs*, 1994, vol. 70, pp. 621–34.
Murray, Leonie, 'Somalia and the "Body Bag Myth" in American Politics', *International Politics*, 2007, vol. 4, pp. 552–71.

Ornstein, Norman J., 'Foreign Policy and the 1992 Elections', FA, 1992, vol. 71, pp. 1–16.
Powell, Colin, 'US Forces: Challenges Ahead', FA, 1992–93, vol. 72, pp. 32–41.
Pastor, Robert A., 'The Clinton Administration and the Americas: The Postwar Rhythm and Blues', *Journal of Interamerican Studies and World Affairs*, 1996, vol. 38, pp. 99–128.
Remnick, David, 'The Wanderer', *The New Yorker*, 18 September 2006, pp. 42–67.
Ross, Robert S., 'Navigating the Taiwan Strait: Deterrence, Escalation, Dominance and US–China Relations', *International Security*, 2002, vol. 27, pp. 48–85.
Rubinstein, Alvin Z., 'The New Moralists on the Road to Hell', *Orbis*, 1996, vol. 40, pp. 31–41.
Schlesinger, Stephen, 'The End of Idealism', *World Policy Journal*, 1998–99, vol. 24, pp. 36–40.
Sicherman, Harvey, 'The Revenge of Geopolitics', *Orbis*, 1997, vol. 41, pp. 7–13.
Slater, Jerome, 'What Went Wrong? The Collapse of the Israeli–Palestinian Peace Process', *Political Science Quarterly*, 2001, vol. 116, pp. 171–99.
Steinberg, James, 'A Perfect Polemic: Blind to Reality on Kosovo', FA, 1999, vol. 78, pp. 125–41.
Walt, Stephen M., 'Two Cheers for Clinton's Foreign Policy', FA, 2000, vol. 79, pp. 63–79.
Wills, Garry, 'Bully of the Free World', FA, 1999, vol. 79, pp. 50–9.
Zakaria, Fareed, 'The Rise of Illiberal Democracy', FA, 1997, vol. 76, pp. 22–42.

Index

9/11 terror attacks 1, 4, 8, 21, 44, 135, 137, 170

Adams, Gerry 88–90, 113
Afghanistan 31, 123, 130, 137–9, 166, 169
Africa 26, 67–71, 135, 137
AIDS 21, 131, 135
al Qaeda 135–9, 170
Albright, Madeleine: background 15–17, 128; bureaucratic role 33–4, 40, 168; and Kosovo 19, 42, 56, 60–1, 67, 68–70, 72, 77, 79, 84, 86, 92–8, 110, 115–16, 119, 121, 125, 129, 131, 133, 151–3, 156, 159–64
American Federation of Labor–Congress of Industrial Organizations (AFL-CIO) 49, 51–3, 57
American Israeli Public Affairs Committee (AIPAC) 150, 158
Annan, Kofi 131, 156
Anti-Ballistic Missile Treaty 14, 103, 142–3
Arafat, Yasser 147–9, 151, 161–4
Aristide, Jean Bertrand 71–4
Asia-Pacific Economic Cooperation (APEC) 54, 58
Asian financial crash 56–8
Aspin, Les 18, 29, 31, 63–6, 69, 71, 77, 168
assertive humanitarianism 77–80; *see also* humanitarian intervention; humanitarianism
Australia 71, 132, 167

Baker, James 19, 82–3, 91, 164

Balkans 2, 13, 26, 29, 31, 81–3, 85, 92, 101, 123, 129–30, 169
Baltic States 100, 128–9
Barak, Ehud 3, 160–4
Barshefsky, Charlene 48, 55, 58, 60, 117
Belfast (Good Friday) Agreement 28, 88–91
Berger, Sandy: background 17–19; bureaucratic role 21, 33–4, 168; and economic foreign policy 45–6, 55, 60, 69, 86, 92, 95, 98, 104, 111, 114, 116, 156
Biden, Joe 41, 130
bin Laden, Osama 137–8; *see also* al Qaeda
Blair, Tony 89–92, 95, 97, 156–7
Blumenthal, Sidney 3, 11–12
Bolton, John 68, 102
Bonior, David 53, 56
Bosnia 5, 14, 26–31, 35–6, 60, 72, 81–8, 92–3, 99, 101–2, 128, 130, 135–6, 138, 158, 166–7
Boutros-Ghali, Boutros 68–9, 131
Brazil 48, 74
Brown, Ron 48, 111
Brzezinski, Zbigniew 6, 15–17, 19, 99, 105, 123, 143
Buchanan, Pat 23, 25, 30, 49, 53
Bush, George H.W. (Bush41) legacy and continuity with Clinton 2, 4–5, 8, 18–19, 22–3, 25–6, 32–3, 35, 41, 43, 47–9, 51, 63–5, 68–70, 71–2, 81–3, 99–100, 103, 132, 134, 135, 139, 141, 147, 152–4, 168, 169–70
Bush, George W. (Bush43) continuity with Clinton 1, 2, 4–6, 8, 31, 35, 63,

96, 131, 134–6, 145–6, 154–7, 163, 166–70

Cable News Network (CNN) 15, 24, 62, 68–9, 75–6, 120
Camp David (2000) 160–4
Canada 16, 50–4
Carter, Jimmy: and the Balkans 83, 85, 90; compared to Clinton 123, 168–9; and Haiti 75–6; and North Korea 120–3, 15–20, 22, 25, 29, 33, 35, 42, 56, 63, 69, 106, 146, 148, 161, 163–4
Cedras, Raoul 71–4
Central Intelligence Agency (CIA) 18–19, 34–5, 72, 79, 86, 119, 136–8, 152, 155, 158, 160
Chechnya 102–5, 138
Chemical Weapons Convention (CWC) 40, 136, 144
Cheney, Richard 63, 68, 126
China: and North Korea 116–17, 122; trade issues 48, 55–61, 112–13, 116–17, 21, 25–30, 33, 48, 85–6, 98–9, 106, 111–17, 130–2, 142, 144–5, 156, 167–8, 170; *see also* Taiwan
Chirac, Jacques 86, 133
Christopher, Warren: background 14–15, 19–20; bureaucratic role 32–4, 39, 168; and the Balkans 83–6, 92, 44–5, 66, 70, 74, 78–9, 100–1, 106, 109, 111, 112–13, 120, 124, 126, 128, 130, 134, 141, 150, 154, 158, 166
Clark, Wesley 92, 95–8
Clarke, Richard 136–7
Clinton Doctrine 41–5
Clinton, Bill: autobiography 5–6, 8, 76; background and personality 8–12, 63–4, 88, 111, 170–1; decision making 1, 5, 7, 9, 31–6, 55–6, 63, 76, 162–70; foreign policy assessment 6–10, 165–71; relations with Congress 9, 29–30, 36–40, 50–4, 58–60, 70–1, 73–5, 78–9, 85–7, 94, 96, 103, 105, 109–11, 113, 115–16, 131, 138, 140–5, 157–9, 167–71; relations with military 35, 62–7, 77, 141–5; reputation 1–6, 167–71
Clinton, Hillary: background and role in the administration 6–7, 12–13, 15, 20, 47, 53, 64, 113, 135, 151, 160
Cohen, William 18–19, 33, 43, 71, 92–3, 97, 116, 121, 134, 142–4, 157, 168
Cold War: end 2, 8, 16, 21–5, 26, 34, 49–50, 68, 73, 76, 89, 91, 97, 99, 102, 106, 107, 111, 123, 125–8, 134, 145; *see also* post-Cold War order
Cole, USS 136–7
Colombia 133–4
Comprehensive (Nuclear) Test Ban Treaty (C(N)TBT) 31, 39, 115, 144–5
Congress, US 1, 3, 14, 23, 29–32, 34–40, 49–50, 52–61, 65–6, 71, 73, 78, 92, 100, 102, 107–9, 112, 115, 121, 126, 133, 135, 156, 165–8; *see also* Clinton, Bill: relations with Congress; House of Representatives, US; Senate, US
congressional elections (1994) 19, 29, 36–8, 77
Contract with America 37–9, 65, 127
Croatia 83–5, 94, 158
Cuba 25–6, 31, 37, 72, 102, 106–11, 133, 167
Cuban American National Foundation 107–11
Czech Republic 47, 124, 127–9

Daalder, Ivo 5, 13, 93, 97
Dayton Agreement 87–8, 92–3, 128
defence policy 25, 27, 31, 38, 62–7, 141–5
defence spending 4, 25, 27, 31, 38, 63–7, 141–4
democracy-promotion 28–9, 42–6, 67, 76, 99, 105
democratic peace 29, 42–6
Democrats 6, 15, 17, 19, 25, 48, 51–3, 58, 60, 112, 128–9, 139, 142, 159, 167
Deutch, John 18–19, 35, 86
Dole, Robert 18, 30–1, 37, 79, 87, 102, 106
dual containment 42, 146, 152–61
Dukakis, Michael 17, 25

economic policy 2, 47–8; *see also* foreign economic policy; globalisation

Egypt 135, 138, 146, 160–1
enlargement 42–5
environmental policy 14, 26, 57–9, 123, 139–41, 144
European Union (EU) 29, 54, 83–4, 134, 140, 158

fast-track 51, 55–60, 167
Federal Bureau of Investigation (FBI) 136–8, 159, 166, 168
Ford, Gerald 2, 56
foreign aid 39, 55–7, 61
foreign economic policy 2, 34, 41–61
France 79, 84, 86, 94, 13–14, 145, 156–7
Freeh, Louis 137–8, 159, 168

Gallucci, Robert 118–20
General Agreement on Tariffs and Trade (GATT) 29, 36, 50, 52, 54–5, 58
Gephardt, Richard 49, 53–4, 58, 112, 115
Gergen, David 13, 18, 33–4, 72
Germany 16, 22, 94, 128
Gingrich, Newt 37, 55, 58, 63, 127, 138, 140, 171
globalisation 2, 21, 41–61, 104, 106, 117, 168–9
Gore–Chernomyrdin Commission 96, 101–2, 104
Gore, Al: background 13–15, 17, 20; bureaucratic role 26, 32, 40; and environmental policy 139–41, 45, 51, 58–9, 79, 84, 88–9, 96, 102, 104, 116, 121, 124, 128, 131, 136, 143, 154, 156
Gulf War (1991) 14, 23–5, 66, 69, 83, 92, 119, 146, 152, 155

Haiti 1, 26, 29, 30, 33, 36, 39, 62, 71–7, 108, 167
Harris, John 4, 6
Havel, Vaclav 47, 121
Helms–Burton Act 31, 55, 72, 109–11
Helms, Jesse 30, 39–40, 55, 102, 109–11, 128, 130, 156
Holbrooke, Richard 15–16, 34, 83, 86–7, 93–4, 99, 126, 130, 158, 168

House Foreign Affairs Committee 38, 70, 158
House of Representatives, US 24, 29, 37–9, 49, 52–4, 58–60, 87, 96, 109, 113, 115, 126; *see also* Clinton, Bill: relations with Congress; Congress, US
humanitarian intervention 62, 77–80, 83–4, 94–8
humanitarianism 20, 29, 31, 44, 62, 66–71, 74, 83–5, 98, 123
Hungary 124, 126–9
Hussein, Saddam 5, 14, 152–8

impeachment 2, 8, 28, 93, 98, 158; *see also* Lewinsky scandal; Whitewater
India 24–5, 43, 48, 115, 132, 167
Indonesia 48, 56, 133
Indyk, Martin 146, 150, 152, 154, 159
International Criminal Court (ICC) 130–1
International Monetary Fund (IMF) 39, 47, 55–7, 104
Iran 15, 34, 42, 114–16, 135, 144, 152–3, 158–9
Iraq 4, 33, 39, 42–3, 120, 130, 135, 146, 152–8, 166
Israel 14, 39, 119, 135, 146–52, 160–4, 167

Japan 3, 47, 50, 54, 56, 114, 132, 167
Johnson, Lyndon B. 2, 10, 36, 114, 156, 166
Jordan 148, 163

Kantor, Mickey 48, 50, 54–5
Kennan, George 22, 41, 44, 124
Kennedy, Edward 89–90, 170
Kennedy, John F. 2, 10, 26, 28, 67, 88, 134, 155, 157
Kerry, John 87, 106
Kissinger, Henry 3, 16–17, 111, 149, 164
Kosovo 13, 31, 34, 60, 81, 84, 92–8, 104, 130, 135, 166–70

Lake, Anthony: background and personality 16–20, 168; bureaucratic role 25, 27, 33–4; and humanitarian

intervention 62, 64, 69, 72–4, 78–9, 84–6, 89, 4, 111, 113–14, 118–20, 125–7, 132, 153–5, 168
Lebanon 146, 160
Lewinsky scandal 35, 38, 93, 156, 166
Lewis, Anthony 80, 94
Libya 138, 158
Lieberman, Joseph 65, 82–3
Lott, Trent 92, 94, 138, 156–7
Lugar, Richard 38, 40, 60, 103, 143–5

McCain, John 18, 66, 91, 96, 106, 121, 145
McGovern, George 12, 17, 19, 24, 63
Mexico 30, 39, 48, 50–6, 60, 74, 133, 166
Middle East 2–3, 19, 26, 29–30, 42–3, 81–2, 146–64, 167, 170
Miller, Aaron 147–9, 152, 160–4
Milosevic, Slobodan 84, 92–8
Mitchell, George 16, 89–91, 112
monetary (exchange rate) policy 54–6
Morris, Dick 32, 37, 74, 76
Muravchik, Joshua 38, 67

National Economic Council (NEC) 34, 48–9, 54
National Missile Defence (NMD) 65, 103, 142–3
National Security Council (NSC) 13, 15, 32, 68, 118
National Security Council staff 32–4, 47–8, 70, 85, 92, 116, 126, 138, 164
neo-conservatives 38, 67, 80, 96, 98, 119, 124, 145, 151, 154
Netanyahu, Benjamin 150–2, 160–2
new isolationism 23, 37–8, 40, 46, 56–7, 96, 115
New World Order 23, 41, 43, 83
Nicaragua 14, 18, 24
Nixon, Richard M. 2, 16, 25, 33, 100–1, 105, 130, 166
North Amercan Free Trade Agreement (NAFTA) 23, 26, 29, 36–7, 48, 50–7, 80, 129
North Atlantic Treaty Organisation (NATO): enlargement 38, 92–8, 124–9, 134, 167, 23, 28, 30, 34, 42, 44, 50, 84–8, 101–2, 123

North Korea 30, 33, 43, 58, 75, 99, 112, 114, 117–22, 135, 167
Northern Ireland 2, 3, 13, 26, 30, 33, 81–2, 88–91, 134, 149, 167
Nuclear Non-proliferation Treaty (NPT) 115, 118–20
nuclear proliferation 30, 43–4, 99, 117–21, 144–5, 159
Nunn, Sam 15, 36, 75–6, 103, 143, 145
Nye, Joseph 7, 115, 117

Obama, Barack 6, 13
Obey, David 38, 58, 77
Oslo Accords 147–9

Pakistan 4, 28, 43, 115, 132, 137
Palestine 146–52, 160–4, 167
Panetta, Leon 7, 33, 48
Partnership for Peace (PfP) 101–3, 126–7
Pelosi, Nancy 59, 112
Pentagon 18, 22, 25–7, 32–5, 38, 63–7, 69, 72, 74, 77–9, 84, 87, 92, 97, 112, 114, 117, 118–20, 125–6, 130, 133, 137, 141–7, 167–8
Perot, Ross 24, 26, 30, 51, 53
Perry, William 18, 33, 65–6, 74, 78–9, 84, 87, 112, 114, 116, 119–22, 125–7, 132
Poland 48, 124, 126–9
post-Cold War order 1–2, 9, 16, 20–5, 29, 36–7, 43–4, 50, 627, 71, 77, 82, 86–7, 98–9, 110, 124–6, 136, 146, 168–70; *see also* Cold War: end
Powell, Colin 45, 63–6, 68, 70–7, 122
Power, Samantha 79–80
Presidential Decision Directive 25 (PDD 25) 77–80, 131, 134
presidential election (1992) 24–7, 51, 64, 69, 72, 83, 88, 106
presidential election (1996) 30–1, 57, 65–6, 87, 115
presidential election (2000) 58–9, 143, 145
public opinion 2, 7–8, 23–4, 30, 66, 73–4, 79, 87, 94, 157, 165
Putin, Vladimir 103, 106

Rabin, Yitzhak 136, 147, 151, 160

Rambouillet 93–4, 96–7
Reagan, Ronald 2, 5, 8, 14, 19, 25–9, 35, 37, 47, 72, 76, 139, 143, 145
Reich, Robert 11, 47
Republican revolution 36–40
Republicans 4–5, 18–19, 25, 29–31, 49, 52–5, 60, 64, 72, 87, 105, 112, 115, 126–9, 140, 142–5, 167, 169; *see also* Clinton, Bill: relations with Congress
Revolution in Military Affairs 63, 65, 141–3
Richardson, Bill 11, 34, 131
Rieff, David 80–1
rogue states 42–3, 153–6
Rosner, Jeremy 42, 128, 144
Ross, Dennis 147–51, 162–4
Rubin, Robert 11, 32, 34, 47–9, 54–5, 57, 60, 101, 113
Rumsfeld, Donald 143–4
Russia 21–2, 29–30, 34–5, 41, 61, 82, 93–106, 124–8, 137, 142–3, 145, 156–7, 159, 167–8
Rwanda 78–80, 130, 167–8

Safire, William 18, 42, 51
Salinas, Carlos 51, 55
Saudi Arabia 136, 138, 158–9
Scowcroft, Brent 69, 119, 127
Seitz, Raymond 15, 89
Senate Armed Services Committee 15, 6, 136
Senate Foreign Relations Committee 12, 14, 30, 39–40, 70, 109, 130, 159
Senate, US 16, 18, 24, 26, 28–31, 37–9, 52–3, 60, 74, 79, 83, 87, 89, 92–3, 102, 109–10, 113, 128–9, 136, 138, 140–1, 143–5; *see also* Clinton, Bill, relations with Congress; Congress, US
Shalikashvili, John 73, 78, 87
Sharon, Ariel 162–4
Shelton, Hugh 92, 142
Soderberg, Nancy 25, 67, 69, 71, 79, 86, 89, 91, 119
Somalia 2, 29, 36, 62, 67–71, 77–8, 138, 167
South Africa 27, 48, 135
South Korea 48, 114, 117–21, 132, 167
Sperling, Gene 45, 48

State Department 14–17, 32–6, 39–40, 42, 47–9, 74, 83, 92, 95, 109, 112–13, 118, 124–6, 131, 137, 146–8, 154, 159, 164, 167–8
Steinberg, James 95, 98
Stephanopoulos, George 5, 72, 76–7, 101
Strategic Arms Reduction Treaties (START) 100–4, 125
Strategic Defence Initiative (SDI) 14, 65, 103, 143
Sudan 31, 130, 166–7
Summers, Larry 48, 55, 101, 104
Syria 146–9, 151, 160–1

Taiwan 39, 42, 111, 113–17, 166
Talbott, Strobe 14, 16, 19, 34, 42, 75, 86, 94, 96, 100–6, 124, 126
Tarnoff, Peter 44, 70, 108
Tenet, George 19, 138, 152, 152
terrorism 2, 30, 46, 135–9, 146, 155–6, 158–60, 170
trade policy 29–30, 47–61, 112–14, 130, 134, 166–7; *see also* China: trade issues
Trimble, David 88–90
Truman, Harry 2, 22
Turkey 48, 93
Tyson, Laura 48–9

Ukraine 103, 105, 133, 167
unilateralism 31, 38–40, 98, 123, 130, 142, 144, 153
United Kingdom 82, 84, 86, 89–94, 97, 128, 134, 137, 145, 154–5
United Nations 13, 15–16, 23, 31, 26–40, 65, 67–74, 76–9, 83–6, 93, 102, 108, 117, 120, 130–1, 135, 139, 152–4, 156–8, 170

Vance, Cyrus 15, 17, 19, 83
Vietnam War 11–14, 16–17, 20, 23, 26–7, 34, 56, 62–3, 66–7, 71, 81, 83, 87, 106–7, 114, 156, 168
Vietnam: normalisation 106–7, 109; syndrome 21, 30, 69, 92

War Powers Resolution 38, 70–1, 74, 76, 157

weapons of mass destruction (WMD) 4, 43, 143–4, 146, 153–5; *see also* nuclear proliferation
Weinberger, Caspar 66, 77–8, 95
Whitewater 28, 38, 154
Wolfowitz, Paul 143, 154
Woolsey, James 18, 34–5
World Trade Center (1993 bombing) 28, 135, 154

World Trade Organisation (WTO) 31, 47, 50, 54, 57–61, 115–17, 171
Wye River Agreement 147, 151–2, 160

Yeltsin, Boris 30, 95, 97, 100–6, 124, 127–8

Zelikow, Philip 18, 32, 135
Zinni, Anthony 139, 155

eBooks – at www.eBookstore.tandf.co.uk

A library at your fingertips!

eBooks are electronic versions of printed books. You can store them on your PC/laptop or browse them online.

They have advantages for anyone needing rapid access to a wide variety of published, copyright information.

eBooks can help your research by enabling you to bookmark chapters, annotate text and use instant searches to find specific words or phrases. Several eBook files would fit on even a small laptop or PDA.

NEW: Save money by eSubscribing: cheap, online access to any eBook for as long as you need it.

Annual subscription packages

We now offer special low-cost bulk subscriptions to packages of eBooks in certain subject areas. These are available to libraries or to individuals.

For more information please contact webmaster.ebooks@tandf.co.uk

We're continually developing the eBook concept, so keep up to date by visiting the website.

www.eBookstore.tandf.co.uk